SHAPING THE COMMON LAW

Jurists: Profiles in Legal Theory

William Twining, editor

Shaping the Common Law

FROM GLANVILL TO HALE, 1188–1688

Essays by Thomas Garden Barnes

EDITED AND WITH AN INTRODUCTION

by Allen D. Boyer

STANFORD LAW BOOKS

An imprint of Stanford University Press

Stanford, California 2008

Library of Congress Cataloging-in-Publication Data

Barnes, Thomas Garden.
Shaping the common law : from Glanvill to Hale, 1188–1688 / essays by Thomas Garden Barnes ; edited and with an introduction by Allen D. Boyer.
p. cm. — (Jurists—profiles in legal theory)
Includes bibliographical references and index.
ISBN 978-0-8047-5714-0 (cloth : alk. paper)
1. Common law—History. 2. Common law—England—History. I. Boyer, Allen D. II. Title
K588.B37 2008
340.5'709—dc22 2007049988

Printed in the United States of America
on acid-free, archival-quality paper

Typeset at Stanford University Press in 10/13 Galliard

À Jeanne-Marie

Les mariages se font au ciel et se consomment sur la terre.
—Antoine Loisel

Contents

Author's Preface ix

Introduction by Allen D. Boyer 1

1. Glanvill 11
2. Magna Carta 23
3. Thomas Littleton 32
4. John Fortescue 46
5. Richard Hooker 61
6. James VI and I 79
7. Francis Bacon 98
8. Sir Edward Coke 114
9. Michael Dalton 136
10. William Hudson 152
11. John Selden 167
12. John Milton 177
13. The Laws and Liberties of Massachusetts 195
14. Trial of Charles I 205
15. Matthew Hale 221

Notes 239 *Further Reading* 261 *Index* 273

Author's Preface

While I toiled amidst the dry-rot, fallen timbers, and primitive plumbing of a family home in southwest Nova Scotia in the summer of 1982, a telegram came to the Plympton post office, relayed by the postmaster to his mother, who phoned the neighbor across the road, who walked over to deliver the message. It was an invitation from Leslie Adams, Esq., of Birmingham, Alabama, lawyer and publisher of the Gryphon Library of Classics, to assemble an editorial committee to oversee a new venture, The Legal Classics Library. A few moments' thought, then I crossed the road and used the neighbor's telephone to respond to Les, settle terms, accept the offer, and choose the first half-dozen volumes. A second call directed Maritime Tel & Tel to install a telephone.

In 1783, my great-great-great-grandfather Nathan, a Loyalist, fled to these same acres from Waltham, Massachusetts. Before 1982, Plympton provided me a similar sort of refuge from Berkeley, California. There had been pastoral bliss in escaping for the summer, to labor tool-in-hand, research, and write without the interruption of modern communications. That evaporated. The telegram was cause and my response had its effect. Now the house, barn, and garage are festooned with cord and cordless phones, my study mounts fax and desktop, and the TV cable provides ISP.

In the quarter-century since that phone call, I have written ninety-nine introductory essays of some 20–25 printed pages, printed separately as pamphlets to accompany works reprinted in The Legal Classics Library. Chronologically, these "Notes from the Editors" ranged from Hammurabi's Code to William Rehnquist's *The Supreme Court: How It Was, How It Is.* Multivolume works demanded Notes to accompany each volume: the eight essays for William Blackstone's and Chancellor Kent's respective *Commentaries* together totaled almost two hundred pages. English and American works I entered upon with verve, considering them less formidable than in the event they proved to be. The volumes on Plato, Greek trials, Justinian, Vico, Montesquieu, Beccaria, the *Code Napoleon,* Savigny, Tocqueville, and Kovalesvsky, were all unfamiliar territory, but they provided relief from Storrs Lectures. They also taught me a great deal about the history of law that I would not have learned in any other way. Notes for other volumes, particularly in Roman and civil law, international law, and jurisprudence, were supplied by distinguished colleagues from both sides of the Atlantic.

Both "Legal" and "Classics" were liberally construed. Included in the series were some less-than-legal work by lawyers, some works trenching on law by non-lawyers, and a few trials. "Classic," besides encompassing the conventional meaning of the word, also included significant, even recent, works touching the law.

Here are fifteen of the Notes, the first written in 1982 and the last in 1998. They are essentially vignettes of jurists, works, and events which over five centuries, 1188 to 1688—from Glanvill's *Tractatus de Legibus et Consuetudinibus* to the revolution the apprehension of which moved Sir Matthew Hale not to publish his *History and Analysis of the Common Law of England*—played a formative role in the making of the common law. Not every candidate for the distinction is here (alas, The Legal Classics Library never found available a worthy vehicle via which to present Bracton). Two subjects are avowedly obscure: William Hudson and Michael Dalton. Magna Carta and *The Book of the General Lawes and Libertyes of the Inhabitants of the Massachusets* are both documents, but nonetheless, like the trial of Charles I, they are cardinal events which warrant their inclusion.

The Notes rested on the proposition that an important work of law is inscrutable if separated from the historical context that produced it and without an appreciation of the personality responsible for it. Ideally, connecting the text to its author and era involves a survey of the past on its own terms and a conscious disregard of the desire to draw connections to the here and now. With regard to the individual jurist, even when what can be known about the author is slight and the whole person irretrievable, the attempt to make a personal appraisal is necessary. A life-and-times level of understanding may be all that can be attained, but each writer and each law-book can be fitted into the particular epoch and its challenges. To a considerable extent, each reveals something of a *genius loci*, a presiding deity of the law, for its particular time and circumstances. Often the personal can be inferred or intuited, or read outright in the force of the words on the page. Sir Edward Coke's almost mystic juristic zeal was unmistakable and inimitable. James VI & I was virtually transparent by the standards of the age—which proved a chief source of his difficulties as king.

In preparing these essays for this volume, I have not attempted to update them. Subsequent scholarship, some of which is referenced in Further Reading, may condition the portraits here, but does not radically alter them.

No agenda drove the enterprise. I did not seek to impose any continuity, which would have been impossible since the Library chose and printed works without respect to chronology. What coherence there may be among these essays comes from a guileless reverence for the achievement of these jurists and their books, and from a humble awe at the role played by historical events in the fashioning and development of the common law. From its origins as an amalgam of custom and command, the common law was continuously caught in the tension between king and subject. The climacteric between medieval and modern ushered in religious and political revolution. Although sorely challenged, the common law not only survived but more than any other English institution of Church or State was strengthened by the turmoil. In the process, the common law became the touchstone for English liberties in the New England.

Is this too Whiggish, lauding the common law as a river which despite silt and diversion flows on ever greater and clearer? Such a sentiment cannot survive intact Karl Nickerson Llewellyn's realist skepticism. Yet the resiliency and the adaptability of the common law have always served us well and will continue to do so. What we mean by the "rule of law" is, simply, the common law.

It is with gratitude that I acknowledge both the vision of Leslie Adams in launching The Legal Classics Library and the commitment of his successor, Rick Ritter, in sustaining it. From 1991 until 2007, Christine Valentine in New York was managing editor. A fellow Pittsburgher, and one whose love for France provided a harmony of endeavor that smoothed out the usual strains between editor and author. Her editing was gentle, her own prose sparkling, her literary command wide, and her professionalism incomparable. Notes from the Editor have owed more to her than to any other.

With this undertaking, as with everything else I've done over many years, I've had the assiduous help of my assistant at Boalt Hall, Chris Swain, and I thank him heartily. My thanks also to the editors of the Stanford University

Press responsible for this book. And to Allen Boyer, who is editor and commentator of this volume, this is my (literal) *indebitatus assumpsit*. It was his idea that it should be published and he made it happen. Some fifteen years ago he called me from Wall Street to say he was writing a biography of Sir Edward Coke and asked if I could help him. Thus began a friendship that did not bring us face-to-face until four years ago. I would be delighted to own him my collaborator, but he has taught me more than I have been able to assist him. I am deeply grateful.

Thomas Garden Barnes

All Saints Day 2007
Berkeley, California

SHAPING THE COMMON LAW

Introduction by Allen D. Boyer

Certain law-books become eponymous, and certain authors become authorities. The books wear off their titles and become bodies of work, artifacts of their authors' careers and reputation. The authors become the texts with which their surnames are connected. In this collection of essays, Thomas Barnes offers a brilliant group portrait of a set of farsighted jurists and the books that enduringly bear their names—Glanvill, Fortescue, Littleton, Coke, Bacon, Dalton, Hudson, Selden, Hale—and of two kings and a cleric who figured profoundly in the law. Their lives and works, along with Magna Carta and *The Laws and Liberties of Massachusetts*, shaped legal rights and constitutional theory as they emerged in early modern England, the defining moment for the common-law system and Anglo-American political institutions.

Among these equals, Glanvill is first—Ranulf de Glanvill, justiciar of England, and the treatise *Tractatus de Legibus et Consuetudinibus Regni Angliae*, "commonly called Glanvill." With Glanvill begins "legal memory," the history and era of the common law; earlier there is only "the time before which the memory of the law does not reach."[1] Only rarely can any judge claim a share in the historical glamour of an age. If any law-giver can, it is Glanvill, who was counselor and chevalier to one of history's great kings. At the court of Henry II, Glanvill must have headed the royal judges who deliberated long ("*multis vigiliis excogitata et inventa*," it was said), drafting the writ of novel disseisin.[2] At the battle of Alnwick, when the English scattered the Scottish host of King William the Lion, it was Glanvill who commanded, and who is said to have personally taken King William prisoner.

Of equal moment are the contents of the treatise. In Glanvill one finds the first thorough treatment of the jury—so new and so innovative a mechanism, Professor Barnes observes, that the royal counselors explained its workings in thorough, confident detail. The breaking of further new ground appears in the discussions of the writs. Novel disseisin, praecipe, mort d'ancestor, darrein presentment, utrum—in the clear morning light of the Angevin legal revolution, the writs display the brilliance of a new coinage.

> These were the first writs of course, boilerplate instruments which gave the king's court jurisdiction and demanded the parties' amenableness to it. They were the common law's first forms of action, and so made it truly "common" in the sense of one law, of one procedure and one substance, for each writ was available to any freeman for the assertion of his interest in any free tenement with the mere purchase of the writ.

If Glanvill the justiciar did not actually compose Glanvill the treatise, the book was written within his circle and circulated under his authority; to England's preeminent judge was attributed the first treatise on English law. The book was completed in the last stage of King Henry's reign, between November 29, 1187 and June 7, 1189. The justiciar was elderly, but he was not exhausted. Glanvill put aside his law-books to take the cross. In November 1190, he died on crusade, in the English camp before the walls of Acre. Jerusalem remained in the Saracens' hands, but Glanvill's achievement was already complete.

The customs of England and the rules by which the judges of England decided cases, even though unwritten, Glanvill had maintained, merited the name of laws. Making law in this common-law system has involved the unceasing process of striking a series of balancing transactions. A controversy pending before the court must be decided in a way that addresses squarely the facts of the case, is consonant with relevant legal doctrine, and is consistent with the understandings and practices by which the everyday legal system functions. The balance need not be delicate but it must be careful, and it is customarily done in a manner mindful of tradition—that is, in the awareness of how similar balances have previously been struck.

As the honor paid by the system to eponymous classics illustrates, the common law places a crucial emphasis upon the role of the judge, the author to whom a given judgment or rule of law may be ascribed. In his seminal essay, "The Common Law and Legal Theory," A. W. B. Simpson has worked out with a philosopher's rigor certain conclusions that follow from such premises.

> If all laws are laid down, all laws must have an author, for someone must have performed the act of positing the law. Secondly, there must be some test or criterion for identifying the lawmaker or lawmakers who have authority to lay down the law, or entitlement to do so, for it would be absurd if anyone who cared to do so could lay down law. . . . Thirdly, if law is by definition laid down, all law must originate in legislation, or in some law-creating act. Fourthly, law so conceived will appear as the product of acts of will, and the law which results as the will of the lawmaker. Fifthly, if laws owe their status to their having been laid down by the right author, it cannot be a necessary characteristic of law that it should have a particular content, for its content will depend upon the will of the lawmaker.[3]

Perennially, when the common law's apologists have denounced what the common law is not, they have rejected abstraction, even disparaged it. They have said that the common law, however it may be defined, cannot be equated to the application of unmediated logic, mechanical jurisprudence, neutral principles of adjudication, or economic analysis. Simpson has gone far toward explaining this aversion. He has reiterated what may too easily be overlooked, that the common law is never univocal. The content of a rule of law depends upon the will of the individual lawmaker. Positivists may hear in the law the imperative tone of a sovereign, and natural lawyers may hear rights and duties articulated in whatever tongue the angels speak. By contrast, the common law is to be heard as a consort of human voices.

The greatest subject of the common law is a document that cannot be ascribed to any one common lawyer's hand. Magna Carta figures here in all its guises: as a political concord of sweeping scope and particular detail; as the first statute, the enactment by which all subsequent laws have been admeasured, the outward and visible sign of an unwritten constitution; as a document that has been ignored as well as venerated; as a reference linking the epochal crises of medieval England to Stuart parliamentarians and the eloquent colonial lawyer John Adams.

The *Tenures* of Sir Thomas Littleton and *De Laudibus Legum Angliae*, by Sir John Fortescue reflect a medieval balance of the real with the ideal. Fortescue was a judge to be reckoned with: an experienced local magistrate, a veteran of eight parliaments, a tough-minded partisan of the House of Lancaster, and ultimately so steadfast a servant of the crown that he could make his peace with the Yorkist regime of Edward IV. His ultimate achievement, S. B. Chrimes opined, was credibly "to make up a doctrine that had its roots on one side in abstract political theory, and roots on the other side in the concrete facts of political practice. He contrived to link up what he wanted to say about England with the sanction of high theory."[4]

Like Fortescue, Littleton was a shrewd common lawyer, able to write on the theoretical level because he possessed a deep knowledge of the working law. In the name of critique and reason, he pruned from his *Tenures* the case citation that might have fleshed out the rules that he formulated. "The didactic ends of Littleton did not require authority," Professor Barnes summarizes. "Each short section was an assertion posed by putting a case. It made no difference for analytical purposes whether the case was real or hypothetical." The result was a Tudor best-seller, the first law-book printed in English, "a rose of rational analysis and jurisprudential concerns in a thicket of how-to and what-was-done works."

Richard Hooker was a divine, not a lawyer, but his work may claim a place among the law-books. He may have titled his masterwork *The Laws of Ecclesiastical Polity* to answer the civilian-turned-theologian Jean Calvin, who (following Justinian) had titled his own treatise *The Institutes of the Christian Religion*. Part of the reason that Hooker would exalt reason, "natural reason revealing natural law," may be that he preached to the lawyers of the Inner Temple. Certainly he defined law in terms that his congregation would have understood:

> That which doth assign unto each thing the kind, that which doth moderate the force and measure, that which doth appoint the form and measure . . . we call a law. So that no certain end could ever be attained, unless the actions whereby it is attained were regular; that is to say made suitable, fit and correspondent unto their end, by some canon, rule or law.

Rather than revelation and authority, this outlook relies upon fairness and process. Very similarly, Hooker ventured to explain the religious community in terms of "an order expressly or secretly agreed upon," an implicit consent by the community's members to act and allow for the common good. This idea would later find broader, explicitly political scope. The judicious Hooker, the learned parson would be called—a compliment, fittingly, paid by John Locke.

With *The True Law of Free Monarchies* and *Basilicon Doron*, the Stuart dynasty's most gifted member staked a claim to be considered as a world-class university president born wrong. The starting point for Professor Barnes's consideration of James I is the provocative bon mot of the French ambassador, that James spoke like a despot whenever he tried to sound like a king, and was vulgar whenever he sought to show the common touch. Not the least of James's problems, this essay observes, was that the king's four principal speeches on kingship were delivered, at increasingly greater length, to successive sessions of the same Parliament. His concessions on common-law jurisdiction, his intelligent arguments for an Anglo-Scottish union, his serious attempts to define the partnership of crown and parliament, all such initiatives suffered: "James's repetitiveness doubtless fell on progressively deafer ears." In the end, the Commons heard only the rhetoric and the self-concern, and not the message about the concerns of the realm. The evil done by these speeches lived after them.

The voice and character that Professor Barnes restores to *The Trial of Charles I* are those of the king himself. He emphasizes about Charles what often has remained hidden in plain sight: that the narrative of Charles's career is not merely a chronicle of flawed judgments and disastrous outcomes, but rather the story of the will that drove Charles to persevere in his course, despite a series of disasters—the story of one man's determination to govern his realm. "Charles' destruction is the strongest evidence of his central importance to the age and its events," Professor Barnes writes, in a deceptively simple sentence.

The essay on William Hudson's *Treatise of the Court of Star Chamber* draws deeply on the scholarly work for which Professor Barnes remains best known. Around the Camera Stellata there has settled a black legend almost as sinister as that which envelops the Spanish Inquisition. This essay does not fully dispel that—no one work is likely to dispel that—but it wisely observes that what Star Chamber supplied to the common law was "a not unmixed blessing but a substantial benefaction." In particular, "the law of sophisticated crime" can be traced to this institution:

> Crimes against justice (perjury, maintenance, champerty, embracery, vexatious litigation, contempt); crimes by officers (subornation and extortion); crimes of covin and deceit (forgery, fraud, impersonation, extortion); criminal libel—and in distinction to it the modern civil tort—and sedition; inchoate crime (conspiracy and attempt) were all crimes either largely created and developed by Star Chamber in the exercise of its common-law jurisdiction or else were statutory offenses defined and refined by the court.

How royal laws were translated into legal practice is the theme of Michael Dalton's *The Countrey Justice*. Dalton claimed that "my calling is to a country life," but the countryside with which he dealt was neither peaceful nor bucolic. As William Lambarde had noted, Tudor lawmakers had laid "not loads, but stacks of statutes" upon the rural justices. Dalton offered his fellow justices a guide to follow in exercising the judgment required of them by the new enactments. "From Alehouses to Affray to Armor to Barrator to Bastardy," Professor Barnes comments, *The Countrey Justice* "corresponded to the realities of a single JP's existence." This essay also casts a quick, illuminating sidelight on how the day-to-day government of Stuart England represented an interplay between the central government and the county justices—who not only served in local office, but could frequently count on framing central policy when called to Westminster as Members of Parliament.

The essays on *The Countrey Justice* and Hudson's *Star Chamber* treatise recall that jurisprudence in isolation does not amount to a legal system. So to speak, the justices who paged through Dalton's manual and the robed magnates who made speeches in Star Chamber both represent allegorical figures of law in action. The justices used their discretion and local authority to apply the law. The Privy Council sat in Star Chamber to back up government policy with legal decisions and to adapt the law to changing circumstances. The continuing effort to make new law and reinterpret old precedents was the embodiment of the common law's vitality.

The same interplay between learning and process was one of the concerns upon which Simpson has focused. Simpson concludes that the law is defined by its acceptance by the professional community—that propositions of law have value only depending "upon the degree to which such propositions are accepted as accurate statements of received ideas or practice," and insofar as they are consistent with lawyers' practice. If deciding cases and settling rules remains in each and every case an act of will, for continuing generations of judges, as well as for the judge who first articulated a point, such decisions and principles will be accepted only as long as they persuade.

> The notion that the common law consists of rules which are the product of a series of acts of legislation (mostly untraceable) by judges (most of whose names are forgotten) cannot be made to work, if taken seriously, because common law rules enjoy whatever status they possess not because of the circumstances of their origin, but because of their continued reception.[5]

The tradition of the common law, the mechanism that provides for transmission over time of a received body of knowledge and learning, resembles the rules that govern language.

> Formulations of the common law are to be conceived of as similar to grammarians' rules, which both describe linguistic practices and attempt to systematize and order them; such rules serve as guides to proper practice since the proper practice is in part the normal practice; such formulations are always inherently corrigible, for it is always possible that they may be improved upon, or require modification as what they describe changes.[6]

Change as well as continuity—"corrigibility," as Simpson puts it—is part of a tradition. And the way in which an individual's voice will make itself heard may best have been explained by T. S. Eliot, speaking not of the lawyers but of the poets.

The irony of a tradition, Eliot observed, is that tradition "cannot be inherited, and if you want it you must obtain it by great labor." It requires the engagement of an individual's talent and perspective with the conventions with which other artists have previously chosen to work. Of absolute importance is the historical sense, an awareness "of the timeless as well as of the temporal and of the timeless and the temporal together." Yet tradition is not simple juxtaposition and coexistence. To the contrary, a tradition is a dynamic.

> What happens when a new work of art is created is something that happens simultaneously to all the works of art which preceded it. The existing monuments form an ideal order among themselves. . . . The existing order is complete before the new work arrives; for order to persist after the supervention of novelty, the *whole* existing order must be, if every so slightly, altered; and this is conformity between the old and the new.[7]

In the works of Sir Edward Coke, the *Reports* and the *Institutes* that remade the common law, the process described by Eliot can be unmistakably seen. Coke tirelessly traced into the past the concerns and doctrines of the courts he knew. "He brought the medieval literature of the common law into line with the modern literature," Sir William Holdsworth wrote. "Glanvil, Bracton, Britton and Fleta were made to explain and illustrate Perkins, Fitzherbert, Staunford and Lambarde." Coke hailed Littleton's *Tenures* as "the most perfect and absolute book that ever was written in any humane science," but he changed and conformed the text nonetheless. Coke added discussions of related legal points wherever they were tangentially relevant, turning a carefully structured treatise on the law of real property into a sprawling one-volume legal encyclopedia. The ultimate effect was to put numberless new lives into the old volume's leasehold.

> [Coke] supplied as a thick overlard on Littleton's spare text a discrete commentary on Littleton's scholarship by the addition of cases from the Middle Ages going to support Littleton's citationless assertions. . . . Coke's *Reports* had already begun to revolutionize the way lawyers looked at cases, the purpose they found for cases, the dawning realization that in cases was to be found the law.

Adding old cases gave Littleton new relevance. In making his own contribution to the lawyers' art, Coke changed an old masterpiece, rewriting Littleton in every sense except the literal.

Sir Francis Bacon's perennial projects for the reform of English law found their most eloquent presentation in *The Elements of the Common Laws of England*. Other lawyers were content to rely upon familiar maxims, some to coin new maxims; the bursts of Latin tag-lines that drove home the courtroom arguments of Bacon's worthiest rivals had their counterpart in the bursts of Latin tag-lines with which Marlowe closed scenes in *Doctor Faustus*. Bacon planned to do more. His analysis of the law, the first step of which was to reduce the basic principles of the law to 25 maxims, he presented less as a strategy for winning cases than as a strategy for exploring the balances and subtle connections of the law. Bacon found in his maxims, epitomes of Year Book cases, rules that might be abstracted from the precedents, rather than the reverse—even the first fruits of the harvest for which Bacon hoped, a grand set of the "laws of laws."

In *Areopagitica*, which John Milton published in 1644, one finds the complexity that a brilliant talent brings to a subject with which he has both a political engagement and a personal stake. The framing here is judicious. Milton's reputation as an advocate of freedom of speech is balanced against his record as a zealous pamphleteer in *The Tenure of Kings and Magistrates*, "a hodgepodge of spurious history lightly reinforced by a stringing together of the most fanatical advocates of insurrection and tyrannicide." A second irony, far from humorous, lies in Milton's having been the Interregnum official who, searching for seditious papers, had his pursuivants ransack the study of William Prynne, the same sarcastic historian who had lost his ears by decree of King Charles's Star Chamber. Yet nonetheless, the double-handed nature of Milton's ambitions finally allow for their author's redemption. Ultimately, *Areopagitica* remains known for Milton's call, "Give me the liberty to know, to utter, and to argue freely according to conscience, above all liberties." That eloquence, Professor Barnes suggests, must be heard as the voice of Milton's better angel.

The essay on John Selden, focusing on the *Table Talk of John Selden*, catches the political lawyer and first great English legal historian at his most engaging—both deeply and lightly learned. The wit and insight that Selden characteristically displayed are the more notable for having been sounded against a brooding political silence. As counsel in the *Five Knights' Case* (1627), Selden had the misfortune of seeing contradictory truths. He understood that Charles I had gone too far in imprisoning gentlemen who had resisted the royal Forced Loan of 1626. At the same time, he saw that, bound by existing doctrine, the courts could stretch no English law, not even Magna Carta, far enough to hold that his clients' imprisonment was invalid. The quandary in which Selden found himself forced to act reflected the larger impasse at which the court and the country had arrived.

Other Englishmen were less concerned with the Gordian complexity of mid-century politics. The same year that King Charles was negotiating with Parliament and intriguing with the Scots, the magistrates of New England issued a *Book of the General Laws and Libertyes Concerning the Inhabitants of the Massachusetts.* They had turned their attention to New World problems, to man-stealing, idolatry, false witness, and a widow's right to her husband's chattels. Their mind-set was not experimental; it was responsive, responsible, and quietly but forcefully independent.

> From title-page to the oath for viewers of pipestaves, there is nothing that would indicate that the Bay colonists were subjects of Charles I. . . . The only citation to an institution beyond the Bay is that to "the High Court of Parliament in England" in the proheme. Such silence is deafening.

With Bacon's insights, with Milton entertaining irreconcilable contradictory propositions, with Selden understanding what the age demanded, the first great, honest survey of English law was attempted. Sir Matthew Hale's *History of the Common Law* was the work of a committed Christian who avoided sectarian disputes—of a great advocate who, amid the vicious politics of the Interregnum and Restoration, was noted for his rare ability to walk a middle line and follow principle in doing so.

The *History* was never published by Hale, who did take the trouble to publish two pamphlets on Torricellian fluid dynamics. Hale may have left his best work unpublished, even incomplete, this essay suggests, because he did not wish to perpetuate, even by an honest contribution, an intellectual debate that was savagely charged with politics. Hale rejected the conservative political theory upon which England's radicals relied (the myth of an ancient constitution, of a golden age before the Conquest whose liberties might yet be restored to the English people). He had even less patience with the radical doctrine that conservatives had adopted, Thomas Hobbes's paean to absolute monarchy. *The History of the Common Law* was remarkably fair and intelligently balanced in an age in which to argue for moderation was to challenge received ideas and invite angry rejoinders. Hale's reluctance to put such a document into print only reiterated the caution that it represented.

> By his manifest learning and impartial conduct on the bench, by his 'natural philosophic' speculations published and conveyed by discourse among the intellectuals of his day, and by his exemplary demeanor as a pious and devoted

> Churchman, Hale was held to be a man above partisanship and beyond the corruption of power. . . . Hale's contemporaries understood that to his voice they should hearken because he said so little.

Hale self-effacingly served the common law with the same intense avocation that his friends in the Royal Society accorded to the study of natural philosophy. It was to another body of learned gentlemen, his colleagues of Gray's Inn, that Hale left his manuscripts. In 1688 those lawyers would help bring to the throne of England William III, the monarch whose Act of Settlement would guarantee the political independence of the judiciary.

Lawmakers, law-books, lawyers, and litigants—across five hundred years, these essays ring changes on these elements in the history of the common law. These themes have been marshaled by a remarkable intellect and personality. Thomas Garden Barnes received his A.B. from Harvard University in 1952 and his doctorate from Oxford University in 1955. After teaching history at Lycoming College, he joined the history faculty at the University of California at Berkeley in 1960 and the Berkeley law-school faculty in 1966. After forty-five years at Berkeley he took emeritus status, but he has not ceased to teach or to pursue research. He has long been a Councillor of the Selden Society and has recently completed a term as a board member of the Board of the American Society for Legal History. Outside academia, he has served for a quarter-century as chair of the editorial board of the Legal Classics Library.

The studies selected for this volume contain a wealth of knowledge, and Professor Barnes writes lucidly and piquantly. These pieces are always thoughtful, customarily independent, generous in their insights, and frequently brilliant. In these respects they reflect their author.

CHAPTER ONE

Glanvill

Present at the Creation: here is a claim few jurists can make, a cachet borne by few jurisprudential works. That is, the rare distinction of witnessing, describing, or even effecting the creation of an entire system and structure of law, partaking of the almost mystical experience of discovering the *fons et origo*, the fountain and source, of law, of being Moses on Sinai when the Ten Commandments are handed down, of sensing Beginning as Genesis ("God") or the Gospel according to St. John ("the Word") reveal it. The accolade belongs to Hammurabi, lacking an earlier god-king law-giver in civilization's cradle; to Justinian, of course, as creator and motive force behind one of the great root-systems of law; perhaps to the collected delegates at Philadelphia in 1787; to Bonaparte, though at best grudgingly. Now we must add the late twelfth-century English jurist, whoever he was, author of the *Tractatus de Legibus et Consuetudinibus Regni Anglie qui Glanvilla Vocatur*. We will bow to convention and call the treatise Glanvill, for as the subtitle—"commonly called Glanvill"—indicates, the name is more appropriate to the work than to its author.

Glanvill's fame rests as much upon its temporal situation, in that narrow window of a single generation in which the common law took its frame, as upon the considerable merit and even precocious originality of the work itself. From the outset of consciousness of an historical tradition in the common law, Glanvill has never failed of comment and usually praise. Sir Edward Coke in his *Reports* cited it frequently and invariably with an approbation that verged on reverence. Even John Cowell, a doctor of the civil law and contemporary of Coke whose profound differences with the common law tradition as represented by Coke were unbridgeable, said no more than was enough, that Glanvill "is the ancientest of any [book] extant, touching" the common law of England.[1] Sir William Blackstone, with more inclusiveness than discrimination, wrote of "authors, to whom great veneration and respect is paid by the students of the common law. Such are Glanvill and Bracton, Britton and Fleta, Littleton and Fitzherbert. . . ."[2] The legal historians of the past century who, beginning with Frederic William Maitland, have laid the foundations and gone far towards raising the monument which is English legal history of the first two and one-half centuries after the Conquest, have never stinted him praise. Maitland, in a chapter entitled "Age of Glanvill," cautioned,

> We have no reason to suspect that the writer is giving us his theories instead of the practice of the king's court. What he has borrowed from the new [Roman law] jurisprudence consists first of a few general distinctions . . . and secondly a logical method which we may call dilemmatic.[3]

He concluded by paying Glanvill a measured but very high compliment:

> We can not call Glanvill's treatise the earliest text-book of feudal jurisprudence . . . but in the production of such a book England stands well in advance of France and Germany.[4]

Theodore Plucknett, near the end of a long and distinguished career traced in Maitland's footprints, wrote of the "dilemmatic" challenge Glanvill faced in determining what went on in the King's court acceptable as authority, that

> It must have been a bewildering situation, but we must acknowledge with respectful admiration how brilliantly Glanvill acquitted himself. He saw clearly the points in debate and explained them lucidly. He firmly turned his eyes away from the past, and in effect laid down the law of the future. . . . Glanvill was above all the sentimental talk about the *laga Edwardi* [the putative laws of Edward the Confessor] and wrote—consciously and deliberately it must have been—the law of the future. Written in a moment of supreme crisis in our legal history [the challenge of Roman law], before there were as yet any authoritative documents to guide him, the courage and mastery which produced Glanvill's Book VII are unsurpassed in our legal history.[5]

Admitting some skepticism about Glanvill's clairvoyance (it is a rare achievement ever to write future law even co-incidentally, let alone "consciously and deliberately"), Plucknett's compliment is well taken. Raoul van Caenegem's more cautious assessment is praise enough:

> The Tractatus indeed provided a new start as well as summed up a great period [of legal creativity]. It was a stepping stone for future achievements. It drew the balance, and as it showed what had been achieved, people could better see what was left to be done.[6]

These conclusions resonate in G. D. G. Hall's careful and searching introduction to his edition of Glanvill, which like its subject is original, comprehensive, and persuasive: "free of the tradition and necessity of extensive textual quotation. . . . [reflecting] a freedom to innovate and a reliance on the fruits of practical experience."[7]

We would like to know who such an author was. Derek Hall's rejection of the three magnati most frequently credited by historians over the past century—Ranulf Glanvill, Hubert Walter, Geoffrey fitz Peter—reflects the best recent consensus. His suggestion that the author was a lesser figure, possessed of a modicum of academic training and thoroughly familiar with the practice of the King's courts of Henry II, is both fruitful and frustrating. That Glanvill so long appeared the best candidate was not discreditable. The wealth of documentary materials in the treatise allows dating from internal evidence with great exactness. It was produced sometime in a period of twenty months: Derek Hall, with the medievalist textual scholar's instinctual caution, concluded that there "is nothing in the treatise inconsistent with a date anywhere between 29 November 1187 and 6 July 1189, when Henry II died."[8] This period corresponds with the last years of the justiciarship of Ranulf Glanvill, which began with his appointment by Henry II about April 1180 and ended with his dismissal by Richard I on September 17, 1189. Little wonder the treatise was "commonly called Glanvill." That Justiciar Glanvill played some other role in it than merely providing an ascriptive name is not hard to credit. Maitland, in one of those perilously seductive innuendos with which for a hundred years we have had to contend in order to see the high Middle Ages through our eyes rather than his, suggested, "We may safely say that it was not written without Glanvill's permission or without Henry's."[9] Of course we can safely say no such thing—but even mere probability makes the allusion compelling, reinforcing what for a full eight centuries has been an indestructible ascription.

"Not written without Glanvill's permission or without Henry's"—that begs the bigger issue, which is not what either justiciar or king permitted, but what they had done, in the absence of which no treatise would have been necessary or relevant. The King is far the more important of the two: Henry II, King of England (1154–1189), Duke of Normandy, Count of Maine, of Touraine, of Anjou, and by marriage Duke of Aquitaine, known also as Henry Plantagenet, Henry of Anjou, born 1133. He was the son of Geoffrey Count of Anjou and Matilda, daughter of Henry I of England, who was the relict of the Holy Roman Emperor Henry V. Matilda, with the support of her second husband, Geoffrey, and latterly championed by their son Henry and in his interest, contended with her half-brother Stephen for the English crown throughout his uneasy reign (1135–1154). Henry of Anjou early showed his mettle and his aggressiveness when in 1147 at age fourteen he mounted a filibustering expedition from Normandy to further his own ambitions more than those of his parents. Defeated and deserted by his followers and his mercenaries, the young man managed to raise enough money to pay off his troops and return home—the donor was none other than his uncle and target, King Stephen, whose prudence in thus ridding himself of a youthful adversary nicely complemented the youth's cheek. The episode demonstrated Henry's phenomenal good luck, which deserted him only once in his long life, when his angry and vengeful words led to murder in the cathedral with the martyrdom of Thomas à Becket and Henry's abject humiliation by the Pope. It also prophesied that on whichever side of the Channel the King might be found, his regal authority would have to be as powerful and as palpable on the other. Henry II was destined to spend most of his thirty-five years on the throne outside of England, all but a few months of those absences passed in France. Here was the necessity for the justiciar who would exercise vice-regal powers in the King's absence, and here was his scope and ambit for reform, renewal, and creation in administration and in law, in institutions and in practices.

Henry was a powerful character and personality beyond the martial qualities which were the first attributes of the medieval monarch. He had received considerable formal education for the age: he was literate (and read), commanding languages, including Latin. He enjoyed the conversation and the controversion of scholars in discourse; alas, the film *Becket* slighted the intellectual intercourse between Henry II and his Chancellor Becket in favor of the other kind between them and peasant strumpets. A disposition to corpulence was tamed by relentless exercise, he was lionized for unparalleled feats of strength and stamina, he kept irregular hours and frequently worked throughout the night, and he was at once volatile and energetic, yet always courteous and usually patient. Fearless in action, he was reflective at rest. He was a strong—even unyielding—advocate of what he believed in, of a cause embraced. It might be said of Henry as one detractor said of Theodore Roosevelt, that he was a combination of St. Paul and St. Vitus. He bore a certain resemblance to his namesake, the Eighth of the Henries, in intellect, energy, activity, but differed markedly from him in lacking that murderous ruthlessness which made Henry VIII a monster, the violence which amounted to bloodlust, and the sanguinary martial bellicosity in which he gloried.

Perhaps Henry II's appeal has outlived him, even to our own time. In the fall of 1960, why should the author's students in English medieval constitutional history have been surprised when the arrogant, young, lecturer arrived in a Berkeley classroom with a large homemade campaign button proclaiming "Henry of Anjou for President"? The lecturer had been mad about Harry, twice madly for Adlai, despaired as the nation was gently anesthetized by Ike (especially after what had been done about Suez and not done about Budapest in 1956), could not trust Dick Nixon, and had already sensed the Young Emperor's moral nakedness. Henry II was a man fit to fill the regal boots of an American president when energy and creativity were demanded. Unfortunately, bringing Henry from the Abbey of Fontevrault (not surprisingly, he had died in France) for the inauguration raised an insuperable obstacle. The "draft Hank" movement never got off the ground, not even at the university where everything else always seemed to find its moment.

Henry II's most thorough biographer does not shrink from attributing to him personal contributions to governance and statecraft which the paucity of direct eye-witness literary evidence might cause us to doubt. The biographer's instincts are no less correct than his judgment. For clearly Henry did make a difference: he ruled as well as reigned in a way which even a few centuries later would become less likely and more ambiguous in a monarch. As W. L. Warren weighs Henry's aims and accomplishments, especially in creating the trans-Channel Angevin Empire, he is not using the king as a term for collective government, he is not referring to the crown, but to the head that wore it:

> The territories which came to Henry as the result of two marriages—the marriage of his father [Geoffrey] to the heiress [Matilda] of England and Normandy, and his own marriage to the heiress [Eleanor] of Aquitaine—were almost beyond the possibility of effective control. In other hands than his they almost certainly would have been. Henry II's consolidation and defense of his authority in these vast dominions rested upon his mastery of the art of warfare, and this in turn rested upon his ability to turn his capital resources into available wealth. Henry's technique for enhancing his wealth was not conquest and plunder but efficient management. This meant, above all, the efficient management of England, for England was his principal source of wealth. Of course, if this had been all, Henry II might have been remembered simply as an efficient exploiter; but it was not all, for it was Henry's genius to make efficient management synonymous with sound government.[10]

There is some danger in seeing Henry II's efficient management, including his formative impact on the origins and development of the common law revealed in Glanvill, as motivated merely by profit and dictated only by economic materialism. A useful antidote is provided by van Caenegem, who noted that while there were profits of justice, these amounted to a few hundred pounds against a total revenue of about £35,000 *per annum*: "What an elaborate, onerous and farfetched way of filling the royal chest, when the king could and did use such simple methods as levying huge arbitrary forest fines or leaving some bishopric vacant for a little longer to receive a yearly extra income of over £1000, without any trouble."[11]

We are aware that power is as alluring an objective as money, perhaps more so to any but the most rapacious of rulers. The legal and judicial reforms moved by Henry II with the assistance of his justiciars and other officials made his power palpable among a feudal baronage of a bare three generations' standing. This baronage's great-grandfathers had comprised that knightly band of thugs whose instincts were still hardly elevated above the piratical level of their Norse recent-forebears when they joined Henry's great-grandfather—William the Bastard, Duke of Normandy—in a conquest that was one of the best-rewarded acts of aggression, acquisition, and annexation in history. The essentially centrifugal thrust of the feudal contract, nexus, counsel, aid was erosive of kingship and corrosive of order. It required much curbing—as King Stephen learned, as Henry II knew because he helped teach Stephen, and as Henry's son, John, would learn too late at Runnymede in 1215. Henry could plait in a network of genuine interdependence not only his own barons but the barons of his barons by litigation in his court. There remedy was made freely and cheaply available, rationally and quickly acquirable, efficaciously implemented, and even-handedly extended in that most critical and contentious area of interest, the *meum et tuum* of land. By the end of the reign of Henry II, it was established "law" that no man need answer for his free-tenement, whether he held it of the King or not, save he be impleaded by the King's writ. So popular was this invasion of the long-established feudal responsibility of the lord to do justice to his vassal, that the baronage of England, when it revolted against John for his oppressive actions, demanded paradoxically better access to and more of his justice. Magna Carta, Article 17, provided that the royal court of "common pleas shall not follow our court, but shall be held in some definite place." Article 40 asserted that "to no one will we sell, to no one will we deny or delay right or justice." The *curia regis*, the King's court, of Henry II was a kind of proto-Versailles where a monarch no less enamored of power and cognizant of how to acquire and maintain it than Louis XIV five centuries later and across the water bound up a fractious nobility in law-doing. Historians have long shrugged off the arms/law observation with which Glanvill's Prologue begins:

> Not only must royal power be furnished with arms against rebels and nations which rise up against the king and the realm, but it is also fitting that it should be adorned with laws for the governance of subject and peaceful peoples.[12]

This has been treated as an imitative Romanist conceit, proving Glanvill was familiar with Justinian's Institutes but hackneyed in his use of it.[13] That is to ignore a salient fact of Glanvill's own experience, that law in the hands of Henry II was a powerful "arm against rebels."

Moreover, it can be easily overlooked that the law that Henry fashioned with which to govern his francophone subjects, the barons and greater freemen of the realm, was also applicable to the anglophone race who still bore the Norman Yoke imposed by the Conquest—provided that they were freemen, not villeins (which the vast majority still were), "subject and peaceful peoples." The acculturating power of that law should never be underestimated. It would become the birthright of an undifferentiated English people by the fourteenth century. Old English lambs would finally lie down with Old Norman lions, not to be devoured by them. The process was already well-begun by intermarriage at the level of the aristocracy in Henry II's time, was much advanced after the Anglo-Norman barons lost their Norman lands in 1204 and were forced to bend to domestic tranquility on the island, and was finally accomplished in a merging of language, culture, genetic traits, and social identification by Chaucer's age, two centuries after Glanvill's.

In Glanvill Henry II's revolution stands revealed. This was an emperor with clothes. Most of Henry II's legislation, those famous "constitutions" and "assizes" evocative of what are today sleepy country towns which every legal historian feels obliged to toll in at least one lecture, are explicitly or implicitly evident in the account. At least all of the writs relevant to the King's court find a place, especially the *praecipe quod reddat*, the four possessory assizes, *mort d'ancestor*, *darrein presentment*, *utrum*, and *novel disseisin*, and the first writs of a whole new class, those of gage (if not all in extenso, then at least by treatment). These were the first writs of course, boilerplate instruments which gave the King's court jurisdiction and demanded the parties' amenableness to it. They were the common law's first forms of action, and so made it truly "common" in the sense that one law, of one procedure and one substance, for each writ was available to any freeman for the assertion of his interest in any free tenement with the mere purchase of the writ. Moreover, there are analyses of those specific developments and elements in the law which either did not depend at that time upon a writ (or, more aptly, a writ-form) or were subject to ambivalent approaches leading to ambiguous doctrine underwent treatment, some of it the most brilliant and speculatively powerful treatment: Book VII is the quintessential example of that achievement. Crime receives scant attention, though sufficient (and appropriate, given the work's plan) explanation is accorded those delicts which were repressed in the King's courts. Likewise, writs proper to the old jurisdiction of the shire-reeve are dealt with summarily. But what is not stinted is Glanvill's detailed treatment of the almost cosmically important institution of the common law, the recognitors or jury. This institution's critical role as a better probative mousetrap went an almost incalculable distance in promoting the jurisdiction of the King's courts. So complete is Glanvill's analysis, modern scholarship can occasionally escape lengthy explanation with, "Glanvill has given such a clear explanation of the procedure followed in a grand assize that a brief outline may be sufficient here."[14] In any case, when we begin discussing the jury, we begin—as in so many areas of our law—with Glanvill.

Henry II's revolution was more than a personal triumph and it was more than an extension of the dynastic vigor brought by the Conquest of 1066. Like every revolution, it was in part the product of certain "preconditions." These were complex and mixed, even confused. But they are worth sorting out, because they determined the emergence of that peculiar institution which is the common law and many of its attributes.

First and foremost, Henry II was a new-style monarch without any single contemporary exemplar and no regal peer in Latin Europe. Neither the Germano-Roman emperors, even the inimitable and energetic Frederick Barbarossa (1152–1190), nor the Capetian kings of France, least of all Henry's contemptible challenger Louis VII (1137–1180), wielded a regality commensurate with Henry's. The reasons are not difficult to discover. First, both German and French feudal governance were consequences of a long process in which confrontation between lord and vassal—king and baronage—had fashioned checks and balances resulting at critical moments in stalemate. Not so in Anglo-Norman England. William, Duke of Normandy, had introduced feudalism in 1066—and he was prudent never to allow his vassals the power-base, stance, and attitude to challenge him which he, vassal of the King of France as Duke of Normandy, had so effectively turned against his lord. In short, William and his sons, William II and Henry I, fashioned their own particular brand of feudalism, more feudal in form than in substance.

Secondly, William consciously and explicitly found the substance of his monarchy in the hegemonic and unifying qualities of Anglo-Saxon and Danish kingship, which had obtained since the West Saxon king, Alfred the Great, had created a unitary Anglo-Saxon kingdom holding sway over the whole of southern England in the latter part of the ninth century. In the two centuries before the Conquest, Alfred's construct had waned and waxed again, never so extensive but internally more cohesive and culturally more resistant than it had been before. It had survived Norse pillaging, absorbed conquest from the Danes to the north, and withstood internal rebellion. It was a monument to survival and resilient statecraft. William claimed he was nothing more than the rightful heir, successor, and assign of the last true Anglo-Saxon king, Edward the Confessor, and he let slip none of the powers and pre-eminences which the last Danish king, Cnut, had enjoyed a generation earlier. Anglo-Saxon kingship had created centralized institutions, notably the gathering of great landholders and great ecclesiastics in the *witenagemot*, a precursor of the Anglo-Norman *curia regis*, blended with local jurisdictions based on the shires or counties with aeolderman and shire-reeve responsible for the preservation of order and the administration of local government. Anglo-Saxon kings had legislated, within a consensual framework which fell short of the feudal *consilium* but went well beyond the constraints characteristic of Germanic tribal chieftainship. Anglo-Saxon kingship presented an attainable ideal of what monarchy could achieve by unitary action even in the pluralistic world of feudatories. All of the Anglo-Norman kings—even Stephen, the weakest and worst positioned of them—were ready to attempt the ideal.

Another significant precondition was what the great American medievalist of a couple of generations ago, Charles Homer Haskins, called the "twelfth century renaissance." The allusion is a bit too studied, one supposes (renaissances are always diaphanous enough without multiplying them), but it calls attention to the remarkable intellectual and cultural efflorescence of the century. The phenomena are well-known, and a checklist of the more prominent will do: the foundation and rise of the universities; the rediscovery of classical learning (especially Aristotle); the creation of jurisprudence under the influence of Justinian's Roman law and the stimulation of papal hegemony in the raising of canon law; the new and more rigorous forms of Benedictine monasticism and the new worldly orders of friars, Dominicans and Franciscans; the soaring openness, almost pyrotechnical brilliance, and daring of Gothic architecture in contrast to the more stolid, solid, and less imaginative qualities of the Romanesque; the new plasticity and suppleness in painting and sculpture; the broadened horizons created by the outward imperialistic urge loosed by the Crusades; the new wealth, commercial activity, and civic self-awareness and pride of the towns of Europe;

the sudden, dramatic, absence of any pagan or particularly parlous infidel threats directly aimed at Latin Europe. It was an epoch in which there was enough leisure from getting and spending, killing and being killed, fearing and terrorizing, that energies could be released to gentler and more civil ends of mind and spirit. The most immediate result was something akin to an educational revolution. More people of more modest background were finding more opportunity to acquire more education and better prospects for better utilizing that education. This is the first age of an intellectual elite in Europe which was accorded a universal recognition outside the narrow confines of its own academies and *fora*. Perforce, much of that elite found role and function in the Church as clerics, though also serving the state in an age when the best theory saw Church and state as two edges of the same sword of faith and morals. But if the Church claimed most of the educated class, it did not absorb them all. Henry of Anjou could claim to be at least an adjunct to it. And he certainly was assiduous in advancing the perquisites, place, and powers of the intellectual elite to his own ends in his own service. Remarkably he encountered only one "treasonous clerk," and even Becket was able to accomplish only in death the ecclesiological ends that had otherwise eluded him when quick.

England benefited from the twelfth-century renaissance in a way in which it would never again quite partake of a European-wide cultural explosion. Its two universities were early foundations and eminent ones. The new monastic orders, prominent among them the energetic and capitalistic Cistercians, had enormous impact in the more remote parts of England; the friars arrived in a wave, and Robin Hood's Friar Tuck was a caricature of a real enough type. English clerics found ready employment in the services of secular rulers everywhere, and not least in the papal curia. One Englishman became Pope Adrian IV (1154–1159) and, having tangled with Emperor Frederick Barbarossa, confessed he was sorry to have left England. English towns and commerce grew rapidly. English architecture was on the cutting edge of technology and aesthetics by the end of the century as evidenced by Salisbury Cathedral. The new English intelligentsia, in service of Church and state, took second place to none. John of Salisbury (d. 1180) was a Classical scholar of revered learning, and in his *Policraticus* (1159) provided the European world with its first original rather than simply derivative treatise on political theory, advancing the unsettling proposition that under certain clearly prescribed circumstances resistance to regal authority was not merely justified but a Christian duty even if it extended to tyrannicide. And that pragmatic and meticulous analysis of how the financial organ of

Henry II's state, the Exchequer, operated, written by Richard fitz Neal in the later 1170's, had no parallel anywhere for another generation: the *Dialogus de Scaccario*. The *Dialogue of the Exchequer* was a monument to the most sophisticated and efficient instrument of government and bureaucracy that operated it anywhere in Europe—and it was Henry II's, the *deus ex machina* of his state, imperial grasp, and good government. Indeed, *Policraticus* and the *Dialogue of the Exchequer* are not only singularly remarkable achievements, but when taken with Glanvill demonstrate the precocity of English politico-constitutional letters in that age.

Glanvill memorialized, even lauded, the vigorous and peculiar Anglo-Norman monarchy, while maintaining a tacitly respectful appreciation for the dynamics of feudalism. In this its author represented the reality of the age. He was also a child of the twelfth century renaissance. He was aware of and admired the Roman and canonical legal scholarship which was blossoming on the Continent and attracting adherents in England. To a point, as Derek Hall makes clear, Glanvill was prepared to use the new scholarship for purposes of contrast and to assist in clarity. But he did not need it for form or structure: these he created largely by himself for his own ends and uses. Here was the achievement for which all the commentators praise the author of Glanvill, Creator.

In retrospect, Henry II, his justiciars and the curia regis, the common law, and not least Glanvill, arrived together at a critical moment to consolidate old kingship into new monarchy, new feudalism into old statecraft, and create a legal system that united rather than divided, confirmed centralization at the expense of the centrifugal force of provincialism, and worked by a procedure of such simplicity and suppleness that it could carry the substantive law in its interstices. The structure of Anglo-Norman government and its common law matured to a tough amalgam in a single generation, resilient enough to survive a Romano-canonical "reception" of sorts in areas of law-doing outside the arena of the common law, pragmatic enough to adapt new doctrines and new procedures to the common law's needs, and attractive enough not to lose the affection and fidelity of King, judges, lawyers, and litigants. The Age of Henry II—it might be called the Age of Glanvill—built so soundly, so high, and so mighty a law that it survived all challenges and threats, the erosion of routine governance, and outlived all other institutions as well as those who would subvert it. There is something almost eerie in this. Hall remarks, that for Glanvill, "the authorities" upon which he perforce founded his work "were writs, the legislation of Henry II, the practice of the king's court and the opinions of its judges."[15] Analyze that observation for a moment, and one sees that in Glanvill are to be found gathered all the various, and at least superficially antagonistic, ways in which later jurists have looked at common law authority: John Austin's sovereign legislator, Oliver Wendell Holmes' experience, and John Chipman Gray's judge. In Glanvill is the precious pluralism which has been the glory of our law, even when it has been the despair of the litigant.

A final observation. Glanvill's writs assume that the role of the law is to benefit private interests at least as much as to serve public ends. The point is fundamental to the nature of a free and liberal regime of law, for upon it rests not only the difference between private law and public law, but between rights and restrictions, ultimately between the individual and the state. The writs could not help but make the distinction, since they dealt with Blackacre, the very stuff of feudalism and all that flowed into it, through it, and from it. We were reminded of such "dilemmatics" in that year of miracles following the fall of the Berlin Wall, on November 9, 1989, when the long ballyhooed and mightily trumpeted "inevitable" triumph of the Marxist dialectic, of scientific socialism, of the eclipse of private property suddenly evaporated. Revealed stood an emperor not only without clothes, but even without hair. Soon we began to notice, in our law schools, and even in our law firms, earnest young Russian and Eastern European legists, who disavowed any faith in old-school socialist law and, with an engaging innocence that melted even the hardest heart of an old cold warrior, asked how they could restructure law to protect the rights of the individual. They had trouble understanding that there could be no easy solution: the United States Constitution, the rule of law, our criminal code, our jury, all our other institutions . . . even if instituted all together and with the best will in the world implemented with an assiduity and an unflaggingly high-minded unqualified respect for justice, would not answer their need or slake their thirst. We told them that they must start with private law, with the law of property and of contract, the law that does not wait upon Caesar for its being or its authority. They must start where we did. They must start with Glanvill. They too would have to be, as it were, present at the Creation.

CHAPTER TWO

Magna Carta

That irreverent "Memorable History of England" containing "103 Good Things, . . . 5 Bad Kings, . . . [and] 2 Genuine Dates"—*1066 and All That*—lists King John as a Bad King but fails entirely to give 1215 as a Genuine Date. This is a pity, because "Magna Charter" is given exhaustive treatment, under six headings, ending with a triumphant proclamation: "Magna Charter was therefore the chief cause of Democracy in England, and thus a *Good Thing* for everyone (except the Common People)."[1] Over the past two centuries, historians who were more serious, if not necessarily more erudite, have come to substantially the same conclusions. And they have never failed to credit the events at Runnymede as constituting June 15, 1215 a Genuine Date, and therefore entirely Memorable.

Magna Carta claims a unique place in Anglo-American legal and constitutional tradition. But its role has been different on the two sides of the Atlantic because British and American constitutionalism have taken different paths from a point of common departure in the seventeenth century. It is a truism that British constitutionalism is not based upon "fundamental law" and that the whole law—understood as the rule of law—is fundamental to its vitality. Perhaps that is true, and as far as it goes that is determinative. However, even in British law, there has been no law more fundamental than Magna Carta. The circumstances surrounding its promulgation were unique in British history. It was a comprehensive concession of rights wrung from a reluctant monarch by a baronage (for all practical purposes, the political nation) in open rebellion. The concessions were the price of civil quiet, the cost paid by John for his continuation upon his throne, the settlement of a revolutionary situation, which, in the event, failed to avert civil war. In all the other baronial insurrections of the Middle Ages, before and after Runnymede, no such comprehensive concessions were exacted from a King as ransom for his throne. The two other great documents of English liberty which come close to Magna Carta in being accorded attributes of fundamentality did not constitute ransom in a revolutionary situation. The Petition of Right of 1628 was moved by a Parliament vociferous in its sense of grievance but not in rebellion against Charles I, and the Bill of Rights of 1689 was not understood to be a *quid pro quo* for William III's assumption of the throne vacated by the convenient "abdication" of James II in 1688.

Magna Carta was unique, too, in being so often re-promulgated or confirmed in the decades after its creation. In November 1216, John's son and heir, Henry III, confirmed it for the first time, in order to consolidate his accession to the throne and to rally the baronage against the invasion of the heir of the French king in prosecution of his claim to the English throne. With the expulsion of the French in the next year, Henry reissued Magna Carta (shorn of the clauses concerning forests, which were drawn into a separate Charter of Forest Liberties). In 1225, Henry would give, in his third confirmation, the final form to Magna Carta. By 1301 Magna Carta and the Charter of the Forest had been reissued or confirmed at least fifteen times, usually as consideration for a grant of revenue to the king. What is most striking about these repeated re-promulgations of Magna Carta was the wide publicity given to its provisions by proclamation in the countryside. If later, revisionist, historians argued that Magna Carta was a charter of liberties only for a small baronage, in furtherance of the interests primarily of the feudatories, its frequent reissue during its first century, with the widest publicity the age allowed, impressed it on the fabric of the entire polity as the source of liberties under law of all English freemen.

Magna Carta could not have survived, neither would it have acquired (if only for a season) the attributes of fundamentality in English constitutionalism, had it remained merely part of the English historical ethos and a pious declaration, oft-repeated, of liberties in the high Middle Ages. It required implementation, as law. This it also received with remarkable consistency in its first century. Neither the instrument consented to by John at Runnymede in 1215 nor the final version of the Great Charter confirmed in 1225 by Henry III are technically "statutes," if one accepts the proposition that without Parliament (an institution still a half century away even in its most inchoate form) there could be no statute. Yet from the fourteenth century onwards, manuscript collections of the statutes usually began with Magna Carta. The early common lawyers were unaware of our later technical niceties, that statutes were to be made by the King by and with the advice and consent of the Lords Spiritual and Temporal and the Commons in Parliament assembled, but the common lawyers understood that the process by which the Great Charter had come into being, the colloquy of King, prelates and barons in 1215, constituted as broad a consensual base as the practice of government at that time allowed and broader than that which undergirded the great legislative enactments of a half-century earlier under John's father, Henry II, which marked the true beginnings of the common law. As Lady Stenton noted, "The common law received in Magna Carta its first generally recognized statute, written law, authoritative at the date of its publication."[2]

Although henceforth statutes became an increasingly common device for changing the law as need required, and some of those changes modified some of the provisions of Magna Carta, that first statute itself proved unrepealable and its intended rights indestructible. Edward II and Parliament by ordinances in 1311 declared that statutes made by the King's ancestors that were not contrary to Magna Carta, the Charter of the Forest, or the other provisions of these ordinances were to be maintained. In 1368, in once again confirming Magna Carta, Parliament declared that acts contrary to it were void.[3] Even when Magna Carta was not cited explicitly, its rhetoric permeated statute. Another statute of 1368, to prevent abuses by false accusers, enacted that "no man be drawn to answer without presentment before justices, or matter of record, or by due process and original writ, according to the ancient law of the land"—a clear and unambiguous echo of Magna Carta's famous Clause 39 (Clause 29 in the 1225 confirmation).[4] Magna Carta, like all medieval statutes, but rather more emphatically than the rest, was assimilated by common law, even absorbed into it. By *Confirmatio Cartarum* (1297), Edward I and Parliament, in putting Magna Carta on the Statute Rolls, imposed Magna Carta on the courts "as common law."[5] This absorption constituted apotheosis: Magna Carta had become almost solo the law of the land, a veritable fountain of the laws and liberties of Englishmen.

Apotheosis exacted a price. Because Magna Carta became so much an accepted and routinely incorporated part of the common law, the perception of its uniqueness was dulled. Magna Carta itself became a liability in late medieval pleading: counsel who argued the Charter were chided by the judges for taking "frivolous exceptions." The rhetoric of liberty under law used in the courts of law was so much a commonplace that it had become a cliché by the end of the fourteenth century. The Charter was also of questionable relevance when the kingdom faced the hard political realities that came with the Houses of Lancaster and York struggling for the throne in the fifteenth century. Then the threat to liberty under law came less from the King than from the feudatories who fuelled and fought the dynastic civil wars and who bought and sold justice by corrupting juries and intimidating judges, lawyers, sheriffs, and litigants by the menace of their private armies. Political reality dictated strong monarchy, and strong monarchy came with the first Tudor King, Henry VII, in 1485.

After two centuries of being largely ignored by Parliament and the courts, Magna Carta enjoyed a phenomenal revival in the seventeenth century. A century of rigorous Tudor governance worked a religious revolution from the top in the Reformation, expanded enormously the political nation by Tudor monarchy's reliance upon Parliament (a legislature increasingly dominated by a broadly based landed gentry endowed with the spoils of ecclesiastical lands) and, inevitably, introduced political abuses which Parliament-men found increasingly intolerable under the Tudors' successors, James I and Charles I. Why such a fundamental law of the land as Magna Carta would be refurbished to do battle against what was perceived to be a growing tyranny in state and Church is not difficult to explain. How it was possible for Magna Carta, so long ignored and so much neglected, to be revived is more complex. If Magna Carta was to be mobilized and sent into battle against Stuart "despotism," its provisions and the history surrounding its origins would have to have been strongly impressed on the consciousness of the greater political nation.

Early seventeenth-century Englishmen did not have far to look for their history of John, the barons, and Runnymede. For the Latinist, Matthew Paris's *Angli Historia Maior,* a contemporary chronicle of the reigns of John and Henry III, was printed in 1571, and his highly derogatory portrait of John was unforgettable. Much more significant was the publication in 1577 of Raphael Holinshed's *Chronicles of England, Scotlande, and Irelande.* Written in English in a clear, even exciting, prose, Holinshed was a best-seller. The second, expanded, edition of 1587 enjoyed even more success, and was the source for Shakespeare's history plays. Holinshed was a new-style humanist historian, with much didactic purpose, a desire for comprehensiveness of treatment, a good sense of evidence, and a genuine concern to avoid anachronism. His treatment of John and Magna Carta was highly critical of the King and very favorable to the barons. With Holinshed began the historiographic reputation of the barons as the redeemers of English liberties from Norman tyranny. It has been noted that nowhere in Shakespeare's

King John is there mention of Magna Carta. The explanations are either fatuous (Shakespeare did not regard the Charter "as good theatre") or merely wrong (the Charter was forgotten or "there was no Magna Carta to bother Elizabeth").[6] Thanks in large part to Holinshed, Magna Carta was well remembered, evocation of it certainly did bother Elizabeth, and Shakespeare probably thought it politically discreet not to provide a highly dramatic scene of a reluctant John sealing the Charter surrounded by glowering, menacing barons!

For the provisions of Magna Carta had never disappeared from the lawyers' view. Following the long tradition of the manuscript collections, the first comprehensive printed collection of statutes, Richard Pynson's *Magna Charta cum aliis Antiquis Statutis* (1508) established the practice followed invariably for three centuries (until the publication, 1810–1820, of the authoritative compilation, *Statutes of the Realm)* of beginning the statutes with Magna Carta, the 1225 version. Pynson's work, continued by other printers, sometimes translated into English (from 1534), ran to at least twenty editions by 1587. Abridgments of the statutes—also beginning with Magna Carta—appeared in even greater numbers and more editions. By the end of Elizabeth's reign, no lawyer would have been without some such collection, and Magna Carta would meet his eye as soon as he opened the book. Little wonder that Edward Coke of the Inner Temple began to make notes on the early statutes, with pride of place to the Great Charter. Yet long before Coke's famous *Second Institutes*, a thorough if rambling commentary on Magna Carta and the other early statutes, was published (posthumously, by order of the Long Parliament) in 1642, the Great Charter had been increasingly raised in court and Parliament. It would be sent into full battle by Coke and other MPs during the Parliaments of the 1620's. But it fell to two lesser lawyers to fight the first skirmishes soon after Holinshed and the printed statutes worked a new appreciation of Magna Carta.

Robert Beale, Clerk of the Privy Council, and James Morice, Attorney of the Court of Wards and Liveries, in the 1580's and 1590's attacked the Court of High Commission for exacting an oath of the defendant to accuse himself. By treatises and as Members in Parliament they repeatedly summoned Magna Carta, Clause 39, as their authority against such self-incrimination. Their attacks, which earned them both reproof and Morice imprisonment, were the first steps in that expansion of Clause 39 which led ultimately to the Fifth Amendment of the United States Constitution. They also sounded the tocsin that would be tolled throughout the next century in opposition to Stuart abuses. Magna Carta was revived.

Magna Carta served in three ways as a weapon against what was perceived as arbitrary Stuart government. First, as "law," it was held to deny authority to the monarch to impose taxation without parliamentary consent and to imprison or put on trial the subject without due process of law. In the first case it protected the property of the subject, in the second his liberty. These were the two foci of the political and constitutional confrontation in Stuart England between the political nation and the King, and therefore Magna Carta fit the real concerns of the age perfectly.

Secondly, as "fundamental law"—for such Coke and other lawyers argued Magna Carta was—it provided as much constitutional theory in defense of liberty as the political nation of landowners, lawyers, and merchants were prepared to accept as respectable and sufficient until John Locke's *Two Treatises on Civil Government,* published after the Glorious Revolution of 1688, totally recast English constitutional and political theory. Magna Carta strongly reinforced the fifteenth-century notion, revived in the seventeenth, that England was a mixed monarchy, in which the King ruled in concert with the estates represented in Parliament. It was hailed as the first statute, the product of consensus between King, barons, and the Church in 1215, so often reiterated in medieval practice. Both the Petition of Right of 1628 and the Bill of Rights of 1689 were raised on this intellectual foundation, and were seen by contemporaries as being explanations or refinements in particulars of the Great Charter, suited to the new age.

Thirdly, as "history," Magna Carta was the seventeenth-century Englishman's link with the supposed ancient laws and liberties of Anglo-Saxon times, a system of belief in which Parliament and the common law were claimed to be as old, if not older, than monarchy itself. The event at Runnymede was celebrated as the moment when the yoke of Norman tyranny was lifted from the necks of the English people. What had been done on a grassy island *in* the Thames in 1215 could be done again, this time in the Parliament House *by* the Thames. Until 1642, the political nation could pride itself on its growing success in withstanding tyranny, and in avoiding a civil war such as had raged between John and the barons after Runnymede. With 1642, that comforting illusion was shattered. The civil wars of 1642–1648 replayed 1215–1216, with the even more dreadful result of a King dethroned, tried and condemned as the enemy of his people, and publicly executed, with a republic set in the place of monarchy.

It was with these events and the decade of republicanism which followed that Magna Carta's role began in the New World, on a course very different from that which it took in the Old. The revolutionary episode of mid-seventeenth century England turned the nation inexorably away from constitutionalism based on fundamental law. A decade of republican experiment produced five years of haphazard institutional change best described as chaos and one written constitution, the Instrument of Government of 1653, which was a triumph of mixed monarchy with the monarch called the Lord Protector in the person of Oliver Cromwell. Legitimacy eluded the regime; the regime did not survive Cromwell's death. With the Restoration of Charles II in 1660, not upon explicit conditions but by a tacit understanding that he would abide by the early legislation of the Long Parliament which had corrected the abuses of his father, legitimacy was restored in the person of the monarch and in the institution of monarchy. Written constitutionalism based upon fundamental law, tainted by its origins in the Instrument of Government, was discredited. The Restoration settlement avoided it.

English constitutionalism returned to dependence upon the rule of law, the preservation of liberties by the working of law that was less than fundamental law. Magna Carta was cast back to its more modest role of mere "law" protecting the property of the subject and the liberty of his person. It achieved some notable successes: the Habeas Corpus Act of 1679 and, above all, the Bill of Rights of 1689. But it could do no more. If English liberties were to be maintained and even advanced, political rather than constitutional practice would have to provide the impetus and the consolidation of gains. With the rise of Parliament to an indispensable routine function in government, with ministerial responsibility to Parliament, with the enlargement of the Parliamentary franchise, and ultimately with the sovereignty of Parliament over the sovereign King—all of which was accomplished over the two centuries after 1688—political practice was perfected. British constitutionalism, allowing for the protection of liberties by the rule of law, had come to eschew both a written instrument and fundamental law and to rest upon restrained, customary, political activity in a House of Commons elected by a democratic franchise and organized by two competing major political parties. Magna Carta had done its work: it could be enshrined as a once-mighty instrument of liberty of extraordinary historical significance to the nation but no longer of much real utility.

It was otherwise in the New World. All of England's early colonies there were founded upon charters, not a Great Charter, but each a little charter created by the exercise of the royal prerogative in the form of a written instrument of letters patent, the charter defining the powers of government to be exercised by the undertakers of the colonies. Such a charter was, from the perspective of the colonial company and the colonists, "fundamental law." Under the charter, sometimes despite it, practical measures of government were instituted for the unusual exigencies facing the creation of a new polity in a wilderness. The distinction between the normative requirements of the charter and the real institutions and practices of government made the charters even more "fundamental" by making them remote from the routine of governance, and sometimes far away from the hands of those charged with government in the colony. This was true whether the colonial charter remained in London (as in the case of Virginia) or was carried to the colony (as in Massachusetts). Moreover, since the charter was a written instrument, it constituted a written fundamental law. The colonial charter was one foundation of American constitutionalism, and probably the single most important one.

The other was Magna Carta. At the time that Virginia and Massachusetts and the other early colonies came into existence, Magna Carta enjoyed its greatest and widest importance in English political life. In its threefold role discussed above, Magna Carta had something for all Englishmen, on both sides of the Atlantic. For those who were starting anew, it offered even more: they were beginning to build polities from the ground up and they were concerned to preserve the laws and liberties of Englishmen. This was a theme that ran through the early charters and, even more significantly, the early laws and practices of the colonies. To these men, Magna Carta *was* fundamental law. They sought in their new cities-upon-a-hill to preserve it as native Englishmen and to imitate it in their own laws as colonial Englishmen. Thus, John Winthrop, the guiding mind and hand of the Massachusetts Bay colony, noted in his journal in 1635:

> The deputies [of the General Court] having conceived great danger to our state, in regard that our magistrates, for want of positive laws, in many cases, might proceed according to their discretions, it was agreed that some men should be appointed to frame a body of grounds of laws, in resemblance to a Magna Charta, which, being allowed by some of the ministers, and the general court, should be received for fundamental laws.[7]

The fruits of that endeavor were two-fold: Nathaniel Ward's "Body of Liberties" of 1641 and the first printed comprehensive compilation of laws of any English colony, *The Book of the General Lawes and Libertyes Concerning the Inhabitants of the Massachusets*, 1648. The titles almost say it all. The "Body of Liberties" was very much more graven in the image of Magna Carta than was the *Lawes and Libertyes,* but the latter contained all but nine of the ninety-five substantive clauses in the former.[8] America's first statute book provided not only good laws to govern by, but also law to preserve basic liberties. Clearly and forcefully, this echoed the Great Charter. The sitting of the General Court that ordered the printing of the *Lawes and Libertyes* was also quite unambiguous about what it intended when, "to the end we may have the better light for making & proceeding about lawes," it ordered that two copies of "Coke upon Magna Charta" be procured for its use.[9]

Americans never retired Magna Carta to a pantheon of past blessings of slight current utility. As the Great Charter waned in practical applicability in eighteenth-century Britain, it gathered strength in the American colonies as a bulwark against imperial abuses. John Adams in a spirited defense against trial without jury in the vice-admiralty court in Boston in 1769 asserted that "The People of England are attached to Magna Charta." He quoted Clause 39 verbatim, cited Coke to the point, and closed with a demand for the summoning of a jury and that the defendant "be tryed by Magna Charta."[10] The English in America were in fact more attached to Magna Carta than the English in England.

Long after the liberties of the American nation were founded upon the Constitution of 1789 and its first ten amendments—the latter owing so much, some explicitly, more implicitly, to the Great Charter—Magna Carta is still accorded a reverence in the United States that continually astonishes Englishmen by its fervency. On July 28, 1957, a host of British and American legal dignitaries gathered on the tiny island at Runnymede to dedicate a monument to Magna Carta erected by the American Bar Association, which met in London that summer. The Americans were visibly moved as the drape fell from a simple stone column bearing, under a prominent (and very American) star, the legend "To commemorate Magna Carta, symbol of freedom under law." A casual, youthful observer did not appreciate at the time the irony of it all. He does now. For the column, which is massive, is protected from proverbial English weather by a delicate classical rotunda, open on all sides between the columns supporting the cupola, a veritable pantheon indeed. Both peoples, the fathers of Magna Carta and the scions who have cherished the patrimony, are nicely caught, doubtless unconsciously, in the architectural structure: the English in the temple, the American in the altar.

CHAPTER THREE

Thomas Littleton

The motto of Sir Thomas Littleton, Justice of the Common Pleas from 1466 until his death in 1481, was "*Ung Dieu et Ung Roy*," One God and One King—appropriately enough, in the Anglo-Norman French become Law French in which Littleton wrote his *Tenures*. The conventional piety with which Littleton prefaced his will and his provision of a £5 annual endowment for chantry Masses indicate that his belief in the God of the medieval Catholic world was entirely orthodox.[1] About "One King" there is a touch of irony, for Littleton served rival kings. Raised to the dignity of a King's Serjeant-at-Law by the Lancastrian Henry VI in 1455, Littleton served that monarch faithfully as legal advisor and judge of assize. In 1461, when Edward, Duke of York, drove Henry from his throne and took the crown as King Edward IV, Littleton was reappointed King's Serjeant and five years later made one of the three puisne judges of the Court of Common Pleas. Unlike his contemporary, Sir John Fortescue, who lost his place as Chief Justice of the King's Bench and loyally went into exile with Henry's family, Littleton, eschewing such political demonstrations, managed to survive the dynastic changes of the Wars of the Roses.[2]

Littleton's motto might just as well have been "Ung Droict et Ung Livre," One Law and One Book. The One Law was the common law of England, particularly the law of property, of which Littleton demonstrated a peerless mastery in his One Book, *Les Tenures de Lyttleton*.[3] For upon that mastery and that book was built the undying fame of Thomas Littleton, as well as the English-speaking world's understanding of the structure and much of the dynamic of its property law for some three and one-half centuries.

Littleton's *Tenures* was a prodigy, a book that rated as a genuine classic within a few years of its publication. It is a classic by the verdict of history, the first book of English law ever printed, and one of the earliest books printed in England. During the reign of Edward IV, probably in 1481, it came from a press set up by two foreign printers near one of the eight churches of All Hallows in the City of London.[4] When it was reprinted for the first time, only two or three years later, the *Tenures* had embarked on its way to being one of the greatest commercial successes in legal publishing. Between 1481 and 1639 the *Tenures* went to forty-six distinct printings in French, between 1525 and 1661 to thirty-five in English, and in 1671 to one edition in both languages—a total of eighty-two distinct printings.[5] Hardly any major early printer of English law books failed to bring out one or more editions of Littleton, and the famous Richard Tottell alone produced twenty-eight editions in both languages. During the working life of the *Tenures*—that is, from 1481 until it was wholly superseded by Coke upon Littleton in the mid-seventeenth century—only in one decade (the 1500's) was there no edition printed, save for the 1630's there were never fewer than three per decade, and from the 1520's through the 1590's the printers issued an average of more than seven editions per decade. During the sixteenth century, only the Bible in English, with 118 editions, bested Littleton. Indeed, not since Gutenberg first wrought has any legal book come closer to challenging Scripture's printed primacy than Littleton did.

Littleton's burgeoning popularity in the last three-quarters of the sixteenth century was closely connected with that remarkable phenomenon, termed "the education of the gentry," which began just before mid-century and continued until the civil war in the 1640's. It became the vogue for young gentlemen of the landed aristocracy (or those who aspired to join the landed aristocracy) to be sent in their early teens to one of the universities for a few years, and afterwards for a year or two to study at one of the four Inns of Court. It was not intended that these young men would take a degree at Oxford or Cambridge; that was for those bent on taking religious orders, or who sought to be civil lawyers or physicians. Rather, they were to be exposed to the higher elements of basic Classical learning and introduced to polite manners. Likewise, sojourn at the Inns was not meant to produce barristers; it was to expose them to the city life of London and Westminster and to introduce them to the rudiments of law, so much law, particularly property law, as they would need to manage their estates.[6] Between 1530 and 1550, all four Inns of Court together averaged eighty to ninety admissions per year. This rose to over two hundred annual admissions in 1580–1584 and reached to a high point of over three hundred in 1615–1619, then began falling, to a nadir of one hundred and seventy-five admissions in 1640–1644.[7] From 1580 to 1639, one barrister was called for about every six students admitted; and about three-quarters of those who were called to the bar appear to have practiced law.[8]

How did this glut of more-or-less serious young men learn that property law which was, if anything was, the object of their sojourn at the Inns? Principally, by reading Littleton's *Tenures*. The *Tenures* was the only text on the subject, it was relatively small (and therefore relatively cheap), and it had more direct relevance to legal pedagogy than almost everything else that went on at the Inns. (The semi-annual readings, lectures on statutes by senior barristers, could be enlightening; but these could be too erudite for anyone but the most dedicated apprentice-at-law.) Had there been no market for Littleton other than the crowd of gilded youth on the western fringes of London, the *Tenures* would still have been a best-seller. Littleton's popularity reflected a readership that was other, and broader, than merely professional and learned.

The waning of Littleton's popularity also reflected the student market. There was a rapid decline of new editions in the first three decades of the seventeenth century, while the number of entrants to the Inns continued to rise. There is no reason to believe that these young gentlemen were any less assiduous than their grandsires. Rather, the *Tenures* was recognized as becoming increasingly obsolete. While it was a brilliant statement of the classical law of real property and chattels real, it offered little on all those kinds of future interests which the new men of property in later Tudor England and their lawyers sought to manipulate for purposes of estate settlement. What Littleton had said about uses—and it was sufficient for his day—had been rendered irrelevant by the Statute of Uses (1536) and the Pandora's box of creative conveyancing and even more creative interests opened by that act. Littleton had not ignored "equity," for there was no such entity in 1481. But there certainly was "equity" by the early seventeenth century, and—both as a system, and insofar as its doctrines touched upon common law—no property lawyer could afford to turn a blind eye to it. The *Tenures* remained a good starting place for property law. However, a starting place premises a journey. While a serious student of the law, intending to go to the bar, could be expected to note-up in the margins of the *Tenures* a century's worth of developments in property law, the gentleman-sojourner probably lacked the stamina and knowledge to revise an aging text, and had neither the inclination, the time, nor the experience to do so.

One young student of the law at Littleton's old Inn, the Inner Temple, in the 1570's, appears to have taken more than mere pains to digest the *Tenures* and to bring it up to date. He was impelled by much seriousness of purpose, possessed of a vigor that would still drive him even in his eighties, and given to a nostalgia for time and place that moved him to identify with the old judge. Master Edward Coke of Norfolk began in the 1570's that close familiarity with Littleton's *Tenures* which, a half century later, issued in his own magisterial renovation of Littleton's classic. By the time of his death in 1634, Sir Edward Coke had collected two ancient manuscripts of the *Tenures*: a Littleton "Covered with Crimson velvett and gilt Bosses," and the following volume:

> Littleton mixed not onely with [Year] booke cases and many titles of the lawe intermixed therewith, but with many reports of cases in the raigne of Queene Eliza: before the 32 yeare [1589–1590] of the same Q: with a Cover of Crimson Sattine curiouslie imbrodred with gold silver and silke and over that a Cover of Crimson damaske. / in 8°./ [9]

This "Littleton mixed" was the first-fruits of Coke's assiduous redactal efforts. The full harvest, in 1628, would be the publication of *The First Part of the Institutes of the Laws of England: or a Commentary upon Littleton, Not the Name of the Author only, but the Law It Self*—the book better known and forever renowned as *Coke upon Littleton*.

If by the 1620's the *Tenures* looked increasingly moribund, Coke gave the work a new lease on life. He supplied as a thick overlard on Littleton's spare text a discrete commentary on Littleton's scholarship by the addition of cases from the Middle Ages going to support Littleton's citationless assertions. None in his age (and possibly none since) commanded like Coke the Year Book erudition of medieval common law. And none before him used the Year Books as if they were "reports" in the modern sense in which Coke's own volumes of reported cases were reports, sets of substantive precedent that counsel would be expected to follow and with which (the formidable Lord Chief Justice intended) future courts could square their judgments. The first eleven volumes of Coke's *Reports* were published between 1600 and 1615.[10] Coke cited his *Reports* prominently in his *Commentary upon Littleton*. That is less important than the fact that Coke's *Reports* had already begun to revolutionize the way lawyers looked at cases, the purpose they found for cases, and the dawning realization that in cases was to be found the law.[11] By the time he published *Coke upon Littleton*, Coke had already conditioned lawyers and students of the law to look to cases: old cases, new cases, in context, out of context, to the point, irrelevant, it didn't make much difference. In short, Coke's copious citations in *Coke upon Littleton* lent verisimilitude to the enterprise for a generation of lawyers who sought authority in precedent. The master practiced what he preached, and so *Coke upon Littleton* was, even for the old law in it, absolutely up-to-date. In generations to follow, to the very middle of the nineteenth-century, *Coke upon Littleton* maintained the blush of authoritative youth, as subsequent editors piled new cases on Coke's cases. Save for his copious cases, Coke's Littleton, despite the enormous weight of Lord Coke's reputation, would have followed the original into obsolescence and ultimately oblivion. To spin a metaphor that both Littleton and Coke might have appreciated, Coke's new lease on life for Littleton was not for twenty-one years or one life but for one hundred and ninety-nine years!

Coke also rescued Littleton's *Tenures* from falling into a desuetude caused by what was *not* in the text. His commentary supplied the bulk of the developments since Littleton's day which any lawyer in the 1620's had to master. A glance at the index to Coke's Commentary will testify how considerable the new matter is.[12] Even where one might least expect it—in part because many connections that Coke drew were tenuous, tangential, or eccentric—new matter is inserted, so much that in the end the text covers with a remarkable degree of completeness developments which had no origins in or connection with the law of Littleton's day. Very little is missing which any assiduous student of Coke's day would have needed.

Alas, the commentary did in fact presuppose a very assiduous student indeed. Coke in his Preface, with an earnestness which is genuinely moving, commends his labors to "all students of the law in their beginning of their study."[13] In his youth at the Inns, even though he had arrived at Temple Bar on his horse with £10 in his purse, a rapier, and a diamond ring inscribed "O Prepare," Coke had bent himself to learning rather than to lewd boisterousness.[14] Perhaps the old jurist had forgotten how grueling had been the round of scholarship. For more than two centuries, the myriad students of the law who were compelled to plow through *Coke upon Littleton* complained bitterly over the laminations of learning in the volume—but seldom was the criticism aimed at Littleton's contribution. Sir James Fitzjames Stephen showed the Victorian exasperation of a working jurist and devoted codifier when he wrote, "A more disorderly mind than Coke's . . . would be impossible to find."[15] Sir William Holdsworth evinced a starchy Edwardian disdain in characterizing the work as "a legal encyclopedia arranged on no plan except that suggested by the words and sentences of Littleton."[16] Holdsworth's successor as the dean of English legal historians, T. F. T. Plucknett, preferred English understatement: "extremely discursive, but full of valuable information."[17] Percy Winfield, Holdsworth's contemporary, suggested diplomatically that Coke "was overwhelmed by the learning he possessed."[18] Perhaps the best balance was struck by Sir John Baker:

> Coke shoveled out his enormous learning in vast disorderly heaps, piled around Litteton's Tenures to form a phrase by phrase gloss on the text. He delighted in wandering off at tangents, and in doing so covered many aspects of the common law which Littleton never hinted at. Coke seems to have been oblivious to the disorder, but the reader can easily forgive him. He wrote like a helpful old wizard, anxious to pass on all his secrets before he died, but not quite sure where to begin or end.[19]

With subsequent editions the shoveling of learning was not, of course, entirely Coke's work. The edition that is probably best-known and most widely consulted, the eighteenth edition of 1823, piles on the learning of Coke's two most eminent successors as legal scholars, Sir Matthew Hale, Chief Justice of the King's Bench 1671–1676, and Heneage Finch, Earl of Nottingham, Lord Chancellor 1674–1682. Hale and Nottingham had noted-up Coke as Coke had noted-up Littleton. To these contributions were added the antiquarian-historical labors of Francis Hargrave and Charles Butler, stalwarts among eighteenth-century scholars. The heap is high, the weight of learning very heavy.[20]

For the reader already familiar with *Coke upon Littleton*, this criticism may perhaps do no more than confirm established frustration. The author, having had to cope professionally with *Coke upon Littleton* for four decades, has himself used strong language, thought dark thoughts, and foundered in deep despair. He finds consolation in the practical counsel of Coke himself. The reader should begin by reading Littleton's text, Coke directed, then read it again, understand it thoroughly, and only then, finally, read the commentary:

> And no more any one time than he is able with a delight to bear away and after meditate thereon, which is the life of reading. . . . And albeit the reader shall not at anyone day (do what he can) reach to the meaning of our author, or of our Commentaries, yet let him no way discourage himself, but proceed; for on some other day, in some other place, that doubt will be cleared.[21]

Following Coke's advice, the reader can appreciate one of Coke's maxims elsewhere: "*Nemo aliquam partem recte intelligere potest antequam totum per legit*," None can properly understand a part until he has read the whole.[22]

About the life of Thomas Littleton very little is known and not much more is likely to be discovered. Littleton was born about in 1422 in Worcestershire near Birmingham, into a family of the minor gentry. His mother came of better lineage than his father, and consequently Thomas took her maiden name for his surname. There is no evidence that he went to either Oxford or Cambridge, and it is very unlikely that one inclined toward a career in the common law would have done so in the 1430's. Tradition has it that Littleton was a student at the Inner Temple, and that seems probable. We know that around 1540 he gave a reading on the famous property statute *De Donis Conditionalibus* (Westminster II, c.1, 1285) at the Inner Temple—indeed, he was the Inn's earliest recorded reader.[23] At about the same time he became recorder of the city of Coventry in Warwickshire (this also endeared him to Coke, who himself served as recorder of Coventry). His professional rise was rapid if not meteoric: serjeant-at-law in 1453, King's Serjeant in 1455, and Justice of Common Pleas in 1466. He enjoyed the distinction of being instituted a Knight of the Bath in 1475 at a noble and royal conclave. He made his will on August 22, 1481, died the next day, and was interred in a handsome tomb in Worcester Cathedral.

What moved Littleton to set down at the end of a long and distinguished career at the bar and on the bench such a comprehensive treatment of property law containing so much recondite matter? Following the last pages of his treatise (Section 749), he begins a short epilogue with the words, "Now I have made to thee, my sonne, three books."[24] This may refer directly to his second son, Richard, who became an eminent barrister of the Inner Temple.[25] In the late 1470's, when Littleton wrote the *Tenures*, Richard may already have been a student at the Inner Temple. Yet there is evidence that Littleton meant the work for more eyes than Richard's. There are three early manuscript copies (none of which can be termed the original) of the *Tenures* in the Cambridge University Library. One has a note that it was bought in St. Paul's Churchyard, London, on 20 July 1480, a little over a year before its author's death. That the book went to the printer as early as 1481 indicates that though Littleton addressed his book to one young apprentice-at-law, it had circulated sufficiently in manuscript to appeal to others.

Littleton's graceful epilogue also testified to his method as well as to his didactic purpose:

> And know, my son, that I would not have thee beleeve, that all which I have said in these bookes [the three Books of the *Tenures*] is law, for I will not presume to take this upon me. But of those things that are not law, inquire and learne of my wise masters learned in the law. Notwithstanding albeit that certaine things

> which are moved and specified in the sayd bookes, are not altogether law, yet such things shall make thee more apt, and able to understand and apprehend the arguments and the reasons of the law, etc. For by the arguments and reasons in the law, a man more sooner shall come to the certaintie and knowledge of the law. *Lex plus laudatur quando ratione probatur* [the law is most praiseworthy when it is consonant with reason].[26]

This surprising exhortation, with its elliptical playfulness, easily escapes the serious student mining through the *Tenures*. It has been overlooked. Worse, Coke's commentary upon Littleton's text, with its perennial hobby-horse riding of one of the commentator's favorite themes, "reason of law," overshadows and obscures what Littleton meant by reason. Littleton's exhortation is a caveat. He warns the reader that what he offers in the work is not a compendium of the established law of property, but rather a dialectical analysis of the principles upon which that law is founded. Most significantly, it is a dialectical analysis of the principles upon which the law *ought* to be founded.

This normative concern expressed by Littleton was, in the three and one-half centuries between Bracton and Coke, a rarity largely unchallenged by other lawyers and law-books. Fortescue's *De Laudibus Legum Angliae* (c. 1470) and Christopher St. Germain's *Doctor and Student* (c. 1530) are honorable exceptions. Many have given due credit to Littleton's lonely accomplishment in having written a book on law at all in an age when law-book meant that potpourri, the Year Book. But they fail to appreciate the significance of his fundamental jurisprudential concerns. Even the astute T. F. T. Plucknett missed the large contribution of Littleton. Regretting the deepening darkness of common-law literature in the later Middle Ages, a space lighted only by Littleton's candle, Plucknett noted:

> Beside Littleton there is nothing whatever which can be called a law book, however feeble, to represent the professional writing of his age. The Year Books alone remain, and from that precariously sustained series we learn enough to show that the law was in fact developing steadily and usefully according to its own queer lights.[27]

None knew better than Littleton how queer were the lights of the law in his age. Alone among the lawyers of his time, he sought to reduce the oddities to ordinaries, capricious rule to rational order, peculiarities in law to jurisprudential generalities.

Of course Littleton started with the law that was. What he chose to emphasize, however, were those features of existing law—doctrines would be too strong a term for them—which he believed most amenable to development to jurisprudential ends. It was no accident that it is in Book Three that Littleton carefully but vigorously undertook the enterprise of rationalizing and even refashioning English property law. Indeed, Book One on estates and Book Two on tenures and the services and incidents pertaining to tenures were preparatory to Book Three. The first two Books were clearly intended as a necessary foundation, based upon the existing learning of the fourteenth century, the "Old Tenures."[28] Littleton saw them as the predicate for a bold departure in property law.

From this perspective, the putative sins of omission and the puzzles with which later scholarship has taxed Littleton either disappear or appear explicable. That there were few citations to cases in the *Tenures* (and the ones that appear, even wrong ones such as that in Section 420, apparently were interpolated by later editors) has been accounted by many a mystery in a jurist who himself figured prominently in the Year Books during his quarter-century on the King's Bench. However, quite aside from the fact that the Year Books were not "reports" and that no lawyer of the era would have used them as such, the didactic ends of Littleton did not require authority. Each short Section was an assertion posed by putting a case.[29] It made no difference for analytical purposes whether the case was real or hypothetical; it made even less difference for the reader to know whether the case was real or not. If Littleton thought the assertion was open to question, he would put the arguments for and against it, sometimes concluding as to the assertion's validity, sometimes leaving the question unresolved. It was reason, not judicial pronouncements that determined the issue. Littleton did not presume to argue that "all which I have said . . . is law." His epilogue is a good confession and avoidance.

A much more substantive omission has been charged against Littleton by Holdsworth, who, focusing on Section 364, wrote, "There is no hint either that unbarrable entails are things of the past."[30] Unbarrable entails were not things of the past when Littleton wrote, despite the conventional wisdom that *Taltarum's Case* (1472) made them so. Littleton was indeed one of the two Common Pleas judges in *Taltarum* who, by accepting that a third party—not the donor or his heir—might be a sufficient single voucher to warranty to bar an entail, pointed the way to the device that would a half-century later make "unbarrable entails . . . things of the past." But Littleton would have earned credit for clairvoyance had he maintained in 1480 that all entails were barrable. There is no indication that he would have *desired* free barring of entails, because the use of the collusive common recovery to bar entails in his day was primarily to condition the rigor of almost two centuries' interpretation of *De Donis Conditionalibus* in order to allow resettlement rather than to disinherit issue.[31] Indeed, it is not difficult to see why the learned reader on *De Donis Conditionalibus* at the Inner Temple about 1450 would three decades later still respect the thrust of that old statute's purpose, to give effect to the wishes of the donor according to the express words of his grant. If in Section 364 Littleton posited a right of entry by a donor or reversioner to enforce a condition of an entail against alienation by a tenant in tail or his heirs, he did so because of the positive value of the old statute, not because he was breasting a wave of new doctrine and new practice which had already washed away *De Donis*. That wave was only a ripple in 1480.

It is that same sense of conservative probity that moved Littleton in Sections.721–723 to deny the validity of "all such [contingent] remainders in the forme" set down in Section 720. This has been construed as representing the denial of the validity of *all* contingent remainders. Even Coke appears to have mistaken the matter, for he was obviously much discomfited by an assertion which by 1550 had crashed in flames; his summary of these Sections is disingenuous.[32] Later scholars have been merely puzzled that Littleton could have denied the validity of what ultimately became for a season a perfectly acceptable (when bounded by rules against abuse) future interest. In Littleton's day one kind of contingent remainder was admitted by Common Pleas, but all others were discouraged if not damned for sound reasons of law and, perhaps, policy. The one allowed was a gift to the heirs of a living stranger, provided the stranger died while the donor was yet alive. The objections to contingent remainders in the late fifteenth century were centered on three interconnected, doctrines of the common law: that there could be no abeyance of seisin (that is, there must always be a feudal tenant); that a living man had no heir; and that the word "heirs" was a word of limitation, not purchase, and thus an heir must claim by descent rather than by grant. The example above was unobjectionable because it was not in breach of any of these doctrines. There was no abeyance of seisin since seisin was in the donor until the contingent-remainderman heir took it; when the contingent-remainderman took, he was by definition the heir of his dead ancestor; being the heir of a stranger, the contingent-remainderman could not take from the donor by descent. The instance posited in Section 720 was clearly objectionable and it is hard to fault Littleton for roundly condemning it. As to the validity of contingent remainders in general, we do not know what Littleton thought. If he had serious qualms about them, and we might suspect that he did, those qualms were shared by his brethren. It was perfectly in keeping with his normative concerns that he would find contingent remainders perilous to the law's integrity. They had a fraudulent odor to them (they could cheat the lord of his feudal incidents) and they were a potentially dangerous obstacle to liberal alienability. From the vantage point of a century later, whatever misgivings Littleton might have had would have proven well-founded, for the contingent remainder was a loose cannon on the law's gun-deck—a concept that took on a limited usefulness only after the best efforts of many judges, including Coke, to lash it down.

Finally, why did Littleton, who had made grants to feoffees to such uses as he should appoint by his will, have so slighted that portentous development, the use, that apparently threatened to overpower the common law of real property?[33] On the face of it, Littleton appears to have largely ignored uses. Section 115, touching uses, was a later interpolation and not Littleton's work at all. Section 296 dealt with active uses, which posed no challenge to the common law. Section 352 involved uses to convey, a common device that enabled a tenant in fee simple to convey a lesser estate to himself by the Chancellor's intervention if necessary, something that could not be done directly at law. Sections 462–463 raised issues growing out of the employment of uses to devise realty by will, the major and still expanding function of uses at the time. In Section 499 Littleton raised the important issue of the effect of a tortious enfeoffment to uses by a disseisor countered by a release of real actions at common law to render the disseisor vulnerable to a statutory action.

Littleton's slight is more apparent than real. First of all, he discussed the principal kinds of uses employed at the time he wrote. Secondly, proper to his enterprise, he dealt with uses according to their impact upon the common law of property, not as matters of concern themselves. Lastly, Littleton was doubtless aware of what recent scholarship now enables us to appreciate—that is, the extent to which uses were becoming a species of property increasingly subject to legal rather than mere equitable interpretation and thus on the way to becoming subject to the jurisdiction of the common-law courts. This development had already begun by the time Littleton wrote. It would be stimulated by a statute passed three years after his death that explicitly gave jurisdiction over certain uses to common-law courts. It terminated in 1536, with the Statute of Uses, which destroyed the classical uses fashioned by the length of the medieval Chancellor's reach and loosed a swarm of mischievous doctrines in the common law of property.

Until very recently our received learning saw uses as the shock-troops of a vital, expanding, liberating system of "equity," challenging a rigid, ossified, and decadent common law. In the nineteenth century, when Charles Dickens was visiting derision upon Serjeant Buzfuz and Benthamite reformers were visiting wholesale statutory reform upon the common law, equity was vested with almost magical or at least mythopoeic properties—hailed as redeeming, liberating, and cleansing. Ironically, this was the moment when equity was about to be absorbed finally into the common law and its importance, with that of all doctrines bound up with real property, reduced to a shadow of its former self in an industrial and commercial age. But the myth of "equity" was safe and secure in the next generation of legal scholars. Holdsworth evinced an almost chiliastic fervor in describing Littleton's treatment of the law of real property as riven with complications growing from the "enthusiasm of the legal profession for the technicalities of a vicious system of procedure" and "the lawlessness of the age," a "savagely litigious age." Holdsworth went on to bemoan not only the fact that the land law was under the "incubus" of the "barren technicalities of a worn-out system of procedure," but also that unfortunately the "incubus [had been] removed, not by the clean and incisive process of direct legislation, but by piecemeal changes and improvements introduced by the legal profession."[34]

Littleton's silence on procedural matters, which were after all largely irrelevant to his substantive-law emphases, maintains its silence in the face of Holdsworth's purplish criticism. Littleton knew, though, what Holdsworth would probably not have believed had he seen it: that for all of the activity of the great ecclesiastical chancellors of the late Middle Ages, the chancellors had not fashioned a system of equity, and that the singular (and single) device the chancellors had nurtured and protected, the use, was being pared away to destruction in the later fifteenth century by a resurgent common law of property. While Holdsworth vaunted the "clean and incisive process of direct legislation" to effect legal reform, there was never a cleaner or more incisive act than the Statute of Uses of 1536. The misfortune of the way in which the incubus of uses was removed lay precisely in the fact that it was by legislation, rather than by the piecemeal changes of lawyers. The act was fatally flawed. By "executing" uses (converting the beneficiary's equitable interest into a legal estate), rather than by absolutely prohibiting the employment of uses in conveyancing, the Statute opened the common law of property to all of the anomalous interests which unsystematic development under ecclesiastical chancellors had spawned. Later generations of legal scholars, enamored of "equity," failed to see that if uses were a cure for the ills of the common law of property, it was worse than the disease. The only thing worse than both was the Statute of Uses.

Littleton may have chosen to underemphasize uses because he suspected, with reason, that they had little future per se. Instead, he concentrated his greatest efforts on those features of property law which appear to us dreadfully archaic and doomed to such radical reduction as to lose almost all importance in the following two centuries: descents which toll entries, continual claims, discontinuances, warranties, remitters, releases and confirmations. These subjects comprised some 60 percent of Book Three, consisting of Chapters 6–9 and 11–13 of that Book. Commentators who dismiss such detailed treatment as an egregious waste of effort, mere slavish adherence to the shackles imposed by the "technicalities of a vicious system of procedure," should note that in these chapters Littleton was at his creative and normative best. In Littleton's day, the common law, for all of its procedural shortcomings, had reached the point when the true owner (or more correctly, the claimant with the better title) was recognized as the fit subject for protection against the tortious disseisor and the disseisor's feoffees. Another way to put it is, that by the end of the fifteenth century, the common law had finally slipped the shackles first imposed upon it in the twelfth century (albeit for commendable reasons and to admirable ends) by the possessory assizes and the emergence of the doctrine of seisin. This was a considerable advance, and it had been worked largely by weighing some of the doctrines treated in these Chapters against others—continual claims against descents which toll entries, warranties against discontinuances—as well as by new emphases in other Chapters on safeguarding the rights of the true owner. This was indeed complicated, torturously so; it was over-fine, and it displayed some of the worst procedural features of the law. Nonetheless, from the vantage point of a jurist and jurisprudence dedicated to both instructing in the law and providing a rational, even scientific, basis for change in the law, it was not a misplaced emphasis.

How important this was is not yet fully appreciated. The doctrines and features of the subject are only now being opened in new scholarship. Legal historians of the immediate post-Maitland generation largely ignored the subject (and the period as a whole) in favor of the classical formative common law of earlier centuries. With some few exceptions, most notably S. F. C. Milsom, those historians who have ventured beyond the magic year 1307, when Edward I died, have tended to leap from the fourteenth century to the sixteenth. Littleton's century, and so Littleton's learning, conclusions, and purposes, are only now beginning to receive the degree of attention that has revealed so much about the early common law.[35] Until such work is done, we should be leery of standing too adamantly upon Coke's maxim, "*Stabit praesumptio donec probetur in contrarium*," A presumption will stand good until the contrary is proved.[36]

What is known—and not merely presumed—about Thomas Littleton's contribution is that his arrangement of the tenures and the estates of medieval English law passed into the entire literature of the law and the history of medieval English institutions. What none can deny is that his *Tenures* was a masterly summation of English property law as that law stood on the eve of far-reaching adaptations. What all appreciate is that his book was a rose of rational analysis and jurisprudential concerns in a thicket of how-to and what-was-done works. Littleton's achievement was enormous, if for no other reason than that the *Tenures* demonstrated that the common law of property was not all procedures but also substantive rules. The *Tenures* bears more kinship to present-day legal literature in what it sought to do, what it did, and how it did it, than any other law-book written before the last half of the seventeenth century, Coke's work included. If this seems to disparage Lord Coke, remember that he knew better than all other post-medieval jurists the excellence of Littleton. His encomium of the *Tenures* admits of no demurrer or plea in bar:

> this book is the ornament of the common law, and the most perfect and absolute work that ever was written in any human science; and in another place, that which I affirmed and took upon me to maintain against all opposites whatsoever, that it is a work of as absolute perfection in its kind, and as free from error, as any book that I have known to be written of any humane learning, shall to the diligent and observing reader of these Institutes be made manifest.[37]

Made manifest it is.

CHAPTER FOUR

John Fortescue

Few scenes of Shakespeare are more heartrending than the one set on the fatal field at Tewkesbury in 1471 in *Henry VI Part 3*, where Margaret of Anjou, queen of Henry VI, cradles the corpse of her son, murdered before her eyes by Edward IV and his two brothers, and shrieks out her despairing lament,

> O Ned, sweet Ned! speak to thy mother, boy! Canst thou not speak? O traitors! murderers! They that stabb'd Caesar shed no blood at all. Did not offend, nor were not worthy blame, If this foul deed were by to equal it: He was a man; this, in respect, a child. And men ne'er spend their fury on a child. What's worse than murderer, that I may name it?[1]

Sweet Ned was Edward, Prince of Wales, eldest son of King Henry VI of the House of Lancaster, aged seventeen at the time of his death. Prince Edward was indeed a high-spirited youth, held in genuine respect and affection by the doughty old judge, Sir John Fortescue, who attended him for a decade in exile and who instructed him and commended to him the laws of England in *De Laudibus Legum Angliae* against that day which would never be when he should be king.

The Prince is prominent among the dramatis personae of Shakespeare's trilogy. Yet nowhere in *Henry VI* is there mention, directly or by implication, of Sir John Fortescue, and nowhere is there an appearance by that eminent chief justice and servant of the crown—though Fortescue himself was at Tewkesbury, and was taken prisoner when the House of Lancaster finally fell. Fortescue had borne arms before for Henry VI, most notably at Towton Field on that wintry Palm Sunday in 1461 when Henry was driven from his throne and from England. During Henry's sojourn in Scotland,

Fortescue had been, at least by his own account, the King's closest advisor, promoted to Lord Chancellor by the exiled monarch, a mark of favor and appreciation though not of power or function. During the long seven years spent by Prince Edward and his mother in the French dominions of Margaret's father, Fortescue attended upon the queen and her son. It was during that sojourn that Fortescue composed *De Laudibus Legum Angliae* for Prince Edward's edification.

Though Shakespeare chose to ignore Sir John Fortescue, other Englishmen of the era did not. Between the first publication of Fortescue's treatise in 1546 and John Selden's edition of the work (first issued in 1616, the year of Shakespeare's death), the book appeared nine times, at least once in every decade. By sixteenth century standards, the book was a best-seller. In fact, Fortescue became something of a cult figure in Elizabethan England. The title applied to the book by its translator Robert Mulcaster, *A Learned Commendation of the Politique Laws of England*, expressed the Englishness of Fortescue's work, and Elizabeth's England, beset by foreign foes and xenophobic in the extreme, clasped Fortescue to its bosom. When Selden in 1616 gave the book its enduring title, *De Laudibus Legum Angliae*, what was gained in translation, the phrase *In Praise*, trumpeted even more strongly the patriotism of the nation. And for Selden's generation, fearful of a growing "Stuart Despotism," Fortescue's emphasis on Parliament, on a mixed-monarchical constitution, and on the jury as the guardian of the Englishman's liberty seemed a prescription against the infection of tyranny.[2] In 1614, Sir Walter Raleigh termed *De Laudibus* "that notable bulwark of our laws"—as a prisoner in the Tower, enduring a sentence of death that would be carried out four years later, Raleigh can be said to have spoken from the heart.[3] Sir Edward Coke directed his reader to Fortescue for an explanation of why only English common law provided trial by jury. Fortescue's words, said Coke, were "worthy to be written in letters of gold for the weight and worthiness thereof, I will not abridge any part of the same, but refer the learned reader to the fountain itself."[4] In the great parliamentary debates of the 1620's, Coke and his fellow opponents of the pretensions of Stuart monarchy made many trips to that fountain.

John Fortescue is a far less shadowy figure than many of his fifteenth century contemporaries. The high offices he held (he was Chief Justice of King's Bench for nineteen years, from 1442 to 1461), as well as his hard service in the cause of the House of Lancaster, raised him far above anonymity. Those anecdotal didactic notes of cases in the King's Bench and Common Pleas, the Year Books, pay considerable attention to Fortescue's learned comments and memorable quips in Westminster Hall, and the flavor of the man and his wit is caught in them. The official records, particularly of letters patent issued in Chancery, enables us to reconstruct his busy judicial career as a commissioner for trials in the country and on special commissions, and there are occasional glimpses of him in the King's Council in Star Chamber.[5] Those two great mines of information for contemporary life and events, the Paston Letters and the Stonor Correspondence, allude to him.[6] And the public records and private muniments so assiduously sifted by historians of the Wars of the Roses provide a great deal of information about the political activities of such a notable participant in the great affairs centered on that civil war of dynastic factions for the crown of England.

The life of Fortescue by his Victorian descendant, Thomas Fortescue, Lord Clermont, provides the essential detail of Fortescue's life.[7] However, some salient features of Sir John Fortescue's life have become clear only with subsequent research. First of all, S. B. Chrimes argues convincingly that Fortescue was born about 1385, not between 1394 and 1396.[8] There is no evidence that Fortescue was ever a student at Oxford.[9] Fortescue, along with the royal party in its early exile in Edinburgh, was housed in the Dominican house there, Blackfriars—not at Greyfriars, the Franciscan house. Fortescue was also married twice; Lord Clermont was unaware of his first marriage in 1423 to a Devonshire heiress, who died in 1426 without leaving issue.

More significantly, Chrimes's research has established how active Fortescue was as a justice of the peace and as a special commissioner for trials criminal and civil, both before and after he became Chief Justice. This experience is reflected in Fortescue's book. He wrote of English legal institutions—especially trial by jury—from a practical perspective based upon an inimitable experience of that procedure. So it was, too, with Parliament. As Chief Justice, Fortescue attended the House of Lords as an assistant learned in the laws. Most significantly, recent research on Lancastrian parliaments has brought to light that Fortescue between 1421 and 1436 was elected eight times to the House of Commons (seven times for boroughs in his native Devon, for the eighth and last time as MP for Wiltshire). The first great political-theoretician of Parliament, one of its greatest constitutional exponents, was a practiced parliamentarian.

Of course, Fortescue's own writings tell us most about him as jurist, political philosopher, statesman, and politician. It is not to detract from Fortescue's reputation as a learned juristic commentator and political theorist or from the value of his considerable corpus as a scholarly contribution to emphasize that his three major works, including *De Laudibus*, as well as a number of his shorter pieces, were written in the cause of the House of Lancaster. Moreover, the three major pieces were written either during the Lancastrian exile after Towton or shortly after the short-lived restoration of Henry VI in October 1470. Conventional wisdom has assigned to the years 1461–1464, when Fortescue was in Edinburgh with Queen Margaret and Edward, Prince of Wales, the composition of *De Natura Legis Naturae*. Chrimes argued for a later date, sometime during the exile of Margaret, Edward, and Fortescue at the castle of Koeur in St-Mihiel in the Duchy of Bar.[10] The work was by far the largest Fortescue undertook, more than twice as long as *De Laudibus*. *De Natura* is a weighty (indeed, a heavy) work directed to proving by the law of nature that Henry VI had the sole rightful claim to the English crown and that Edward IV was a mere usurper. Though the claims are judiciously weighed and Fortescue's treatment of the law of nature is surefooted, his partisanship is patent.

The shortest of Fortescue's three principal works was *De Dominio Regali et Politico*, better known by the subtitle given it by its modern editor, *The Governance of England*.[11] Its date and provenance are the most disputed of the three longer works. Written around 1470, the time of the restoration of Henry VI, it was revised about a decade later, after Henry VI's final deposition and his murder in the Tower by the Yorkists. And it was addressed to Edward IV. The Lancastrian cause lost and his young pupil slain, Fortescue had accepted the Yorkist regime and penned a repudiation of his former propaganda efforts on behalf of the Lancastrians. In October 1471 Fortescue was pardoned by Edward IV and admitted to the new king's Council. Though written to advise Henry VI, *The Governance* was an equally sound blueprint for institutional and constitutional restructuring by a usurper, particularly one who proved to be an institutional reformer. The book was an extended argument for a constitutional polity as against a despotic system, picking up and developing the contrast between France's merely regal regime (*dominion regale*) and England's mixed consensual and monarchical polity (*dominion politicum et regale*) which Fortescue had first adumbrated in Chapters 9 and Chapters 34–36 of *De Laudibus Legum Angliae*.

The Governance had a very practical side. It dealt with royal revenues, beginning with the point that French monarchical despotism was largely the result of the poverty of the French king, which in turn made him yet more tyrannical in his search for adequate revenue. The English king was warned to consider carefully what charges were likely to be placed on his revenues, and Fortescue suggested to him sources from which it might be drawn. He warned the king of the importance of reducing the powers of the feudal nobility, the "overmighty subjects," who had gained even more power in the tumult brought by dynastic rivalry in the Wars of the Roses. He offered sage advice on the proper choice of the King's Councillors, the structure of the Council, and the distribution of honors. *The Governance*, written in English and not Latin, has been called "the first book about law" in English,[12] but it might better be termed the first constitutional commentary written in English. Recent historical scholarship has demonstrated that many of the institutional reforms that have conventionally been attributed to the Tudors, particularly Henry VII, in fact began in Edward IV's reign from 1471 to 1483.[13] *The Governance of England* may well have played a role in both stimulating and directing the changes which recast English government as it entered the modern age.

De Laudibus Legum Angliae resembled both the other principal works and it was in intention no less a partisan political effort written on behalf of the House of Lancaster. Implicit in its encomium of English law and English political practice was the argument that Lancastrian government—beginning at the turn of the fourteenth century, with Henry IV, first of the dynasty—had assured the virtues of mixed consensual and monarchical polity and secured the liberties that were the objects of that polity. Fortescue was at considerable pains to establish that English law was consonant with the law of nature (Chapter 16), thus reinforcing the proposition developed earlier in *De Natura Legis Naturae*, a work to which he explicitly referred (at the end of Chapter 9, for example). *The Governance of England* clearly owed to *De Laudibus* its central idea (the idea of the *dominion politicum et regale*), but went beyond it in its attention to detailed reform. Both books were exhortations to the Lancastrian king to maintain the English polity which gave him, much more than the law of nature could provide, his legitimacy.

The most striking feature of *De Laudibus* is also its most distinguishing characteristic: it was a didactic work. It was meant to instruct a young prince in the responsibilities which he would undertake when he succeeded to his throne. Fortescue's choice of the tried-and-true rhetorical device of the dialogue, which had a long and honorable history behind it in English letters, gave weight to this didacticism, for a dialogue was usually between a pupil asking questions and a teacher answering them. We should not take the dialogue so literally as to suppose that Fortescue and Prince Edward sat down to discuss the subject. Yet Fortescue was in regular and prolonged contact with the young prince and was undoubtedly one of those in the exile-court to whom the prince's education in statecraft was confided. What is certain is that Fortescue did not write *De Laudibus* as a work for general distribution. It is far too rudimentary for a scholarly treatise directed to a learned audience. It lacks the ponderousness of Fortescue's syntax and rhetoric in *De Natura Legis Naturae* which, while clearly a work of propaganda, was meant for an educated and mature readership. The frame provided by Fortescue's Introduction, where an aged Lord Chancellor calls a princeling out of the tilt-yard to lecture him on the laws of his kingdom, allowing for its conventional third-person detachment and its scene-setting for a feigned dialogue, can be taken at face value.

The most recent effort to date with exactness the writing of *De Laudibus*, if Professor Chrimes is correct, lends weight to the conclusion that Fortescue's purpose really was the instruction of Prince Edward. Chrimes makes a strong argument that the book was composed no earlier than 1470 and quite possibly between October 1470 and April 1471.[14] The tone of *De Laudibus* is one of confidence, expectation, optimism. Until the restoration of Henry VI in October 1470 there were scant grounds for such a positive note. If the work was written in exile—and it was—by an octogenarian who had suffered loss of office, lands, goods and who had even contributed from his own small means to subsidize the cause for which he had given all, it was written apparently at the dawn of a new day for the House of Lancaster. In the pages of this book, Fortescue sounds convinced that Prince Edward would one day be king. In those six months after October 1470 when Henry regained his throne, there was every likelihood that Edward would ultimately succeed to the throne by due hereditary right. Moreover, for reasons that are unclear, Queen Margaret, Prince Edward, and the exile-court, Fortescue with it, remained at Koeur during that hopeful six months. Fortescue had ample time and above all else a motive to see to the education in statecraft of a prince who would by every reasonable expectation some day be a king.

Fortescue's instructional task was a formidable one. Prince Edward had been carried into exile, away from England, when he was less than eight years old, and he knew nothing of the country. He had lived for almost seven years, the critical years of adolescence, in a French ambience, under trying conditions of uncertainty as to the future, surrounded by considerable intrigue and many alarums. His education as a prince was, perforce, in the martial arts; if he were ever to wear a crown, he would have to fight for it. The picture of the young prince breaking lances with his companions-in-arms, as it is given in the Introduction, rings true. At the same time, however, on both sides of his lineage, Prince Edward had scholarly blood.

His great-uncle, Humphrey, Duke of Gloucester, had been a notable patron of learning and letters, his name commemorated in the earliest university library at Oxford which he had endowed and to which he had given his library. Prince Edward's maternal grandfather and benefactor at Koeur, Duke René of Anjou, was not only a patron of arts and letters, but an artist and writer in his own right, who richly deserved the appellation (unusual for his age) of "the Good." Even if the exile-court at Koeur maintained an atmosphere of learning, it would still demand considerable effort to turn the young prince's attention from the lists to the library. It was that which Fortescue had to effect.

Fortescue sought to persuade Prince Edward of the excellence of English law and English institutions and to convince him that as king he should maintain them. *De Laudibus* was an extended initiatory essay on kingship that was only incidentally a legal study—a point little appreciated in later ages when Fortescue's work was hailed for what it (and it alone) said about English legal institutions in the later fifteenth century. What distinguished *De Laudibus* from the myriad treatises on kingship before and after it—from St. Augustine through John of Salisbury, Aquinas, Machiavelli, Bodin, Botero, and James VI & I—was its focus on a particular realm, that of the English king. The treatment of the origins of kingdoms in Chapters 11–13 provided a context and general background for the discussion of English monarchy, and the comparison throughout between the kingdoms of England and of France afforded the opportunity to investigate and illuminate the nature of English kingship. English kingship was the subject; French kingship was the foil. Fortescue observed in Chapter 19: "*Comparationes vero, Princeps, ut te aliquando dixisse recolo, odiose reputantur*" [Comparisons truly are, Prince, as I remember you once said, reputed odious].[15] Though he would conclude this observation with an elegant demurrer to making odious comparisons, clearly Fortescue had little interest in French kingship other than to use it as a worst-case alternative to English kingship.

The glory of English kingship was that it was both regal and political, kingly and consensual, a mixed polity in which the king could not rule alone, could not legislate solely, could not levy taxes by fiat, and could not render justice in person. Fortescue began with the fact of that mixed polity. He located its origins in a particular historical experience, the establishment of kingship by agreement and consensus (Chapter 13)—and not by force, the origin of kingdoms ruled despotically (Chapter 12). The *politicum*, the consensual imperative of English polity, was therefore present from the beginning. But the continued vitality of the *politicum* in the polity depended upon the existence of a political nation represented by the three-hundred plus wise and prudent men who in Parliament made law with the king (Chapter 18). That political nation, in turn, was the particular product of the social and economic conditions of rural England, graced by nature with abundant fertility, which supported a numerous and uniformly distributed middling-sort of prosperous, able, observant, and leisured men who were incorruptible, honorable, knowledgeable, and politically involved (Chapter 29). Fortescue's description of this political nation in reference to jurors was equally appropriate to the same men as parliamentary electors and parliamentary members.

If English polity was clearly in accord with historical and even environmental realities, Fortescue could not rest satisfied with such an explanation. Jurist and theorist, mediaeval man that he was, he felt compelled to summon authority to his aid. He found it, as he supposed, in St. Thomas Aquinas's *De Regimine Principum*: "St. Thomas . . . wishes, that a kingdom could be so instituted, as that the king might not be at liberty to tyrannize over his people; which only comes to pass in the present case; that is, when the sovereign power is restrained by political laws."[16]

Whether or not Aquinas will in fact serve as authority for the notion of *dominion politicum et regale* has been hotly contested by students of Fortescue for a century. Professor Chrimes, having once taken the position that Aquinas's description of the imperial regime was so far removed in time and circumstance from the realities of fifteenth-century England that Fortescue made Aquinas's authority chimerical, later concluded that Fortescue had at least found his inspiration for the notion in Aquinas's *"regimen regale et politicum."* We cannot dispute Chrimes's conclusion:

> When all is said, he [Fortescue] did manage to make up a doctrine that had its roots on one side in abstract political theory, and roots on the other side in the concrete facts of political practice. He contrived to link up what he wanted to say about the government of England with the sanction of high theory.[17]

Fortescue's respect for authority was largely manifested in the first fourteen chapters of *De Laudibus*. This served his purpose to discuss kingship generally before exploring in depth the particular nature of the English realm. Moreover, this was the appropriate place for him to establish his bona fides as a thoroughly orthodox jurisprudent before discussing that peculiar institution, the common law of England. He urged the Prince to study the laws since that was as much a foundation for his discharge of duty to his people as was military practice requisite for protecting them (Chapter

1). He then went on to accept the distinction between divine and human or positive laws but pointed out that all positive laws have divine authority behind them, that through the implementation of positive law the greatest good of human life is assured, that the ruler can establish justice—his responsibility—only by knowing the law, and that the ruler can himself be a just man only by knowledge of the law (Chapters 2–5). The future ruler should learn the law when he is young and best able to do so, that he can learn all the law requisite in a year, and that he can safely confine his study to the laws of England, which are superior to Roman or civil law (Chapters 6–8). These preliminaries set the stage for his discussion of polity and the development of England's *dominion politicum et regale* (Chapters 9–13). In Chapter 14, he introduced a critical, pragmatic question, posed by the Prince: whether the common law of England is as effectual for that one kingdom as is the civil law of the Holy Roman Empire which was accepted as sufficient for the government of the entire world. It was on this question, rhetorically put, that the entire treatment of law in *De Laudibus* turned. As his treatment of kingship demonstrates, Fortescue accepted that, for good or for evil, kingship manifested itself principally in the promulgation and implementation of laws.

The next four Chapters (15–18) were almost as remarkable for what they did not say as for what they did. The three varieties of positive law (the law of nature, custom, and statute) posited in Chapter 15 were given a conventional and even a hackneyed discussion. While he quickly dispatched the law of nature (Chapter 16), Fortescue dilated at length on custom in Chapter 17 and on statute law in Chapter 18. But there was not a word about the statutory origins of the Roman or civil law; it was damned implicitly in a backhanded way by the emphatic praise that Fortescue heaped on the way in which the English promulgated statutes by the king in Parliament, rather than by the will of the king alone. The civil law received its explicit condemnation in Chapters 19–32, when Fortescue contrasted English criminal procedure of proof by jury with the civil law procedure of proof by witnesses and, in France, the use of torture to obtain the moral certitude afforded by the accused's confession. After an excursus into arbitrary rule, *dominion regale*, Fortescue contrasted English common-law rules on succession and descent, legitimization, and wardship with what the civil law held on these substantive points, concluding with a note on the commendable rigor of English law against theft and an equally commendable preference for the freedom of a serf once freed, in Chapters 38–46. On no point in these two lengthy comparisons of English common law and civil law did civil law win a skirmish.

At first glance, the topics which Fortescue chose to contrast between the two legal systems appear eccentric. Why such emphasis upon proof by jury? Perhaps the explanation is already provided in the point made above that the jury was the procedural manifestation of the political nation which provided the *politicum*, the consensual element, in the English *dominion politicum et regale*. This is part of the explanation, but probably not the whole of it. The fifteenth century witnessed the rapid expansion in juridical activity by non-common law tribunals, which proceeded by bill rather than indictment or writ, and provided for proof by witnesses' testimony rather than by a jury's sworn findings, with the tribunals' benches finding the facts. These were the tribunals which would later be called English-bill courts, notably the King's Council (usually sitting in the Star Chamber), the Duchy Chamber of Lancaster, and, above all, the Lord Chancellor in a jurisdiction that a century later would be termed equity.[18] So much arrant nonsense has been written about the so-called rivalry between such courts and the old common-law courts, especially in the seventeenth century, that a historian of one of them (Star Chamber) is very reluctant to give any credence to the notion that there was inbred hostility between the jurisdictions. Yet, from the perspective of the quondam Chief Justice, the English state's increasing recourse to such tribunals doubtless raised the threat of insidiously encouraging a method of proof which he only reluctantly admitted existed in England (Chapter 32) and which might lead to pernicious results.

On this reading, the excursus on arbitrary rule, Chapters 34–36, which otherwise seems out of place immediately following the long disquisition on the jury, makes sense of Fortescue's motivation in giving such attention to the jury. The excursus was introduced by the Prince's astonishment (Chapter 33) that his ancestors should have attempted to repudiate the "laws of the land"—not least, perhaps, to subvert the jury. The remainder of the excursus was devoted to arguing that the powers of the purely *regale* King of France and the *politicum et regale* King of England were equal, that arbitrary rule did not increase power but merely served to produce those palpable evils which beset France, and that the English king, if he held to the *dominion politicum et regale*, was in fact more secure than a merely *regale* king.

The substantive law topics which Fortescue contrasted in Chapters 38–46 were not eccentric either. Legitimization and female succession were the major topics. In discussing the latter, the Lancastrian partisan shone through clearly. If the civil law's preference for female succession was valid the House of Lancaster would lose the bulwark of its legitimate title against the claim of the House of York, a claim which depended upon descent through the female line. Fortescue had argued this before in *De Natura Legis Naturae*, and it was natural that he should reemphasize the point again in *De Laudibus*.

We can reasonably ask whether Fortescue's distaste for civil law had any substantial basis or was merely rampant prejudice fed by chauvinism and xenophobia? He appears to have been a close observer and given to considerable curiosity about law and politics. His seven years' sojourn on the Continent afforded him opportunity to study the French legal system in operation, and it is difficult to believe that he would choose to ignore the opportunity. What he saw could not have pleased him. The reception of the civil law in juridical practice, particularly the procedural law, was far advanced by the later decades of the fifteenth century throughout the domains of the King of France and the Imperial territories immediately to the east, including those of Fortescue's host, René, Duke of Bar and Lorraine. This new system was displacing the older customary laws. Even where customary law maintained its substantive vitality, the reception of civil law introduced new rigor into the procedures of the courts. Behind reception was the unquenchable thirst of the Valois kings for more revenue and more centralized control. The instrument for implementing the king's wishes was a bureaucracy that was increasingly recruited from lawyers trained in the law faculties of the universities, trained in "both laws," that is, the canon law and the civil law. These jurists were impatient of local peculiarities and customs, and for them nothing that was not the civil law was worthy to be called law.

In Chapters 47–51 of *De Laudibus*, Fortescue asserted the excellence of the recruiting, training, and advancement of the common lawyers in England, in their Inns of Court. He would have had the conventional common lawyer's suspicion of the logic-chopping Schoolmen of the universities before he went upon his Continental travels. What he had seen in the French courts confirmed him in his suspicions and persuaded him that university-trained lawyers constituted a threat to the established polity and time-honored laws indigenous to his English homeland. Much of Fortescue's most powerful argument in praise of the laws of England is to be found in these luminous chapters on the legal education and legal profession of English common lawyers. He had seen the enemy, and in these chapters he took up sword against him. Indeed, the threat was apparently so real in Fortescue's eyes that he could extol as virtues the vices of dilatoriness that as Chief Justice he had been called upon to combat (Chapters 52–53). He ended on the triumphant note, which married the excellence of English law to the glory of the English polity, that whatever shortcomings English law might have, these failings could be remedied by the king in Parliament, in the *dominion politicum et regale* that was England (Chapter 53).

Sir John Fortescue and his eminent contemporary and fellow judge, Sir Thomas Littleton, have been called the two earliest Renaissance jurists of English common law.[19] "Renaissance" is too imprecise a term when applied to English law and lawyers of the era to be useful for much more than decoration; it is best left to literati in English departments! Still convention dictates analysis. It is hard to see how Littleton, author of *The Tenures*, that thoroughly mediaeval treatise on the English law of real property, can be called a Renaissance man. The work itself, as its title suggests, was backward-looking in an age when the key to mastering property law now lay in understanding estates rather than tenures. And it has none of the ebullience and self-assuredness of tone, none of the self-satisfaction, which characterized Renaissance letters.

Fortescue and *De Laudibus* are another matter. Fortescue was a genuinely learned man, engaged with a wide range of scholarly subjects, including religion. The citations in *De Laudibus* indicate a familiarity with the entire corpus of scholarship available to a fifteenth-century writer—sources ranging from antiquity through the Church Fathers and mediaeval Scholasticism to Renaissance letters—and, significantly, the Bible (the most commonly cited source in the work). The Biblicism of the fifteenth century owed a great deal to the Renaissance ideal of a return to the origins of knowledge. Moreover, the didactic, even pedagogic, objective of *De Laudibus* exudes the Renaissance spirit and reflects the Renaissance belief in education. It might stretch the evidence, but a close reading of *De Laudibus* leaves the definite impression that its author was imbued with the Platonic ideal that swept through Italian humanism in the decades when Fortescue was writing: the striving for perfection, the sensitivity to beauty as a constituent of good.

Perhaps the best proof of Fortescue's membership in the Renaissance pantheon is the fact that Tudor commentators on law and politics found *De Laudibus* a thoroughly modern model for their own endeavors. Christopher St. Germain's *Dialogue between a Doctor and a Student* (c. 1530), weighing the various merits of the civil law and the common law through the mouths of a doctor of the former and a barrister of the latter, bears in both form and substance an uncanny resemblance to *De Laudibus*. St. Germain cited Fortescue's work, and it clearly inspired and influenced his own book.

Sir Thomas Smith's *De Republica Anglorum* (1583) bears certain marks of Fortescue's influence, especially in its treatment of English kingship and its concern with comparative politics.

Where Fortescue and Littleton join hands in innovation is in the emphatic new departure their works brought to English legal literature. Not since the formative age of the common law and its literature—in the twelfth and thirteenth centuries, when Glanvill and Bracton gave frame to the law's principles—had the common law produced a literature that was much more than practice books, formularies, and instructional tools. With *De Laudibus* and *The Tenures* the common law began a jurisprudential flowering that gathered force in the sixteenth century and reached its climax in the seventeenth with the works of Coke, Selden, and Hale. Littleton's role is clear, when one reflects that *The Tenures* became Coke's *First Institutes*, "Coke upon Littleton"—the very Bible of the common law of real property, the most considerable and most complex branch of the common law.

Fortescue rendered a further service. The brevity, didacticism, and chauvinism of *De Laudibus* gave it enormous popularity in the sixteenth century. As it was originally meant to instruct a Lancastrian prince so it could also teach less exalted Tudor Englishmen. It possessed the appeal of a good textbook: directness, clarity, vigor, wit, and a touch of style. Its small size made it eminently printable and printing made it cheap. Above all, it preached to the converted. Its Englishness and praise of Englishness resonated the patriotism and xenophobia of a nation that proclaimed itself liberated from the yoke of Rome's religion and armed against its Catholic foes. Fortescue was easily Protestantized and Anglicanized. All of his strictures against the tyranny of the civil law system and the degrading despotism of European kingship raised on mere regality were given double force in the age of the Reformation and the beginnings of Continental absolutism. In Elizabethan England, only editions of the Bible outsold editions of Littleton's *Tenures*, and only *Foxe's Book of Martyrs* had more lasting political influence than *De Laudibus*.[20] Consequently, like Foxe, Fortescue was destined to play a major role in the great political confrontation within English politics and society which marked the first half of the seventeenth century, destroyed a king in 1649, and continued to reverberate until the end of the century.

An English constitutional historian has remarked, of the debates that framed the English Civil War, that "Everyone spoke the same language."[21] Indeed, the rhetoric of King Charles I and his supporters was largely indistinguishable from that of their antagonists in Parliament. To great extent, *De Laudibus* had taught them all that same language. In June 1642, a bare two months before the resort to arms, Charles I pronounced his last formal words in the continuing verbal exchange that had gone on between King and Parliament since 1621. His reply to the Parliament's Nineteen Propositions, written by his advisers Viscount Falkland and John Culpepper, was an echo of *De Laudibus*:

> There being three kinds of government among men, absolute monarchy, aristocracy and democracy, and all these having their particular conveniences and inconveniences, the experience and wisdom of your ancestors hath so moulded this out of a mixture of these as to give to this kingdom (as far as human prudence can provide) the conveniences of all three, without the inconveniences of anyone, as long as the balance hangs even between the three estates, and they run jointly on in their proper channel.[22]

Here was a classic statement of mixed monarchy, of the *dominion politicum et regale*. Falkland and Culpepper were as stalwart and devoted disciples of Fortescue as their adversaries, John Selden and John Pym, on the other side of the great divide between King and Parliament. The English Revolutions of the seventeenth century were not fought between contending systems. All agreed on the proposition that England's polity was a mixed monarchy and that it was the best polity vouchsafed any people. The battle was over the mix.

The mix was not settled constitutionally until James II was expelled from his throne in 1688 and his daughter and her husband were confirmed in their enjoyment of it by a convention. It was not settled practically until the new joint-monarchs reached a routine working relationship with Parliament, and it was not settled theoretically until John Locke, in the early 1690's, published his *Two Treatises on Government*. Though written before the Glorious Revolution of 1688, the *Two Treatises* were relied on to explain and justify the final act of revolutionary confrontation. What is remarkable about the *Two Treatises* is how much Locke owed to Sir John Fortescue. Chapter 14 of *De Laudibus* enunciated a social contract theory of the origins of the English polity. A social contract, albeit more figurative than literal, was the foundation of Locke's political theory. That is not to say that Locke's social contract theory owed nothing to Hobbes's *Leviathan* of a generation before. But Hobbes's social contract was a compact of servitude, while Fortescue's was a compact of liberty; it is not hard to determine to which prior theorist Locke owed most. Even more striking is the fact that Fortescue's political nation is also Locke's. Locke was concerned to justify only one kind of revolution, that of men of property against a tyrant. Men of property alone possessed the right to declare the social contract dissolved by the tyrant's breach of it. That right had its corollary in the exclusive right of men of property to participate in political life. Through such participation, tyranny (and so revolution) could be avoided. The key to understanding why only men of property formed the political nation, in Locke's view, was their singular leisure, their dispensation from the drudgery of labor by virtue of their economic ability to hire others to do it, and consequently the time which they had free to reflect upon and act in politics. Fortescue's middling-sort of men, jurors and electors, in Chapter 29, were indistinguishable from Locke's men of property—or is it the other way around?

Perhaps the great glory of Fortescue is that in *De Laudibus* he prefigured so much of the political theory of the next two centuries. Besides Locke's debt to him, all those English polemicists, most of them in the Stuart camp, who were so fond of the anatomical and physiological metaphors for the body-politic, must acknowledge their obligation to Chapter 13, with its metaphor of the king as the head of the body politic and the laws as the sinews that bind the polity together. What a marvelous irony that perhaps two of Fortescue's disciples must be numbered among those downtrodden French, groaning under the yoke of *regale* tyranny! For Jean Bodin, in his treatise *Les Six Livres de la Republique* (1576), also advanced an explanation for the particularism of a polity based upon its social and economic peculiarity. Bodin was, however, much less thoroughgoing in his adherence to the notion than was Fortescue, for in comparing democratic, aristocratic, and monarchical government, Bodin clearly could not rid himself of the French vice of believing willy-nilly in pure monarchy. More to old Sir John's liking would have been the discipleship of Montesquieu. In the *Spirit of the Laws* (1748), with a high degree of refinement, Montesquieu would attribute political and constitutional particularism to the environment of the polity in question. Even better, Montesquieu would agree with Fortescue's explanation for the flourishing state of consensual governance in England. Montesquieu not only admired English institutions—he urged their replication in the France of his day, a nation repressed by the last and heaviest deadweight of absolutism. And in Montesquieu's idea of checks and balances between executive and legislative (regardless of how far he misread the actual political functioning of the British constitution in the mid-eighteenth century) one hears more than only an echo of Fortescue's *dominion politicum et regale*. Such a disciple Fortescue would have appreciated. With his fondness for Scripture, he might have said of that one Frenchman as it was said of Saul of Tarsus, "And straightway there fell from his eyes as it were scales, and he received his sight" (Acts 9:18).

CHAPTER FIVE

Richard Hooker

"Laws, as all other things human, are many times full of imperfection," a learned divine once observed,

> and that which is supposed behoveful unto men, proveth often-times most pernicious. The wisdom which is learned by tract of time, findeth the laws that have been in former ages established, needful in later to be abrogated. Besides, that which sometime is expedient doth not always so continue: and the number of needless laws unabolished doth weaken the force of them that are necessary.[1]

Such a categorical embrace of the mutability of law and the pragmatism inherent in its creation and evolution as the Reverend Richard Hooker (1554–1600) displays here was rare among churchmen in the age of the Reformation. The competing certainties of ecclesiological authority and dogmatic theology of the last medieval schism and the first modern revolution left little room for ascription to mere human agency of anything governing belief or behavior. So few were those things divine that the combatants agreed were not necessary to be believed or practiced that one is reminded of the redoubtable bookseller, a citizen of the People's Republic of Berkeley in the 1970's, who produced a stunningly sardonic poster with the caption "Everything not prohibited is compulsory." In the mid-sixteenth century, on the same lines, Lutheran believers quarreled violently over whether ceremonies not enjoined or forbidden by Scripture were permissible. The term applied to such ceremonies by those who would accept such diversity was the Greek term *adiaphora*, "things indifferent." It took a quarter-century for the German Lutherans to agree that there were indeed things indifferent and that the individual Churches still grasping a scintilla of hope of Christian reunification might determine what they were and how far they might be observed.

The tradition of *adiaphora* found its happiest home for a season in the Church of England of Hooker's day. In fact, underlying Hooker's pragmatism was a belief that there were some things that Christians might agree upon and many things that Christians might agree need not be agreed upon. He was preeminent among those Anglican adiaphorists who responded to the challenge not only of Rome but of Geneva by seeking common ground in accepting as indifferent uncommon beliefs and practices, while still maintaining the fundamentals of the Faith and the integrity of the Church of England.

Rome saw the Church of England as heretical, schismatic, and apostate. It had first broken with a pontifical authority when Henry VIII (1509–1547), in order to obtain an annulment of his marriage to Katherine of Aragon, expelled papal jurisdiction and secured from a pliant (though not Protestant) Parliament statutory recognition

> that the King our sovereign lord, his heirs and successors kings of this realm, shall be taken, accepted and reputed the only supreme head in earth of the Church of England called *Anglicana Ecclesia*.[2]

With Henry's first heir, Edward VI (1547–1553), the English Church under its regal Supreme Head became avowedly "Reformed Protestant," that is, looked increasingly to Swiss Protestantism, ultimately Calvin's Geneva, rather than to Luther's Germany. When the boy-king died, succeeded by Henry's eldest daughter, Mary (1553–1558), the issue of Katherine of Aragon, England and its Church were reconciled to Rome. The nation's schism and apostasy was absolved under the watchful, brutal, and rigidly orthodox-Catholic eye of Mary, who dissembled the royal style of Supreme Head by cloaking it under an "etc." Those clergy and laity who would not recant or reconvert either fled—many to the Reform Protestant havens in Switzerland and the Rhineland of Germany—or else faced immolation at the stake, which claimed one archbishop, four bishops, and sixteen priests along with almost three hundred resolute and strident laymen and laywomen. With the last of Henry's children to take the throne, Elizabeth I (1558–1603), the royal supremacy over the Church of England was restored, not merely recognized but granted by act of Parliament. The Lords and Commons conferred upon the Queen the title and style of "Supreme Governor," which continued to remain hidden by an "etc." After a decade of studied ambiguity in worship, practice, and doctrine in the Church of England, Pope Pius V's excommunication of Elizabeth in 1570 and virtual mandate to her subjects to depose her brought Roman Catholics under increasing disabilities and forced them to conform or suffer financially and risk punishment for treason if they aided or entertained missionary priests. It also solidified the Protestantism of the Anglican Church and emboldened the demand for further reform along Genevan, Calvinist, lines.

Largely under the influence of clergymen returned from Reformed centers whence they had fled during the Marian persecution, the Anglican Church became substantially Reformed Protestant on the Genevan model: in its dogmatic theology, by accepting John Calvin's categorical soteriology, the doctrine of Predestination; in its worship by the least possible ritualistic observance in its liturgy and emphasis on the sermon at the expense of the prescribed rites; and in its government with an alternative authority structure based on congregationally imposed discipline aimed at the eventual substitution of presbyterian governance for that of episcopacy. The mentality and the agenda of what was soon called Puritanism left little scope for *adiaphora*. It also demanded a response and rebuttal to its challenge, an exercise in apologetics, by which a reasoned defense of and rational explanation for the faith and practice of the Church would be advanced.

This is what the Reverend Richard Hooker undertook. Though he was neither learned in "both laws"—*viz.*, civil law and canon law—nor an "apprentice del ley" at the Inns of Court, he executed a compelling defense which went far beyond any existing *apologia* for any ecclesiastical body, sect, or cult of the day. Moreover, he did it as a legal treatise. In the process, Hooker's thorough and thoughtful apology both reflected the influence of the common law tradition and in turn influenced that tradition.

The preeminence of Hooker's concern with law is clear from the title of his monumental treatise, the first four (of eight) volumes of which were published in 1594: *Of the Laws of Ecclesiastical Polity*. Of the three elements in the title, "laws" demands treatment at some length. "Ecclesiastical" raises no inherent difficulty, since it refers to matters pertaining to the Church as an organized body of believers admitting one faith under one spiritual authority. A slight ambiguity at Hooker's hands results from the fact that in ecclesiastical matters the English state was no less intimately involved than the Anglican Church, the temporal authority (Queen) no less important than the spiritual (Supreme Governor), and neither easily distinguishable from the other.

"Polity" demands attention, because it was in Hooker's time a neologism, and never achieved common use. In what may have been its earliest use, in the 1530's, polity was defined as the civil order without which man existed only in a state of nature. A state of nature was what Thomas Hobbes decried a century later: "No arts; no letters; no society; and which is worst of all, continual fear and danger of violent death; and the life of man, solitary, poor, nasty, brutish, and short."[3] Hooker used polity in that sense in discussing whether any single form of civil order in religious usage was obligatory:

> But we must note, that he which affirmeth speech to be necessary among all men throughout the world, doth not thereby import that all men must necessarily speak one kind of language. Even so the necessity of polity and regiment in all Churches may be held without holding any one certain form to be necessary in all of them.[4]

It is difficult to recapture that meaning. Post-Lockean as we are, we think of a state of nature as merely a heuristic device, never a historical reality. We also find it difficult to see either a first cause or a prime mover in history. Hooker and his contemporaries were creationists in the fullest sense of the word, not doubting the reality of God's intention and exercised will manifested over time. Polity was civil order and civil order carried every denotation of "civilization." As civilization itself, polity subsumed the existence of government. Yet polity was something more than governmental structure or mere anatomy, more than the constitution; polity also included the dynamic that we call "politics," the play of policy. Indeed, as Hooker used it in the broader sense, "polity" could be seen analogously with "regiment," or rule by government, though it denoted an active or fluid state whereas government denoted a static one. Polity was both *government* and *governance*. Therefore, in *The Laws of Ecclesiastical Polity*, Hooker set out to describe, justify, and warrant the authority, structure, and operation—the polity—of the *ecclesia anglicana*, the Church of England, the Church by law established, as it was under its Supreme Governor, "Elizabeth, Queen of England, France, and Ireland, Defender of the Faith, etc." in the final decade of her long reign.

In order to do this, Hooker posited that that polity must be ruled by law, by laws that were divine in origin and sanction but human and positive in prescription and promulgation. This rested upon the Christian tradition that had obtained from the Church's beginnings, founded upon the Decalogue that Moses brought down from Mt. Sinai, the stern and awesome elaboration of those injunctions in Leviticus, and Christ's own assurance:

> Think not that I am come to destroy the law, or the prophets: I am not come to destroy, but to fulfill. For verily I say unto you, till heaven and earth pass, one jot or one tittle shall in no wise pass from the law, till all be fulfilled.[5]

The Latin Church, as it recovered from the onslaught of the barbarians who had destroyed the Roman Empire and received the Roman law codified by the Emperor Justinian, fashioned a universal code of ecclesiastical regulation, the canon law. The canon law, refined in that new institution of higher learning, the university, asserted the authority of a supreme pontiff who, not content to be simply the successor of the Apostle Peter, now claimed to be the Vicar of Christ. By the time of the Reformation, next to the Sacraments and the liturgy, the canon law had become the most powerful, ubiquitous, and defining dimension of the Roman Catholic Church. It had become the surrogate for pastoral theology, one of the strongest voices in apologetics, and the most palpable instrument of doctrine.[6] Easily overlooked in seeing the Reformation as a revolution in ideology, worship, and doctrine is the fact that the Reformation was also a revolution that attacked ecclesiastical authority as expressed in legislation and implementation of law. In a word, the Reformation demanded a revolution *in* law, sometimes vehemently *against* law.

There was a notable precedent for a lawyer-become-theologian producing a great work of dogmatic theology profoundly marked by legal construct and rhetoric: Jean Calvin's *Institutes of the Christian Religion* (1536). But it was less common for a theologian to turn lawyer. If Richard Hooker seems at first glance an unlikely figure to write an apologetical ecclesiological treatise fundamentally legal in form and substance as well as in title, tone, and objective, his background, education, and professional formation fitted him well for the undertaking.

Richard Hooker was born in March 1554 in a suburb of Exeter, the county seat of Devon and the largest city in southwestern England after the great port, Bristol. He came of a distinguished provincial-bourgeois family, Vowell alias Hooker, that played a leading role in the affairs of the city and its hinterland for some generations. Hooker's great-grandfather and grandfather both had been mayor of Exeter. Though his father was in reduced circumstances, his uncle John Hooker alias Vowell was both schoolmaster of Exeter grammar school and city chamberlain, Exeter's chief financial officer. John Vowell (1529–1601) was educated at Oxford, and in a long life—his nephew Richard would pre-decease him—produced numerous antiquarian works, most devoted to the topography and history of Exeter, a biography of a noted Devonshire warrior of the age, and a new edition of the chronicler Raphael Holinshed, whose work undergirded the age's historical understanding. He was a Member of the Irish Parliament in 1568 (keeping a journal of the proceedings), and he sat for Exeter in the English Parliament of 1586. It was uncle John who taught young Richard the essentials of Latin grammar, mathematics, and the other subjects requisite for university study. In the process, Richard learned a great deal about the way a polity worked, the manageable discrete civic polity of Exeter.

It was also John who brought Richard to the attention of his friend and fellow antiquarian, John Jewel, Bishop of Salisbury. Jewel interviewed the fourteen-year-old Richard at Salisbury, was impressed by him, settled a modest pension on his parents for his support, and in 1568 secured him a clerk's place at Corpus Christi College, Oxford.

Bishop Jewel's patronage and friendship, which endured unabated until his death in 1571, had an enormous impact on Richard Hooker. It determined where Hooker received his higher education, since Jewel had been a fellow of Corpus, 1542–1553, until deprived of his position by Mary's churchmen. While Jewel had been forced to flee to Frankfurt, and thence to Strasbourg and Zurich, he was less radically infected with Reformed Protestantism than many of his fellow Marian exiles, in great part because he eluded the dogmatic grasp of Geneva and Calvin. At Frankfurt he opposed the unyielding, fanatical, Calvinist radical, John Knox, who was destined to bring Reformed Protestantism to Scotland with profoundly revolutionary results, the effects of which have resonated since in all of the British Isles (most recently in the explosions that terrorized Londonderry, Belfast, and London). Returning to England on Elizabeth's accession, Jewel debated and defeated Roman Catholic divines, and in 1560 was appointed to the see of Salisbury. He demonstrated thoroughly orthodox Anglican tenets in his treatise *Apologia pro Ecclesiae Anglicanae* (1562). While written to defend the validity of the Church of England's reform against attack by Roman Catholic polemicists, the book also served to blunt Puritan demand for further "godly reformation." Jewel's apologetic was the first attempt in a thoroughgoing and rational way to explain what Anglicanism stood for against all of its detractors on both sides of the ecclesiastical divide. Testifying to its importance was the order to parish churches that it be placed, chained, on a lectern beside the Holy Bible. And what Jewel began would be brought to final form and full fruition three decades later by his protégé Richard Hooker in his treatise.

Hooker's scholarly formation owed most to his college. Corpus Christi College was a very young institution, founded in 1517 by one of Henry VII's and Henry VIII's most astute ministers, Richard Fox, Bishop of Winchester.[7] Corpus was to nurture and teach the Christian humanism of the Renaissance, and its first professor was the luminous Spanish humanist, Ludovico Vivès. With twenty fellows and twenty scholars, a handful of clerks and others, Corpus endured the change in religion and worked to ensure the increase of learning in Church and commonwealth. Fox's intention had been that Corpus should institute and endow the teaching of Greek in the university in furtherance of the new learning of the Renaissance. The new learning was built on new scholarship and new skills applied to old learning, and that by thorough command of the three languages of antiquity, Greek, Hebrew, and Latin. While Latin had been the vernacular of Western learning for a millennium, Greek and Hebrew were recent novelties. No less a figure than Erasmus prophesied that the *trilinguis biblioteca*, the college's library containing as many works in the three antique tongues as Fox and his faculty could secure, would make Corpus famous in the world of learning.[8] A half century after its foundation when Richard Hooker went up to Corpus it was still *the* college of new learning, full of vitality, graced with a learned faculty, and enjoying a deserved reputation for scholarly excellence.

In 1573, Hooker became a scholar, which brought him full maintenance, even though he was technically over the age limit—a clear sign of the esteem in which he was held by the president and fellows. Processing through the BA and MA, he was made a probationary fellow in 1577. In 1579, he was made a regular fellow and was appointed by the university to give the public Hebrew lecture. In effect, he became professor of Hebrew, and he held that post until he left Oxford in 1584. This was a mark of genuine distinction, not only because of the rarity of those commanding Hebrew well enough to teach it, but because that language exacted particular linguistic skills that sharpened rhetorical logic and inculcated minute respect for the use of words. The great clarity of Hooker's English prose, which has helped to keep current *Of the Laws of Ecclesiastical Polity* over the course of four centuries, owed much to the Hebrew of the Old Testament, and almost as much to the Greek of the New. Hooker's command of those two ancient tongues effectively "de-Latinized" him, and thus helped "English" him. Hooker was also a lecturer in logic, and so mightily equipped for the exacting labors demanded later by his apologetical masterpiece.

Hooker's sixteen years at Oxford was a relatively long tenure by contemporary standards. He made full use of them, and all of his subsequent theological scholarship was founded in those years, spent at the great presses in the library holding the chained books, printed and manuscript, which provided Scripture, the Latin and Greek Fathers of the early Church, liturgical works, the full range of systematic theology, and much of the history and muniments of the Catholic Church. Hooker also made lasting friendships with his contemporaries and students, many of whom would hold important places in the Church or government. Yet a college fellowship was not a career in itself but a stage in professional development. Having been ordained deacon in 1579, Hooker was in due course ordained priest. Upon marrying a London draper's daughter (who apparently was so disliked by his numerous friends that she has been roundly calumnied ever since), Hooker in 1584 was required to give up his fellowship and to leave Oxford for a country vicarage. Though anyone other than Richard Hooker might have rested satisfied with the cure of souls in a bucolic setting, performing with assiduity and compassion pastoral duties and following a strict regime of fasting and private prayer as he did, he never gave over study and scholarship.

One of Hooker's ex-students, whose father was Archbishop of York, was so disgusted by Mrs. Hooker's petticoat tyranny that he moved for Hooker's appointment as Master of the Temple—in essence, as chaplain to two of the Inns of Court, the Middle Temple and the Inner Temple. As the candidate of John Whitgift, Archbishop of Canterbury, the hammer of the Puritans, Hooker received this wealthy living in 1585. His cure was the Templars' old round church by Temple Bar, tucked in between the two Inns. The Master was nominated by the Crown but paid by the Inns; he preached at the Sunday morning service during law terms. The Temple also had an unendowed stipendiary preacher who preached at the Sunday afternoon service and on other days of the week. Since 1580 the preacher had been the Reverend Walter Travers, one of the most prominent and raucous Puritans, a devoted disciple of Calvin's successor at Geneva, Theodore Beza. Travers had not received Anglican—episcopal—ordination because he refused to subscribe to the articles required. His loathing of bishops was exceeded only by his rapture with presbyterianism. Whitgift had become archbishop in 1583 after having strenuously and successfully fought Puritan influence at Cambridge. That he was able to put in Hooker at the Temple instead of Travers (who enjoyed the support of Elizabeth's chief minister, William Cecil, Lord Burghley) was more than a political coup; it signaled that Puritanism faced such a challenge as it had not known before.

Travers, disgruntled and made harsher yet in word and spirit, remained preacher. Hooker, not one to turn away from a challenge, entered into a sustained polemic that lasted for more than a year until in 1586 Travers was inhibited from preaching by Whitgift because he was not in Anglican orders. The polemics were antiphonal: Hooker preached Sunday morning, Travers on Sunday afternoon, so that "the forenoon sermon spoke Canterbury and the afternoon Geneva."[9] The stakes were high. A contemporary noted that "to suffer one opposite to the English discipline [to preach at the Temple was] in effect to retain half the lawyers of England to be of counsel against the ecclesiastical government."[10] So high were the stakes, by virtue of this dispute, that Richard Hooker was moved to write *Of the Laws of Ecclesiastical Polity*.

It is significant that as early as the controversy with Travers, Hooker posited his fundamental canons of interpretation by which the "laws" governing "ecclesiastical polity" were to be determined and construed. The two minor prefatory pieces of his treatise, the sermons on the "Certainty and Perpetuity of Faith in the Elect" and "Justification," drew their texts from Habakkuk, 1: 4, and were preached in the Temple.[11] Both argued, contrary to Travers, that reason attending Scripture, rather than mere Scripture alone, was the source for authority, the source for law. Nowhere is this more powerfully put than at the outset of "Certainty of Faith in the Elect":

> That which we see by the light of grace, though it be indeed more certain; yet is it not to us so evidently certain, as that which sense or the light of nature will not suffer man to doubt of. Proofs are vain and frivolous except they be more certain than is the thing proved: and do we not see how the Spirit every where in the Scripture proveth matters of faith, laboreth to confirm us in the things which we believe, by things whereof we have sensible knowledge? I conclude therefore that we have less certainty of evidence concerning things believed, than concerning sensible or naturally perceived.[12]

This exalted the use of reason, natural reason revealing natural law. In the eyes of the literal Scripturalists of Travers's confession, it was not only erroneous, and conceivably heretical, but also verged on blasphemy. Similarly, Hooker appealed to reason in the matter of "Justification," the central contention of that sermon being that those in faith are justified though they slip from grace:

> The case is clear, *long experience hath made this manifest, it needs no proof*. I grant we are apt, prone, and ready to forsake God; but is God as ready to forsake us? Our minds are changeable; is his so likewise? Whom God hath justified, hath not Christ assured, that it is "his Father's will to give them a Kingdom?"[13]

Here in brief is the ground upon which Hooker would challenge the Puritans' Biblical fundamentalism in Book II, especially Chapter 7, "An examination of their opinion concerning the force of arguments taken from human authority for the ordering of men's actions and persuasions."[14] And here is the seed that blossomed in the triumphal Chapter 8, "A declaration what the truth is in this matter,"[15] in balanced condemnation of both extremes of the Reformation's great disputation over the source of authority:

> Two opinions therefore there are concerning sufficiency of Holy Scripture, each extremely opposite unto the other, and both repugnant unto truth. The schools of Rome teach Scripture to be so unsufficient, as if, except traditions were added, it did not contain all revealed and supernatural truth, which absolutely is necessary for the children of men in this life to know that they may in the next be saved. Others [Puritans] justly condemning this opinion grow likewise unto a dangerous extremity, as if Scripture doth not only contain all things in that kind necessary, but all things simply, and in such sort that to do any thing according to any other law were not only unnecessary but even opposite unto salvation, unlawful and sinful.[16]

This was a goodly reminder, less directed at and less relevant to Rome than to Geneva, that while Scripture is indeed God's Word, fallible humans do not always hear it the same way, though all admit its authority. Luther's soteriology, Justification by Faith, was raised on St. Paul's Epistle to the Romans (10:9): *That if thou shalt confess with thy mouth the Lord Jesus, and shalt believe in thine heart that God hath raised him from the dead, thou shalt be saved*. Calvin's soteriology, Predestination or Election, was raised on the same letter, by the same apostle, to the same Church (Romans 11: 5–6): *Even so then at this present time also there is a remnant according to the election of grace. And if by grace, then is it no more of works: otherwise grace is no more grace. But if it be of works, then it is no more grace; otherwise work is no more work*. These two passages of the New Testament are just a page apart. Their respective exponents in the Protestant Reformation were a world apart.

One of the most astute historians of English Christianity, who brilliantly surveyed in five volumes the interaction of worship and theology from the Reformation to the present day, has written: "Hooker gloried in a church freed of the superstition of Rome and the scrupulosity and intensity of Geneva, affirming that Anglicanism's first loyalty was to Scripture, its second to the pure traditions of the primitive and undivided church, and its third to reason."[17]

Horton Davies's use of the word "loyalty" is apt, for it avoids the categoricalness and rigidity of "belief," or "commitment," or "postulate," or any one of a number of other terms that bespeak unyieldingness. Hooker's three "loyalties" are not mutually exclusive, they are complementary, and they admit of varying emphasis depending upon circumstance and necessity. Hooker would not accept that anything clearly repugnant to Scripture could be believed. At the same time, he believed that the tradition of the primitive Church, the Church of the Apostles, of the first century of the

Christian era, configured Scripture to speak to the explicit needs of the Christian. One of the best illustrations of this is to be found in the matter of ministry. The New Testament speaks of two orders, bishops and deacons; it is silent with regard to a third order, presbyter (priest). Nonetheless, in the primitive Church, a priesthood developed to share the bishop's responsibility and burden for the liturgical life of the congregation. Thus evolved the three orders that obtained in the Church, Latin and Greek, until in the Reformation in the West the principal Protestant bodies came to deny the necessity for and the authority of the bishop.

Geneva equated presbyter with bishop, and denied the validity of the subsequent development of the episcopal office with its increasing powers.[18] Opposing this, Hooker argued that by the use of reason the tradition of the primitive age completed Scripture and revealed what Scripture meant as well as what it said, thus establishing a place for both episcopal and priestly offices and reason and confirming the wisdom and necessity of recognizing both roles. If Scripture spoke clearly about bishops and was silent on presbyters, to admit a role for the latter did not require jettisoning the former. It only meant respecting the divine wisdom which reason in the primitive age had revealed and which reason in the present age confirmed. For Hooker, reason was not merely a tool—it was the hook on which hung all the law and the prophets of Anglicanism!

Why speak of "laws" for the Church's polity? The most superficial reason—but not a negligible one—is simply that the debate giving rise to the treatise took place before lawyers in their chapel. As his ideas developed, Hooker might well have decided to address in their own language his congregation of men trained and experienced in the laws, themselves masters of logic, the grave and learned men whose professional consensus was what Edward Coke of the Inner Temple called the "artificial reason" of the law. Coke himself produced a dozen or more aphorisms on reason in law: *Ratio est legis anima*, for example—or *Lex semper intendit quod convenit rationi*, or *Nihil quod est contra rationem est licitum*. None of these commonplaces was inconsistent with what the Temple's Anglican chaplain was asserting about the laws of the Church, and all of them would encourage the framing of theological arguments along legal lines.[19]

Moreover, Hooker's principal adversary, behind Travers and his fellow Puritans—an adversary dead for a generation, yet always present—was Jean Calvin, and the thesis to which Hooker's work was to be the antithesis was Calvin's *Institutes of the Christian Religion*. A small volume of six chapters published in Latin in 1536, Calvin's reform manifesto grew to seventeen chapters in 1539, and thereafter steadily expanded until the last edition in 1559 comprised eighty chapters, a massive tome that carried conviction by sheer weight rather than a sharp point. (Such a phenomenon should not be strange to lawyers.) Calvin displayed his early professional deformation as a lawyer in continually updating his work to account for new "cases" to deal with changed circumstances, recent criticisms, and new insights. The very title *Institutes* is more closely associated with legal works—from Justinian to Coke—than theological. In taking up the Calvinist challenge, Hooker recognized that his response to it would have to reflect those rigorous legal attributes of form and rhetoric dominating Calvin's work.

The increasing prominence of law in Tudor England should not be overlooked. There was a marked increase in litigation over the course of the century. The creation of new tribunals answered the demand for it; so did expanded jurisdiction in existing courts, sometimes by fictions such as *latitat* (by which King's Bench achieved a large civil jurisdiction) and *quominus* (by which the Exchequer acquired a civil equity role). Increased litigation was largely an unintended consequence of the Reformation itself. Between 1536 and 1547, Henry VIII's dissolution of the monasteries and Edward VI's suppression of chantries put roughly a quarter of all the real property in England and Wales on the market. This property endowed a new stratum of landowners, the gentry. The gentlemen of England increasingly made their weight felt in Parliament in legislation favoring property owners, even at the expense of the Crown. They sent their sons to the Inns of Court to learn enough law to make them learned lay clients, able to talk knowledgeably with the barristers who would conduct their litigation over real property. The new litigants bought the legal talent that invented a myriad of innovative devices to fashion proprietary interests that at the beginning of the century would have been unthinkable. No conveyancing device is worth more than its survival in court, but so many such devices—those that failed as well as those that succeeded—resulted in an enormous amount of clouded title, which multiplied litigation exponentially.

By the time of Hooker's death in 1600, not least because of such endemic litigation, the jargon of the law, even more than the rhetoric of the law, had penetrated areas of thought and speech that had nothing necessarily to do with law.[20] This was true for the poets and the dramatists—witness the manor-court proceedings that provide the shaping metaphor for Shakespeare's Sonnet 46—and it was true of the theologians. The apex of the phenomenon came in the next century with the "covenant theology" of the Puritans, so influential in New England.[21] A British historian of the French

Revolution, A. B. Cobban, noticing that in the generation before the fall of the Bastille Frenchmen, including Louis XV himself, used rhetoric that 1789 unleashed, remarked that the French had begun to talk revolutionary talk even before they had thought revolutionary thoughts. So it was with the English and their law, analogously, in Hooker's day.

Finally and most pertinent as to why "laws" of ecclesiastical polity is the simple fact that English ecclesiastical polity was raised upon and depended upon secular municipal law, as distinct from God's law, natural law, or canon law. Henry VIII did not "found" the Anglican Church any more than Constantine founded the Roman Church. What Henry VIII did was fundamentally to sever from the polity of the Roman Church the polity of the Church in England, two polities that had been tightly joined for almost a millennium. Henry's revolution had been effected by a series of discrete legislative enactments of the "Reformation Parliament," which sat for nearly seven years, from November 1529 until April 1536. During this Parliament's eight legislative sessions, the organic connection between England and Rome was whittled away by a thousand cuts that stripped the pontiff of his revenues, his jurisdiction, his powers, and finally even his title insofar as they pertained to England. Whatever was done henceforth to the Church of England could only be done ultimately by the King in Parliament. Even the devoutly Roman Catholic Mary had no choice but to undo by acts of Parliament the schism worked by Henry and the Protestantization effected by Edward, and it was by Parliamentary legislation that Elizabeth re-edified a Protestant establishment. Though the term did not become common until the eighteenth century, the Church by Law Established came into being in the sixteenth. It was the reality with which any apologist for it had to deal. It was the reality with which any who would attack its validity or its regularity would have to deal, or else lose the argument. Therefore, if the Church was to be defended and justified by Richard Hooker, he had to do it by an argument framed in legal terms that reflected an institution which if divine in origin was regal in operation.

The achievement of Hooker was to cast his argument for the laws of the English Church's polity in so wide a jurisprudential context that his treatise contributes to legal learning as a whole. His definition of law is set out early, clearly, emphatically, and comprehensively:

> All things that are, have some operation not violent or casual. Neither doth any thing ever begin to exercise the same, without some fore-conceived end for which it worketh. And the end which it worketh for is not obtained, unless the work be also fit to obtain it by. For unto every end every operation will not

> serve. That which doth assign unto each thing the kind, that which doth moderate the force and power, that which doth appoint the form and measure, of working, the same we term a Law. So that no certain end could ever be attained, unless the actions whereby it is attained were regular; that is to say made suitable, fit and correspondent unto their end, by some canon, rule or law. Which thing doth first take place in the works even of God himself.[22]

Not only is law not arbitrary in its creation, it is also not arbitrary in its motivation. It stems always from necessity, some felt need. And there are various levels of necessity, of well-doing:

> In Goodness therefore there is a latitude or extent, whereby it cometh to pass that even of good actions some are better than other some; . . . Degrees of well-doing there could be none, except perhaps if the seldomness and oftenness of doing well. But the nature of Goodness being thus ample, a Law is properly that which Reason in such sort defineth to be good that it must be done. And the Law of Reason or human Nature is that which men by discourse of natural Reason have rightly found out themselves to be all for ever bound unto in their actions.[23]

Here the canon is settled: the law, with an exquisite economy founded on necessity, pragmatically ranging to attain goodness, capable of amendment to remove imperfections and to fit circumstances, is the means by which humankind fashions a "life fit for the dignity of man." That law is the basis for society:

> Two foundations there are which bear up public societies; the one, a natural inclination, whereby all men desire sociable life and fellowship; the other, an order expressly or secretly agreed upon touching the manner of their union in living together. The latter is that which we call the Law of a Commonweal, the very soul of a politic body, the parts whereof are by law animated, held together, and set on work in actions, as the common good requireth.

Yet unless man is understood to be averse from obedience to the laws of his nature, such "laws politic" to impose external order cannot be perfected:

> in a word, unless presuming man to be in regard of his depraved mind little better than a wild beast, they [laws politic] do accordingly provide notwithstanding so to frame his outward actions, that they be no hinderance unto the common good for which societies are instituted.[24]

By agreeing to polity, some form of a civil body politic, humans overcame the baneful consequences of their depravity.

Here, Hooker posited that such an agreement constituted consent. He was silent on precisely what kind of consent and (more to the point) what continuity and longevity of consent was necessary. What he gave with one hand, elsewhere he seemed to take away with the other. We cannot make him a founding father of representative government. We can however with John Locke, who a century—and two revolutions—later spoke of "the judicious Hooker," greet a kindred spirit for the proposition underlying the social contract, and a spirit moreover that understood that there was no single optimum polity:

> Howbeit not this the only kind of regiment that hath been received in the world. The inconveniences of one kind have caused sundry other to be devised. So that in a word all public regiment of what kind soever seemeth evidently to have risen from deliberate advice, consultation, and composition between men, judging it convenient and behoveful; there being no impossibility in nature considered by itself, but that men might have lived without any public regiment. Howbeit, the corruption of our nature being presupposed, we may not deny but that the Law of Nature doth now require of necessity some kind of regiment; so that to bring things unto the first course they were in, and utterly to take away all kind of public government in the world, were apparently to overturn the whole world.[25]

Indeed, Locke's *Second Treatise on Government* sanctioned no more strenuous action in defense against tyranny: government might change, but the society undergirding it and for which government existed could not be dissolved, the social contract abrogated.

Hooker's intention was considerably more limited than either to prescribe law for the temporal polity of England or to contribute to political theory. He sought to justify the existing polity of the Church of England as it had developed under the Elizabethan settlement of religion, founded on the first two statutes of Elizabeth's reign in 1559, the Act of Supremacy and the Act of Uniformity.[26] The former recreated in the monarch the supremacy over the Church, giving full jurisdiction to the Supreme Governor to exercise the authority and the powers wielded by the Pope over the whole Catholic Church before the Reformation. The latter prescribed uniform services, rites, and the administration of Sacraments by a newly revised Book of Common Prayer sufficiently ambiguous to admit either a Roman or a Genevan interpretation of the function of the Eucharist. Both acts assumed the traditional order of an historic episcopate, presbyters, and deacons; the validity and efficacy of the Sacraments; the structure of cathedral and parish churches; the continued existence of canon law courts; the maintenance of orthodox theology and the Christology of the Fathers of the early Church; the primacy of Scripture—in short, all of the fundamentals of Catholic ecclesiology short of the Papacy itself. In the course of the next four decades, theology came to be mightily tempered by Calvinist soteriology and worship, and the drumbeat for further reform, banishing remaining "popish practices" (vestments, ring in marriage, kneeling) and formal ceremonies and ritual, substituting the sermon for sacramental prayer, and even abolishing episcopacy in favor of Genevan presbyterianism. The principal defender of the Elizabethan settlement against further reform was Elizabeth herself. The Supreme Governor's prominence has earned for the Settlement the appellation, "Erastian," which means the supremacy of the state over the Church.[27] This term, as applied by historians, has been usually pejorative. But it tends to smudge the centrality and primacy of the nontemporal and nonsecular dimensions of the Church. It was these that Hooker intended to explain and justify. His ecclesiastical polity was genuinely ecclesiastical.

The remaining three books of Hooker's treatise spring from Book I's disquisition on law. Book II establishes the Scriptural and primitive origins and Patristic development of authority for Church polity. Book III challenges directly the Puritan (and obliquely the Roman Catholic) critics of the Anglican Church's polity, making the essential distinction between what is *grounded* in Scripture and what is *commanded* by Scripture. Book IV, with remarkable vigor and candor, argues that the Anglican Church maintains continuity in practice with the universal Catholic observations in rites and ceremonies, certainly shorn of features without Scriptural warrant but not damned merely because they remain yet in Roman usage. In defense of continuity, Hooker went far beyond either Rome or Geneva in recognizing the Judaic origins of Christian practice. He ends on a note of exultation:

> Wherefore, if any refuse to believe us disputing for the verity of religion established, let them believe God himself thus miraculously working for it, and wish life even for ever and ever unto that glorious and sacred instrument [the Church] whereby he worketh.[28]

The first four books were published—notably, in English, in keeping with their intended audience—in 1593. Hooker cut his final ties with the Temple in 1595 and retired to a country living in Kent (in the Queen's gift), there to continue on the project. He was still at work there when he died in 1600. He had published Book V in 1597. The subsequent three books were published posthumously, very late, VI and VIII in 1648 and VII in 1661. Hooker appears to have written the posthumous books, but they were in various states of completion, especially VI and VIII, which are clearly drafts. The posthumous books are detailed examinations of the basic structures of both spiritual and civil power, a coda to the more general meditations of Books I-IV. Book VIII, especially, is a brilliant analysis of the Supreme Governorship, reflecting as deeply on the theory of monarchy as on the theory of supremacy.

The posthumous publication, along with the continuing currency of Books I-V, is the highest compliment that the English could give to them. Hooker's texts were appealed to by the New Anglicans of a high-church persuasion, skeptics of Calvinist predestination, ceremonialists with a commitment to Sacramentalism and liturgy, and loyalists to a fully episcopalian polity. These churchmen came to dominate the higher clergy in the first half of the seventeenth century—such clerics as Lancelot Andrewes, Bishop of Winchester, John Donne, Dean of St. Paul's, and William Laud, Archbishop of Canterbury. All were disciples of Hooker, and he can rightly be seen as the morning star of that new tradition. At the same time, those Puritans who stood in diametric opposition to the New Anglicans and who achieved political and ecclesiastical triumph over them in the mid-seventeenth century English Revolution—taking off in the process the heads of Archbishop Laud and of King Charles—also appealed to Hooker. They cited Hooker for his spirit of *adiaphora*, irenic tone and disposition, and certain latitudinarian acceptance of different usages which Laud and his set appeared to threaten. A half-century after his controversy with Walter Travers, Hooker had become a prophet with honor almost everywhere. His judicious and exacting labor reflected St. John's Gospel: "In my Father's house are many mansions. . . ." So it became in the course of the following, tortured, century in England and its Church.

Richard Hooker would not like that to be his epitaph. He had contended too long and too strenuously with those who denigrated the practices and observances of the Church by Law Established to go so gentle into that good night. Book V, devoted particularly and in detail to liturgy, is in many ways the most explicitly New Anglican exposition of the *Laws of Ecclesiastical Polity*. In it he manages to give eloquent voice to the governing aesthetic of the rites prescribed in the Book of Common Prayer, which perhaps more than any other single feature of the Anglican tradition distinguished it:

> That which inwardly each man should be, the Church outwardly ought to testify. And therefore the duties of religion which are seen must be such as that affection which is unseen ought to be. Signs must resemble the things they signify. If religion bear the greatest sway in our hearts, our outward religious duties must shew it as far as the Church hath outward ability. Duties of religion

> performed by whole societies of men ought to have in them according to our power a sensible excellency correspondent to the majesty of him whom we worship. Yea, then are the public duties of religion best ordered when the militant Church doth resemble by sensible means, as it may in such cases, that hidden dignity and glory wherewith the Church triumphant in heaven in beautified.[29]

Nunc dimittis, Lord, now lettest thou thy servant depart in peace. . . .

CHAPTER SIX

James VI and I

King James the Sixth of Scotland (1567–1625) and the First of England and Ireland (1603–1625) was to his contemporaries an object of considerable derision. Henri IV of France, his necessary ally in European politics, was reputed to have called James the "wisest fool in Christendom." Henri certainly managed the cruelest taunt when he said he accepted that James was indeed the "Scottish Solomon," because he was the son of David—a nasty allusion to the vicious rumor that his father was not Lord Darnley but David Riccio, the Italian secretary of his mother, Mary Queen of Scots. James never forgave Henri for that crack, which made the round of European capitals, and the animosity it engendered between the two kings contributed to the failure of England and France to make common cause against Spain. Lesser potentates were not loath to add insult to such injury. Maurice of Nassau, the chieftain-prince of Dutch independence, suspicious that James was conniving with the Dutch merchant oligarchy to make peace at any price with Spain, insulted him publicly and was forced to apologize for it. Even those who owed everything to James, the succession of handsome young favorites, were wont to abase him by transgressing from impudence to insolence. James's stinging letter to Robert Carr, Earl of Somerset, who had received seven years of regal largesse, was pathetic:

> For although I confess the greatness of that trust and privacy betwixt us will very well allow unto you an infinitely great liberty and freedom of speech unto me, yea even to rebuke me more sharply and bitterly than ever my [school] master durst do, yet to invent a new art of railing upon me, nay to borrow the tongue of the devil . . . is but a gentle admonition, that cannot come within the compass of any liberty of friendship.[1]

The most contemptuous words ever offered to James were offered to him face-to-face by Andrew Melville, a Scots presbyter of the tough-as-leather sort, who informed the king directly that he was no more than "God's sillie vassall."[2] It is hardly surprising that at Hampton Court in 1604, sitting among the English bishops and Puritan clergymen who were airing views on how the Church of England might be further "reformed," James thanked God "for bringing him into the promised land, where Religion was purely professed; where he sat among grave, learned and reverend men; not, as before, elsewhere, a King without state, without honor, without order; where beardless boys would brave him to his face."[3]

Though Andrew Melville was almost three-score years and bearded, he can be counted among those whom James was glad to have escaped. It was not a clear escape. There must be some temptation to believe that James drew resentment and mockery because he was a pedant and a didact who never hesitated, when addressing an issue, to deliver himself of everything he knew. Moreover, because James put his views in print, he offered a solid and substantial target for anyone who wanted to challenge him. The mystique of monarchy, into which James constantly sought to cloak himself, was impossible to maintain when the king was literally an open book to even the meanest of his subjects and, more dangerously, to those who felt moved to oppose him. The king's collected works, originally published in 1616, demonstrates how open the window of his mind was, and how transparent was so much of his learning. Here are the essentials of the best-published and most scholarly of any European ruler of his age, a monarch whose rule often appeared to fall far short of his kingcraft and regal aspirations. The abridged reprint by Harvard University Press in 1918, entitled *The Political Works of James I*, omits some of the original's polemical pieces against Roman Catholic apologists and all of James's writings on witchcraft and demonology, a subject in which he took a keen and too credulous interest. But the reprint provides the important theoretical contribution of a vitally interested participant in the statecraft of the age as those new entities, the European states, escaped from the traditional dependencies and authorities that had become the norm since the death of the Emperor Charlemagne in the middle of the eighth century and Pope Gregory I in the early seventh. If the book is a masterpiece of political theory (and Charles H. McIlwain, the editor of the Harvard reprint believed it was), the political writing was also a particular reflection of James's uniquely kingly experience, beginning even before he was capable of knowing it when he was barely a year old. Much of the misunderstanding surrounding James's theory disappears when it is framed in terms of biography.

The least uncharitable and possibly most acute observation of James was that of the Comte de Tillieres, the French ambassador to his court. He noted that when James wanted to play the king he sounded like a despot, and when he stooped to conquer, he was simply vulgar. The first part of that proposition will demand most of our attention below. The last part is relevant to the more general disparagement of James, both during his lifetime and posthumously.

Even in an age when the term "gentility" referred to social status denoted by the right to a coat of arms and not to any refinement of manner, James's salacity and fondness for the scatological were often remarked upon. Negligent of popularity with the masses (unlike his predecessor, Elizabeth, who radiated an aloof graciousness), James seldom showed himself to the crowd, and once when urged to do so, snapped back, "God's wounds I will pull down my breeches and they shall also see my arse."[4] At the Hampton Court Conference in 1604 when the priggish bachelor president of Corpus Christi College, Oxford, the Reverend John Reynolds, objected to the Prayer Book wedding service's vivid "With my body I thee worship," James quipped, "Many a man speaks of Robin Hood who never shot in his bow," scandalizing worldly bishops and puritanical parsons alike.[5] James was more direct with Scots presbyters, reacting to their homiletic extravagances with a lusty "I give not a turd for your preaching."[6] His vigor of expression seemed more absurd than compelling, and often the reaction to it was the kind sought by burlesque house comedians: derision.

James's ghost suffered ridicule no less than his person. Not immediately. At the time of his death in March 1625, while some spoke ill of the dead others found virtues in him. William Laud, Bishop of St. David's, whom James had denied major preferment because he thought his rigor against Puritanism disruptive (St. David's was about as far away from Whitehall as a bishop could be), had little reason to be grateful to him. Yet he wrote a brief memorial noting James's clemency, moderateness, patience, justness, sweetness, his peaceable entry into England, his ability to forgive, his pacifism in avoiding war abroad and rebellion at home, his kindness to those who served him, his support of religion, his learning, and the fact that in his English reign "he took away the life of no one nobleman, but restored many."[7] If "nobleman" was narrowly, though properly, construed—Lord Cobham's brother George Brooke was beheaded in 1604, and Sir Walter

Raleigh was beheaded in 1618—and the "many restored" an artful way to observe James's prodigality in creating peers, the point was still a compliment.

The drumbeat of posthumous condemnation began only after the horrendous events of 1640 to 1660 that took the life of James's son, Charles I. Sir Hammond LeStrange, writing from the perspective of 1655, was categorical:

> And though those dismal calamities which befel his Son, were doubtless ampliated by a superfetation of Causes; yet was their first and main existency derivative from those seminalities. Let Court-Pens extol the calmness of his Halcyonian Reign with all artifice of Rhetorick, yet can they never deny but that admired Serenity had its set in Cloud; and that he left to his Successor, both an empty Purse, and a Crown of Thorns.[8]

LeStrange echoed the old derision of the king's lifetime and gave it explicative force in the light of subsequent events. Arthur Wilson, writing in 1653, saw the seeds of Charles's destruction in James's failures growing in great part from his "remiss comportment," a clear allusion not only to errors in governance and a noticeable want of regal bearing in the king but also to his excessive, perhaps felonious, intimacy with his comely young favorites:

> And the Tongues at those times more fluent than my Pen, made every little miscarriage (being not able to discover their true operations, like small seeds hid in earthy darkness) grow up and spread into such exuberant Branches that evil report did often pearch upon them. So dangerous it is for Princes by remiss comportment, to give growth to the least Error; for it often proves as fruitful as malice can make it.[9]

The posthumous scandalization of James's conduct, particularly his relationship with his last and greatest favorite, George Villiers, Duke of Buckingham, occurred shortly after James's death in 1625, because Buckingham's already overweening power actually increased with Charles's accession. Allusions to Buckingham's homosexual intimacy with the old king was the vehicle for the attack, and the absence of any suggestion that the deep friendship between the new king and the old favorite was tainted by homosexuality spared the living crown while tarring the dead one. In Michaelmas Term 1627, a troupe of itinerant minstrels were heavily sentenced in Star Chamber for a slander on Buckingham which they had sung around London. Among its stanzas:

> What other goodnes could ever arise
> Come love me whereas I lay

From a master [James I] that was soe sincere and wise
The cleane contrary waye.

Whoe if he could now from his grave ascend
Come love me whereas I lay
He surely would the truth of his service commend
The cleane contrary waye.

Although common people his glory would stayne
Come love me whereas I lay
Heele live yett to gett their prayse againe
The cleane contrary waye.[10]

In our sexually explicit age "the cleane contrary waye" demands no clarification; the other refrain is clearer when rendered as "Come love me where ass I lay." These stanzas reflected the rumor that Buckingham had poisoned James in order to accelerate Charles's accession. (Some went so far as to suggest Charles's complicity.) Sir Anthony Weldon, whose career in James's household had ended when he finally said too many nasty things about Scots courtiers, was still traducing Buckingham in 1650, in the process giving a degree of indelibility to the unprovable but certainly plausible scandal that James's relationship with Buckingham was carnally homosexual.[11] To the present day, those historians most unsparing in their judgment of James and his reign have been those most convinced of his active homosexuality.[12]

George Villiers's meteoric rise from a minor gentleman to Duke of Buckingham cannot be explained by mere deviancy. James relied increasingly upon the comely young gentleman for what became almost the entire governance of England and Wales—though notably and emphatically, not of Scotland. Handsome, athletic, vivacious, and of noble bearing, Buckingham was in almost every respect, including ability, better than all the king's previous favorites. By 1621, he was the indisputable vicegerent. He had also become the bosom friend of the king's second son and heir-apparent, Charles—even a surrogate older brother, for Buckingham resembled James's eldest son, Henry Prince of Wales, who had died tragically in 1612, aet 18. A regal youth, Henry had seen the prince's vocation as that of a soldier and man of the world. He was everything that Charles, crippled as an infant by rickets and shunned by his parents, until Henry's death left them no other male heir, was not. Whatever weight can be attached to James's ambivalent allusion in a letter to Buckingham, "And so God bless you, my sweet child and wife, and grant that ye may ever be a comfort to your dear dad and husband," the king's almost invariable reference to himself as "your dear dad" and his epistolary joint address to Buckingham and Charles as "my sweet boys" strikes a consistently paternal note.[13] Buckingham filled a genuine void in James's affections caused by the death of his son that none other, not even his second son, could fill.

Considered dispassionately, and considered separate from the disasters into which he guided the realm during the reign of Charles, Buckingham's services to James were considerable. He worked the destruction of the Howard clan in James's counsels and government, facilitated by the fall of Somerset who was the stalking horse of that enduring, corrupt, and jobbing gang. If the disastrous collapse of the Howards afforded Buckingham personal satisfaction, it also enabled him to promote better and more competent people to take their places. He was more discerning than James in his understanding of the domestic political and the foreign diplomatic obstacles to the marriage of Prince Charles to the Infanta of Spain (the "infamous" Spanish Match, which made perfect dynastic sense given James's inherent pacifism). Buckingham was also more perspicacious in realizing when it was time to abandon these negotiations. Where Buckingham failed was as strategist. Taking England to war against Spain in 1624 was built upon the strategic miscalculation that he could win quickly and the political myopia of not realizing that if he did not win quickly he could not sustain enough popular support to furnish the revenues necessary for a long conflict. Buckingham's ignorance of the art of war and his arrogance in believing he was a warrior led directly to defeat on land and sea, both for his forces and his cause, and to his own death in 1628, at the hand of a disgruntled officer.[14] The crises amid which the Duke died became the first failures of the young king's reign.

Buckingham's presence as vicegerent (and incidentally as tutor-companion to the heir apparent) relieved James of a great deal of responsibility for political routine. It made possible, even if not advisable, the marked decline in James's assiduity in affairs of state that set in about 1616—the year that James published his political works—and continued with gathering momentum until the king's death in March 1625. That decline was certainly marked by increasing illness, especially after 1618, with bouts of severe arthritic pain, feebleness, and something akin to neuropathy, possibly from a genetic metabolic disorder, acute intermittent porphyria.[15] James's passion for hunting, dancing, and the sybaritic good things of court life increased with age (as the author's old teacher at Harvard, W. K Jordan, said, "James liked to watch the boys and girls play"). The king spent more time with his books and scholarly interests, in long and rambling discussions with bright and accommodating clerics, not least the dean of St. Paul's, whom he had called from the long robe to the cloth. To James, John Donne as theologian was more acceptable than John Donne as poet: the king is supposed to have quipped that Donne's metaphysical poetry reminded him of the peace of God, which passeth all understanding. James always found time and reserves of energy for theological argument. During the great controversy over free will centering on the Dutch theologian Jacobus Arminius, particularly during the Synod of Dort in 1618–1619, James played a heavy, if not quite weighty, and very ambivalent role, sending missives from Whitehall, ceaselessly badgering the hapless English delegates and anybody else who would listen to him. He skirted the details of government more than he had at any time before. Less inclined to play the king, he was also less likely to sound like a despot, if we are to credit Tillieres's crack.

Just how despotic did James sound? The obvious place to look for an answer to that question is in the speeches he delivered to Parliament. There is much assertion of his regality, with varying degrees of stridency. Moreover, all four speeches in his *Political Works*, from 1604 to 1610, were given to the same Parliament, composed of the same members. Between its assembly on March 19, 1604, and its final prorogation, on December 6, 1610, this parliament sat in five sessions totaling twenty-five months. During this period, as James addressed his subjects, his speeches grew longer (save for his address of November 9, 1605, which was the shortest for a very good reason), from just under an hour for the first to one and one-half hours for the last.[16] Consequently, James's repetitiveness fell on progressively deafer ears, each succeeding homily on kingship being less convincing than its predecessor. The leadership in the Commons, which was increasingly disinclined to cooperate with the crown and was beginning to take control of the House's own debate, found the king's sorties beginning to rile as well as pall.[17]

The king's earliest speech, delivered to both Houses at the convocation of the first Parliament, on March 19, 1604, was relatively succinct and markedly gracious.[18] James stooped to conquer without a hint of vulgarity. Touchingly, he ecstatically recalled the welcome extended him by his new subjects a year before, "their eyes flaming nothing but sparkles of affection, their mouthes and tongues vttering nothing but sounds of joy."[19] His evocation of peace, foreign and domestic, was heartfelt, as was his plea for a union of his two kingdoms as well as his two crowns. His invocation of God in support of his project for the union was to take a liberty, but would have seemed entirely appropriate to contemporary ears. His careful confession of faith and analysis of religion in England were brilliant. What he believed as a mildly Reformed Protestant Anglican he revealed to all his subjects from the bully pulpit of Parliament. His clearly drawn distinction between Roman Catholic clerics (to be banished if they continued to maintain Papal supremacy) and laity (to be tolerated and not punished in their bodies for the error of their minds if they eschewed sedition and subversion) was adumbrated in an appropriate forum: Parliament was the place for dealing with such problems. His curt dismissal of "the *Puritanes* and *Nouelists*"—he considered their demands disposed of by his proclamations of the year before following the Hampton Court Conference—neatly preserved his prerogative as the Supreme Governor of the Church not to treat ecclesiastical matters in Parliament.[20] And in his exhortation to the episcopate to be diligent in their care of souls, reference to himself as God's "Lieutenant" over the Church was no arrogation in the Supreme Governor.

When he turned to the judges (the twelve of the courts of King's Bench, Common Pleas, and Exchequer attended Parliament as assistants to the Lords), he emphasized his responsibility to God, in some ways jointly with them, in others singularly as their master. He did not let slip the chance to both inveigh against too much legislative activity and to distance himself from tyranny as a "righteous and just King."[21] He gave away most in his defensive discourse on patronage, why he had rewarded many and yet not enough from the perspective of most of his auditors, while dealing with the implication that too many Scots and too few English supped at his ample table. His promise to do better, especially if his disappointed English suitors would only be less importunate, was unconvincing but not derisory.

The sting of the speech was in its tail. The king's apology for lacking eloquence concluded with a faintly veiled threat:

> That it becommeth a King, in my opinion, to vse no other Eloquence then plainnesse and sinceritie. . . . [the former to avoid ambiguity, the latter so that] as farre as a King is in Honour erected aboue any of his Subiects, so farre should he striue in sinceritie to be aboue them all, and that his tongue should be euer the trew Messenger of his heart and this sort of Eloquence may you euer assuredly looke for at my hands.[22]

James was as good as his word: that is what alarmed his auditory.

The second speech, delivered on Saturday, November 9, 1605, was four days after James I, the Lords Spiritual and Temporal, and the Commons in Parliament assembled were to have been blown up by a cache of gunpowder placed under the Parliament house. Word of the Powder Plot, or Guy

Fawkes Plot—a conspiracy organized by a small group of well-born but madly fanatic Roman Catholic laymen who hoped the act would unleash a rebellion strong enough to return England to the fold—was leaked by one of the conspirators before it could be executed. The attempt had a profound effect upon James. It was heightened by a fear of death which for the king had begun in the womb. When his father Darnley murdered Riccio in the presence of Mary Queen of Scots, Darnley's companion the Earl of Gowrie had held a sword to the belly of the Queen, six months pregnant with James. Less than a year later Darnley was strangled, possibly by the Earl of Bothwell with Mary's connivance, and his quarters blown up by gunpowder—a fact that James learned very early. As a young king James lost his first regent (his uncle the Earl of Moray) to assassins in 1570 and his second regent (his grandfather the Earl of Lennox) in an affray in 1571—James saw the mortally wounded man carried into his house. His fourth regent (the Earl of Morton) James himself sent to the ax in 1581 for complicity in Darnley's murder. James, aged sixteen, was for ten months held prisoner by a group of noblemen, Presbyterian ultras, after being kidnapped as a political pawn—by the same Earl of Gowrie. The lad had reason to fear for his life, and his rescue by the conservative noble faction threatened civil war. Eighteen years later, in 1600, another Earl of Gowrie, son of the first, along with his brother threatened James's life at Gowrie Castle; in the confusion that followed, James made sure that the two younger Gowries were slain by his retainers. James's fear of assassination was obsessive but in the circumstances it was not neurotic. The king always wore in public a quilted doublet, perhaps with a mail-coat underneath, to ward off an assassin's blade.

Addressing his Lords and Commons, after the Gunpowder Plot had been thwarted, James expressed the deep satisfaction that, had he been launched heavenward on the Fifth of November in company with the Parliament, at least he would not have died with ignominy in a bar or a brothel. This illustrates Tillieres's point about the king's vulgarity in stooping to conquer.[23] Although this announcement fell far short of the conventional paean of thanksgiving, it was heartfelt. The sentiment was also consonant with James's careful exposition, in this same speech, of the respective roles and responsibilities of king and Parliament in what James graciously called "this Honourable and high Court of Parliament":

> which is nothing else but the Kings great Councell, which the King doeth assemble either vpon occasion of interpreting, or abrogating old Lawes, or making of new, according as ill maners shall deserue, or for the publike punishment of notorious euill doers, or the praise and reward of the vertuous and well deseruers.[24]

There was nothing here that was not agreeable to the traditional understanding of mixed monarchy—the interactive, interacting, balanced cooperation of king and estates to avoid the polar extremes of absolute monarchy and democracy. James spoke of what Sir John Fortescue had described, and it was the antithesis of absolutism in theory and in practice in the seventeenth century.[25]

The third speech, March 31, 1607, was not delivered at the opening of Parliament. It was delivered more than half way through a stormy session which served up the most serious political defeat that any monarch had yet suffered at the hands of the estates since Henry Tudor captured the crown at Bosworth Field in 1485, or would suffer again until James was fought to a standstill over the Spanish Match by the Parliament of 1621. In 1607, James was in part the author of his own misfortune. The most reasonable and balanced of any of the king's speeches to Parliament, and the one that sounded his highest praise of England's institutions of governance and law while fulfilling his promise to speak his heart and the truth, this address was marred by an ineptly tendentious opening, full of cant and hyperbole. James preached all the oratorical virtues he himself did not practice. From "fewest wordes with most matter doeth become best," to "*Rex est lex loquens*, . . . That the Kings will and intention being the speaking Law, ought to bee *Luce clarius*," to "I am euer for the Medium in euery thing," the phrases rang false.[26] He gave the distinct impression that *Rex est lex Loquens* is best rendered as "The King is loquacious law," and that so much talk provided more smoke than clear light.

"The errour was my mistaking," James said at one point; "I knew mine owne ende, but not others feares." That statement was all too painfully true. It can stand as the epitaph of this disquisition. What a pity: for after the first ten minutes the speech was a statesmanlike and brilliantly composed analysis of what would be gained by both England and Scotland by the organic union of the two kingdoms. The king's transparent sincerity in wishing only the welfare of both his peoples gave passion and persuasiveness to an astute rebuttal of the arguments against union. James dealt with the Scots' reservations, conceding that "there are many *Piggots* amongst them," an allusion to the English MP, Sir Christopher Pigott, a Buckinghamshire patriot who a month before had launched a vitriolic attack against all things Scottish and the Scots as beggars, rebels, and traitors (in ascending order of depravity?). James showed himself able to compare intelligently his two kingdoms' institutions, and his reiterated preference for the common law could only be pleasing, and his intention that the union would extend it to Scotland flattering, to his auditory. His argument that the union would solve both the continuing threat posed by the Auld Connection, the Franco-Scottish alliance which was a sword at England's back, and the disorderliness of the Anglo-Scottish border was incontestable. Finally, his careful and temperate discussion of the Antenati, those Scots born before his accession as James I, and whether they would be accorded the same rights as native subjects in England was conciliatory and entirely correct in its prediction that in time this would cease to be a problem, if it really was one at all. Alas, more than words and assurances were needed to counter the issue, because the single greatest fear of the English governing classes was a horde of ravenous Scots immigrants. That chimera was the rock upon which the proposal for union was wrecked.

James and his experienced and sagacious chief minister, the Earl of Salisbury, then committed an inexplicable political mistake. Immediately following the king's speech, they adjourned Parliament for a three weeks' Easter recess, which prevented the speech from gaining momentum. It would have been better received had the speech been given upon the reassembly of the Parliament. In the event, Parliament refused the union, and James, to his everlasting regret, had to abandon it.

The last of James's four parliamentary speeches in *The Political Works* was given on March 21, 1610. Considering the gravity of the speech's context, much of it seems irrelevant to the great concerns of the session, though that was less James's fault than the Commons'. The session had opened six weeks earlier with a forthright demand pressed by Salisbury that Parliament supply the King's fiscal needs by an extraordinary and comprehensive grant of taxes. This would retire the debt, provide for defense, and create an emergency reserve. Coupled with this demand was a request for an annual supply sufficient to meet about a third of the king's income and afford a sizable surplus over his existing expenditure (which had been prodigally high). The demand hinted at concessions, and the Parliament took up the challenge. While this meant routinely redress of grievances, it also had the larger potential of an agreement by the King to give up certain sources of ordinary revenue inhering in the crown in return for a settled annual supply. Much of that ordinary revenue, including wardship of underage heirs, other feudal dues and incidents, and forced supply of the royal household with goods and services, were notable grievances because of their increasing exploitation by a financially embarrassed crown. Thus began the negotiation between King and Parliament for what Salisbury termed a "Great Contract," a financial settlement that would certainly have made the crown less dependent on Parliament for revenue and therefore more negligent of grievances. No sooner proposed, the business was blindsided by one of those fugitive issues that a restless leadership in the Commons found useful to keep the MPs in line. The Commons caught the scent of an academic scandal. The king had, by his recurrent homiletics on the nature of kingship and statecraft, sensitized the House to just such a challenge as that presented by Dr. John Cowell, a civil lawyer at Cambridge, whose *The Interpreter*, published by the university press in 1607, was a useful and comprehensive dictionary of law.[27] James's imperious rhetoric on the divine origins and the quasi-divine character of monarchy, the rights of kingship, and the exaltation of the kingly person, the subordination of all other persons and all institutions to him, and the prerogatives that undergirded his power was balanced by repeated enunciation of the king's obligation to his subjects and responsibility to God. Dr. Cowell, however, had failed to be so measured and conciliatory in preparing his dictionary's entries for *Prerogative*, *Parliament*, *King*, and *Subsidy*. The clear thrust of *The Interpreter*'s treatment of these topics was that the king's power was so absolute that the king alone—without the estates—could make law. The Commons gave chase. James and Salisbury snared the quarry first: the book was suppressed and ordered burned by the public executioner. Salisbury informed Parliament, on March 8, that

> His Majesty said further that for his kingdom he was beholden to no elective power . . . [and] that, though he did derive his title from the loins of his ancestors, yet the law did set the crown upon his head, and he is a king by the common law of the land. . . . But withal he did acknowledge that he had no power to make laws of himself, or to exact any subsidies [revenue grants] *de jure* without the consent of his three Estates.[28]

James's speech a fortnight later was to bear this point home and make a pretty acknowledgment of his care to redress grievances while warning the estates that the hue and cry after grievances would have to stop short of sedition and self-interested promotion. Though he argued the value of other legal systems, including the civil law, James was at pains to exalt the common law, albeit admitting that in important respects it would bear reforming. He sought to end the unseemly free-for-all of jurisdiction expansion by the courts for fees and forum shopping by litigants, recently made hotter by the Common Pleas' use of the writ of prohibition directed at ecclesiastical courts and courts of equity—including Chancery—to enhance its own jurisdiction. The king was frank in charging the Commons to provide supply, and equally candid in disclaiming any greediness for more than the nation could reasonably provide or more than he needed, "For that were to giue me a purse with a knife."[29] He advanced an able defense of his moderation in dealing with Roman Catholics (that required some courage, for memories of the Gunpowder Plot were still fresh) by pointing out that his own new treatise, "An Apologie for the Oath of Allegiance" (1607) had challenged not only English Catholics but Rome itself. And he ended by appealing to any subject who loved the chase with a call for preservation of game and woodlands.

In this address to the Parliament, what must stick above all else, were the king's two unequivocal statements:

> For the King with his Parliament here are absolute, (as I vnderstand) in making or forming of any sort of Lawes.
>
> I shall euer be willing to make the reason appeare of all my doings, and rule my actions according to my lawes.[30]

These were not despotic utterances. They would satisfy Bracton, and we suppose Coke.

James's charge to the judges of assize, on June 20, 1616, can be grouped with the parliamentary speeches. It was delivered on the post-term day of Trinity, the last day of the legal year, just before the Long Vacation when the twelve judges of the common law courts prepared to go on their summer assize circuits. As was customary that day, the judges attended the Privy Council in the Court of Star Chamber to assist on points of law raised by pleas in mitigation of sentence. This work was done in camera after a copious dinner about one in the afternoon The charged ended the morning sitting which had been devoted to motions in Star Chamber.

Though the charge was usually pronounced by the Lord Chancellor, this time the king himself gave charge. In opening it, James purposely chose as his text that most monarchical of King David's songs, Psalm 72, "Give thy judgments to the King, O God, And thy righteousness to the King's son." He would play judge for the day, to remind those lions under his throne that the frame of jurisprudence was the law of the king, which the judges were to interpret just as the king settled the interpretation of God's law. The charge's thrust was appropriate to a jurisprudent who was not, and made no claim to be, a *jurisperitus*, one learned in the law: settling the jurisdictions of the courts and repressing the common law courts' prohibitions. Chief Justice Sir Edward Coke, before he was booted upstairs from the Common Pleas to the King's Bench in 1613, had been the most frequent offender, and remained so.

What James had to say about the law here, how it should be reverenced, how it might be reformed, how it must be limited, was a well-argued essay in jurisprudential analysis that could not be excepted against, not even by James's most captious critics. It comports well even with our understanding of the rule of law. Most of what James had to say specifically about the law, he said to Coke. The king warned darkly that the "Starre-Chamber Court hath bene likewise shaken of late, and the last yeere it had receiued a sore blow, if it had not bene assisted and caried by a few voices." This could be laid entirely at Coke's door.[31] Two years before, Coke and two other Common Law judges sitting in Star Chamber, carrying a Privy Councillor with them, had almost managed to limit the court's jurisdiction in a critical way with demeaning results.[32] In fact, this speech was clearly monitory to Coke. In his wonted arrogance Coke chose to ignore the warning. Five months later, after a final act of obstinate, even contemptuous, defiance, he was removed from the bench.[33]

Was Tillieres right? Read carefully, the speeches lead to a guarded "no." Whatever categorical language James used there in exalting the kingly authority *jure divino* was balanced in good part by equally clear statements of the King's responsibility to God and hence to man, his subjects in particular. There was nothing despotic about this. And if one seeks the tone of tyranny—which was really Tillieres's point—then he can find it only by much contextual wrenching. James might well have better chosen to soften his assertiveness. But he really was a plain-spoken man, sincere in delivering his heart and his mind. If that was less than politic, it did not make him a despot. The problem of course with the spoken word is that it registers differently on different ears, in minds differently disposed. Parliamentary speeches raise particular perils, and James tended to lead with his best line of defense. In the whole debate, when analyzed by reading it retrospectively, James appeared less extreme, his arguments better balanced and properly qualified. Yet, in dealing with Parliament he could have heeded his own adolescent advice in a poem he wrote about 1582:

> Since thought is free, think what thou will,
> O troubled heart, to ease thy pain.
> Thought, unrevealed, can do no ill;
> But words passed out come not again.
> Be careful aye for to invent
> The way to get thy own intent.[34]

Perhaps at sixteen James was too cynical. With age and regal success he had become more confident of himself, less fearful and more open. A mute king must appear to be so by malice, and he cannot hope to rule voiceless. Still, James talked too much, too often.

There has been one persistent Whiggish slander of James I: that he was a Scot and so did not understand English institutions, least of all Parliament. Some of the mud in this statement may stick but the slander is false. James was not a skilled parliamentary manager, but that was never a king's job. He has been blamed for not having chosen better parliamentary managers (an accusation now undergoing some revision in the light of a new appreciation of the obduracy, immunity, and autonomy of Parliament during the later years of Elizabeth's reign). Insomuch as he sought to perform a leader's role in the estates, he increased the risk of the fate that stalked him in England, talking too much and too often. He had no doubts about the sufficiency of his knowledge of English government and governance. In the speeches he refers once to his "experience" and twice to his "apprenticeship" of English governance, emphasizing that he had served two successive apprenticeships, long seven-year stints. He was a quick study—and, as he reminded the auditory in the Star Chamber, he was an old king when he came to England's throne. If he erred at all in England in dealing with the estates, it was in giving his first Parliament's members too much time and continuity to become experienced in their own right and in pursuit of their own agenda. He did not repeat that mistake: 1614 saw one Parliament of a few weeks' duration, followed by seven years without another. Even 1621, harsh though it was, saw no concessions from the King to the Parliament in defeasance of his singular prerogative to conduct foreign affairs. His catastrophic failure in 1624 was the work of his immature son and his ambitious favorite, inordinately driven by intemperance, hubris, and gratification with a vague and ephemeral popularity. It was small comfort to James that 1624 saw the king more popular with his Parliament than ever before; that popularity came at the cost of his lifelong passion for peace as England, with an unfortunate and ill-advised enthusiasm, went to war against Spain. If James demonstrated any frailty in his handling of the Parliament at Westminster it was in believing that he could persuade by authority and reason what was becoming an increasingly sophisticated and articulate, politically coherent, legislative establishment, a body that after 1603 would not accept what earlier members had been prepared to put up with in a previous century, in an age of schism and rebellion. Though James did not get everything he wished from his parliaments—most notably the union of the two kingdoms—and never enough supply (his extravagance assured that), James was far from the parliamentary failure that his son proved to be and which cost him his head. James was pragmatic, Charles merely duplicitous.

Indeed, James VI and I was an experienced king as far as estates, their cultivation and uses, were concerned. Despite the considerable differences between the Parliament of England and that of Scotland, the role of each within a "free monarchy" was much the same: supply, legislation, and maintenance of a national consensus in support of good order at home and defense against foreign threats. Mixed monarchy was the objective on both sides of the river Tweed. The estates offered the "free monarch" the arena within which his domestic enemies could be domesticated. Probably no crowned head of his age knew better than James VI the risks of noble factionalism. Few were more successful in curbing those risks by astute political cultivation, including coercion, conciliation, prison, patronage, and parliamentary action. In the 1590's, as an adult king, increasingly aggressive and confident in his role, James fashioned the Scots Parliament into a bulwark of the monarchy. This meant advancing the interests and security of the lairds, the Scots gentry, in order to counterweigh the great lords. It was also advanced by reinstituting an episcopate as a parliamentary class capable of both bridling the earls and hobbling (though never quite gagging) the radical clergy, their noble adherents, and the town laity. For if James VI understood the dangers of aristocratic factions, he saw the real enemy as theocracy, or at least a clerocracy, with dominance by the clerical First Estate much more than by the noble Second Estate.

Three of the pieces in the *Political Works*, "An Apologie for the Oath of Allegiance," "A Premonition to all Christian Monarches, Free Princes and States," and "A Defence of the Right of Kings, against Cardinali Perron," were launched against the greatest clerocracy and most thoroughgoing theocracy of all, the Bishop of Rome and his claim to a triple-crowned supremacy over secular governments and polities. These essays had a universal appeal, among Roman Catholic kings and princes as well as Protestant ones. Political theory had developed a line of argument during the sixteenth century—the route stretched from Niccolo Machiavelli to Jean Bodin to Giovanni Botero—that ultimately posited that the state was an ethical entity. The state, even if a collectivity of souls, is not a conscientious and ethical being. To attempt the equation would raise a true monster more terrible that Thomas Hobbes's Leviathan, in a word Jean-Jacques Rousseau's "general will" that has underlain totalitarianism for over two centuries. Therefore, against a papacy that claimed its authority was *jure divino* vested in the Pope, the highest authority to raise a counterclaim was a truly "free monarchy" headed by a servant responsible to God, not to God's vicar on Earth. James did not invent divine-right monarchy, but he refined it, armed it with a compelling rhetoric, and sent it off to battle the red-hats and triple crown itself.

McIlwain, in his introduction to the *Political Works*, comprehended the foundations of James's enmity toward Roman Catholic doctrine and ecclesiology:

> James's real attitude toward Catholicism springs from the same root as his views on Puritanism. In both cases his hostility is more political than religious. . . . what made him hate equally a Scottish synod and Roman pontiff was their common denial of his royal power as supreme governor in matters and causes ecclesiastical, and nothing else.[35]

"The Trew Law of Free Monarchies," written in 1598 and first published in 1603, and "Basilikon Doron," published 1599, were directed against the greater clerocracy closer to home and more dangerous to a free monarch. The Scots Kirk in the hands of the Presbyterian ultras went far toward proving that "new presbyter" was less "old priest" than old pope "writ large." "The Trew Law" was in fact a Te Deum sung over the near-prostrate form of the ultras who, since Melville had called the king "God's sillie vassall" in 1596, had increasingly lost control over the Kirk to the king. Save for the most extreme Presbyterians among the nobility, who were effectively excluded from positions of power around the king and his government, James had turned the nobility onto a parliamentary path that divided them and their interests from those of the ultras. James managed to reduce the influence of the urban laity in their support of the ultras, even removing his capital from Edinburgh to Leith for a season until the city fathers of the former made a full, humiliating, and financially costly submission to the King for his return there. He reinstituted a parliamentary episcopacy. He secured increasing control over the agenda and the timing of the Kirk's General Assembly. And he managed to swamp the ultra influence by directly subsidizing and encouraging attendance at the Assembly by northern delegates, who generally favored royal powers. By the time he published "The Trew Law" upon his accession to the English throne, God's vassal had become a free monarch and equally the free governor of the Scots Kirk, and there were no longer Melville's "two Kings and two Kingdoms" in Scotland.[36]

"Basilikon Doron" has been characterized correctly as traditional in its approach to Scottish secular politics, albeit unconventional in its assertive and *jure divino* stance against the Kirk.[37] James's sound and sage advice given to young Prince Henry in matters of state, family, mores, and society certainly reflected conventional theory. The work was a thorough, unexceptionable example of mixed-monarchy analysis. Here, more than in the speeches or in "The Trew Law," the King's obligations weigh heavier than his powers: of the whole, the Second Book, "Of a Kings Dvetie in His Office," is both the longest and the most earnest. James is here the schoolmaster, the Scots dominie, and his pupil is his son.

James had not known a father. If he had marked and inwardly digested a *testament politique* he found it in the hard lessons of his perilous childhood and challenging youth. But he had had a schoolmaster: George Buchanan (1506–1582), who tutored the young king throughout the 1570's in Classical letters, modern languages, philosophy, religion, statecraft, and political theory. An elegant Latinist, accounted among the foremost Classical humanists who succeeded Erasmus, More, Colet, and d'Etaples, Buchanan was strict, demanding, laconic, and unsmiling. He frightened the boy-king with his displeasure and hardly reassured him with the small and infrequent tokens of satisfaction that greeted the lad's best work. A layman, but a staunch and early convert to Calvinism, Buchanan had served as moderator of the General Assembly of the Kirk, and was an ultra. In his last years he finished a Latin treatise that was intended as much for his student as for the learned world and his countrymen to whom it was addressed. Buchanan's *De Jure Regni apud Scotos* (1579) treated royal law, but it was founded on premises diametrically opposed to those that underlay James's works. For Buchanan, the source of political power is the people; the king is bound by the terms on which he receives the supreme power from the people; and a tyrannical king can lawfully be resisted, and even destroyed. Clearly this was an argument to frighten the uneasy head that wore the crown, and not surprisingly the Scots Parliament, with James's blessing, condemned the book in 1584. Buchanan's ghost acquired a more alarming aspect after that notable exercise of his doctrine of tyrannicide which took place outside the Banqueting House at Whitehall on January 30, 1649, when the public executioner cut off the head of "Charles Stuart, tyrant." In 1683, Oxford University—always more royalist than the King and traditionally the home of lost causes—burned its copy of the work. That did not stop the English, five years later, from disposing of (without bloodshed) another Stuart king.

James VI and I might almost seem to have devoted almost his whole scholarly life to refuting Buchanan and counteracting Buchanan's poisonous doctrine. That appearance is deceiving. The one prevailing, consistent note in all of James's political works is the centrality of the king's divinely ordained and divinely derived obligation truly to imitate God in justice and righteousness. The just and righteous king was the kind of king Buchanan taught James to be. James never repudiated this branch of Buchanan's teaching. However imperfectly and despite his notable human frailties and regal failures, he had tried to uphold that model of kingship. If he failed, this was the ideal that he failed at. Moreover, James always had before his eyes not only the divine displeasure and condign judgment that God would at the end of time visit upon him for his regal demerits, but also the present, temporal, fatal threat of the scorpion tail of Buchanan's doctrine. Charles McIlwain made few mistakes in his learned introduction to James's works, but he made a horrendous one in trying to explain the word "burreaux" in the "Basilikon Doron."[38] After reminding Prince Henry that "a good King (after a happie and famous reigne) dieth in peace, lamented by his subjects, and admired by his neighbours," James drew a stark contrast:

> Where by the contrarie, a Tyrannes miserable and infamous life, armeth in end his owne Subiects to become his burreaux: and although that rebellion be euer vnlawfull on their part, yet is the world so wearied of him, that his fall is little meaned by the rest of his Subjects, and but smiled at by his neighbors.[39]

"Burreaux" is the plural of the French word *bourreau*, the public executioner. James, always the pragmatist, wholly distanced himself from his old master's approval of tyrannicide. But he was his old master's apt pupil in teaching his own pupil and beloved heir apparent that life does not always imitate theory, even the best of it, and that the crown of thorns that a tyrant wears in the next world might well be put on his bodyless head in this one. We suppose Prince Henry's younger brother, Charles, read "Basilikon Doron." If he did, he ought to have heeded it better.

CHAPTER SEVEN

Francis Bacon

At the outset of his career, in the first sentence of his first substantial literary endeavor, Francis Bacon (1561–1626) wrote:

> I hold euery man a debtor to his profession, from the which, as men of course doe seeke to receiue countenance & profit, so ought they of duty to endeauour themselues by way of amends to bee a helpe and ornament thereunto; this is performed in some degree, by the honest and liberall practice of a profession, when men shall carry a respect not to descend into any course that is corrupt, and vnworthy thereof, and preserue themselues free from the abuses wherewith the same profession is noted to bee infected; but much more is this performed, if a man bee able to visite and strengthen the roots and foundation of the science it selfe; thereby not onely gracing it in reputation and dignity, but also amplifying it in perfection and substance.[1]

Very nearly the last words he wrote—appropriately, in his will, on December 19, 1625—four months before his death from pneumonia, were "I bequeath my soul to God above. My body to be buried obscurely. My name to the next ages, and to foreign nations."[2] There is a vaulting irony in the juxtaposition of these two quotations. Bacon's career as legist and judge ended in disgrace, when in 1621 he was convicted upon impeachment for accepting bribes as Lord Chancellor in cases in equity in Chancery. He had freely confessed the facts, attempting only to avoid their moral implications. In the latter he did not succeed, and every shift and excuse attempted by his admirers then and since have not exonerated him. Indeed, the most recent scholarship has drawn the noose tighter.[3] As far as his will was concerned, the testamentary directions for the disposal of his soul and body were simple enough: they were followed to the letter, his mortal remains interred near those of his mother in an obscure parish church in Hertfordshire, a monumental statue erected only later in the chancel by his old servant, friend, and protégé, Sir Thomas Meautys. As to his soul, what success he made of that disposition waits to be revealed at the last trump. More complex, both in intention and in consequence, were the directions for disposing of his reputation. Certainly the next ages even unto our own have not forgotten him, and denizens of foreign nations then and since have esteemed him. But the verdancy of his name has depended upon his published contributions to philosophy, particularly natural philosophy (the contemporary term for the new science of the sixteenth and seventeenth centuries), not on his professional scholarship as a lawyer.

Bacon's scholarly undertakings generally remained unachieved, not least his ambitious and varied contributions to philosophy, especially natural philosophy. His *Advancement of Learning* (1605), even after enlargement and translation into Latin as *De Augmentis Scientarum* (1623), remained undone at his death. *De Augmentis* was to be the first part of his Great Instauration, or Great Renewal, a radically comprehensive rethinking of the entire realm of philosophy directed at understanding and commanding nature to ends as much pragmatic and material as pure and ideal. The second part of the Great Instauration, published in 1620 and Bacon's single most significant philosophical work, was *Novum Organum*. The title constituted a little conceit and a large arrogation in its allusion to Aristotle's *Organon*, or instrument of logical method. It also did not quite deliver all the novelty the title promised. Bacon managed better the demolition of the old, Aristotelian, system of logic than the erection of a new instrument (*novum organum*) suitable for scientific investigation. Even the vehicle for his novel worldview, the charming utopian fable *New Atlantis*, was incomplete when published three decades after his death.

His literary works achieved a greater degree of finality. Very little if any aspect of the human condition, from "Truth" (Essay I) to "Of Vicissitude of Things" (Essay LVIII) were wanting in the fifty-eight elegant *Essayes or Counsels Civil and Moral* (in its first form published in 1597, final form 1625). This remains his most widely read, affectionately regarded, even revered work. The extended essay, *The Historie of the Raigne of King Henry the Seventh* (published in 1622 and dedicated to the future Charles I), was a finished work of remarkable accuracy and interpretative rigor that remains the cornerstone of analytical historiography of the first Tudor monarch. Similar attempts for Henry VIII and Elizabeth, and an incursion into contemporary history, *The History of Great Britain*, remain only as tantalizing introductory scraps. The *Apophthegms*, anecdotal gleanings that are usually amusing, sometimes cutting, and always informative to a student who knows the context of the tales and those who figure in them, rightly begs the question of completeness; one only wishes there were many more of them. Yet, such didactic gems were too easily ignored or forgotten, even by the author himself, *viz.*

> Sir Thomas More [Lord Chancellor] had sent him by a suitor in chancery, two silver flagons. When they were presented by the gentleman's servant, he [More] said to one of his men, Have him to the cellar, and let him have of my best wine: and turning to the servant, Tell thy master, if he like it, let him not spare it.[4]

Bacon's legal writings were less a matter of unachievement than of underachievement. From a purely professional perspective, the most considerable and important of his legal pieces is the Reading on the Statute of Uses (1536) that he delivered at Gray's Inn in the Lent vacation, 1600. Such a reading was a highly conventional exercise, a series of lectures usually on a statute delivered at an Inn of Court either in the Lent vacation or the Summer vacation by a senior barrister for the instruction of students in statutory interpretation. It signified the barrister's preparation for call as a bencher on the governing body of the Inn (in Gray's Inn, Pension). An exceptionally learned bencher might be moved to give a second reading, as was the case with Bacon's reading on the Statute of Uses. Students and junior barristers were to moot relevant cases after a lecture. The reading was the major formal instructional instrument (if mooting is excluded as a separate form, then the only one) for training barristers.

Enough readings from the period exist, often as students' notes, a number of which were printed posthumously in the later seventeenth century, to give us considerable insight into the way that lawyers of Bacon's generation dealt with statutory enactments and interpreted them using the intellectual process that was already called legal reasoning. Alas, the bulk of the readings testify to jurists who were more artisan than artist, solid advocates eschewing legal principles as far as possible and sticking to the narrowest *explication de texte.* Giving a narrow clarification of obtuse laws that baffled students and slightly inattentive junior barristers pressed the reader to avoid much architectonic grandeur.

Bacon's reading exists as a fragment, six of probably fifteen lectures, published posthumously in 1642. It was the product of a mature lawyer of unparalleled intellectual gifts, and it dealt with one of the half-dozen most important statutes touching common law ever enacted by Parliament. The quality of Bacon's reading is an exception to the norm, as Sir William Holdsworth observed:

> The only reading which is really illuminating is Bacon's unfinished reading on the statute of Uses. His wide intellectual outlook and gift of style, united to his complete mastery of the technical rules of the common law, gave him the power to state and explain and criticize its rules in a manner comprehensible to a student and illuminating to a lawyer. We have already seen how great a light it sheds, not only on the statute, but also on the history of Uses. . . . This one reading gives him a place beside those few great teachers who have appeared at infrequent intervals in the history of English law—beside men like Blackstone and Maitland.[5]

Hyperbole overcomes Holdsworth only in the first and last sentences. A good many other illuminating readings are extant in manuscript (more than Holdsworth chose to be aware of), and even by the wildest reckoning Bacon the preceptor does not rank with the author of the *Commentaries on the Laws of England* and one of the authors of *The History of English Law*.

The best of Bacon's juristic writings is *The Elements of the Common Lawes of England*. Or at least the first and most considerable part of it, *A Collection of Some Principall Rvles and Maximes of the Common Lawes of England, with Their Latitude and Extent*—hereafter, *Maximes*—about the authorship of which there is no question. The second part, *The Use of the Law, Provided for Preservation of Our Persons, Goods, and Good Names, According to the Practise of the Lawes and Customes of this Land*, though ascribed to Bacon and bound up with the *Maximes* since the first edition in 1630, is probably not Bacon's work.[6] In any case, the dead Bacon was poorly served by the assigns of John Moore, who rolled the two tracts off their press in 1630 under the title *The Elements of the Common Lawes of England*. The text is full of little errors that are not always minor, errors, even to the description of the author on the title page of the *Maximes*, who had never been "Sollicitor general to the late renowned Queene Elizabeth" though a decade later was solicitor-general to James I. No matter. The reputation as a juristic writer of Sir Francis Bacon, Baron Verulam, Viscount St. Albans, quondam Queen's Counsel, King's Counsel sworn, Solicitor General, Clerk of the Council in Star Chamber, Attorney General, Lord Keeper of the Great Seal, and finally Lord Chancellor, depends upon the twenty-five *Maximes* set down with learned commentary over 104 pages, preceded by a dedicatory epistle to Elizabeth I full of exhortation to undertake law reform and an elegant preface making clear the possibilities and the perils of finding general principles in order to determine what the law is. On the title page, if Bacon himself did not indicate the audience intended, the publisher did: "Explicated for the more facile

Introduction of such as are studiously addicted to that noble Profession." There is nothing particularly facile about the explication, and as the reader soon realizes the *Maximes* demands not much less than an addiction to law and legal scholarship to work its magic.

There is magic. Because of Bacon's stylistic vigor and the rigorousness of his thinking, the breadth and the depth of each maxim or rule is made very clear very quickly. His almost excruciating meticulousness in banishing the inherent ambiguity of the maxims seems almost legerdemain. It is, however, neither chicanery nor sophistry that Bacon works here, the intellectually dishonest slights and leaps that a crooked advocate advances with orotundity and theatrics in search of forensic success. Bacon had an enviable forensic reputation, but one honestly earned. His appearance at bar always attracted a large and rapt auditory. Rapt, because he always made sense and seldom failed to carry the audience (if sometimes not the bench) to a higher appreciation of the issue at trial. His submissions were usually masterpieces of persuasive clarity. He had the capacity to carry a legal argument with almost contrapuntal harmony of elements that would, if attempted by a less eloquent advocate, have been a cacophony of unrelated and disparate notes. One sees in the *Maximes* the skill that Bacon exercised in all those causes célèbres, from the prosecution of his old mentor the Earl of Essex to the *Case of Richard Brereton* that impelled James I personally to sit in Star Chamber and instruct the judges concerning the regal prerogative to determine the boundaries of their respective jurisdictions.[7] It is the *Maximes*, read in conjunction with the records and reports of cases, along with Bacon's own papers in modern editions, that has enabled recent scholarship to retrieve Bacon's juristic reputation from damnation by the faint praise voiced by nineteenth-century legal commentators—that he was a jurist of marginal writings, mere forensic pyrotechnics, dilettante dabbling. Bacon has finally achieved the stature of being taken seriously as a legal theorist.[8] It is surprising that it has taken so long. Bacon's jurisprudential powers, that is, his ability as a philosopher of law, ought not be surprising. After all, for one who boldly conceived and argued convincingly for a whole new way of seeing nature and humankind's place in it, who fashioned the appropriate logical tool—inductive reasoning—to master knowledge, a systematic jurisprudence was feasible and, in his scheme of things, essential.

To capture the jurisprudential Bacon, the legal philosopher at full pitch, we are less dependent on the twenty-five *Maximes* than we are upon a cognate form of the genre of pithy phrase so prominent in Bacon's writings. To the twenty-five rules or maxims in *The Elements of the Common Lawes of*

England must be added a further ninety-seven aphorisms that found a place in the 1623 *De Augmentis Scientarum*, Book VII, Chapter III. While the use of the terms *maxim* and *aphorism* suggests a distinction, the difference between the two is subtle. A maxim (from the Latin *maxima*, greatest) is a general truth drawn from science or experience. It governs or controls—and, as indicated by the Latin term for a legal maxim, *regula* or rule, carries with it an implicit sanction for its violation. An aphorism, no less pithy, has the less forceful quality of definition, appropriate to its Greek origin (*aphorismo*, definition). It serves to clarify a concept rather than mandating it. For most purposes—and ours hereafter—the distinction can be ignored and maxims and aphorisms dealt with as one, but the distinction obtains in comparing the twenty-five maxims and the ninety-seven aphorisms. The ninety-seven aphorisms Bacon saw as "laws of laws," *legum leges*, defining those terms, concepts, and principles of law requisite to determining what good or ill any law might do. In short, the ninety-seven are propositions which through argumentation can lead to a general jurisprudence. Bacon included this aphoristic review of jurisprudence in *De Augmentis* in furtherance of his intention in that part of the Great Instauration to provide a survey or inventory of what was known preparatory to the thoroughgoing reinterpretation of existing knowledge and the fearless search for the new that was his goal. The aphorisms have the smell of clichés, of the most conventional of conventional wisdom. They also tend to be dullingly dialectical: *altera*, *vel*, and *sed* are the most common Latin conjunctions in the aphorisms; on the one hand, on the other hand. But the aphorisms are strung together with a forward dynamic that provides them with a coherence otherwise lacking in a merely random collection of pithy sayings. In seeking the source of law to be applied in a case in the absence of promulgated law or law that is unclear, Bacon directs a comparison to similar cases (aphorisms 11–12), then to interpretation using tools of rhetorical inductive logic (13–20), precedents (21–31), equitable principles (32–46), and retrospective legislation (47, 51). The result is remarkably comprehensive and singularly plausible, even to modern eyes.

Bacon said that he had three hundred aphorisms and maxims at hand. One winces in contemplation of a treatise of commentary and explication incorporating so many pithy Latin expressions. In this case, Bacon's wonted inability to complete an undertaking has spared posterity. Yet we might regret the loss when we reflect on what Bacon did manage with the genre, perhaps not so much with the greater jurisprudential undertaking in *De Augmentis*, where the pithy phrase served the function of dialectical proposition, as with the lesser, manageable, and quintessentially legal enterprise represented in the *Maximes*.

At the outset of determining what Bacon meant to do with the *Maximes* and what he accomplished, the genre of the pithy saying itself requires attention. The early modern epoch might almost be called the Age of Aphorism. One product of the classical revival in the Renaissance was that the weighty sayings of the ancients were discovered (even if not lost, given renewed emphasis). The Latin tongue lends itself to aphorism; its syntax is peculiarly felicitous for the pithy device. Classical pre-Christian Roman letters had a large role for aphorism. Similarly, Roman law, particularly Justinian's Digest, was a fertile source for legalomoral aphorisms, and later civilian and canonical commentators increased the number of them. The vernacular languages of post-Roman Europe might almost be gauged in their developing sophistication and literariness by the growth of aphorism in them over the course of the Middle Ages. This was clearly imitative of Latin, and it was a long time before the developed vernaculars evolved a large range of aphorism. Europeans long preferred their dalliance with aphoristicity in Latin! Indeed, that is a principal reason why Bacon made no attempt in the *Maximes* to render the maxims in English.

The vernaculars early developed an indigenous aphoristic form, the proverb. The proverb was less sonorous and less elegant, without the pretension to authority or the didactic import of the maxim-*cum*-aphorism. The proverb, born in folklore, expressed in the vernacular and preserved in oral tradition, did provide, for common discourse, conventional wisdom similar to that which the maxim-*cum*-aphorism provided the more exalted written word. Despite its humble origins, the proverb also benefited from the Renaissance, finding a place in literature, thereby democratizing letters to an extent previously unknown. But this tended to preserve the Latin aphorism long after it might otherwise have disappeared in professional and scholarly letters: there was something inherently vulgar and ignorant in using the vernacular to express high ideas in the vernacular. Or even to express low notions. Listen to this maxim: *Testis lupanaris sufficit ad factum in lupanari*.[9] It doesn't have quite the same ring to it in English: A whore is a sufficient witness of what happens in a brothel.

Just how widespread was the phenomenon of the maxim in sixteenth- and seventeenth-century English law is evident from the ubiquity of maxims in legal literature, printed and manuscript. This is different in kind from the earlier literature of the common law. Glanvill and Bracton certainly turned an aphoristic phrase on occasion. There is no greater one than

Bracton's *Rex non debet esse sub homine sed sub Deo et lege quia lex facit regem*, The king ought be under no man, but under God and the law, for the law makes the king.[10] Here we correctly detect the Roman influence on both of those great early treatise-writers. Still, the two most important forms of medieval legal literature, the practice books (such as the *Natura Brevium*) and the Year Books, reveal a small role for aphorism in the common law then. It is with the advent of the modern case reports, especially with the eleven volumes of *Reports* that Sir Edward Coke published, that the legal maxim begins to loom very large in the common law's literature. Coke's contribution is clear. In a current collection of maxims in English common law, of the 1102 maxims set down (many of them not ascribed), 547 are cited to Coke.[11] Relatively few of these can be pushed further back than Coke. Coke argued that the maxim provided the most certain authority and was sufficient proof in itself of what the law is. It is well not to take this at face value, because Coke was less than candid in his use of maxims. Sam Thorne has caught him out:

> As a rule of thumb it is well to remember that sentences beginning "For it is an ancient maxim of the common law," followed by one of Coke's spurious Latin maxims, which he could manufacture to fit any occasion and provide with an air of authentic authority, are apt to introduce a new departure. Sentences such as "And by these differences and reasons you will better understand your books," or "And so the doubts and diversities in the books well resolved," likewise indicate new law. If I may formulate a theorem of my own, I advance this—the longer the list of authorities reconciled, the greater the divergence from the cases cited.[12]

After more than five decades of grappling with Coke, Coke's *Reports,* and Coke's maxims, the author is convinced that Professor Thorne let him off too lightly.

Other lawyers did not so abuse maxims. Maxims as used by other advocates and judges seldom made a claim to authority or to proof. Rather, they were used illustratively and for rhetorical effect. Sir Thomas Egerton, Lord Ellesmere, Bacon's immediate predecessor as Lord Chancellor, was at great pains over his twenty-one years presiding in Chancery and Star Chamber to preserve and neatly arrange maxims with which to dress his opinions. These he set down on separate sheets of paper and in a distinctly different, Italic, hand.[13] Appropriately sorted by subject matter and (where known) the source cited, they range over legal literature, civilian, canonical, and common law, classical letters, and philosophical writings. From Ellesmere's notes of Star Chamber cases it is clear that few of them were expected to bear authoritative weight. The most common one that can be so characterized is without citation (and so far undiscoverable), used time and again by Ellesmere in Star Chamber when the high and the mighty were called to judgment: *Dignitas delinquentis auget crimen (culpam)*, The dignity of the delinquent increases the crime (guilt). So obvious is the notion, there can be no deceit here.

Neither will Coke's deceit be found in Bacon. For Bacon's maxims are real enough, and even insofar as some of them are his own confection, none of them are intended to give a false authority to his argument. Bacon's assertion in *De Augmentis* that maxims were laws of laws should not be understood to give them the effect of some kind of fundamental law, with all of the immutableness and preeminence that fundamental nature warrants. The mistake is easy enough to make, for the maxims appear to be "the law." That is, each maxim exudes a positivist categoricalness, a legislative imperative, exacting absolute literal and verbatim implementation. Certainly rhetoric plays a role in this, but the larger source of the maxim's apparent positivism is simply that, by being the starting point, it dominates the subsequent discussion and commentary. The singular role played by the maxims collectively, as the taxonomic structure of the whole undertaking, also comes into play. Once the reader gets into the commentary, however, the maxim seems less categorical, more subject to exceptions, a heuristic device more than an injunction. The first maxim dispels all misapprehension of diktat or ukase, fundamental and immutable prescription. Granted, the maxim itself is unambiguous, ringing in its declarativeness, and unequivocal in its assertion: *In jure non remota causa, sed proxima spectatur*, In law not the remote cause but the nearest cause is to be considered. However, the entire commentary on it is as painstaking in demonstrating where the "rule faileth" directly or constructively (where remoteness and proximity cannot be distinguished) as where it applies.[14]

Such ambivalence, if not downright contradiction, was, of course, inherent in the nature of the common law process. The substantive common law developed by growing in the interstices of procedure, dependent upon the forms of action as the instruments for the evolution of remedies that, unlike Athena, did not spring full-grown out of the head of God (or the Anglo-Norman kings). Such ambivalence in the law would, almost two centuries later, undergird Mr. Justice Blackstone's most famous dissent, wherein he insisted that the immediate tortious cause was actionable in trespass but that the remote tortious cause was actionable only in case.[15] This distinction disappeared with the erosion of the forms of action in the next century and the rise to dominance of negligence in tort. Yet the modern American lawyer might remark somewhat ruefully that the distinction of remoteness and proximity still lurks in deep pockets in tort law. Bacon is not yet irrelevant.

It is also clear that, as soon as one gets beyond the sonorous maxim, the stuff of the law is here. The cases are real. Bacon asserted that many of the cases are judged cases, "either within the books [Year Books] or of fresh report, and most of them fortified by judged cases, and similitude of reason."[16] We should take him at his word, despite his refusal to cite his authorities, "judging it a matter undue and preposterous to proove rules and maxims a regrettable practice that grew from a sensitivity less exquisite than arrogant, that he would not derogate from the authority of the rules, by vouching of any of the authority of the cases."[17] It is revealing that the assigns of John Moore had no such compunction, and where the provenance of the cases in the commentary could be determined citation was provided. By 1630, with my Lord Coke's *Reports* in printed form and a vast, widely circulated corpus of manuscript reports of other eminent lawyers and judges, the English lawyer was already beginning to judge the weight of a case's authority by the heft of its citations. The day was long past when Bacon could sneer at John Perkins's *A Profitable Booke Treating of the Lawes of England* (1530) and William Staunford's *Plees del Coron* (1557) for their care in citing authorities. Court, counsel-contra, and client all demanded that the advocate provide chapter and verse.

In his aphorisms in *De Augmentis*, Bacon makes clearest, explicitly, what the relationship is between the rule and the law:

> It is a sound precept, not to take the law from the rules, but to make the rule from the existing law. For the proof is not to be sought from the words of the rule, as if it were the text of law. The rule, like the magnetic needle, points at the law, but does not settle it.[18]

If the reader approaches the *Maximes* with that advice in mind, there can be no mistaking Bacon's purpose and no misunderstanding the function and role of the maxims. There can also be no doubting Bacon's intellectual honesty in the use of maxims. Coke stands diminished in comparison.

But why rules at all? To the Westlaw eye there is something anomalous about trying to condense law existing in the form of cases into a neat table of rules, especially if we are told that we are not to find the letter of the law in the rules. However, Bacon's enterprise might not seem so anomalous to a generation of American lawyers raised on the Uniform Commercial Code, Restatements, and American Legal Institute Model Codes if the rules and maxims are seen as the foundation of a thoroughgoing reform of the common law based on a restatement of its principles. When Bacon wrote the *Maximes* in 1596 there were high hopes that the common law might undergo considerable reform. The portents were good. The Queen herself seemed well disposed. In the *Maximes*' Epistle Dedicatory to the Queen, Bacon referred to the Queen's speech to Parliament in 1593 in which she had alluded elliptically (Elizabeth's preferred manner) to undertaking "a generall amendment of the states of your lawes, and to reduce them to more breuity and certaintie."

Moreover, in these same years, a new generation of lawyers were rising to commanding positions of influence and juridical power. From 1592 to 1595, fourteen new serjeants-at-law were coifed, four of them Queen's Serjeants sworn of her counsel learned, the largest promotion to the apex of the legal profession in any four-year period in Elizabeth's reign. Both King's Bench and Exchequer acquired new chiefs in 1592 and 1593, respectively—and the new Chief Justice of King's Bench, John Popham, would prove a particularly vigorous and assertive jurist. There were two new puisne justices of the Common Pleas appointed in 1593–1594 and a new Baron of the Exchequer in the latter year. In short, five of the twelve judges of the three great common law courts, including two chiefs, were appointed within three years. In 1592, Edward Coke was appointed Solicitor General. In 1594 he was promoted Attorney General, and in 1595 Thomas Fleming succeeded him as Solicitor. In 1592, Thomas Egerton was appointed Attorney General, in 1594 he was promoted Master of the Rolls, and in 1596 he was elevated to the highest office as Lord Keeper of the Great Seal (retaining until 1603 the Mastership, thus effectively dominating Chancery at all levels). Last but not least, Francis Bacon was named (but not sworn) to the Queen's counsel learned, serving without patent or fee, a poor consolation prize for having lost the attorney-generalship to Coke and the solicitor-generalship to Fleming.

From the greatest of these jurists to the least of them (and by virtue of rank and emolument Bacon was the latter), they were a remarkably learned and energetic cohort. All of them had been formed in the old construct of the mediaeval common law, of writs and Year Books, but all of them recognized that the age demanded procedural reform, greater emphasis on substantive law, and more certainty as to what constituted authority in the law. The clearest statement of the tasks they faced, one to which all gave at least substantial tacit consent, was in Bacon's Epistle Dedicatory, where he set down the benefits to be enjoyed and the perils to be avoided by general law reform. His objective was the better to establish and settle "a certaine sense of the law, which doth now too much wauer in incertaintie."

Bacon's device to achieve certainty was the enunciation of rules (*regulae*), laws of laws (*legum leges*), drawn from the cases. When completed, all of some hundreds rules (possibly thousands) would be reconciled and arranged in the form of a restatement of the common law. This would be the compass guiding the jurist into the law, not the law itself. Clearly, new cases would find a place under the old rules. The restatement done, the law would become at a stroke a structure much more centered on substantive law and much less dependent upon the adjective, procedural law which had been the mother, nurse, and governess of the common law from its origins. Indeed, the great task facing the common law at the end of the sixteenth century—the end of the Middle Ages so far as the common law was concerned—was how to get away from nanny. This is what reform according to Bacon's precepts would have accomplished.

To bring certainty to the law this way would have been a painful labor. After all, this method is that underlying every codification or statute law revision, and though precious little Latinity is visible in the Uniform Commercial Code, its rules are still identifiable as *regulae* of an older dispensation. The assumption behind the process is that there is a body of law and that however it has come into existence "there are rules & grounds dispersed throughout it."[19] Every codificatory exercise has worked on that assumption, and the work of Justinian and Tribonian was no exception. Their Digest was Bacon's model. The Digest (or Pandects) had gathered together, reconciled, and reduced some 2000 treatises of two score jurists of Republican and Imperial Rome into fifty books containing several titles and altogether about 9000 separate extracts. However, the ruling principles in the Digest, determining the arrangement of the extracts, were taken from the a priori dictates of the Codex compiled a few years before. Bacon apparently had no intention of producing a code, and he had profound misgivings about the legislating sovereign being preferable to custom as the authority for law. In a 1616 proposal to James I for law reform itself—a sad reflection on what had not been accomplished since the new jurists arrived in the 1590's—Bacon made clear his position on the fundamental issue that codification raises:

> It is too long a business to debate whether *lex scripta aut non scripta* [law written or unwritten], a text law or customs well registered, with received and approved grounds and maxims, and acts and resolutions judicial from time to time duly entered and reported, be the better form of declaring and authorizing laws. . . . In all sciences, they are the soundest that keep close to particulars; and sure I am there are more doubts that rise upon our statutes, which are a text law, than upon the common law, which is no text law.[20]

Bacon would not begin with a code but rather with those "laws of laws," which careful sifting through the existing law of cases, living custom more than sovereign exigent, revealed. And he would stop there. There would be a digest of case law and a digest of statute law. The case law would be shorn of prolixity, obsolescence, and contradiction by the judges and, if necessary, by Parliament. In *De Augmentis* (Book VIII, Chapter III, Aphorism 92), Bacon suggested that points of law be referred to the judges by the king for authoritative determination, upon argument but without a real case stated. This was hardly novel, since it had become a relatively common procedure under James I. It was also doomed, since its use had been stoutly opposed by the judges, not least (but not exclusively) by Coke, whose translation from the chief justiceship of Common Pleas to that of King's Bench in 1613 and sacking from the latter in 1616 turned in part on his opposition to such apparent regal interference.

The Justinian model was, in Bacon's order of things, to be carried one step further beyond the two digests. There would be four other books. The first would be *De antiquitatibus juris* (antiquities of law), *viz.*, collected writings about laws and judicial pronouncements *quae ipsum corpus legum tempora praecesserunt* (which came before the body of the law).[21] It is not entirely clear what practical function this book was meant to have. It would be drawn from muniments and archives as well as treatises, rigorously summarized albeit as fully as possible, and while having value as precedent would not have binding authority. Since Bacon was reluctant to let advocate or court look behind the digest of cases and the digest of statutes, and certainly would not allow the old, overruled, and obsolete cases and enactments any forensic vigor, the book of antiquities would probably be limited to the small role of preserving the tradition of the legal culture. The other three books were intended to pedagogical ends. The first would be institutes, similar to Justinian's *Institutes*, for instruction in the law. The second would be a compilation of terms of the law, old and new, arranged not alphabetically but by logically related concepts, something like *Roget's Thesaurus*. (Bacon had a horror of that ubiquitous, alphabetically ordered, aide-mémoire of the lawyer, the commonplace book.) The third book would be *De regulis juris*—maxims once again—directed at opening the leading principles of law, through a logical process essentially dialectical and inductive. Those principles were the general dictates of reason, which run through the different matters of law, and are like legal ballast (*Saburra Juris*).[22] So, the maxim in nautical metaphor thrives, though we have descended from the compass on the quarterdeck to the keelson and the bilge! But the maxim remains seaworthy and afloat in fulfilling a vital and august role in Bacon's *novum organum* of law and jurisprudence.

Bacon never completed his ambitious undertaking of not just law reform but the whole recasting of the common law. He failed even to begin it, beyond the few pieces discussed here. Nonetheless, he had his disciples, those who saw merit in maxims as more than mere illustration or forensic decoration. John Doddridge's *The English Lawyer* (1629) made abundant use of maxims for the ready instruction of lawyers (through memorization). William Noy's *Principall Grounds and Maximes of the Lawes of the Kingdome* (1642) was also primarily aimed at students. Edward Wingate's *Maximes of Reason* (1658), including religious and philosophic maxims as well as legal ones, had great currency. And Henry Finch's *Nomotechnia*, first published in law French in 1613 and in English in 1627, was most directly influenced by Bacon and emphasized maxims as principles. Finch's book had a wide influence, continuing into the latter half of the next century. There is, though, pathos in the paucity of Bacon's disciples. The fertile product of the greatest legal mind of the age had been replicated only in student texts.

The future direction of English law was not determined by Francis Bacon. It was by Edward Coke. This is not the place to recount the deep and disordering rivalry between the two men that was personal, professional, and political. Neither man's considerable stature and gravity are improved by the confrontation, face to face, knife to back, delating lips to ear. Coke's latest biographer has seen the rivalry as reflecting

> the tension between the practical lawyer and the philosopher, the independent man and the chronic debtor, the ally of Cecil and the friend of Essex . . . the lack of sympathy between the industrious poor relation [Coke] and the talented, indolent, prodigal son [Bacon].[23]

None who studies the events of the late Elizabethan and early Stuart epoch can escape the tension. It crops up in unlikely places and times, involved in seemingly innocent events. One sympathizes with Bacon: he was, after all, the greater loser of fortune, place, honor, and reputation. One also sees the justice of Coke's victory and accepts with professional satisfaction its result. Yet, in the scheme of English history, wherein, despite two domestic revolutions in the seventeenth century and an overseas one in the next, there is only one acceptable and therefore viable interpretation of what happened: the Whig Interpretation of History, which celebrates the peace, order, good government, representative institutions, constitutionalism and ultimately democracy which prevailed against Stuart Despotism. The Coke-Bacon confrontation is too easily read as a collision of good and evil, and tends to divide historians into partisan communities. Even Coke's most impassioned biographer (whose lengthy encomium of the great common lawyer was greeted by one English reviewer as applicable to any lawyer, in any age, anywhere) was a partisan, though Catherine Drinker Bowen gracefully changed her mind about Bacon after she wrote a biography of the philosopher-essayist.[24] There is a tinge here of the Dreyfusard/Anti-Dreyfusard split that divided France at the end of the nineteenth century, albeit one without the disfiguring animus of anti-Semitism or the larger issue of Left and Right unresolved after a century of French revolutions. But had Bacon and not Coke triumphed in determining the direction of the modern common law, our law today, on both sides of the Atlantic and throughout the common law world, would be considerably different.

Coke eschewed radical reform, and he possibly never entertained a single abstract jurisprudential thought. He was also suspicious, and more to the point, impatient, of principles in the law. He believed that there was a vast body of existing law that could be summoned by the artificial reason of the judge for application to the concrete case at hand in order to arrive at a just conclusion of an issue and afford appropriate remedy for the wronged party. But that body of law provided discrete directions to solve real situations, not principles for ratiocination. Coke had enormous faith in the probity and the capacity of the judiciary. He believed that the court almost unerringly managed to find the right solution by the right way. Coke's *Reports,* or simply *the* Reports in English citation, were less scripture than hymnal—praising the justice emanating from Westminster Hall, celebrating the steady ritual acts of the common law. He was almost naive in his confidence. Dismissed from the bench in 1616, summoned back to the Star Chamber as a Privy Councillor in 1618, he emphasized the judicatory nature of that tribunal and never doubted that it was indeed the High Court of Star Chamber. Finding a seat, a voice, and enormous influence in the House of Commons in the 1620's, he fashioned the High Court of Parliament. Thus, he played a large role in reviving the mechanism of impeachment, the most notable victim of which—deservedly—was Lord Chancellor Bacon.

Coke's contribution was above all else to sum up the existing mediaeval law in its most important branches, as for real property in the *First Institutes*, Coke upon Littleton, and largely ignore the rest. In his reports he bridged the gap that separated the anecdotal and ambiguous content of the Year Books from the necessarily factually precise, conclusion driven, and explicitly reasoned modern report. Here his spurious maxims were useful, because while he denied them the authority of principles, or "laws of laws," he used them to short-circuit the interminableness of pleading in the Year Books. This enabled him to fashion new law less hindered by the trammels of the old. In this he showed the way to other lawyers of the age, who whether knowingly or not came to use maxims to the same purpose.

What a strange fate for the maxim! In 1616, Bacon had confidently predicted to his royal master, James I, in promoting his larger scheme for law reform,

> And I do assure your Majesty, I am in good hope, that when Sir Edward Coke's Reports and my Rules and Decisions shall come to posterity there will be (whatsoever is now thought) question who was the greater lawyer.[25]

It was not to be. Perhaps the bitterest defeat of all was that not only did Coke found the modern common law upon his *Institutes* and *Reports*, he used *regulae* not to sum up the old law as Bacon did, but to isolate it and destroy it as authority.

CHAPTER EIGHT

Sir Edward Coke

Having playfully suggested in the essay on Sir Thomas Littleton that the appropriate motto for Littleton would have been "One Law and One Book," the author must reveal at the outset that the tomb of Littleton's great commentator, Sir Edward Coke, carries a Latin inscription exalting the deceased as "*Duodecem Liberorum Tredecim Librorum Pater*," Father of Twelve Children and Thirteen Books.[1] The tally of the children is accurate and thirteen books is dead-on for the eleven volumes of *Reports* published in Coke's lifetime, his *Book of Entries* (1614), and his *First Institutes*, the volume known as *Coke upon Littleton* (1628). But the real contrast between the two judges is that between the motto of Littleton, "*Ung Dieu et Ung Roy*," One God and One King, with the motto chosen by Coke at his call as serjeant-at-law: "*Lex Est Tutissima Cassis*," Law is the Safest Helmet.[2] Littleton's motto reflected the conventional Catholic piety of the twilight of the Middle Ages and asserted a fervent, even prayerful, monarchism that had marked relevance in the England of the Wars of the Roses. In 1606, Coke's England was no longer Catholic, and a century of strong Tudor monarchy had banished the specter of civil war between rival royal houses; and indeed, instead had raised the ogre of a monarch so strong as to be fearsome unless restrained by the law. Coke's motto was a perfect and complete statement of his guiding principle, his singular devotion to the primacy of the law.

Coke's reference to "helmet" strikes the right note of bellicosity. Throughout his life and long career as advocate, judge, councillor, and parliamentarian, Coke was a fighter: toughly adversarial, aggressive, never wont to lose a case by faint prosecution. Like the true soldier, he was courageous under fire, resilient in defeat, and magnanimous (only) in victory. But "helmet" also bespeaks a certain defensiveness—it is a device of protection rather than a weapon. *Justitia* in European iconography has always been represented holding scales in one hand and a sword in the other (whether she is blindfolded or not varies). Never, though, does she wear a helmet. Perhaps in Coke's day she needed one. Justice fared poorly in an age of assertive, absolutist, monarchs, and as she needed protection so was her law the armor of the liberties of the monarch's subjects. If this was not entirely apparent to Coke in June 1606 when he basked in the favor of King James I—who that balmy summer rewarded his servant's fourteen years as counsel-learned by naming him Chief Justice of Common Pleas—it would become evident enough a decade later when the servant was driven from the bench as if he were a treasonous clerk.

Edward Coke came from an old and modestly well-to-do family of Norfolk gentlemen. Born in 1552 at his father's manor house at Mileham, he was the only boy among seven sisters. At the grammar school in the cathedral close in Norwich he acquired a mastery of Latin grammar and rhetoric that got him into Trinity College, Cambridge, in 1567 and never deserted him. Coke's reputation for learning owed a great deal to his Latinity, in an age when education meant a command of that language above all else. The rhetoric of Latin was the foundation of his logic. Its grammar, vocabulary, and syntax furnished the mortar, stone, and chisel of those finely wrought Latin maxims which he tossed off with abandon to embellish his obiter dicta and lend them an antiquity and authority that seduced his contemporaries and corrupted his successors. Its philology and etymology provided the foundation of his grasp of English and Law French and the source of his legal-historicism. Absent his Latinity, Coke might have been easier reading, but his written corpus would have been poorer in substance and lessened in persuasiveness. He left Cambridge without taking a degree, but that university, which he would always revere as alma mater, made no mistake in later conferring upon him the degree of Master of Arts, for although Coke wore the lawyer's robe and not the parson's surplice he was marked by his bookishness and his accomplishments as a true son and disciple of scholastic learning.

Coke was of the last generation of English barristers who as a matter of course would pass a year or two at one of the inferior Inns of Chancery before going on to an Inn of Court. The commendable justification for such a sojourn was that the fledgling barrister would learn something about the chirographic and procedural, the clerical and "paper," side of the law before proceeding to the superior Inn of Court to learn the law. The denizens of the Inns of Chancery were court clerks and attorneys, clearly inferior in professional function and also—almost by necessary deduction—inferior in social status to the advocate-barristers who peopled the Inns of Court. In Elizabethan England, an increasing definition of the distinction in status (rather than a distinction in function) impelled the governing barristers of the Inns of Court, the benchers, to exclude the attorneys from their "company" and to confine them to the Inns of Chancery. The benchers acted not only from their own inflated self-esteem but also responded to the reality that the sons of noblemen and squires flocking to the Inns of Court for a year or two introduction to the common law would not tolerate the company of their social inferiors or admit that anything useful could be learned from them. The clerks and attorneys were to keep their place in the Inns of Chancery, while *real* gentlemen maintained their exclusivity in the Inns of Court. What was lost to the future barrister was intimacy with the entire adjective dimension of the law, an immediate comprehension of how and even why so much of the law was process rather than substance. Young Edward Coke was lucky in a way his successors would not be. His year at Clifford's Inn, after he left Cambridge and before he entered the Inner Temple in 1572, reinforced his almost medieval scholastic bent, enabled him to perceive the law from the bottom up, and taught him all of the method and some of the skills of the legal draftsman. In short, the year at Clifford's Inn formed Coke in an institutional frame and a pedagogy that more closely resembled the world of Justice Sir Thomas Littleton a century earlier than it did the world of Chief Justice Sir Edward Coke less than a half century later.

In his six years' studentship at the Inner Temple—he was admitted in April 1572 and called to the bar in April 1578—Coke progressed rapidly through the exercises: moots, which were exceptionally long and complicated at the Inner Temple; simple "case-putting"; attendance at readings, the twice-yearly lectures on statutes; residence; court-sitting. In the twilight of his career, Coke would deprecate the value of the readings as "long, obscure, and intricate, full of new conceits, liker rather to riddles than lectures, which when they are opened, they vanish away like smoke."[3] One supposes that he excepted from this harsh judgment his own readings, one at Lyon's Inn in 1579 and the other at the Middle Temple in 1592.[4] Yet Coke's own experience as a student at the Temple gave point to the convention that the informal activities at the Inns were as much a feature of legal education as the formal exercises. Tradition has it that during his last year before his call to the bar, Coke led a student rebellion against the Inn's cook for the poor food served in hall. He drafted a Latin bill of particulars against the cook, arguing that the cook in his malfeasance had breached his engagement with the Inn (and its students), and presented the case personally before the benchers to the admiration of his fellows and the favorable notice of his superiors. The records of the Inn are silent as to the outcome, indeed, silent as to whether or not the incident actually occurred.[5] But henceforth, thanks to the so-called "The Cook's Case," there would be no end of puns on the name of Edward Coke, pronounced "cook" by his contemporaries. Few, though, surpassed that of his inveterate foe and rival, Francis Bacon: too many Cokes spoil the law.

Coke's early rise in the profession was meteoric. He held a readership at Lyon's Inn a year after his call—a rare, perhaps unique, honor for one of such short continuance at the bar. He soon enjoyed a large practice; he rode the Norfolk circuit, and many of his early clients came from his East Anglian home counties, Norfolk and Suffolk. Within a decade he had joined the front-rank of leaders, men who were widely sought after as advocates and counselors, enjoying practices that were genuinely national. His appointment in 1586 as recorder of Norwich—that is, as counsel to the urban corporation and judge of its criminal courts—was a belated recognition of his regional reputation; the year before, he had been named recorder of Coventry in the west Midlands, a clear mark of his national reputation.

Coke early gained a reputation as a masterful conveyancer. His years as a practitioner corresponded with the heyday of attempts to create extravagant, even bizarre, interests in property by pushing the Statute of Uses beyond the extremes of logic to allow legal interests to be created which were in complete defiance of the rules of the limitations of estates at common law. Most of these interests were created to settle landed estates, and a good many of them raised the threat of perpetuities.

Coke patently did not like perpetuities: he reported, with ill-concealed glee, a number of the cases in which the courts averted the threat by judicial surgery. The contingent remainder was the first culprit. No sooner had that interest been fully accepted, in *Colthirst v. Bejusin* (1550),[6] than the peril of perpetuities was perceived, and the courts turned to cutting back the contingent remainder. This surgery was largely completed in *Shelley's Case*,[7] decided the year after Coke's call—his first great case, and perhaps the first one that he reported. But perpetuities was like the hydra-headed monster. *Shelley's Case* notwithstanding, if the contingent remainder was created by way of uses, it could be a valid legal interest by action of the Statute of Uses and by virtue of the fact that the courts were prepared to accept limitations by way of uses that they would not accept by way of limitations at law. Not until *Chudleigh's Case* (1595) was the danger of such perpetuities by way of uses broken, by the simple expedient of holding that the legislative intent of the Statute of Uses was to make limitations by way of uses subject to the rules governing estates at common law.[8]

From the property lawyer's vantage point, these were exciting times. Coke's practice, like those of his less eminent contemporaries, relied on the fast legal footwork necessary to keep at least one step ahead of the courts and one step away from the crash of an instrument. He wrought well. A conveyancer's form-book in its fifth edition in 1683 contains an exquisite settlement drafted between 1584 and 1592 for Henry, 9th Baron Scrope, by a number of counsel, *inter alios* Edward Coke.[9] The longevity of this device owed all to the fact that its settlement was limited by way of two life estates, which put it outside of the strictures against contingent remainders, successive life estates, and even the legal executory devise (which was developed sometime after 1620) as devices creating perpetuities. The Scrope settlement epitomized the modest, cautious, device of two lives which proved a thoroughly workable means to effect settlement without raising the specter of perpetuities. It was also the foundation of the brilliant device of Orlando Bridgman in the mid-seventeenth century, the "strict settlement," which passed muster under Lord Nottingham's rule formulation of the rule against perpetuities in the *Duke of Norfolk's Case* (1681) and served the landed aristocracy of England well for two centuries until the Settled Land Act of 1882 made all settled land alienable.[10]

Coke was honored in his own land when the Inner Temple made him a bencher in 1590 and called him Reader in 1592. In 1592–1593, Coke also entered upon a higher career on a greater stage. He was appointed Solicitor-General, the second law officer of the Crown; made recorder of London, a post that almost invariably went to a barrister high in regal favor; and named Speaker of the House of Commons in the Parliament of 1593. This last was also a mark of royal favor, the role of the Speaker being to maintain the monarch's interests in the House. Coke had sat only once before as MP for a Suffolk borough in the previous Parliament of 1589. In 1593 he enjoyed the greater prestige of being returned to the Commons as one of the two knights of the shire for Norfolk. As Speaker, Coke presided over a contentious but productive session, during which the House and the Queen clashed, over parliamentary meddling in ecclesiastical matters. His skill in serving both the jealous master which was the House and his even more jealous mistress the Queen damped controversy. Coke's reward came exactly one year after Parliament ended. He was appointed Attorney-General on April 10, 1594.

The Attorney-Generalship was a mixed blessing for a lawyer who hoped to attain judicial office. It meant foregoing the chance to become a serjeant-at-law and thereby to practice in Common Pleas, where serjeants alone had audience, and to enjoy the fairly steady odds of becoming a judge of King's Bench, Common Pleas, or the Exchequer. The Attorney-General had at best a vague *spes successionis* to a chief-justiceship, at worst to the post of Master of the Rolls (the second highest office in Chancery). In terms of income from fees, the office was not inferior in profit to that of a serjeant's practice, and usually was worth more. The Attorney-General was not barred from private practice; rather, the office attracted clients as none other did. The greatest drawback might well be the work it entailed. The Attorney-General was required to appear in all prosecutions brought for the Crown in Star Chamber, all major prosecutions in King's Bench, all cases enforcing regal rights in the Exchequer, and prosecutions in great matters of state before any court. He was also involved in criminal investigation touching important matters, requiring his presence at interrogations of suspects (sometimes by torture). He drafted proclamations, pardons, and Crown bills for Parliament. He was constantly called upon for legal advice to the Crown, opinions on points of law, and drawing cases to be put to the judges for advisory opinion. He represented the Crown's interests in such rudimentary appeals as the law allowed. He also attended the House of Lords during the Parliament in an advisory capacity. He enjoyed considerable procedural privileges in all judicial proceedings and he was accorded precedence over all other barristers. But he worked hard for such advantages as the office brought, and if it brought him a large private clientele, he dared not favor those clients in the performance of his official duties.

Coke's tenure of a dozen years as Attorney-General proved particularly onerous. High taxes, Continental markets closed by war, and a succession of crop failures brought want and economic dislocation, creating a threatening undercurrent of unrest. It was a period marked by growing political disgruntlement, religious divisiveness, acts of subversion, conspiracies against the monarch's person, and divisions in the principal organ of state, the Privy Council. Because of the necessity to raise money for a sea war against Spain and civil war in Ireland, Parliament became almost a routine institution, which meant that dissent could be voiced and local feuds were pursued at Westminster. Attorney-General Coke was called upon to bring to the brutal justice of the age Roman Catholic priests, rioting apprentices, bumpkins who talked of seizing armories, and traitors who plotted against the Queen's life, including her own physician. More ominous, if less numerous, were the first prosecutions resulting in death for Protestant sectaries. As Attorney-General, Coke managed the prosecution in three of the greatest state trials in England's history: the trial of the Earl of Essex and his followers for the coup d'état attempted in 1601; the trial of Sir Walter Raleigh and co-conspirators, shortly after James's accession, for planning to kill the monarch and put the king's cousin Arabella Stuart, on the throne; and the trial of the Catholic fanatics who in 1605 attempted the most spectacular stroke of political terrorism in history, to blow up the King and the entire Parliament with gunpowder. Coke's vigorousness and harshness in prosecution were remarked upon by his contemporaries only as manifestations of remarkable patriotism and loyalty to his sovereign. Victorian Englishmen, largely unfamiliar with war or treason, enjoyed the luxury of roundly condemning Coke for his choleric severity. Our age ought to be better disposed to understanding him.

In 1605, the first chief-justiceship (that of the Common Pleas) to open since Coke became Attorney-General fell vacant with Edmund Anderson's death. It was filled by another ancient Templar, Francis Gawdy. Coke's disappointment ended when Gawdy died less than a year later. In June 1606, Coke was made serjeant-at-law—a requisite step to the Common Pleas bench, though pro forma in his case—and a day later was made Chief Justice of the Common Pleas.

At fifty-four, Coke was old by contemporary standards. He had buried one wife (Bridget Paston, who had brought him a fortune, died in 1598) and he might well have wished to bury the second, a harridan he had married after less than six months' mourning for Bridget. His second wife, Lady Elizabeth Hatton, had been the young, high-spirited widow of an elderly knight; her grandfather, Lord Burghley, had he lived the few months required to see Elizabeth marry Coke, would have approved, if for no other reason than Coke's having beaten Francis Bacon to the widow. Elizabeth was given to histrionics and angry demonstrations. Self-willed, demanding, a prodigal spender, she gave Coke two daughters, denied him peace, sued him in Star Chamber, deserted him and stripped his house of its furnishings. Having outlived him, she spoke a venomous epitaph of him: "We shall never see his like again, praises be to God."[11] The scandal and indignity visited upon Coke by this unfortunate union placed him at considerable disadvantage at critical points in his judicial career. It eroded his reputation for integrity, pushed him to excesses in conduct, and played into the hands of Bacon. Bacon never forgot Coke's having been preferred for the Attorney-Generalship or his success in winning the widow Hatton and a fortune that Bacon desperately needed. Whatever else led to two great falls by Chief Justice Coke, Bacon's enmity contributed mightily.

The rapidity with which Coke as Chief Justice of the Common Pleas assumed an adversarial, even hostile, stance toward regal policy has puzzled generations of scholars. As Attorney-General he had been the quintessential "king's man." As a judge, Coke repeatedly took positions that appeared inimical to the Crown interest. The explanation must be complex, if for no other reason than that Coke was a complex man. What can be largely excluded from consideration at the outset is the notion that the explanation lies in some external factors, in regal policies or regal ambitions, in some changes in royal personnel that both signaled and effected basic changes in direction of government. If one looks for the explanation in some seismic change in royal policy to which Coke responded, he will not find it. James and his political and legal advisers did not forsake goodness for evil, not even gradually, let alone suddenly clamp down on previous constitutional practices or English liberties. Rather, the explanation must be sought in Coke himself, in the context of his learning and of his role.

The first thing to be noticed—and it can be easily overlooked—is that Coke was the first judge of Common Pleas in almost a century who had never practiced in that court as an advocate. He had been a serjeant for only a day, and this lack of experience markedly distinguished him from his predecessors and his three brother judges on the court. That is not to say that he was ignorant of what went on in Common Pleas; his *Reports*, presenting cases decided in Common Pleas before he joined its bench, indicates that he was intellectually familiar with its doctrine and even its procedures, and well aware of the nature of its peculiar and limited jurisdiction to party-and-party property litigation. What Coke lacked was immersion (the phrase is his own) in "the course of the court." Coke would have been the last to have disparaged the importance of that experience, for he recognized the course of a court as the true foundation of precedent to be followed by that court.[12] He did not, however, *think* like a Common Pleas jurist. Untouched by the tradition of the court, Coke was impatient of the experientially imposed intellectual and sentimental limitations on the way a Common Pleas jurist thought.

Coke came to Common Pleas, then, fully formed, without the *deformation professionelle* of his brother justices. Moreover, his experience at the bar had been gained in two courts where the common law was undergoing most rapid development: King's Bench and Star Chamber. In great part, that development meant the rapid expansion of jurisdiction. In the years in which Coke had practiced there, the King's Bench had acquired a wide and growing jurisdiction in civil actions; during his tenure as Attorney-General, Star Chamber, ostensibly a court of criminal jurisdiction, became even more openly a tribunal for obtaining civil remedies.[13] Indeed, in the case of Star Chamber, Coke had himself played a large part.

Judicial development also meant an increasing emphasis on precedent as the basis for legal change. Here, a fine line must be drawn if we are not to misunderstand Coke's view of precedent and its relationship to the law. One of his more striking maxims makes clear his meaning:

> New adjudication does not make new law, but makes plain the old; adjudication is the dictum [saying] of law, and by adjudication law which was before hidden is newly revealed.[14]

The law existed; it was not created by the court. Only statute could make new law. Therefore legal change, as Coke understood it was the process and result of revelation. There was a close analogy here to the concept of theological revelation as the medieval Church had understood it. Coke, ever the schoolman, with his fondness for the Vulgate and his shelves of religious tracts, was well-equipped to appreciate this.

To believe that the existence of the law was revealed by adjudication was not a discouragement of judicial activism. On the contrary, it invited it. It reassured the judge that he need not let go the old in pursuit of the new, the established for the novel, the real for the merely theoretical. The idea was almost a license for judicial activism. a patent authorizing the discovery of new law. Coke was, above all else, an activist. As a judge he was a judicial activist.

What was a judicial activist to do on a court which was mired in the most exquisitely sophisticated doctrinal construct of the most fully fashioned body of substantive law—property law—that the age knew? He could, according to the lights of that "artificial reason of law" which Coke posited as the jurist's method, refine the law to broad jurisprudential policy ends in order to suit the existing corpus of law to new requirements. As far as he could, Coke certainly did just this in his seven years on the Common Pleas bench, as his own reports testify, carrying his brethren with him in most instances and, when they differed with him, ignoring them in favor of his own position. But there was something else the judicial activist could do, especially if he enjoyed the latitude for individual initiative in procedural matters which the presidency of the court afforded him (and him alone). He could battle, indeed would feel himself bound, to maintain and expand the jurisdiction of the court against all other tribunals. This too, Chief Justice Coke certainly did, employing an old common law writ: the writ of prohibition. Prohibitions had already been used against the ecclesiastical courts and had elicited episcopal complaint before Coke took his seat on the bench, but Coke used prohibitions with a hitherto unknown prodigality and broadened scope. The writ could be directed against any court, secular or ecclesiastical, to prevent the continuance of a case which the court issuing the prohibition claimed was not within the other court's jurisdiction. During Coke's tenure as Chief Justice of the Common Pleas, most of the shower of prohibitions loosed by him fell upon the ecclesiastical courts because of their determination to maintain jurisdiction over cases for tithe, but prohibitions were also directed to Chancery, Requests, Wards and Liveries, the regional Councils in Wales and the North, the High Court of Admiralty, and a number of other jurisdictions. Two major courts were excepted: King's Bench and Star Chamber. The reasons are many and difficult to apportion, but among them was Coke's residual reverence for those courts and how they were refining the law to proper ends *pro bono publico*.

Prohibitions brought Coke into confrontation with all those vested interests represented in the courts to which they were directed, not least the litigants. Coke made enemies, including Lord Chancellor Ellesmere and two successive Archbishops of Canterbury. And his enemies were closer to the king than Coke was. Prohibitions became a standing grievance against Coke, and not without reason, for Common Pleas's issuance of prohibitions could be seen as mere dog-in-the manger attempts to acquire more business for Common Pleas and profit for its judges, as a restrictive practice on the free-wheeling forum-chasing which characterized litigation at the time, and as a pernicious device to unsettle the harmony of judicature. This is not to question the motives of Coke. It is to explain why he was no sooner on the bench than he began to stir up opposition to his own person and fall afoul of the king, who was the ultimate arbiter of judicial propriety and who stood to lose the most if judicature fell warring within itself.

More than a court's business and jurisdiction lay behind Coke's activism. He took an exalted view of the role of the judiciary, based upon his historical perception of the institution's antiquity, its integrity in the civil polity, and its responsibility for the maintenance of its charge, the law. In 1600, a reporter of the Star Chamber noted: "A sayinge of Mr. Atturnie [Coke] often used by him in his arguments, that it is his duetie to informe ther lordships of the trueth and state of the cause and then that the judgement is thers."[15] Judgment imposed a unique burden upon the judge, one not shared by counsel whose "duetie" was to open the truth of the matter so far as he was able. And as Attorney-General Coke acknowledged, even his client the monarch did not share the burden of judgment if the crown were before the court in a legal way. Coke understood perfectly the adversarial dialectic of the law. For all of the monarch's prerogative and privileges, despite his immunity to prosecution and suit by others, admitting him to be the fount of justice, when the king was at law he was substantially on the same footing as any other party. He was to be heard, but judgment belonged to the judges. Here was the point of friction between Coke and James. For James saw the judge as merely his delegate, with revocable powers, an advisor whose counsel was to be accepted or rejected as the principal willed. James would not interfere with the ordinary course of judicature. But when he believed a vital interest of the crown was at stake in law, the king expected his judges to advise him and recall that they held their offices as his delegates.

Had it not been for a practice of long standing, Chief Justice Coke and his profligacy with prohibitions would have been merely a painful nuisance. What caused Coke to become increasingly considered a threat, by the king and his ministers, was the attitude that Coke struck with respect to advisory opinions elicited from the judges by royal command. Obtaining judicial opinions had been an infrequent practice from at least the middle years of Elizabeth's reign, but was considerably expanded by James. At the outset Coke did not object to the procedure, but he early showed himself prickly toward regal interests in such matters. In the fall of 1608, James and the Council conferred with all the judges on the validity of prohibitions upon the complaint of the clergy. Coke spoke for his brethren in upholding the legality of prohibitions. But he went further, speaking only for himself, in answering James's claim to be able to decide such matters himself. Coke told the King that though the law was reason and the King had natural reason, he could not personally exercise judicature because he lacked training and experience in applying the "artificial reason" of the law, an attainment that could be acquired only by long study. James exploded: then he would be under the law? Coke's rejoinder became legendary. He cited Bracton's immortal axiom, that the King was under God and the law (ignoring the likelihood that Bracton meant natural law, not the common law). During a further series of confrontations between James and the judges, the dispute ended with a frightened Coke on his knees if not his face before an outraged monarch.[16]

In these instances and in others, even if he sometimes spoke rashly, Coke had acted responsibly and in a way supported by custom and precedent. But in 1608 Coke seconded Chief Justice Thomas Fleming of the King's Bench in objecting to the entire procedure of advisory opinions. The issue touched whether or not the four English counties bordering Wales were within the jurisdiction of the Council of the Marches of Wales. At a Privy Council meeting at which eleven of the twelve judges were present, Fleming spoke for them all in refusing to deliver their opinions, on the ground that the judges were to deliver opinions only "as the causes and the cases fell out before them judicially between partie and partie."[17] At that point, James himself, with the Prince of Wales in tow, entered the chamber and launched into a warm disquisition on the power of the King in judicature. He ended by putting the question himself. In the ensuing row, growing from the continued obstinacy of the judges, Coke argued that whether the four counties were intended within the Statute of Wales was a question of fact that should be addressed to a jury, not a question of law. James replied, correctly, that it was a question of law and the judges should decide it (so far was his "artificial reason" sound). The conference broke up with an angry King, tearful judges, and no opinion rendered.

Beyond bad law, Coke's and Fleming's proposition that advisory opinions were wrong was simply untenable. Coke as Attorney-General and Fleming when Solicitor-General had both drafted briefs to put such questions to the judges for advisory opinions. The jurisdiction of the Council in the Marches of Wales was not the last question that the crown sought to settle with an advisory opinion. In 1615, Coke, who had replaced the defunct Fleming as Chief Justice of the King's Bench, objected to advisory opinions in the case of the Reverend Edmund Peacham, a West Country puritan facing trial for treason. Here the judges were being polled individually as to whether they believed the misconduct of the defendant amounted to treason. Coke denounced this as without precedent. This argument would not wash, though it was a refined one addressing a genuine threat to judicial integrity, for polled separately even the most resolute judge might accede to what the crown demanded. As early as his first year on the bench, Coke and the then Chief Justice of the King's Bench had given opinions on impositions, without consultation with the other judges. In 1611 Coke had refused to give his personal opinion on the validity of proclamations as legal instruments without consulting the other judges; only when all the judges had been brought together were opinions rendered by Coke and his brethren. Coke would not win the next round. In *Peacham's Case* (1615) the other judges deserted Coke. His obstinacy was added to the long list of demerits that brought about his final fall in 1616.[18]

Coke's removal from Common Pleas to King's Bench in 1613 constituted a fall in all but name. A judge's profits from litigation in King's Bench were considerably less than in Common Pleas, and Coke took a major financial loss. The translation to King's Bench was also perceived popularly as a rebuke. Coke wept. Bacon, who had suggested the ploy, was gleeful. In fact, Bacon and the King had made a mistake, for Coke was capable of greater mischief on a grander stage in King's Bench, where the criminal cases touched the Crown directly. To soften the blow, Coke was made a Privy Councillor; this also increased his potential for being troublesome.

If the King thought the boot would be admonitory, he was soon disabused. *Peacham's Case* had been preceded by a confrontation in Star Chamber that saw Coke come close to inflicting a "sore blow"—as the King put it—on that court.[19] *Peacham's Case* was followed the next year by a cause célèbre between King's Bench and Chancery, Coke and Ellesmere, over Chancery's entertainment of actions that sought to undo judgments entered in King's Bench. Coke fetched from his bag of historical relics the ancient action of praemunire, triable in King's Bench, to threaten Chancery. Praemunire had lain unused since Henry VIII had menaced the entire clergy of England with it to pry them away from Rome at the beginning of the Reformation. Coke's threat spurred the King to an extraordinary sitting in Star Chamber in 1616. The king lectured the judiciary on their duty and cataloged the attacks by King's Bench on other courts, reproving Coke obliquely, and settled jurisdiction by a Solomonic threat to cut at least one chief justice in two.[20]

The final stroke was precipitated by the famous *Case of Commendams* (1616), touching the King's right to permit a clergyman to hold more than one ecclesiastical charge. Coke alone among the twelve judges of the common-law courts refused categorically to promise obedience to the King's will in such matters in the future. As eleven judges knelt in obeisance to the King, Coke stood upright. To color the King's determination to break Coke, his *Reports* was searched by the King's counsel-learned for points derogatory of royal prerogative, and upon Coke's spirited defense of the few items with which they taxed him, he was sacked as Chief Justice on November 10, 1616. He was merely the first judicial martyr of Stuart England. Charles I would, with varying severity, punish a Chief Baron, a Chief Justice of the King's Bench, and a Chief Justice of Common Pleas on one or another pretext, for one or another reason. In 1640, an outraged opposition in Parliament would exact their revenge on the King's judges by impeaching those who had supported Ship Money on appeal in 1638.

With Coke's fall, his work as a judge was over. His career, however, was not at all finished. Because he was considered a financial genius by no less a man than his foe Bacon, he was readmitted to the Privy Council within a year of his fall. Addressing fiscal issues gave Coke a renewed outlet for his energies, one that very nearly restored him fully to favor. Coke's contribution was characteristic of him, and quite in keeping with his wonted judicial activism. We cannot be sure that he suggested the brilliant move of prosecuting wholesale wealthy miscreants in order to raise revenue from their fines or by allowing them to compound for their fines. We do know that as a Privy Councillor sitting in Star Chamber and giving early voice in judgment, by virtue of his lowly precedence, he played a critical role in setting the fines that would ultimately be imposed. These were enormous: against the dowager Countess of Shrewsbury for aiding and abetting misconduct by Arabella Stuart, £20,000 (1618); against the Earl and Countess of Suffolk for the earl's peculation as Lord Treasurer, £30,000 (1619); against Secretary of State Sir Thomas Lake and certain of his relatives for libel, £16,666 (1619); against thirteen Low Country merchants for exporting gold and silver, a total of £136,333 (1619). Altogether these great sums amounted to exactly one-quarter of the total sum of Star Chamber fines estreated between 1596 and the court's abolition in 1641. While not even the greatest part of these fines were collected, the fact that they had been imposed was effectively used to persuade others to make fiscal peace with the Exchequer. Coke had the considerable satisfaction of settling some old personal and political scores in these cases: Suffolk and Lake had been among his chief enemies in the Council. Their fall was brought about by the rise of the King's new favorite, George Villiers, Duke of Buckingham. Coke's fortunes rose with the new favorite, and he assured himself of Buckingham's favor by forcibly abducting his youngest daughter from Lady Hatton's house and marrying the girl to Buckingham's older brother.

Financial shifts did not avail to provide adequate revenue, and in 1621 James was compelled to summon Parliament for the first time in seven years, to provide funds for the conduct of a costly and contradictory foreign policy. Sir Edward Coke, a loyal Privy Councillor, was returned as MP for a borough in the King's control. Whatever hopes James had that Coke would be in the vanguard of those directing and defending royal policy in the Commons were disappointed. Coke found again a forum worthy of his talents, his learning, and his activism, but the House of Commons was one in which these attributes would be more appreciated by those who doubted or opposed royal policy than by the king. This is not to depict Coke as a weathervane or a mercenary. On the contrary, what Coke saw at stake in the Parliament of 1621 was the preservation of the integrity of the law against the encroachments of royal ministers who were bent upon policies that were wrong, even pernicious, and who were prepared to subvert the law if necessary to effect those policies. The grievances of the King's subjects were to be redressed in a legal way, under protection of the law, in a preservation of the subjects' liberties, by the "High Court of Parliament."

The High Court of Parliament was not quite entirely the confection of Coke, but it relied upon the torturous and tortured history propounded by that oracle of the law for its substantiation as anything more than a notional fiction. Coke's developed brief can be easily consulted as, appropriately, Chapter One, "Of the High and Most Honourable Court of Parliament," in his *Fourth Institutes*, on the judicial structure of England. *Coke upon Littleton*, sect. 164, contains Coke's long disquisition on "this high court of parliament" with its "so transcendent" jurisdiction, tracing its history back to Anglo-Saxon times. No matter that Coke confused matters in finding a history as early as the ninth century for an institution which began in the mid-thirteenth. No matter that the strictly judicial function of parliament had enjoyed something less than a consistent and even development, and was greater at its origins than since, that it had lapsed and been revived to lapse again and be revived again, as a modest instrument of appeal: the faint fire could be stoked up to white-hot heat, and in the Parliament of 1621 Coke blew hard on the embers. He was rewarded by the emergence of an institution which having revived impeachment, turned it on a hapless and obscure Catholic lawyer in Wales, crushed monopolists, broke the Attorney-General, and finally dragged down Lord Chancellor Bacon. In the next Parliament, 1624, impeachment ousted Lord Treasurer Middlesex; later in the decade, in the early Parliaments of Charles I, only dissolution saved the King's great favorite and chief minister, the Duke of Buckingham, from destruction. None stood higher in that "High Court" than Sir Edward Coke. None was busier in patiently explaining the law, passionately urging action or restraining rashness, managing, cajoling, arguing, discoursing, debating.

For his pains in 1621, Coke with several other prominent leaders of the opposition was committed to the Tower for some months. In 1624, he enjoyed the rare favor of Prince Charles and Buckingham as they countered James's pacifism and took England to war with Spain, with Parliament cheering them on and, so that they might conduct the war, voting a modest supply for the first time in fifteen years. In the Parliaments of 1621 and 1624, it may fairly be said that Coke was the most influential man in the Commons. In 1625, the first Parliament of Charles I, although Coke had to share that honor with two others, his influence as the *jurisperitus* of that High Court was still dominant. In 1626 Coke was prevented from sitting in Parliament by being made sheriff, a fate that befell other opposition stars. He came back into his own with the first session of the Parliament of 1628. The Petition of Right, a unique instrument cast in the form of a reconfirmation of Magna Carta and passed by the Parliament to safeguard the subject's liberties and to redress grievances, a document to which Charles gave his reluctant assent, above all the efforts of others, was Coke's own creation.[21]

Coke, along with other prominent opposition leaders, withdrew from center stage in the Commons in the second session of the Parliament of 1628, leaving the initiative with hotter, more radical, men. One suspects he had a singular motive for his silence. Parliament might be a High Court, but it was also a political organ responding to other imperatives than the cool judgment of the artificial reason of the law. Parliament had begun to manifest a taste for power that seemed to beg the limitations of law as Coke understood the law and the role its judges played.

This was Coke's last Parliament. There would not be another for eleven years. On September 3, 1634, Coke died, in his eighty-third year. His death was noticed in high places. As the old judge lay dying at Stoke Poges, Secretary Windebank, in execution of the King and Council's warrant, quietly sent men to search through Coke's mansion and his chambers at the Inner Temple, carrying off his papers. Nothing treasonable or seditious, nothing that had it reached the public would have shaken the kingdom to its foundations, was discovered. Probably no corpse in England's history was ever so posthumously terrifying as that of Sir Edward Coke. The king had paid him a high honor.

Coke was secure in his reputation among his contemporaries, in the fears of his King and in the love of his fellow MPs, in the admiration of lawyers for the legal learning displayed in the *Reports*, in the respect of clerks of courts for his helpful and practical little *Book of Entries* and among those students for whom he undertook his *First Institutes* to bring them all of Littleton's lore, and masses more of his own. Perhaps most significantly, Coke was famed among the widest range of his countrymen for his stalwart defense of their liberties under law and the maintenance of the supremacy of the law that assured them liberty. When the revolution that Coke could not have imagined overtook the nation and destroyed or maimed all its institutions, he was revered as a hero by the Levellers, who sought a new order with a broader franchise for a continuous Parliament. At the same time, Thomas Hobbes condemned Coke for his medieval obscurantism and the irrationality of his belief that law was custom and not the command of Leviathan. One can be exalted for the enemies he makes as much as by the friends he keeps. Coke's renown went far beyond his partisans. It touched such old adversaries as the civil lawyer, Sir Julius Caesar, whom Coke had bombarded with prohibitions at the Court of Requests, but who remembered Coke's kindness in admitting him to the Inner Temple. Coke's fellow Norfolkman, the parson Thomas Fuller, the uncritical admirer of any figure he deemed worthy of inclusion in his secular hagiography, managed despite himself to achieve truth to the measure of his hyperbole in his epitaph of Coke: "His works will last to be admired whilst Fame hath a trumpet left her, and any breath to blow therein."[22]

Coke is one of those rare figures of genuinely major historical importance who has fared worse at the hands of his subsequent admirers than at those of his contemporary detractors. His contemporaries knew him better than we do and they certainly better knew the age in which he acted, the constraints under which he acted, and the objectives for which he acted. Coke was a complex man. He was not complicated, though too many historiographers have worked arduously to demonstrate that he was. Indeed, to consider Coke's treatment at the hands of historiographers—let us separate the term from biographers—is the clue to understanding the incubus that bears down Coke's subsequent reputation. It has often been remarked in the past that Coke has never found a decent biographer.[23] Virtually all biography of seventeenth-century figures (the most notable exception is Oliver Cromwell) is nearly intractable. In Coke's case, thanks to the fact that most of his papers have disappeared or been dispersed, not least because of the king's paranoia, the task is made yet more difficult. But the problem is compounded in its difficulty by the fact that Coke has been required by historians, ancient and modern, to serve as a symbol of something begun and not yet completed. In short, he has been robbed of eternal sleep, of the mere mortality that permits blissful oblivion for lesser men. We are like Charles I, less fearful, but still apprehensive of what Coke's cadaver can do, what it still means, what it still signifies.

The Whig historians, who flourished in the eighteenth and nineteenth centuries and were enamored of the rise of Parliament, the emergence of the rule of law, the achievement of liberties of speech and association and religious observance, and the evolution (though not too fast, please) of democratic government, saw Coke as the harbinger or proto-epitome of all those developments. Therefore, Coke's beastliness to Sir Walter Raleigh, or his abducting his daughter of fourteen to marry her to a feeble-minded courtier, or the xenophobic anti-Hispanicism that he manifested in the Commons in 1621 demanded some explanation, even justification. The record had to be spun sufficiently that these episodes would not detract from Coke's good qualities or embarrass the sensibilities of his admirers. Recent historians tend, however, to fall into a similar trap in seeking to understand Coke. In the 1930's, Coke was hailed as an early exponent of "economic liberalism," a precursor of Adam Smith.[24] In the 1970's, two admirable works appeared devoted entirely to Coke. One, by a French scholar, argued that Coke must be seen as a precursor of Locke and Montesquieu and accorded him a place in the history of anti-absolutist political theory just a step behind them.[25] What was intended as a handsome compliment is in fact the grossest flattery: Coke was a political theorist in the sense that anyone who can think straight, is involved in politics, and has had recorded what he said in the political process is a political theorist. He might rank with Locke as a significant Englishman of their century, but Locke owed virtually nothing to Coke, whose vaunting of the common law's primacy, in Locke's view, represented as great a peril to the civil government as monarchical absolutism. The other work, by an American scholar, credited Coke with development of "constitutional positions" which would permit English law to adapt to "new social and economic conditions."[26] There is merit in the suggestion of the interpretation, but it presupposes an understanding of constitutionalism on Coke's part that could not have emerged in seventeenth century England until after one bloody revolution and another bloodless one. Not even Coke was capable of such perspicacity.

There is little evidence that Coke had a coherently thought-out constitutional position beyond that medieval, traditional understanding of English polity called mixed-monarchy. Emphasizing consensual governance by the King and the estates, the latter being the clergy, the nobility, and the commonalty, represented in Parliament put a premium on compromise as the means to obtain it, and the law the regulator of relations within the mix. Not surprisingly, Coke devoted much of his attention to the last element, both when he was judge and afterwards as parliamentarian. Coke believed the law served as a surrogate for constitutionalism, and he was wont to stress the regulator as mediator when king and estates fell out. He had ample opportunity to urge this in the 1620's. He did not like either the word or the concept "sovereign," since it suggested not a mixture of equals but a hierarchy of unequals. Yet in standing against the King's penchant for asserting sovereignty he was not unaware that Parliament was drifting toward a counter-assertion suspiciously like sovereignty. Consequently he exalted the role of law, which as mediator could function only if its primacy was accepted by both king and estates as binding upon them severally and jointly. He had no doctrine of separation of powers, judicial review, or other ideas that would develop beyond his own time. But Coke cast the function of the law in civil polity to a higher plane than any other of his contemporaries in the political struggles of the age, and thanks to his posthumous fame as the common law's greatest oracle he influenced a later generation of lawyers to believe that the law was an essential power in a constitution raised on the separation of powers.

Coke's saving grace as jurist and politician was an almost perfervid ignoring of the future. He seldom alluded to it, let alone dwelt upon it, save in the most immediate future. In fact, he preferred the past, always the distant past, of the Year Books, of Magna Carta, or Edward I. In the debate on the Petition of Right in May 1628, in taking strong exception to a clause added by the Lords saving the King's "sovereign power," Coke thundered:

> I know that prerogative is part of the law, but "Sovereign Power" is no parliamentary word. In my opinion it weakens Magna Charta, and all the statutes; for they are absolute, without any saving of "Sovereign Power"; and should we now add it, we shall weaken the foundation of the law, and then the building must needs fall. Take we heed what we yield unto: Magna Charta is such a fellow, that he will have no "Sovereign."[27]

The old man must be taken at his word: Magna Carta was a living person to him.

Coke's past-mindedness differed from that which the modern historian seeks to inculcate in his student. His was all anachronism, the past living in the present, distinct from our attempt to see the past on its own terms rather than on ours. We fail repeatedly. Coke, never having tried for the simple reason that our sublime sensitivity is the product of nineteenth century German positivism, could only succeed in his endeavor. The result was determinative of the future of whole areas of the common law. This was not because Coke planned to achieve that outcome, but because his contemporary authority among lawyers was such as to convince them that his vision of the living past as present was the law. As the historian is struck by certain great events into which all the past appears to have flowed and out of which all the future issued—the Reformation of the sixteenth century and the French Revolution of the late eighteenth century are such—so he sees something of the same phenomenon in the history of the common law, with Coke as aperture.

Coke upon Littleton effected just such a convergence-divergence for the law of property. Coke did not only update Littleton, he made Littleton's terse sections the foundation for all subsequent property law. There was no need to go behind Coke. Littleton was to be found there, a kind of groom to Coke. One result, and an immediate one, was an almost instantaneous stopping of lawyers' recourse to the Year Books. There was no need to extract law from the Year Books; Lord Coke had done it. Judge Littleton was there to bear witness to the completeness of Coke's compilation, and Coke's Latin maxims with their ring of authenticity not only lent credence to the effort but supplied the point in a short, sharp sentence of a few elegant Latin words. Perhaps it never occurred to lawyers to question how there could have been so much Latinity in the "book-law" of medieval England written in Law-French. It didn't matter. Even if the spuriousness was perceived, the maxims were a pithy summation of the law. Even today, in a popular handbook of maxims for lawyers, of the eleven hundred maxims given, just half are directly ascribed to Coke's works.[28]

Coke was quite prepared not only to make up maxims, but also to shape the doctrine to fit them. While Professor Samuel Thorne provided the rule of thumb by which we can detect when Coke was up to creating law out of whole cloth,[29] he also pointed out that such new departures were small and often very technical. It should also be observed that Coke probably believed that in lost cases he was not creating law but merely enunciating law already in existence, though it had been hidden or had previously wanted explicit evidence to establish it. The process was for Coke a matter of discovery, or at least recovery, not of fabrication.

What Coke did for property law in the *First Institutes* he undertook to do for other branches in the succeeding three which he managed to complete but understandably, because of their political sensitivity, did not publish in his lifetime. None of the latter three *Institutes* attained the bulk, comprehensiveness, or profundity of *Coke upon Littleton*. The *Second Institutes*, on Magna Carta and the statutes, was polemically inspired, and its unevenness of treatment from one statute to another was dictated less by the importance of the statute to the law than to the contemporary political concerns of Coke's later years. The *Third Institutes*, on the criminal law, suffered severely from the author's past-mindedness and his tendency to concentrate on treason and felony to the diminution of the growing (in number and importance) misdemeanors which were adjusting criminal law to the repression of more sophisticated crime in a more complex society. The *Fourth Institutes* was the best ordered and the most evenly executed of the *Institutes*, demonstrating powers of organization and sustained argumentation that eluded Coke in everything else he wrote (with the notable exception of *The Complete Copyholder*, a posthumously published treatise on customary estates). Because the *Fourth Institutes* was descriptive of the courts of his day, it had a much shorter useful life than the three other *Institutes*. It was also the most politically controversial, since it bore down heavily and caustically on the ecclesiastical and non-common law courts.

The *Reports* had extraordinary contemporary impact. They appeared to contain all the requisite case-law from 1572 (when Coke entered the Inner Temple) to 1616 (when he was removed from the King's Bench). They were, in fact a monument to Coke's career and in critical points in important cases often represented what he thought the law to be than what the court had declared it was. That the case reports were often rambling and sometimes so opaque as to be virtually incomprehensible mattered less than the fact that they bore the stamp of authenticity of Coke's reputation and his authoritative assertion. They were ampler than either Dyer's or Plowden's reports, though lacking in the systematic method Plowden employed in his *Commentaries*. They generally set out the pleadings, a necessary pedagogical device since Coke put great emphasis on a student learning sound pleading. More often than not, especially in the earlier cases, Coke was at pains to advance general propositions of law, emphasizing the substantive matter of the case and providing analysis of it. In part the *Reports* became the model for all subsequent reporting. They were probably the most frequently cited and most often argued-over reports the common law has known. Their "authority" was not seriously questioned until well into the nineteenth century, and even then the courts found it both difficult and inconvenient to deny their credibility. While uncritical admiration for them disappeared, they remained part of every learned lawyer's armory of argument until this century.

If Coke remained the legal oracle in his own country by virtue of the *Reports* and the *Institutes*, especially *Coke upon Littleton*, he became the founding father of the common law in England's American colonies. On November 11, 1647, the General Court of the Massachusetts Bay Colony ordered that "to the end we may have the better light for making & proceedings about lawes, that there shal be . . . procured for the use of the Courte from time to time" two copies each of Coke's *First* and *Second Institutes*, Coke's

Reports, and Coke's *Book of Entries* (as well as Michael Dalton's *The Countrey Justice* and John Rastell's *Les Termes de la Ley*).[30] For over a century thereafter, generations of fledgling lawyers in all the colonies wrestled with *Coke upon Littleton* to learn the land law, resonated to Coke's encomium of Magna Carta in the *Second Institutes*, and sacked the *Reports* for all the case-law they could find. Thomas Jefferson, studying the law under George Wythe in Virginia in the 1760's, took more readily to the *Institutes* than might have been expected of one of his fastidious reading habits. Coke's history was a curative against David Hume's *History of England* and its Tory revisionism of the Whig Triumph, and we can guess that Jefferson's detestation of Hume commended Coke to him all the more. John Adams found it difficult to conduct a case in Boston without some reference to Coke. In 1774 when Adams, under the pseudonym "*Novanglus*," asserted that Parliament had no authority over the colonies and that each was a separate realm under the King with its own independent legislature, he started from Coke's *Institutes*. His fellow Bostonian, James Otis, in arguing against writs of assistance, raised his whole case on Coke's perverse assertion in *Bonham's Case* that the courts would control acts of Parliament, even to the extent of voiding them.[31] Yet it fell to a non-lawyer, a single-minded foe of British rule over the colonies, a Harvard-trained rabble-rouser, Sam Adams, to recruit the ghostly oracle to the Patriot cause: "whether Lord Coke has expressed it or not . . . an act of parliament made against Magna Charta in violation of its essential parts, is void."[32]

Of such boundless assertions and fungible authorities are revolutions made. Do not examine too closely the extent to which Sir Edward Coke fell in behind Citizen Sam. Scores of others of our Founding Fathers had no doubt which side Lord Coke was on, and none questioned the magnitude of the aid he gave them.

CHAPTER NINE

Michael Dalton

Some years ago, Sir Nikolaus Pevsner, a noted British art historian, began a short history of European architecture with the categorical assertion:

> A bicycle shed is a building; Lincoln Cathedral is a piece of architecture. Nearly everything that encloses space on a scale sufficient for a human being to move in is a building; the term architecture applies only to buildings designed with a view to aesthetic appeal.[1]

The distinction is a sound one, and at a remove applicable to legal literature, in which many landmarks have been built on architectonic lines. William Blackstone in his *Commentaries on the Laws of England* likened the common law to "an old Gothic castle," while the work itself achieves the symmetry and proportionality based on mathematical modularities characteristic of the simple harmoniousness of eighteenth-century Classicism. Nothing less could be expected of the All Souls don who wrote a short treatise entitled *Elements of Architecture*.[2] There can be no doubt that Edward Coke's *First Institutes*, "Coke upon Littleton," was a Jacobean capital messuage, for here indeed was a veritable eclectic pile, neither mediaeval nor Renaissance but pure Mannerism!

Michael Dalton's *The Countrey Justice* does not present, or claim to present, aesthetic appeal. Here is our bicycle shed—and hardly more than that, notwithstanding the title page's classical (and conventional) decorative chaos of obelisks, strapwork, columns, fruit garlands and grapevines, lion's head, crown, Tudor rose, and two putti. This purse remains a pig's ear. The work is a functional vessel, useful without any claim to beauty, about as stimulating to read as a computer guidebook, wanting in any literary embellishment beyond the Epistle Dedicatory and the Epistle to the Benchers of Lincoln's Inn. Nonetheless, *The Countrey Justice* was a best-seller, maintaining its popularity for almost a century and a half. First published in 1618, it went to six more printings by 1635, eight printings between 1643 and 1697, and was frequently reprinted until 1742, being superseded only by Richard Burn's *The Office of Justice of the Peace and Parish Officer* (1755).[3] Old editions of Dalton did not lose their currency: the present author's copy has on a flyleaf a name struck out and a barely legible note, "Jasper Barker [?] his book, anno 1699," indicating that it was still in use almost a half century after its publication and the appearance of six newer editions.[4]

Being a best-seller does not guarantee the status of classic absent some other quality. If it is difficult, given *The Countrey Justice*'s intrinsic demerits, to assert its status as a classic work of legal literature, the book's extrinsic merits more than make the case. First, *The Countrey Justice* provides the most comprehensive and readily obtainable introduction to seventeenth-century English criminal law, both at common law and by statute, available. Second, it opens for the discerning reader a singular institution without parallel elsewhere—lay magistracy—at a critical juncture in its history with long-lasting results for the common law's understanding of justice and the rule of law and for Anglo-American constitutionalism. Third and finally, in substance and in form *The Countrey Justice* proved to have at least modest influence on the early development of the law in the New World, making it one of a handful of English legal works with direct applicability to early American colonial law.

Michael Dalton was Cambridgeshire born and bred. His birthdate is unknown. Since he matriculated at Cambridge as a commoner of Trinity College in 1580, he was probably born about 1565. He died in 1644, by contemporary standards a very old man indeed. Of a gentry family seated at Hildersham nine miles southeast of Cambridge, Michael, the eldest son and heir of Thomas Dalton, gent., and Eleanor Jellebrand, was admitted to Lincoln's Inn in 1581 via Furnival's Inn. Called to the bar in 1589, he was an active participant in the life of Lincoln's Inn, sitting on a committee to appoint a new preacher in 1594, encouraging his younger brother Philip to enter the Inn (1586, called 1594), and in due course securing the admission there of three sons and a grandson. As an "old possessor," he had chambers with Thomas Parmenter on the second story of New Building, being assessed £25 for repairs and alterations in 1609.[5] Dalton was the nephew of Thomas Spencer, a bencher of Lincoln's Inn (his patronage is prayed in the Epistle to the Benchers of Lincoln's Inn) whose arms can still be seen in the west window of the inn's chapel.

Unlike Spencer, Dalton does not appear to have been a well-practiced barrister. In the Epistle, he declares,

> I confesse my self a long, yet an unprofitable member of your honourable Society, but seeing that my calling is to a Countrey life, and considering that he which is of the meanest condition, and that hath the smallest talent, may not (without just reprehension) retire himself so to his private pleasure, or profit, as that he should neglect to shew some fruit and token of his love to his Countrey . . . .

Allowing for the self-deprecation conventional to this genre, there is some circumstantial evidence to indicate that the author was in fact "unprofitable" so far as practice was concerned. He is not to be found among some twelve hundred barristers who, between 1603 and 1625, signed pleadings in Star Chamber. Such involvement is a relatively good indication of the nature and the extent of a barrister's practice. The vast majority of counsel signing Star Chamber pleadings did so fewer than a half-dozen times, usually for clients from the county in which the barrister also resided. Not to have signed any at all is a rare phenomenon.[6]

Equally revealing is the fact that Dalton, "an ancient Utter Barrister," was called an associate to the bench of Lincoln's Inn in 1622, paying £20 before taking his place and £20 to the chapel.[7] Benchers of an inn were those successful barristers at the height of their careers who governed the inn, in an increasingly autocratic way. Associates to the bench, as distinct from benchers proper, were barristers holding senior clerical or quasi-judicial offices in the courts. This fit Dalton. At least as early as 1632, Dalton was one of the dozen Masters of Chancery, the subsidiary judges of the equity court of Chancery and active referees and masters in the entire range of Chancery practice. He probably had the office even earlier, and before that perhaps an appointment as a Master of Chancery extraordinary, which by the end of the sixteenth century was a recognized path to a regular mastership and would have qualified him for associate to the bench of Lincoln's Inn.[8]

In any case, Dalton should be taken at his word, that his "calling was to a Countrey life." He settled in a comfortable house in West Wratting, four miles east of his birthplace, close by his younger brothers (the family was remarkably nucleated even for that time), in Chilford Hundred. In 1609, he was assessed £20 annual value in lands, which made him a substantial squire aside from any other income from profession or office.[9] From West Wratting he served alma mater in a role appropriate to a country lawyer: he was deputy-steward of Cambridge University by 1604, presiding at its courts baron and handling some of its legal matters.[10] Early in James's reign he was in the commission of the peace for Cambridgeshire, in 1608 ranking second from the bottom among the mere Esquire justices of the peace.[11] By 1621, he was "of the quorum" (a JP of the quorum was usually necessary when more than a single JP acted), a status readily accorded a barrister and probably conferred upon him much earlier.[12] He was doubtless still in the commission for Cambridgeshire at his death in 1644, though the last extant list is almost a decade earlier.[13] He served four decades as a justice of the peace.

Dalton apparently managed to avoid other county offices appropriate to his rank. He was, perhaps, somewhat too august to have been the Exchequer's chief investigative officer in the county, the escheator. He never undertook the laborious task of serving as sheriff. This is curious, since Dalton was also the author of the only handbook relating to that office, *Officium Vicecomitum: The Office and Authoritie of Sherifs*.[14] He was never a Member of Parliament, though a substantial squire of his rank (and learning) in a shire within one hundred miles of Westminster might well have been drawn to seek a seat in the tumultuous parliaments of the 1620's and the Long Parliament that in 1640 ended the eleven-years' Personal Rule of Charles I and went on to make a revolution and breathe its death rattle only in restoring Charles II in 1660.

Had Dalton served in these parliaments, where the issues between the King and his ministers on the one hand and the Commons on the other were defined in increasingly narrow and uncompromising terms both political and religious, his position would have been clear enough. His loyalty to the institutions of the common law under God and the King was unquestionable: *The Countrey Justice* makes that evident. In his religious sentiments his dutifulness was more ambivalent. In 1642, he wrote—but did not publish—a cranky, detailed chronology of the Roman Catholic Church entitled, "A Breviary of the Roman or Western Church and Empire, Containing the Decay of True Religion and the Rise of the Papacy."[15]

Beginning with Christ and ending with Luther, he unfolded the sorry tale of the full and final manifestation of "anti-Christ" in the sixteenth-century papacy in more than two hundred pages of mostly obscure facts (real and supposed) and vitriolic interpretations. Dalton was clearly an advanced Puritan of the sort that in his generation Cambridge University produced and Lincoln's Inn nurtured (William Prynne and Henry Sherfield being the prime examples of the visible saints of Lincoln's Inn). Dalton also shared the widespread distaste for the Court of High Commission for Causes Ecclesiastical, which was increasingly calumniated as nothing but the tool of the oppressive Archbishop William Laud. Dalton had particular cause to dislike the High Commission, although the fact that he suffered at its hands had nothing to do with religious heterodoxy. In 1631, Dalton and his brother-in-law, Sir Giles Allington, were censured in High Commission for having connived at the marriage of Dalton's daughter, Dorothy, to Allington, who was her mother's half-brother, hence her uncle. All the parties were Cambridgeshire gentry, and if they did not scruple at keeping the union not only in the county but also in the family, canon law clearly did, such being well within the forbidden degrees of kinship and affinity. Dalton's penal mulct of £2000 was, however, later remitted.[16] His morals aside, given Dalton's position on religion and given the political environment of Cambridgeshire, we can safely assume that Dalton at least favored the Parliamentarian side in the great rebellion. His grandson and namesake, Michael, served as a Parliamentarian commissioner for the sequestration of Royalists' lands in Cambridgeshire, and, under the revolutionary regimes of the 1650's served as a JP for the county.[17]

The Countrey Justice bears the indelible traces of Michael Dalton's bucolic preference. In the Epistle, in referring to "his love to his Countrey," and to "seeing some others amongst you, whose fortunes prove (as mine doth) to withdraw themselves into their Countreys," Dalton uses the term in its common contemporary sense of "county." The vast majority of examples of instruments that he offered as precedents are taken from Cambridgeshire justices' records, and many of those from Dalton's own commonplace book. A good example is the precept to the sheriff (in the nature of a venire facias) to return a jury for trial of offenses which by statute two or more justices could hear and determine out of quarter sessions: the precept is Dalton's own, tested before him at West Wratting.[18] There are more than twoscore explicit references to judges of assize at Cambridge assizes—their jury charges, directions, opinions, and cases between the years 1605 and 1633. In every instance but one, Dalton spoke from his own knowledge, having clearly been present at the assizes. In the case of the exception, he reported, "as I have heard," the advice given to a coroner at the Bury St. Edmunds assizes by Chief Justice Coke.[19] Cambridge was a shire town on the Norfolk Circuit, the most desirable of the six assize circuits, and since the choice of circuit was by precedence based on rank and seniority among the twelve judges of the three common-law courts, invariably one of the two circuit judges was a chief justice and the other a senior puisne judge. Consequently, Dalton had the opportunity to hear the law construed by six Chief Justices—John Popham, Edward Coke, Henry Mountagu, James

Ley, Ranulf Crewe, and Nicholas Hyde—as well as old hands like Justices Peter Warburton, John Doddridge, and Francis Harvy. Dalton likely knew little of what happened on other circuits in an age when reporting rarely took account of assize cases, but, when tolled by Dalton, these judges' pronouncements carried great weight and resonated well beyond Dalton's own "countrey."

Moreover, Dalton enjoyed a certain intimacy with the judges. On the question of whether JPs could suppress excessive numbers of alehouses, following an assizes at Cambridge (probably in 1621), "Sir James Ley told me after at his lodging in Trinity Colledge that this was the opinion of all the other Judges upon late conference had among themselves."[20] Dalton was not timid about alluding to his own magistratical experiences, whether demonstrated by an unusually weighty supplicavit from Chancery to himself and other JPs;[21] his initiative, later approved of by the judges of assize, in binding to good behavior one who fed grain mixed with rat poison to his neighbors' chickens;[22] or his agreement with "worshipfull and grave matrons" that, despite "received opinion," a mother could deliver a stillborn child without help, thus making nonsense of the presumption that a dead newborn of a woman unattended at birth must have been born live and murdered.[23] Some experiences had been fraught with peril: a warrant of arrest from the Lord Chancellor that did not give the cause or grounds for the arrest raised the possibility of an action against the JP.[24] In any case, *The Countrey Justice* so well captures the presiding deities of its author's locale that it might well be entitled *The Cambridgeshire Countrey Justice.*

That provincialism would not explain the book's popularity. Neither would its uniqueness. It was the fourth handbook on the role and practice of the justice of the peace to appear since the advent of printing. The first handbook had been the *Boke of Iustices of Peas, The Charge with All the Processe of the Cessions*, which was directed more at the clerk of the peace, the officer responsible to the justices of the peace at their general quarter sessions, than to the JP. The demand for such a text is clear: first published by that early and enterprising legal printer Richard Pynson in 1506, this book was printed twenty-nine times, for the last time in 1574.[25] The second handbook was a version of the first, pirated by Anthony Fitzherbert, under the title *Loffice et Auctoryte des Justyces* (later as *The Newe Boke of Iustices of the Peas*), which also had a long run in the sixteenth century.[26] The third handbook was a far more serious and even scholarly undertaking by a notable Elizabethan lawyer and antiquarian, William Lambarde, a Master of Chancery. *Eirenarcha: Or the Office of the Justices of Peace* went to thirteen editions between 1581 and 1619.[27] Lambarde was a learned man of great curiosity, a skilled researcher of expansive grasp, always reluctant to abandon a subject until he had fully fathomed it and even more fully explained it. With such assiduity and thoroughness went verbosity and pedantry. With Lambarde the well-turned phrase often became the purple passage, and while that made *Eirenarcha* good reading, it also made the book hard to use. The handbook's size and type—it was a small octavo in dense black-letter—and arbitrary arrangement of topics did not help the reader. It was strongest on the collective role of JPs in quarter sessions, somewhat neglectful of the work done of an individual JP or a handful of JPs out of sessions. It is not accidental that the last edition of *Eirenarcha* appeared the year after the first edition of *The Countrey Justice*. Between the two, there was no contest.

Format alone would commend *The Countrey Justice*. A small folio with good margins, Roman type for English and distinctive Italic for other languages, it was arranged into relatively short chapters containing clear subject matter, divided into succinct paragraphs of a few concise sentences each. Its overall arrangement was by alphabetical title, the fundamental taxonomy of the age, to be found in the ubiquitous commonplace book that literate and literarily inclined persons kept for purposes of record, reference, and recall. Alehouses to Affray to Armour to Barrator to Bastardy . . . This begs logical arrangement, but it did allow quick recapture of a particular subject without any other index or finding guide. It corresponded to the realities that an individual JP would confront, faced in his manor house's "room of office" (which was in way of being called his "courtroom") by a constable with a miscreant in tow. Whether the latter was an alehousekeeper, an "Egyptian" (gypsy), a felon, a laborer, a pauper, or a rogue, the party was clearly someone fitting into a recognized category in Dalton. Most important of all, Dalton was always explicit about what things a single JP might do, what things required more than one JP, what things were to be left to the justices of the peace in quarter sessions, and what things must be sent to the judges of assize. These distinctions took on a new urgency by the end of the sixteenth century, the result of a rapid increase in the duties, responsibilities, and powers of justices of the peace by legislation, ordinance, and direction, matched by heightened surveillance and accountability.

Lambarde first detected the shift, having felt its weight as a Kent JP in the 1580's. He remarked plaintively: "Then, how many Justices, (thinke you) may now suffice (without breaking their backs) to beare so many, not loads, but stacks of statutes, that have since . . . [Henry VII's] time bene laid upon them?"[28] Dalton, no less than Lambarde, grasped the significance of the work, and he realized as well that the shift worked by Tudor statutes put power and discretion in the hands of JPs out of sessions:

> The Commission of the Peace in it self doth leave little (or nothing) to the discretion of the Justices of Peace; but doth limit them to proceed *secundum Leges, Consuetudines, Ordinationes & Statuta* [according to the laws, customs, ordinances, and statutes] . . . . But by some late Statutes, some things are (therein by speciall words) referred to the discretion of the Justices of Peace; some out of Sessions, and some at their Sessions.[29]

Dalton goes on to list particularly those areas in which they were to exercise discretion outside quarter sessions. The magistrates' increased discretion was the corollary of the profound change taking place in their role and function. It was less discretion in judicial matters than in administrative affairs. They had, in the course of the sixteenth century, been transformed from judges into the principal county administrators:

> Even at the beginning of Elizabeth's reign, the justices were still basically judicial officers. By the time of the Queen's death [1603] there could be no mistaking the fact that they had become administrators as well.[30]

The weight of administration fell upon them out of sessions, on the individual JP or group of two or three JPs. The two final statutes of the Tudor "stack"—the Poor Laws of 1598 and 1601—were the heaviest of all. In the four decades following their promulgation, these two statutes, the second building upon and advancing the first, radically changed the nature of magistracy.

Those four decades were precisely the ones during which Michael Dalton exercised his "calling" as a country justice. The first edition of his handbook, 1618, was both somewhat simpler and shorter than later versions, reflecting merely the beginning of a current that would become a tidal wave. In the last edition prepared by Dalton himself, that of 1635, the tidal wave is evident, especially in those chapters dealing with alehouses, bastardy, bridges, cloth manufacturing, highways, laborers, maltsters, the poor, rogues, stock of the shire, and weights and measures. Beginning in the later 1620's and continuing through the 1630's until rebellion and revolution overtook all institutions of Stuart England, Charles I's Privy Council dictated vastly increased activity at the local level to deal with dearth and poverty and public order. This was the manifestation of "strict and strait" governance, the intention of King and Church to rule with a reforming vigor. Much of this program was promulgated in the *Book of Orders*, published in 1630 and distributed to all the justices of the peace in England and Wales;

Dalton refers to it explicitly.[31] The Book of Orders and various cognate demands fell upon the justices of the peace as a continuous responsibility, essentially a weekly round of duties, and resulted in "petty sessions," the regular activity of two or more JPs meeting within their local division. This was no longer merely "out of sessions" work; it was a recognized gathering to implement the Council's directives and to do such other business, administrative and judicial, as was required of two or more JPs. Petty sessions, becoming fundamental to magistracy's routine administration of local government, survived the Interregnum to become an established institution of government and judicature after 1660.

With added powers and responsibilities came vastly increased oversight. The ultimate and final overseer was the King and his council of ministers. The Privy Council of Dalton's era was a remarkable body. It was trim and muscular, well-organized, and served by a very small but effective professional bureaucracy. It aspired to something approaching omnipotence and almost achieved omniscience. Very little that happened anywhere in the realm escaped its attention, and it moved swiftly and ruthlessly to deal with situations that posed the slightest threat of disorder. The Litany of the Book of Common Prayer, by which the English perforce worshiped in the state Church, struck the right prudential, perhaps even slightly hysterical, note: "From all sedition, privy conspiracy, and rebellion; from all false doctrine, heresy, and schism; from hardness of heart, and contempt of thy Word and Commandment, *Good Lord, deliver us.*"

The Privy Council's concern was particularly the first triad of evils. High Commission could take care of the rest. For both intelligence concerning and the execution of its orders, the Council had to rely upon the loyalty, assiduity, and discrimination of the JPs. There was no other primary agency on the ground to serve as the eyes, ears, arm and hand of the Council than those unpaid and increasingly overworked country squires.

The Privy Council frequently summoned JPs to appear before it, explain themselves, and stand such correction and punishment for malfeasance and misfeasance as the Council thought fit. That was a cumbersome and time-consuming method of surveillance. Coevally with the "stacks" of Tudor statutes there developed a more immediate mechanism for overseeing the justices' work: the assizes. Dalton's Chapter 120, "Certain Advices to the Justices of Peace," soundly and prudently admonishes them as to their comportment, both as matters of simple justice (a party "cannot be a Judge indifferent," etc.) and because statutes provided specific penalties for failure to do right.[32] Further to these, "there are certain other things principally tending to the publike good, and lately commended from His Majesty, (by the Judges of Assise) to the care of the justices of peace"; and Dalton sets down ten articles to that effect.[33] These are arresting, both substantively and adjectively. Substantively because they were precisely those matters of stricter governance to which Charles and his Council gave extraordinary prominence in the 1630's; adjectively, because the agency for both direction and oversight was the judges of assize. The judges were the link between the Privy Council and the local magistrates. Dalton drives home the importance of the judges in a concluding paragraph, part Latin, part law French, quoting from a Year Book of 1484: while justices who acted in ignorance of the record or for want of knowledge would not be punished, or punished for things done in a judicial way, "the justices of assize are able to hear and punish the defaults of justices of the peace, to wit, for their contempts, omissions, negligences, favours, affections, corruptions, and other defaults whatever."[34] That gave a wide discretion to the judges of assize, and one that the judges freely exercised in Dalton's time. Little wonder that Dalton found it advisable to cite repeatedly what the judges said at Cambridge assizes. Or that he devoted seven pages to "Resolutions of the Judges of Assises, 1633," on thirty-eight critical questions arising out of ambiguities surrounding the Poor Laws of 1598 and 1601.[35]

From 1596 until the rebellion of the 1640's, the judges of assize, before departing on their semiannual circuits, received instructions as to what they were to move the JPs to do. The government's agenda was presented in the form of a solemn charge given to the judges (and to such JPs as happened to be in the metropolis and would attend) in the Star Chamber. This was usually the task of the Lord Chancellor acting for the King and Council. Twice, significantly, the charge was undertaken by another. Before the summer in assizes 1616, James I himself gave the charge in a notably abrasive speech intended to bring to heel the judges of the three great common-law courts—who were also the judges of assize—for unrest that they had manifested in the court of Star Chamber and elsewhere at the instigation of the Chief Justice of the Common Pleas, Sir Edward Coke.[36] It was an admonition Coke did not heed, and five months later he was sacked. Before the Lent assizes in 1628, the charge was given by Bishop William Laud, a charge full of episcopal (though not divine) exhortation directed against the Puritans, serving to spotlight a new power in Church and state.[37]

As the JPs were reprehended by the judges of assize, so the latter were accountable to the Privy Council. Sometimes it was in a very direct way, and especially after William Laud rose to prominence in Charles I's counsels and used both ecclesiastical and civil power to harass Puritan believers. In 1633, Sir Thomas Richardson, Chief Justice of the King's Bench, when sitting as a judge of assize on the Western Circuit, lent himself to the opposition of more than half the Somerset justices of the peace to disorderly parish fêtes—much detested by Puritans—despite regal and ecclesiastical approval of the fêtes. The Chief Justice was swiftly brought before the Privy Council, so roughly handled by Bishop Laud that he wept, and was assigned to the least desirable circuit for the rest of his short career on the bench.[38]

To emphasize the administrative labors of JPs in fulfilling the exigencies of Tudor monarchy and Stuart strict and strait governance should not obscure the marked increase of activity in the magistrates' traditional judicial role. Overall, Tudor legislation increased the number of crimes prosecutable, either by creating new offenses or redefining common-law offenses. Some were statutory felony (buggery and Roman Catholic subversion), but many more were misdemeanor (perjury, forgery, various forms of unlawful force, fraud). Dalton devotes to "Felonies by Statute" every page of his very long Chapter 106, indicating those statutory felonies that the JPs could hear and determine in quarter sessions, as well as those that they could not.[39] Statutory misdemeanors were often triable by two or more justices out of sessions. Driving the machinery of justice, even at the justice's humble level, was the rapid development of the criminal common law by the superior courts. First and foremost of these was the High Court of Star Chamber, which by the time of its abolition in 1641 had fashioned a remarkably well-structured and quite sophisticated body of misdemeanors of the sort that today we would call white collar crimes. The most astute contemporary commentator on the criminal law, Ferdinando Pulton, devoted the first nine of a total of sixteen chapters in his treatise to misdemeanor, and the remaining seven to treason and felony. He argued that the king's peace was less threatened by the old rough-and-tumble violent felonies than by the new and more sophisticated misdemeanors of covin and oppression.[40]

These new crimes were readily absorbed by the common-law courts, particularly the King's Bench and the assizes. A miscreant convicted at assizes in 1639 for criminal libel by tokens (a lamb's skin with sheep horns) set over a cuckold's door was punishable there exactly as he would have been in Star Chamber, where the offense itself was created and developed.[41] This creative urge was felt and given effect even by the JPs. Though there were no statutory or common-law offenses of the sort that waited for criminalization until the later nineteenth century's Offences Against the Persons Act—gross indecency, indecent assault, etc.—quarter sessions indicted and tried perpetrators of such acts for simple assault but with enough aggravating circumstances to make the penalty very harsh. "Countrey justices," within limits, could play as well at quarter sessions as Privy Councillors did in Star Chamber in extending the law to newly appreciated depredations and newfound delicts.

The criminal law activity that weighed most heavily on the single JP out of sessions was enjoined by two acts of Mary Tudor in the mid-sixteenth century. By those acts a JP was required to examine a suspected felon brought before him by a peace officer and to depose on oath the accusers and witnesses against, write down what was said, and either commit the suspect to gaol or bind him over to the next assizes or quarter sessions for indictment and trial. (The accusers and witnesses were also bound over to testify.) While the suspect was not questioned on oath, this was likely to be the best chance he had to put his case clearly, and often the justice's examination was lengthy. Depositions always were. The process was extremely time consuming, it occurred fitfully and often most inconveniently, and it required the examining JP to come to a prima facie conclusion, no matter how tentative, as to the facts of the case. Either at assizes or quarter sessions, the JP would have a hand in drawing the indictment and might speak at trial of his own knowledge. And inevitably, though the statutes enjoined this elaborate pre-indictment procedure only for felony, because that crime might not always be distinguishable at first blush, JPs applied the same procedure to crimes that appeared to be only misdemeanors. In Chapters 111–113, Dalton goes into this procedure at great length and provides a profile of a felon to guide the JP in his examination, showing a subtlety that would have made John Henry Wigmore proud.[42]

It is because of this pre-indictment activity that *The Countrey Justice* provides such a useful and compendious overview of contemporary criminal law, from high treason to the pettiest misdemeanors. Pulton's *De Pacis Regis et Regni* is both rare and difficult to use; despite its simple arrangement, it is very full, verbose, and in places plainly opaque. Sir Edward Coke's *Third Institutes*, devoted to the criminal law, is as intractable in both taxonomy and prose as anything Coke wrote. Sir James Fitzjames Stephen damned it by faint praise; it was "less ill-arranged" than Coke upon Littleton, he remarked, and then added, "for each offence is put in a chapter by itself, but where any arrangement is wanted it is very bad."[43] In Dalton the twentieth-century reader can come to a working command of the substantive criminal law of the seventeenth century with the least possible difficulty and with real confidence in its accuracy.

Most significantly, *The Countrey Justice* reveals in stark outline how heavily late Tudor and early Stuart government weighed upon the justices of the peace. It reveals their vulnerability to the scrutiny, suasions, and strictures of the protomodern state, with all of its ambitions and absolutes, sure in its power and assured in its authority that it could do almost anything. For the absolutist polity of early modern kingship in Tudor and Stuart England was no less a reality than it was in France or elsewhere on the Continent. It was simply not as absolute in its results. Though more highly centralized than the French Bourbons were ever able to achieve, the English state lacked the legal and institutional dependency on the solo-monarch that *ancien régime* France managed. English absolutists never established an adequate system of prosecution, as the Valois-Bourbon kings achieved by attaching a royal procurator to each court; nor did English monarchs possess an effectual, reliable, and obedient police force like the Valois-Bourbon gendarmerie. The Tudors and Stuarts were unable to fashion a judicial hierarchy with a system of appeals and reviews that ultimately concentrated all juridical force in councillors intimately beholden to the monarch; Star Chamber was different in kind and in degree from the *Conseil Privé* in France, which was able to subvert the ancient sovereign courts of the French provinces and control their noble judiciary. No Tudor or Stuart monarch could pluck out of the university the Roman law, with all of its imperial resonance and reverence for the purple and the ermine. and make it the law of the land, as French kings did from the fifteenth century onward. Finally, Tudor-Stuart monarchy never managed to put to sleep the ancient institution of medieval mixed monarchy, the "estates" of clergy, nobility, and commonalty. While the personal rule of French monarchs began in 1614, when Louis XIII dismissed the Estates-General, and lasted until 1789, when until Louis XVI facing rebellion was forced to summon it again, Charles I's Personal Rule survived only the eleven years from 1629 to 1640 and ended emphatically with the Long Parliament that would finally destroy him and make England a republic for a long and nasty season.

Whatever the inclination of English monarchs for absolutism on the continental model, their failure to reduce their nation's political and legal institutions to dependence and craven obedience was due to the vigorous common law and vigorous common-law judges. In the common law all of the old strengths survived unimpaired: Magna Carta (thrice cited by Dalton), the juries of indictment and trial, the reduced scope for wholesale legislative reform, the inescapable fact that the King alone could not legislate because the power to make new law lay only in the King-in-Parliament. In the case of the judges, though the early Stuart judiciary would be roughly treated and in some cases judges would be sacked for reasons unclear even to them and nearly irretrievable historically, the judiciary was never subverted.[44] The judiciary even survived the revolutionary republican regime that proved a greater threat to its probity and independence than "Charles Stuart, tyrant" had ever been. The seventeenth-century reader who on page 500 of the author's copy of *The Countrey Justice* contemptuously restyled Oliver Cromwell, Lord Protector, "ould rednosed Noll that Grand Tirant," knew what he was talking about.

And then there were also the vigorous justices of the peace. They played a special role. They were never wholly dependent upon the king. They were substantial country gentlemen of landed worth, and they had a natural claim to the leadership of their communities and the direction of their neighbors. The king's commission gave them powers to be used to lawful ends, albeit not entirely without some personal advantage. But it did not make them powerful. Their power relied ultimately on their inherent social status and capacity to command their countrymen. They received no financial reward for their labors; the office was one of expense, not profit. If the justices lost office, they did not lose everything.

If, however, the king lost the justices, he could not govern. If he lost their allegiance, not only could he not govern, but they might become a formidable enemy. The 1630's, during the Personal Rule of Charles I and the almost frenetic activity to which the JPs and other local officials were then called, was the period in which the King not only began to lose the support and affection of those local governors, but he also stood to lose their allegiance. Of the 547 men who served as Members of the House of Commons in the Long Parliament before Pride's Purge in 1648, more than two-thirds had served as local governors, most of these as JPs, in the 1630's. They had had a grandstand view of the Personal Rule. They knew how disastrously most of its policies had failed, despite their best efforts and the enormous pressure that Charles and his councillors had put them upon. As the Long Parliament got down to business on November 4, 1640, to dismantle the Personal Rule—successfully, since almost everything attempted by the king had been undone by the summer of 1641—it was these local governors who knew just how wrong everything had gone. Their bitterness was an ill omen for Archbishop William Laud and Thomas Wentworth Earl of Strafford, the king's two great councillors, both of whom would perish on the block on Tower Hill at the hands of the Long Parliament. Worse, in the bitterness of those ancient local governors, or at least in their newfound neglectfulness and growing undutifulness toward King Charles, there was an even chillier omen, as raw as the January day in 1649 when Charles lost his head at Whitehall.

On such a note one does not leave Michael Dalton or any other mere "country justice" in his old age. Indeed, there is something verdant about Dalton. He can still excite anyone aware of how much our legal tradition owes to lay judges, to one facet of that "trial by peers" that we celebrate unceasingly in Magna Carta. The author confesses that in leafing back through Dalton to write this essay, he embarked upon the recall of *souvenirs du temps perdu*, not so much a sentimental journey as a reinvigorated sense of what the common law means by the rule of law. The author bought his copy of Dalton for five guineas at a London bookshop in 1952 as he set out to learn all there was to learn about justices of the peace and other local governors in a certain county in the West of England. This was to fulfill the University of Oxford's statutory requirement that a D.Phil. thesis be an original contribution to knowledge in fit form for publication. No one reckons in guineas anymore, and the statutory requirement seems to be honored nowadays much in the breach. Dalton's usefulness, though, has not diminished a whit. It remains amazing how much can be learned about the law in Dalton, and how little devoted research of the last five decades has changed the detailed picture retrievable from *The Countrey Justice*.

One also hymns the country justices' longevity. In the last half-century, a succession of British governments (mostly Tory, as distinct from anything rationally called conservative) have changed the face of English institutions. The ancient counties, that had existed virtually unchanged from Anglo-Saxon days, were rearranged, one disappearing entirely, others hacked out of all recognition (the county in the West losing its top third to become something called Avon); pounds, shillings and pence went, replaced by a decimal currency; the old line regiments of the British army were amalgamated or stood down; etcetera, etcetera. Some of the largest changes have been in legal institutions. By the Courts Act of 1971, the court of quarter sessions was abolished, its extensive jurisdiction (as that of assizes, also abolished) being assumed by a new Crown Court, with about seventy centers covering England and Wales, which became the superior criminal court at first instance. But petty sessions is with us yet, in the magistrates' court, with three JPs, still unpaid laymen and laywomen, exercising substantially the same judicial powers that they have had since local administration was removed from their hands in the 1880's. They have lately acquired a sizable family civil-law jurisdiction involving children, and their juvenile court has become the youth court for purely criminal matters. There are some

30,000 lay magistrates manning 400 petty sessions with the same powers as about 200 stipendiary magistrates (who are paid lawyers), the latter in larger urban centers. Magistrates' courts handle more than ninety percent of all criminal cases from start to finish and have a significant civil jurisdiction. The number of jury trials before the Crown Court are much reduced by allowing a wide range of less serious offenses to be tried before the magistrates without a jury. The magistrates, "especially lay magistrates, are the unsung heroes of the English legal system," according to a close student of English criminal law.[45] That high compliment echoes still from Michael Dalton's day.

The Countrey Justice, like Madeira, traveled well. On November 11, 1647, the General Court of Massachusetts ordered that two copies of six legal works (including Coke upon Littleton and Coke's *Second Institutes*, on Magna Carta and the statutes) were to be purchased for its use. One of those works was *The Countrey Justice*. Significantly, and perhaps not coincidentally, that same sitting of the General Court ordered *The Laws and Liberties of Massachusetts* to be prepared for the press. *The Laws and Liberties* is arranged by alphabetical title; its resemblance to *The Countrey Justice* is remarkable. Whether *The Countrey Justice* was or was not the model, we do know that an energetic magistrate on the westernmost frontier, in the settlement of Springfield, Massachusetts, William Pynchon, used Dalton and commended it as a sound guide to the law.[46] In any case, Michael Dalton, like so many other *jurisperiti* of Old England, took a new lease on life in New England. In a word, he was part of the reception of the common law and so a founding father of our legal birthright. Quite an accomplishment for a mere, unprofitable country justice.

CHAPTER TEN

William Hudson

The opening lines of Shakespeare's rollicking *Merry Wives of Windsor* are the braving words of country-justice Shallow: "Persuade me not; I will make a Star-Chamber matter of it: if he were twenty Sir John Falstaffs, he shall not abuse Robert Shallow, esquire." This was sure to raise a laugh in the Globe—not only because the idea of twenty weighty Falstaffs was a sight too risible to contemplate seriously, but because in Shakespeare's day hundreds of his countrymen every year made some contretemps into a "Star-Chamber matter."

Clearly, Star Chamber was popular in its day. It would not have been popular had it not provided what its litigants wanted of it. Yet in 1641 it was abolished by an act of Parliament which declared that "the Proceedings Censures and Decrees of that Court have by experience beene found to be an intollerable burthen to the Subjects and the meanes to introduce an Arbitrary Power and Government."[1] Following its destruction, the very name of Star Chamber entered the English language as one of three genuinely odious words, a dubious honor it shares with "Inquisition" and "Machiavelli." A radical pamphlet of the 1760's was entitled *The Court of Star Chamber or Seat of Oppression*. Judges, legislators, and lawyers today cannot resist calling any irregular or unjust proceedings "Star Chamber justice." The author still recalls with a mixture of amusement and anger how during the student disturbances of the 1960's, when as a disciplinary hearing-officer on the Berkeley campus he was called upon to expend more time and energy than circumstances warranted in trying to do justice to young miscreants (all acting in a good cause, of course, in support of a dozen non-negotiable demands), his efforts were pilloried in the student paper as "Star Chamber" judicature. He took cold comfort in the fact at least that the students were passingly aware of his research interests. Moreover, Star Chamber's bad name goes on. Roderick Taylor and Peter Hyams' film, "The Star Chamber," released in 1983 by Twentieth Century Fox, stars Hal Holbrook as a Los Angeles judge who meets secretly with his colleagues on the bench to order the murder of notorious felons who have escaped justice. Every evening, perhaps, VCRs and DVD players provide a medium to continue traducing the High Court of Star Chamber!

Star Chamber did not meet in secret. All trials in the court were public, in a chamber of Westminster Palace, the Camera Stellata, decorated on the ceiling with plaster-relief six-pointed stars (hence its name). In fact, perhaps even more than Shakespeare's Globe, Star Chamber trials provided one of the most engrossing spectacles in the capital. A notable case between great persons would draw in scores of spectators, so many that they crowded in almost to the bar of the court. Every day saw a number of young men, students at the Inns of Court, sitting on the benches at the rear of the court, doing what students always do (taking copious notes) seeking for themselves a practical education in the law. The judges of the court were the most august men of the realm: the Lord Chancellor presided over other great officers of state—the Lord Treasurer, the Lord Privy Seal, the Lord President of the Council—the Lord Steward, the Lord Chamberlain, the Secretaries of State, other Privy Councillors, at least one archbishop or bishop, and the Chief Justice of King's Bench and Chief Justice of Common Pleas (or, in their absence, other justices of the great common-law courts). The nation's most eminent lawyers appeared there as advocates: the Attorney-General was present on every sitting day (usually Monday and Wednesday in every week of the law term), and the King's Serjeants and other serjeants at law led for important and wealthy clients. Star Chamber proceedings were open and prominent. The only time that the judges of the court sat privately, in camera (in the Inner Star Chamber where the Privy Council transacted its business of state), was on the last day of term when, after hearing counsel plead for mitigation of sentence imposed on their clients at trial previously, the court retired to decide whether mercy was warranted.

What did happen outside the court—and that was before trial—was the entry of pleadings and the taking of evidence. With the exception of the extraordinary and rare procedure called *ore tenus* (by which the Attorney-General prosecuted orally before the court a defendant who had previously upon examination confessed the facts), Star Chamber proceeded by written bill of complaint (or information in cases brought by the Attorney-

General). To this the defendant was required to put in a written answer to the facts alleged or a special plea in law. This was done in the office of the clerk of the court, located in Gray's Inn, although the defendant's answer might be taken in the country by ad hoc commissioners if he were unable to travel to London. The defendant was also examined upon oath to interrogatories drawn by the plaintiff's counsel, and his examination constituted evidence that could be used against him at trial. Witnesses on both sides were examined and cross-examined on oath upon interrogatories drawn by counsel, either in the office or in the country by commission. This was done in total secrecy in order to prevent evidence that might affect the testimony of other witnesses from being known to them. Only after all the testimony had been taken down in writing was it "published," that is, made available to the parties and their counsel on both sides, and a day set for trial.

The only objection that could be taken to such "secrecy" was a purely functional one from the advocates' point of view: it made cross-examination very difficult in the absence of the witnesses' evidence in chief. Not only was the procedure not inherently unjust, it served the interests of both parties, since it provided the testimony of witnesses in extenso in a written form that encouraged careful weighing of the evidence. What was lost at trial was the opportunity to observe the demeanor of witnesses. By the same token, so carefully was the testimony reported that it was possible to assess minute discrepancies in the evidence of a witness—indeed, from the Star Chamber records, even four centuries later the historian can often detect perjury.

Another charge in the indictment commonly (and mistakenly) leveled at Star Chamber was that its proceedings were "summary." Obviously, with forms as elaborate as the bill procedure and the taking of written evidence, there was nothing summary about a Star Chamber matter. By the time of Star Chamber's abolition, an average case took upwards of three years from the subpoena intended to bring the defendant in to answer to the trial of it. This was without undue dilatoriness on the part of either party—and Star Chamber through special pleading (demurrer, pleas in bar, exceptions) gave plenty of scope for dilatoriness.

What was genuinely summary in English criminal procedure of the day was trial by jury at common law upon indictment for felony. It was common for a number of indicted defendants to be tried at the same time by the same jury though each prisoner had been charged with entirely separate offenses.[2] An indicted felon had no right to counsel, no right to have his witnesses deposed on oath, and no right to give evidence on oath on his own behalf. Trial for felony did not take very long. And if convicted of felony—for as little as the theft of goods worth a shilling or more—the defendant would swing (unless reprieved to await pardon or transportation to Ireland or, after 1607, the colonies).

To have the gibbet before one's eyes is to put the "cruel punishments" of Star Chamber in proper perspective. Because the trial of felony was so deeply rooted in the common law's jurisdiction, Star Chamber was prevented from trying those crimes which carried the penalty of death. Star Chamber could not touch life or limb. Its punishments were severe enough: a fine to the King, usually in a sum onerous enough to be *in terrorem*, and imprisonment until the fine was paid; "exemplary infamous" punishment, such as riding to the pillory facing rearward on the horse with a poster on the head indicating the nature of the offense, begging forgiveness of a party offended, loss of office, etc.; corporal punishment, including whipping, standing in the pillory, the loss of an ear, the slitting of nostrils, branding on the cheek with letters indicating the offense (*e.g.*, "FA" for false accuser). The common law could, and did, inflict the same corporal punishments—even to the amputation of limbs, a punishment that Star Chamber could not inflict. It was a cruel age, and the deterrent value of punishment was not often questioned.

Emphatically, Star Chamber did not use torture—another false charge that has been laid at its door. Torture was occasionally used in England, though not as a matter of course, as it was in Continental criminal procedure. In England, torture was an extra-judicial procedure inflicted by warrant of the Privy Council to discover the names of suspected accomplices. The evidence obtained by the rack could not be used against the defendant tortured. And if such a matter came to trial, since the case would be treason or misprision of treason, the evidence against the accomplices would be opened in the common-law court where such serious crimes were tried.

To all of these allegations against Star Chamber was added a final charge of unusual breadth: that it was an "un-English" court, more specifically a "prerogative court" employing a "foreign" and "inquisitorial" procedure, that its substantive law was "Roman law," and that the lawyers practicing in the court were "civil lawyers." Such an argument presupposes a norm of Englishness—a norm, of course, that would have to be the common law. But the Englishness of the common law was entirely a product of the passage of time. In its origins in the late twelfth century, its procedure and substance were fundamentally Norman-Angevin, to give due credit to King Henry II and the French-speaking officials who a century after the Conquest fashioned the writ system and tied it to the institution of the jury. Indeed, this common law was thoroughly "prerogative," since it sprang from the exercise of the king's will and his duty to do justice. The influence of Roman law on the common law can be detected in the attempt of Glanvill in the late twelfth century to fit the writ system into a thoroughly Romanist framework, and Bracton's effort, half a century later, more tenuous and less successful, to adopt for his *De Legibus et Consuetudinibus Angliae* the arrangement of subjects that Justinian had followed. But subsequent centuries of development re-fashioned the common law as a peculiarly English institution, forgot its origins, and enveloped them in the myth of the realm's ancient constitution. It gave the common law an Englishness that was venerable, becoming the glory of Coke's age and the repository of Englishmen's and latterly Americans' liberties in succeeding generations.

Star Chamber didn't have the time to become venerable. It was the product of the late-mediaeval King's Council tying up judicial loose ends and filling lacunae in the implementation of the established common law by entertaining petitions for relief and justice. Therefore, it was the twin of the Chancellor's jurisdiction which would later be called equity. Originally, the Council would act on such petitions, perfunctorily but collectively. Since the business was time-consuming, and the councillors had other important political and administrative functions to perform, most of the petitions were hived off to the one councillor who had the bureaucratic resources to handle legal paperwork, the Lord Chancellor. Those matters that involved important persons or were politically sensitive were retained by the King's Council, which sat in the Camera Stellata. From the beginning of the fifteenth century the Chancellor's judicial activities in handling such petitions were clearly and continuously recorded. Because the records of the Council's entire activities were only fitfully preserved, it was not until almost the end of that century that the Council's judicial work became evident. This was largely due to a statute of 1487 dubbed *Pro Camera Stellata* which was subsequently curiously misunderstood to have "created" the court of Star Chamber.

Everything procedurally particular to Star Chamber also obtained in Chancery, save that in Chancery the defendant usually was not examined. The procedure used in both these courts—the bill and answer, interrogatories and depositions method of pleadings and proofs—appear in fact to have originated in English practice, even though they resembled the methods used on the Continent. This offered a model of judicature that was more rational, simpler, and, for busy officers of state, whether the Lord

Chancellor solo or the King's councillors collectively, less time-consuming, and it was a common phenomenon in the sophisticated high-Middle Ages. Moreover, whatever relief was sought in Chancery in that epoch could also be obtained from the Council sitting in the Star Chamber, if the Council thought the matter or the parties important enough. It was not until the early 1500's, when the tribunal established by the 1487 act *Pro Camera Stellata* was merged into the Council in the Star Chamber (and that for perfectly practical bureaucratic reasons), that the Star Chamber became ostensibly a court of criminal as well as equitable-civil jurisdiction.[3] The 1487 act provided for the Attorney-General to prosecute certain specified offenses by information in the Star Chamber. This grant of jurisdiction was grafted onto the older jurisdiction of the court to hear and grant petitionary relief brought by bill by private parties. Not until the 1560's did Star Chamber stop doing equitable-civil justice. Even afterward, the private litigants who used Star Chamber as a forum to bring prosecutions for criminal actions typically did so in order to support civil suits and actions that they were already contesting in other courts, common law and equity. In the period from 1603 to 1625, for which ample proceedings in Star Chamber exist, four-fifths of all 8228 extant cases (including most of the informations brought by the Attorney-General, which were brought on relation of private litigants) concerned some species of property, real or personal, and over half of the extant cases explicitly indicate that the parties were already at law in Star Chamber or some other court.[4]

Chancery, unlike Star Chamber, did become venerable. It survived the revolution which destroyed its twin, to take its place in the late nineteenth century reform of English judicature as one of three divisions of a "Supreme Court" which preserves still its procedural and substantive distinctiveness. Chancery lasted long enough to have its Englishness assured.

Only utter-barristers, readers and benchers of the Inns of Court, and serjeants-at-law had right of audience in Star Chamber, as in King's Bench (and for that matter, Chancery) from at least the late Middle Ages. This fact demolishes the charge that the lawyers who practiced in Star Chamber were civil lawyers trained in Roman law, with all of the insinuations of popish sympathies and inquisitorial predilections.

If Star Chamber was not what its detractors have said it was, then what was it? Appropriately enough, the answer is to be found in a detailed written document, *A Treatise of the Court of Star Chamber*. The author, William Hudson of Gray's Inn, Esq., utter-barrister, is untypical of the practicers in the court only by virtue of the size of his practice—the largest in the court's history—and his profound understanding of the court's procedure, substantive law, and even history. Hudson pointed the way to an answer to that question in his treatise, which was written in 1621, when the court was at the apex of its power and importance in England's judicature.

Not published until 1792 (an act of historicist piety by that indefatigable eighteenth-century barrister and antiquarian, Francis Hargrave), Hudson's treatise had circulated widely in manuscript recensions of varying accuracy and thoroughness from the time of its compilation until the abolition of Star Chamber two decades later rendered this extremely practical work useless to the profession. It was a model treatise of practice for the age, better arranged, more clearly argued, and more stylishly written than all others of that genre. It was learned in every sense of the word, and it carried the authoritativeness of its author's pre-eminent reputation as both a former official of the court and the greatest practitioner at its bar.

Mr. Hudson had a definite purpose in 1621 in composing his treatise, a purpose that had little or nothing to do with its usefulness for his fellow barristers. The treatise hints at a crisis, or perspicaciously posits a potential crisis, in the reputation of Star Chamber. It demonstrates that Star Chamber was already in danger of derogation at the hands of detractors and had reason to fear the erosion of its authority, power, and integrity at the hands of its officers and jurists. The historian who will not accept Hudson's disquietude refuses to accept the best evidence available of the origins of the court's internal weaknesses, which contributed to its downfall when radical politics governed events fast becoming revolution.

The modern reader can appreciate Hudson's treatise for something else that it offers: insight into the substantive law implemented in Star Chamber. The second part, which comprises about one-third of the treatise, is a concise and accurate summation of the criminal law of the court, complete with case citations and illustrative use of cases. It remains today, as it was in the last years of Star Chamber, the quickest means of surveying and understanding what the court did. Hudson's treatment of the substantive law when tested against the thousand plus reports of cases in Star Chamber from the 1590's to 1641 (some in the early printed reports, notably Coke, Croke, Moore, Noy, and Popham but most still available only in manuscript) stands up as a subtle and rigorously analytical treatment of case-law. And what Hudson's treatise reveals is the lasting contribution of Star Chamber to the common law, English and American.

That contribution is nothing less than the law of sophisticated crime, the offenses which today we characterize as "white collar crime." Crimes against justice (perjury, maintenance, champerty, embracery, vexatious litigation, contempt); crimes by officers (subornation and extortion); crimes of covin and deceit (forgery, fraud, impersonation, extortion); criminal libel, and in distinction to it the modern civil tort and sedition; inchoate crime (conspiracy and attempt)—all these were crimes either largely created and developed by Star Chamber in the exercise of its common-law jurisdiction or else were statutory offenses defined and refined by the court. These crimes stood in sharp contrast to the bulk of the criminal law at the outset of the early-modern era in England, the old felonies of the Norman-Angevin origins of the "King's Peace," the rough-and-tumble crimes of violence and force which led to the gallows. The later medieval "trespasses" had already been truncated into misdemeanor and tort before Star Chamber took up its criminal-law jurisdiction seriously in the sixteenth century. Still, it fell to Star Chamber to evolve case by case a corpus of misdemeanor law over the course of the last half-century of its existence.[5]

A corpus it was. The fourth edition of Ferdinando Pulton's popular and inimitable treatise on the criminal law, published about the time Hudson wrote his treatise, devoted two and one-half times more space to misdemeanor than to treason and felony, reflecting the age's preoccupation with covert crime. Pulton wrote:

> I shall not farre digresse from my theame [the King's peace] by treating of Forgerie, Periurie, Maintenance, Deceit, Extortion, and Oppression, wherein though a man be not assaulted by the Rapier and Dagger, Pikestaffe, or Bilbow-blade, as he is in a fray, forcible entry, or riot, yet a forged deede that conueyeth his land from him, a false oath which depriueth him of his lease, or unlawfull maintenance that wresteth his credit or goods from him, do longer disturb the peace of his mind, sticke in his stomach, and infireth a deeper and more durable impression of sorrow in his heart, than a bore on the ear, a duff in the neck, or a blow with a cudgel given on the sodain, will do. . . .[6]

That preoccupation was clearly shared by the Privy Councillors and common-law judges who sat in Star Chamber. Moreover, because the 1487 act *Pro Camera Stellata* instituted for the first time in England's history routine criminal prosecution by a procurator regularly attendant in the Star Chamber (in the person of the Attorney-General), the repression of crime became a practical rather than largely a theoretical responsibility of the crown and its great officers. The same act dictated the routine presence and involvement of the two Chief Justices in the proceedings, and so brought to the task of defining crime by case-law the best talent on the bench. Because the crime prosecuted was misdemeanor and not felony, the accused had right to counsel, and where learned lawyers are employed on both sides of adversary proceedings, sophisticated law is produced. So it was in the Tudor-Stuart Star Chamber. To answer the question posed above—what was the Star Chamber?—it is enough to say that it was a particularly aggressive and activist court of the greatest eminence, owing less to its origins in the royal prerogative than to parliamentary statute, and relying upon neither for its motivation, which in a manner that was entirely consonant with the traditional common-law method of creating and evolving law by cases fashioned the modern law of sophisticated crimes.

Repression of crimes against justice was the objective of the 1487 act, and it remained a staple of Star Chamber's jurisdiction to its end. In its later years, such offenses were alleged in one-quarter of the informations and bills filed. Maintenance, actively supporting and furthering litigation in which the accused had no valid legal interest, was the most common. Champerty, a misdemeanor still in English law which on the western side of the Atlantic is the pot-of-gold contingency fee for the plaintiff's lawyer, was less common. Embracery, that is, corrupting a jury, was still frequently charged. Perjury, no less a staple, had statutory origins, but Star Chamber expanded the range of what constituted the offense and brought testimony given in any court, secular or ecclesiastical, within its scope. As for vexatious litigation, the court went a long way towards defining what constituted valid grounds for litigation and adequate standing to bring suit by the simple expedient of heavily fining private litigants *pro falso clamore* for groundless actions. It also took the old medieval ordinance outlawing the agreement of parties to bring false prosecution for capital crime and made it into an effective instrument in its own right, as well as expanding its thrust to create the inchoate crime which contemporaries still called "combination" and which we know as conspiracy. It was Star Chamber, as well, rather more than the Lord Chancellor sitting in Chancery, which created the very rigorous English rules concerning contempt of court, both on contempts committed in the face of the court and, more significantly, contempts committed beyond its precincts.

Crimes by officers, particularly bribery and extortion, were almost entirely the creation of Star Chamber and were expanded by the court to cover virtually all officialdom. The court went further by extending the doctrines under these heads to the legal profession, not only to attornies (who were officers of their respective courts) but also to barristers, defining professional malfeasance beyond the older parameters of ambidextry. Crimes of covin and deceit revealed Star Chamber in its most activist and ambitious role. Forgery and fraud were expanded far beyond their statutory limitations, and became a large part of the court's jurisdiction. Arguably, impersonation for fraudulent purposes was not a crime until Star Chamber made it so. Blackmail by private persons was also criminalized by Star Chamber.

Probably nothing else that Star Chamber did contributed more to the development of an important branch of the law, both on the criminal and civil sides, than what it did with libel. The old medieval offense of *scandalum magnatum*, defaming great persons, was democratized, so to speak, by being applied to libel committed by writing (or tokens) of anyone injured in his or her reputation. Because this expansion addressed what was avowedly an offense against the king's peace, Star Chamber never drew a real distinction between libel and sedition, and thereby set the two essential ingredients of criminal libel which obtain in England to this day, that publication is not requisite and the offense does not die with the person defamed. In this, libel as Star Chamber developed it differed from the tort of slander that was a product of the ecclesiastical courts and action upon the case for words in the common-law courts. But written defamation, as distinct from spoken defamation, libel as distinct from slander, even in the civil jurisdiction owed its origins to Star Chamber's protection of the reputations of a myriad of parsons parodied by itinerant players, barristers accused in broadsides of every imaginable corrupt practice, and cuckolded husbands held up to ridicule by horns nailed over their doors.

Sedition, which Star Chamber treated as defamation of the greatest magnate, the King, and the state, has a noxious reputation in our liberal times (made even more pronounced in the United States by virtue of its condemnation by partisan political opinion in the 1790's and the subsequent interpretation of the First Amendment to provide protection for political argument. In the seventeenth century, however, the development of sedition as an offense distinct from treason signaled a considerable advance in the criminal law. Star Chamber's creation of the offense slowed the tendency of Tudor and Stuart governments to expand the law of treason—with its gruesome penalties of annihilation of person and inheritance—to include words and even thoughts—and to apply to treasonous acts, words and thoughts. The law against sedition sufficiently served to protect the modern state, polity, and society at a particularly vulnerable stage in their development, before the formation of adequate instruments to maintain public order, the genesis of political means and *forae* to domesticate dissent, and the conceptualization of democratic ideals of participation in the political process for the preservation of the state.

Inchoate crime, conspiracy and attempt, have their origins in Star

Chamber. The birth of modern conspiracy is *The Poulterers' Case*, sentenced in the court in 1611. The dictum of Sir Edward Coke, "that a false conspiracy betwixt divers persons shall be punished, although nothing be put in execution," is marred by his wonted hyperbole, but it is substantially true as a report of what Star Chamber held.[7] The first clear conviction for a mere attempt to be found in the reports of any jurisdiction in England is *Ryman v. Bickley* (1617), in which Star Chamber overruled an exception that the intended crime was a "thing not effected" and fined the defendant.[8] Modern criminal law is inconceivable without the crimes of conspiracy and attempt. Thanks to Star Chamber they began to develop at a very early stage in our modern law.

How was it that a court dashed as an instrument of despotism created so much public law for the repression of crime that has been accepted into the common-law system and survived? The 1641 statute abolishing Star Chamber explicitly transferred its jurisdiction to the common-law courts, particularly King's Bench and the assizes. However, what is clear from a careful sifting of indictments in the common-law courts before 1641 is that at least as early as the beginning of the seventeenth century, the assizes, as the principal venue in which criminal offenses were tried, were already receiving and accepting from Star Chamber the new misdemeanors. This should not be surprising: the Chief Justices and the other common-law judges who rode the assize circuit also sat in Star Chamber. In Star Chamber the justices became increasingly prominent in the court's deliberations during the last half-century of its existence. Sir Edward Coke is the best example: he had practiced in the Star Chamber as Attorney-General from 1594 to 1607 and participated in Star Chamber's lawmaking as Chief Justice of Common Pleas and King's Bench from 1606 to 1616. After his removal from the bench, Coke returned to Star Chamber as a Privy Councillor in 1617, where he proved an active and sometimes disruptive jurist. Among Coke's most prominent publications, from *The Reports* to the *Third Institutes* and the *Fourth Institutes*, are panegyrics on the High Court of Star Chamber. The common-law judges were apt teachers in Star Chamber; they were also apt learners there, and they went out from Westminster Palace to teach rude country jurors what they had learned there, to propound and to promulgate the law they had created there.

To teach and to learn. That is an appropriate way to describe the roles played by the judges of the common-law courts in Star Chamber. What they taught was the learning of the law, based upon their professional training, professional role, and professional experience. What they learned was the exigencies of policy and the limitations of politics, the requirements of state and the imperatives of duty. Not since the crucial formative decades of the common-law system, in the last half of the twelfth century when the King's Justices sat in the King's Court, the undifferentiated *Curia Regis*, had the English judiciary been so continuously and so intimately involved in affairs of state as they were in the latter part of Elizabeth's reign and the reigns of James I and Charles I, the last half-century of Star Chamber, by virtue of their routine service in that court. Not for four centuries had the judges been so immersed in a process that united political policy and judicial decision-making. There never would be so close a linkage again. In 1640, at the outset of the revolution that would engulf Star Chamber in 1641, a number of the judges of the common-law courts were impeached in Parliament, primarily for the opinions that they had rendered in cases that had come before them during the 1630's—decisions that had been essential to supporting the policies of King Charles's "personal rule." Aggravating such charges, in the eyes of the parliamentarians who brought them, was the judges' participation in those Star Chamber *causes célèbres* that had condemned to heavy fines and corporal punishment some of the most notable dissenters to regal policy, men now identified with the radical, revolutionary, leadership in the Long Parliament.

One lasting result of the English Revolution—an intended one—was to take the judiciary out of politics, if not quite to take politics out of the judiciary. That was assured by the supremacy of Parliament, accomplished within two generations after the demise of Star Chamber. Never again would policy affecting law be so evident and so significant in English judicature. Much was gained, obviously. Much was lost, including the potential for the English courts to play the role in judicial review which the United States Supreme Court has played since John Marshall's interpretation of Article III of the Constitution of 1789. Another casualty was the ability of the state, in collaboration with the learned sages of the law, to create necessary new law, so fast, so freely, and so thoroughly as had Star Chamber.

Two elements have been neglected: "Robert Shallow, Esq." and, one also supposes, "Sir John Falstaff." They were not negligible, and we dare not omit them. Until the last decade of the Star Chamber, the Shallows and the Falstaffs, beyond any other force working on the court, determined its direction, dominated its time, and even dictated its law. Case-law is profoundly the creation of the litigants: they set the courts to work, demand, and pay for the ends they seek in litigation, and vote with their feet and their purses if they are dissatisfied with the justice accorded them by a court. If to some extent this is always true, it was especially so in that period because there were many courts with jurisdiction over any matter *in lite*, litigation was essentially a business practice in furtherance of business negotiation, the ambit of the law was much concentrated on issues of property (and especially real property), the litigants were neither ignorant of the law nor meekly dependent upon the good offices of their counsel to attain their legal objectives, and the courts from clerks to judges relied entirely on the costs of litigation for their incomes. Solemnly and conventionally, historians often declare that Star Chamber was "popular" until the last decades of its existence. Indeed it was; any court that did the roaring business that Star Chamber did was "popular." A court that was not popular was one starved of the business that it needed to flourish. What was true of Star Chamber was true of the King's Bench. King's Bench flourished in the period because it developed an egregious legal fiction, the *latitat* action, which allowed it to attract for the first time a sizable civil jurisdiction. Star Chamber flourished because it was a forum where parties could expeditiously sue for damages, bring collateral actions to support or embarrass lawsuits pending elsewhere, and because the prestige of the court had had enormous appeal for the private litigant who could win a victory there.[9]

All these features of Star Chamber can be detected in Hudson's treatise. Sometimes they are too subtly stated and not always self-evident, but there is nothing ambiguous about this statement:

> For damages to the wronged party this court is the best jury; and when they have justly discerned the wrong, they make the most ample recompence, and requite the wronged person's labour and travel and sometimes with all his injury.[10]

Perhaps Hudson was too embarrassed to admit that this had not been the case before the first decade of the seventeenth century—only then did Star Chamber began to award damages. The damages that a litigant could receive in Star Chamber had qualities particularly advantageous to a victorious plaintiff. A levy against goods to satisfy damages awarded a private party in Star Chamber took precedence over even a fine to the King. Not only was this was a reasonable consequence of Star Chamber's implicitly civil role in litigation; it was also advantageous in maintaining the volume of the court's business.

Star Chamber's tenderness for the private litigant was good business. It also had a perhaps unintended corollary, but a cosmically significant one. The concern of the vigorous monarchy of the Tudor-Stuart period for maintaining public order and sustaining the state was a major consideration in the formulation of much of the legal doctrine that emerged from Star Chamber. The councillors and officials who sat in Star Chamber saw to that. At the same time, however, the demands of the private litigants who brought cases in Star Chamber ensured that Star Chamber would not be reduced to a mere instrument for executing state policy.

Until the 1630's, private litigants and what they sought held a clear predominance in the workings of Star Chamber. That began to change during the "personal rule" of Charles I, after 1629, when the king resolved never to call another Parliament and to fund his government by every fiscal expediency that had the slightest shadow of legitimacy. To cloak this expediency in legitimacy and to overcome resistance to his policies, the king turned to his courts. All were called upon to do their duty to their sovereign. All did, including Star Chamber, which saw some of the hardest and most effective service. Beginning in 1631 and continuing until the abolition of the court ten years later—the proceedings were heaviest from 1632 to 1636—the Attorney-General brought more than 175 actions for essentially fiscal ends, *pro Rege* (for the King) rather than on relation of a private party. Of these, about 40 cases came to trial and determination. Convictions in these actions persuaded scores of subjects who feared prosecution on similar grounds to compound with the Exchequer for their offenses. The more complex of these cases took many days of hearing; one action, against the City of London and its livery companies for fraudulently procuring a grant of the Londonderry lands in Ulster, consumed the whole of Hilary Term 1635 and ten more sitting days in the vacation following. The Attorney-General also increasingly (and notoriously) prosecuted political dissidents against Church and state.

The Attorney-General had the privilege of pre-emption of hearing in the court. If he rose to proceed *ore tenus*, then other cases set down for hearing that day were stood over. During the personal rule, the Attorney-General claimed the same privilege in cases brought by information, resulting in increasingly long delays in private-party actions as the cause-lists grew longer and longer. Patently, Star Chamber had ceased to be a court that catered to private litigants; it had become in fact as well as in name the High Court for the trial of the king's actions. This made more severe a considerable procedural deceleration which had set in over a decade earlier with a marked increase in the incidence of special pleading (which if it was not dilatory in intent certainly occasioned delay in effect). Private-party suits fell off steadily over the 1630's.[11] By the time the court was demolished as an instrument of tyranny it had already lost the bulk of its clientele. The

Shallows and the Falstaffs had deserted it. The famous act of 1641 abolishing Star Chamber was essentially a coup de grace. William Hudson did not live to see that unhappy moment, for he died in 1635. The execution would not have surprised him.

Star Chamber has its monuments, not the least of which was the order it helped impose in a society coming out of the chaos of the last century of feudal rivalry, in an age of profound religious and ideological disorders ushered in by the Reformation, in the first centuries of the perils of new nation-state rivalries. The law it created and bequeathed to its heirs, successors, and assigns, a not unmixed blessing but a substantial benefaction, deserves a substantial cenotaph. Mr. Hudson's treatise is perhaps less monument than epitaph. He ends with a quotation from Bracton that is as good a renvoi or *nunc dimittis* for Star Chamber as it was for Hudson's own careful and painful labor:

> I ask the reader, if he finds in this work anything superfluous or erroneous to correct and amend it, or pass it over with eyes half closed, for to keep all in mind and err in nothing is divine rather than human.[12]

Star Chamber erred; much of what it did was superfluous. A high court it was, but it was not divine, and its judges were all too human. Too long have historians looked at its shortcomings with eyes entirely closed. Eyes even half open can appreciate that without Star Chamber the common law of the English-speaking world would have been vastly different.

CHAPTER ELEVEN

John Selden

John Selden (1584–1654) would doubtless take a certain sardonic pleasure in knowing that from among all his large and wide-ranging corpus of written works *Table Talk* has been chosen for discussion. A sardonic pleasure, because Selden enjoyed the reputation of skeptic and even cynic and reveled in it; because he was naturally charged with wit and humor of a suitably acerbic and derisory kind. Sardonic pleasure, because he also had a large streak of well-cultivated perversity in his temperament, choosing to breast popular waves by assuming unpopular positions, telling admirers as well as denigrators what they did not want to hear, and always getting in the first word on any subject as well as the last. A sardonic pleasure, because while the foundation of Selden's acclaim as well as of his own self-esteem was the number and weight of his scholarly works, *Table Talk* was the least of them all, and not even his own confection. Full of the savant's disdain for the masses, convinced that his travails of search, discovery, and exposition constituted so many gems cast before swine, Selden would find confirmation of all his worst fears and firmest prejudices in the fact that the great works of his scholarship were so soon forgotten and the most negligible of literary mementos of his life so long remembered.

What gems the great books were! Selden's earliest works, written while he was still a student at the Inner Temple, were three studies of early English and British history: *Analecton Anglo-Britannicon* (1607), *Jani Anglorum Facies Altera* (1610), *England's Epinomis* (1610). These early established Selden's reputation as linguist and historian. He edited Fortescue's *De Laudibus Legem Angliae* in 1616. And in his 1623 edition of the early twelfth century chronicler Eadmer's *Historia Novorum*, he included in appendices to it a great deal of information derived from Domesday Book, thus giving increasing prominence to what was becoming the foundation document to the study of early English medieval history.[1] By the 1620's, Selden was increasingly involved in research on Classical antiquities, particularly centered on the notable collection of Greek and Roman statuary acquired by the second Earl of Arundel and Surrey, the "Arundel Marbles," and the Earl's collection of other objects and manuscripts. This work bore fruit in the path-finding description and analysis of the collection published in 1629, *Marmora Arundelliana*. Throughout his life, from his student days, Selden maintained his interest in oriental studies, especially Hebrew and Arabic, with some linguistic materials in Persian, Turkish, and even Chinese. In 1617 he published *De Dis Syris*, an early, not entirely successful, and long-since superseded attempt to deal with Syrian mythology. Selden, as an orientalist, was at his best as a commentator on rabbinical law. From the 1630's to the eve of his death in 1654, Selden published six works, comprising seven volumes, on the subject, all astute and some even brilliant expositions on difficult and often opaque subjects in Judaica. *De Jure Naturali et Gentium juxta Disciplinam Ebraeorum* (1640) had a wide appeal, and today is rightly cited as an important stage in the development of natural law tenets of human rights and liberties.

It was also at an early stage of his scholarly activity that Selden began to make those contributions to English law and legal history which were a major source of his contemporary fame—and which, when a century ago the founding fathers of modern English legal history cast about for a name for their new society, moved them to honor Selden. His first work was a luminous legal-historical study entitled, *The Duello, or Single Combat, from Antiquity derived into this Kingdome of England* (1610). This work, besides in great part standing the test of later scholarship on trial by battle, has added significance in the fact that it was one of the earliest English legal monographs, a scholarly study on a limited area as distinct from the large and ponderous legal treatises which obtained from Glanvill's *Tractatus* in the twelfth century to Coke's *Institutes* in the seventeenth. Indeed, this vehicle Selden as juristic author made peculiarly his own. *Titles of Honour* (1614) was a comprehensive treatment of dignities including kingship extending backwards to before the Flood, ranks and degrees of nobility, and the rules and laws of precedence: the very stuff of the new-found passion for precise status that an age undergoing unsettling social change found reassuring. In 1617, he wrote, but did not publish, *A Brief Discourse touching the Office of Lord Chancellor of England*, which he presented to Sir Francis Bacon on Bacon's appointment to the Lord Keepership.

In the same year Selden published what was probably his finest legal monograph and certainly his most controversial work, *Historie of Tithes*, still called "the classical study" of the subject.[2] Beginning with Melchizedek's gift to Abraham (Genesis 14:17–20), Selden established origins that were entirely human and positive-law, rather than divine and moral, for that most important revenue in support of the clergy. Predictably, the book raised a storm of protest from every episcopal palace, deanery, canonry, and parsonage in England. The book was suppressed. Selden was questioned about it in the Court of High Commission for Causes Ecclesiastical, forced to make his submission, and inhibited from printing any reply to those who attacked him over it. This was merely the first time Selden fell afoul of authority. Yet even in the peril there lay future advantage: James I, always inordinately confident of his intellectual prowess in matters theological, thrice summoned Selden to discuss tithes with him.

Selden was thus encouraged to capitalize on such marks of regal favor by writing a tendentious and misdirected counterblast to Hugo Grotius's assertion in his treatise, *Mare Liberum* (1609), that the high seas were open to all traffic. Selden, in his appropriately titled *Mare Clausum*, written in 1618 but not published until 1636, made the preposterous assertion that the law of nature and the law of nations both permit the sea as fully as the land to be made subject to proprietal right and that the crowns of Great Britain, now joined in James I of England who was also James VI of Scotland, enjoyed the circumambient seas as a perpetual appendage. Though the work was gratifying to James, he refused to license its publication in 1618 for fear of offending his brother-in-law (and creditor) the king of Denmark. Charles I of England and Scotland was even more enamored of the argument and ordered Selden to take up the work again. Charles lent Selden his full support in completing the project, and, after the book's publication in 1636, directed that it be consulted as an essential reference work in the Privy Council, Exchequer, and Admiralty Court. While the future and the preponderance of juristic opinion in international law proved to be with Grotius, Selden may prove a prophet redeemed. During recent decades, the intense debate over sovereign-nation control of the seas, replete with unilaterally redrawn territorial boundaries and 200-mile limits asserted to protect fisheries and the environment, smacks more of Selden than of Grotius. Indeed, notable (albeit risible) among such strident assertions are those of an heir and successor of Charles I, who in right and title of her Crown of Canada and by her Canadian ministers, claims the entire Arctic to the North Pole in a sector between Canada's eastern and western extremities, encompassing vast quantities of the Arctic Ocean.[3] The oceans are fast becoming characterized, jurisdictionally speaking, as more like drainage ditches than open water, and the nations responsible for this arteriosclerosis—mostly of the second and third rank, in terms of power—owe a considerable debt to *Mare Clausum*.

It is significant that, with two exceptions, neither of them extraordinary, Selden did not write any major work on English law or legal history after 1618. The least considerable of the two exceptions was a 1647 edition of *Fleta*, a pale thirteenth-century reflection of Bracton's treatise. Selden took the opportunity in editing the text (which was a unique manuscript in the possession of Selden's friend, political ally, and fellow antiquarian, Sir Robert Cotton) to add an extensive essay dealing discursively with a great many topics, the most important and useful of which was the influence of the Roman law on English law. Rather more considerable, in light of its auspices and currency, was *Privilege of the Baronage of England*, which Selden prepared at the behest of the House of Lords, and which he submitted in December 1641. This treatise was comprehensive, dealing with the privileges of the House as a whole and of the peers individually. But the subject was fraught with hazard as the Lords were drawn along, increasingly recalcitrantly, in what was clearly becoming a tumultuous change in the polity. What is fascinating about the work is its exquisitely maintained balance. It is peculiarly passionless, level in tone, and muted in assertiveness, quite unlike Selden in full cry. He seemed at pains to observe his own dictum, "the wisest way for men in these times is to say nothing."[4]

Clearly, that dictum, prudence in the face of risk, was one reason for Selden's turning away from English legal scholarship during the 1620's. There was hardly any subject in English law that was not potentially dangerous: that decade witnessed the increasing gap between king and Parliament, with both sides appealing to the law and legal record in support of arguments becoming more intensely polemical and less capable of reconciliation. *Mare Clausum* was safe to publish, an unexceptionable work, for every Britisher could agree that Britannia should rule the waves. But, perforce, *how* to rule the waves had to be begged. This question Selden carefully avoided, for it turned on, first, whether Parliament was prepared to raise the revenues to put a fleet to sea under the command of royal ministers whom it did not trust; and, second, whether if Parliament did not vote such revenues, the king could raise them by a tax on all the counties of England. These questions were anything but safe, during the 1630's, as ship-money became a burning political issue with revolutionary overtones.

Another reason that Selden gave over legal scholarship in the 1620's may have been his increasing personal involvement in the political process, to which he brought peerless skills as a legal and historical researcher. Discrete questions which began as political disputes were rapidly framed as issues at law and consequently subjected to legal examination and interpretation. No political issue arose that did not drive first the parliamentarians to the Tower of London and its records, followed by the searchers and the apologists for the crown, as the king's ministers felt compelled to counterattack over the same terrain. Both sides became adept at fashioning factually overlarded "precedents," which, true to the methods of the age, were counted more than they were weighed. This process was implicit in parliamentary debate as early as the final session of James's first Parliament, in 1610. It did much to disorder the very brief Addled Parliament of 1614, and reached a remarkable level of sophistication in the boisterous Parliament of 1621. It was less prominent in 1624, because Parliament and king could make common cause in war, but it surged back in the first two Parliaments of Charles I, 1625 and 1626.

In the Parliament of 1628, with its two sessions, a new and dangerous spin was given to such disputation. What before had been merely "legal" was now in the process of becoming "constitutional." Polemical antiquarianism, the ransacking of the records for precedental facts, was transformed into metahistoriography, creating whole explanations for the present by reference to past developments that were determinative and carried an import beyond the facts themselves. This represented a proto-ideology positing an ancient constitution (Saxon or even British) that had been subverted by Norman kings, who had fixed upon the realm a Norman yoke of regal tyranny. This ancient constitution was almost a cliché in parliamentary rhetoric, expounded with varying degrees of sophistication, rigor, and truculence. Even a skeptic, if caught up in harrowing political debates amid which liberties actually were at stake, made some obeisance to the idea of the constitution. While Selden knew more about Anglo-Norman England than almost any other man alive, he could not fail to genuflect, though he remained a skeptic and, with unusual perspicacity and realism, saw the disputes as more limited and less grandiloquent than the ideology of the constitution puffed them up to be.

Selden's involvement began in 1621. Though not a Member in that Parliament, he was part of the brains-trust who avidly searched the records on behalf of a group of prominent MPs who were openly questioning sensitive issues: monopolies that the crown had granted, James's foreign policy (or lack of it), and the failings of certain servants, including Lord Chancellor

Bacon and Attorney-General Henry Yelverton. Selden was so active and prominent that, along with the MPs he had counseled, he suffered a brief incarceration for his efforts. Entering Parliament in 1624, he was not bashful in speaking, though the subjects debated involved fewer of the historio-constitutional issues which were his forte than had been the case before or would be again. He did not sit in Charles I's first Parliament in 1625, but was elected to the second in 1626. This Parliament saw the exclusion of the most prominent opposition MPs, including Sir Edward Coke, Sir Robert Phelips—who had led the attack against "grievances" in 1625—and Sir Thomas Wentworth. The leadership vacuum was filled by Sir John Eliot, John Pym, and John Selden. Selden played a major role in preparing and moving the impeachment of the king's favorite, the Duke of Buckingham, blamed for the military disasters of the previous year. Charles's dissolution of Parliament saved Buckingham; Eliot was arrested, and Selden was in some danger of the same fate. As it was, he withdrew to the estate of his patron and friend, the Earl of Kent, to launch himself on the study of orientalia. His reverie lasted less than two years, ending with the summoning of Charles's third Parliament in March 1628.

It was in the Parliament of 1628, particularly in the first of its two stormy sessions, that Selden took a leading role, second only to that of Eliot. The great grievances of the first session turned on extra-Parliamentary taxation, unlawful imprisonment, and illegal military exigencies. The first two grew out of the notorious Forced Loan (1626) by which Charles and Buckingham had sought, in the face of Parliament's refusal to provide support, to raise enough revenue to simultaneously prosecute war against both Spain and France. The last grievance centered on the billeting of troops in private homes, the execution of martial law by military officers in peacetime, and local taxation for logistical support of the impressed army, phenomena which since 1626 had seemed prominent and permanent. Behind all such issues were matters of precedent: what had been done before, and under what circumstances, and with what success? Here, Selden came into his own as parliamentarian.

Selden's scholarly sojourn had been interrupted, during the fall of 1627, by his appearance as counsel in the Five Knights' Case. The Five Knights were gentlemen who had refused to contribute to the Forced Loan, and who, after they were jailed by order of the Privy Council, had applied in King's Bench for habeas corpus against their imprisonment without cause shown. In his argument, Selden, true to form, had led with the strongest of his precedents. Yet he had recognized—it was the acuity of a legal mind rather than any partisan heart—that the statutory foundation upon which precedent had to be raised was unequal to the task without supplying more meaning than the act would bear:

> The statute of Magna Carta . . . that statute [which] if it were fully executed as it ought to be, every man would enjoy his liberty better than he doth . . . out of the very body of this Act of Parliament, besides the explanation of other statutes, it appears, *nullus liber homo capiatur vel imprisonetur nisi per legem terrae*. My Lords, I know these words, *legem terrae*, do leave the question where it was, if the interpretation of the statute were not. But I think, under your Lordships' favour, there it must be intended, by "due course of law," to be either by presentment or by indictment.[5]

The court was not prepared to supply so much new cloth—rightly, by contemporary canons of statutory interpretation. Judgment went against the prisoners, and Chief Justice Hyde heavily impressed upon Selden and his fellow-counsel the limitations, as understood in the Stuart age, of a defense based entirely on precedent. It was a salutary lesson, applicable to any age, that precedent is only as good as the factual similarities between the instance cited and the current question:

> Then the precedents are all against you [the prisoners], every one of them, and what shall guide our judgments, since there is nothing alleged in this case but precedents? . . . [I]f no cause of the commitment be expressed it is to be presumed to be for matters of state, which we cannot take notice of. You see we find none, no not one, that hath been delivered by bail in the like cases, but by the hand of the King or his direction.[6]

On March 27, 1628, in the committee of the whole, the Commons took up the Five Knights' Case. Selden, speaking as an MP, noted, "I have spoken for my fee in this case already, and now I speak to discharge a duty to my country," reiterated his precedents. Though he would "not meddle with state" and avoided commenting on the argument that the prisoners had been committed for reason of state, he concluded that "state, methinks, should not alter nor cross law." Yet Selden still was stalked by the fact that the precedents would not support the conclusion sought. And as parliamentarians were increasingly prone to do, he cast the matter higher, making an appeal beyond English law and even English experience:

> I will speak in reference to other states. They [the king's supporters] tell us of foreign governments. I have read stories and lately and for this purpose (for you know where I have use of them in abundance). I will make it good in point of law; there is no prince in Christendom that claims this right, there is neither step nor sign of it in any history.[7]

Of course there were an abundance of signs to be seen, in history and in the divided present, and Selden could no more make his argument good in history or contemporary practice than he could in law.

The point ought not to be labored. The political process, even with constitutional overtones, readily spills out of the metes and bounds of law—surely this is the best argument for the separation of powers. What is taught by the reality that Selden had to confront is that even new positive law innocent of ambiguity does not necessarily settle everything, not even the disputes that called it into being. The first session of the 1628 Parliament witnessed the king's reluctant, pinched consent to the Commons' carefully wrought Petition of Right. Cast in the form of a reconfirmation of Magna Carta, the Petition sought—and the king offered words that promised—redress of grievances that most troubled the Commons. Yet events would prove the Petition of Right unenforceable, and its provisions would be ignored within a matter of months. Worse, the second session of the Parliament would end in a riot, on March 2, 1629, with the Speaker forcibly held in the chair as the House of Commons voted three intemperate resolutions. Charles, determined never to call another Parliament, set about his Personal Rule. And as a first order of business, the king and his Council moved against Eliot, Sir Robert Cotton, and John Selden. An unpublished polemical tract was discovered in Cotton's study and was deemed seditious. For two years, Selden languished in prison under varying degrees of rigorousness. This drained his courage (he got out by a sadly craven submission) and interfered with his scholarship.

Selden never again played as prominent a role in politics, though he had more than a score of years left him, and would be elected to both the Short Parliament and the Long Parliament. Indeed, in 1641, in the first session of the Long Parliament, he took a markedly unpopular but legally correct stand against the legislative destruction by act of attainder (impeachment having failed) of the king's chief minister and Parliament's nemesis, Thomas Wentworth, Earl of Strafford. Religion was another field in which Selden also lacked the stomach for zealotry. He was a passively loyal, often irreverent, adherent of the Church by Law Established—certainly not a member either of the Puritan party within the Church or the Separatists without it. That, if nothing else, took the revolutionary fire out of him in the 1640's, as the revolution-become-civil-war grew more divisive over ecclesiological issues than constitutional ones.

Not least, Selden also came to enjoy creature comforts, the solace of luxury, and the opportunity to pursue his intellectual interests. Early in his career, he became steward and counsel to Henry Grey, ninth Earl of Kent. Common bruit had it that after Selden moved in with the Earl and Countess at their seat in Bedfordshire, the relationship developed into a *menage à trois*. It is pretty well established that after the Earl's death, Selden clandestinely married the widowed Countess; and there is no question that following her death, Selden was comfortably provided for during his life, with realty as well as goods and chattels. Though Selden had achieved the professional recognition of being called bencher at his Inn, the Inner Temple, in 1633, his legal practice was very slight. There seems to have been some merit in the scurrilous relation of the seventeenth-century gossip, John Aubrey, that "I remember Mr Sadler (who wrought many years to that Family) told me that Mr. Selden had got more by his Prick than he had done by his practise."[8] In any event, Selden pursued his scholarly endeavors without letting other men's politics, any more than his legal practice, get in the way.

Neither would Selden allow the study of English law to intrude on his passion for orientalia. If caution here moved him almost to muteness, even more did his developing scholarly interests. On a broad range of matter of law and legal history about which he had thought much and studied hard, and to which he could have contributed extraordinary and unique insights—both to contemporaries and to us who remain intrigued by that earliest "modern revolution"—he largely kept silent. Almost mute, nearly silent, but not quite. That is why *Table Talk* must serve as sufficient monument to an extraordinary jurist. It contains a myriad of insights into a cosmos of contemporary concerns. Each heading in its alphabetical arrangement, so much like the contemporary commonplace book dear to the lawyer's heart, bears witness to abundant knowledge and to a lively intelligence. Moreover, each demonstrates the skepticism that provides balance even in the most hotly contested arena of ideas. The irreverence with which almost all religious matters are treated serves as an antidote to the toxin of contemporary reverences doing battle as prophecies armed. The majesty of the law comes in for very subtle diminution, as its imperfections are revealed and the useful and oft-ignored contributions of other legal systems noticed.

Above all else, perhaps, the beauty of *Table Talk* is that unlike such other great anecdotal compilations as Dr. Johnson's Gospel According to Mr. Boswell, which relied upon the groaning board for site and situation, Selden's ruminations reflect an age of unusual turmoil and crisis in which accepted notions, practices, arrangements, and beliefs were fundamentally challenged and ideas were forged that move us to this day. Selden was one of the great smiths, and each apothegm, aphorism, and epigram in *Table Talk* rings with the clarity of a hammer striking the anvil. Each is worth our attention and our time, for consciously or unconsciously we and our forebears in the common law world since have been in some part formed by those notions. None more so than this:

> Wit and Wisdom differ;
> Wit is upon the sudden turn,
> Wisdom is in bringing about ends.[9]

We seek ends, and for that wisdom alone works.

CHAPTER TWELVE

John Milton

Mention John Milton's *Areopagitica* to a gathering of civil libertarians and eyes will mist, lips quiver, and knees bend. Milton is the patronal apostle of modern American liberalism, *Areopagitica* his Epistle to the new Romans. Votaries of civil liberties are still called upon to laud both man and book and to undertake *dulia* if not *latria,* reverence due a saint if not God himself. The founders of our nation reverenced Milton no less, and with the energetic John Locke and the phlegmatic Montesquieu he is generally accorded the honor of being one of the great Founding Forefathers of the Constitution. The volatile Milton made a contribution in *Areopagitica* that was revolutionary in the way that Montesquieu's careful tractate on social engineering could never be. Locke's *Two Treatises of Government* was a proto-revolutionary analysis written as a theoretical contribution to a constitutional debate that served to justify the revolution after the fact. *Areopagitica*, by contrast, burns with revolutionary ardor. A strident polemic, a tract-for-revolutionary-times, it had great appeal to those New Men, the Americans, who, having achieved independence by the sword, sought to give effect to its blessings by the pen, in a written constitutional instrument assuring basic rights and liberties.

What we run some risk of not realizing—though the Founding Fathers certainly did—are the full implications of the historical context in which Milton wrote and to which *Areopagitica* was his most memorable contribution. Milton has suffered mightily at the hands of the English Department post-modernists who have so thoroughly "deconstructed" his works and the politically correct critics who have reduced him to the negligible status of just one more dead white European male poet. But there are great truths, objective facts, about John Milton that must be weighed if we are to appreciate that multifaceted mind and spirit in a tumultuous age remote to our own and its concerns.

One such truth is that the apocalyptic poet who transports us, sometimes against our will though never against our better judgment, with *Paradise Lost* (1667), *Paradise Regained* (1671), and *Samson Agonistes* (1671), the two epics and the tragedy of his later years, is not absent but only hidden in his polemical prose works. Another truth is that while Milton produced virtually no poetry in the 1640's and 1650's, his polemical prose works did not constitute merely misapplied genius and misspent energy. In fact, we must appreciate how far his polemical prose works gave spirit and texture to his later poetry even while the "active phase of the mass movement" (as Eric Hoffer put it) that called them into being and made of Milton an archetypical "true believer" prevented him from turning his creative powers to verse. Hoffer wrote:

> Milton, who in 1640 was a poet of great promise, with a draft of *Paradise Lost* in his pocket, spent twenty sterile years of pamphlet writing while he was up to his neck in the "sea of noises and hoarse disputes" which was the Puritan Revolution.[1]

Hoffer failed to give the devil his due. Perhaps only after twenty years in the wilderness of civil strife and spiritual disorder revealing Hobbes's state of nature could Milton have achieved the irenic comprehension he gives Samson:

> All is best, though we oft doubt,
> What th' unsearchable dispose
> Of highest wisdom brings about,
> And ever best found in the close. . . .
> Of true experience from this great event
> With peace and consolation hath dismiss'd,
> And calm of mind all passion spent.[2]

Without the polemical prose that he wrote, a Nahum-like exaltation of God's unerring wrath directed at the enemies of His people and God's promise of safety to them in their fidelity, Milton might not have found for himself Job's patience in the darkness of his growing blindness. Nor might he have proven able to accept the fulfillment of paradise regained in expectation of Paul's crown for the course run:

> "Doth God exact day-labour, light deny'd?"
> I fondly ask; But Patience, to prevent

> That murmur, soon replies, "God doth not need
> Either man's work or his own gifts. Who best
> Bear his mild yoke, they serve him best, his State
> Is Kingly. Thousands at his bidding speed
> And post o'er Land and Ocean without rest:
> They also serve who only stand and wait."[3]

Milton the revolutionary did not know how to merely stand and wait.

It was in his polemical tracts, especially *Areopagitica*, that Milton evolved a dynamic and a dialectic for change with which he sought not only to reform a corrupted polity but also to reconstitute a shattered ethos, the great matter of his greatest poetic visions. David Loewenstein makes the point:

> No other revolutionary prose work of Milton's, I think, shows a more resilient capacity to embrace social conflict as the essential element of the historical process—a fact that seems especially striking when we consider that *Areopagitica* (despite its rhetoric of warfare) is so much less abusive and emotionally vehement than Milton's other polemical tracts. The drama of history for Milton is always dynamic, yet here he has highlighted its regenerative consequences: when some momentous historical change is about to occur, Milton writes towards the end of *Areopagitica*, "God shakes a Kingdome with strong and healthfull commotions to a generall reforming."[4]

Milton was the child of a revolution that began as a spontaneous generalized phenomenon, reactive to events, political stimuli, ideological pressures, and the surprising accidents of opportunity occurring in the twelve months that led to the convocation of the Long Parliament on November 4, 1640.

John Milton (1608–1674) had embraced poesy in childhood and turned all his learning, heavy in the languages ancient and modern to becoming a poet. He achieved recognition while still at Cambridge, for his ode "On the Morning of Christ's Nativity" (1629) and a poem "On Shakespeare" (1630). He spent the years from 1632 to 1637 living in his father's house in a Buckinghamshire village twenty miles northwest of London. The elder Milton, an Oxford graduate and prosperous scrivener given more to letters and music than to the formulary copying and banking that characterized his profession, took delight in his son's company and provided him with an almost idyllic ambience in which to write much poetry and even a masque. It was a time of intensive study of the Classics for the younger Milton, which he only gave over in 1637 to undertake the virtually compulsory grand tour on the Continent. He favored Italy, though its fleshpots that drew most young English travelers there had little allure for the priggish and puritanical poet.

There he met Galileo. That illustrious martyr for Truth, persecuted by the inquisition for his new science, figured in *Areopagitica* for very personal and substantial reasons. Milton also visited Hugo Grotius in Paris: another suffering worthy, who had fled his native Holland because there he faced persecution not only for his political activity but also for his theologically suspect jurisprudence.

Milton returned home in 1639 to watch the nation slide into division, disorder, something like anarchy, and finally revolution. His Puritan sentiments were more advanced than those of the presbyterian persuasion who took up the cross against "prelacy"—that is, bishops, Anglican no less than Roman—when their Scots co-religionists rebelled against the imposition of a new order of worship at the hands of that prelate of prelates, William Laud, Archbishop of Canterbury. By 1640 Milton was already an Independent (congregationalist), well along toward sounding that cynical aphorism of congregationalists, that new presbyter was but old priest writ large. His tracts against prelacy, addressed to the Long Parliament and the Westminster Assembly of presbyterian divines in 1641–1642, were violent and vitriolic. These writings also denied the better angel of Milton's nature, which embraced reason and would seek persuasion in religious discourse and intellectual intercourse. Thus he concluded the last of his five broadsides against the bishops:

> And if yee thinke that soundnesse of reason, or what force of argument soever, will bring them [bishops] to an ingenuous silence, yee think that which will never be. But if ye take that course which *Erasmus* was wont to say *Luther* tooke against the Pope and Monks, if yee denounce warre against their Miters and their bellies, . . . [they] will soone be dumbe, and the *Divine right of Episcopacy* forthwith expiring, will put us no more to trouble with tedious antiquities and disputes.[5]

This was a far cry from his prayerful peroration in *Areopagitica*, raised on "those neighboring differences, or rather indifferences . . . whether in some point of doctrine or of discipline, which though they may be many, yet need not interrupt *the unity of Spirit*, if we could but find among us *the bond of peace*."[6] Such an irenic sentiment would have been sufficiently adiaphoristic to satisfy Richard Hooker.

In fact, *Areopagitica* stands in greater distinction to the anti-prelatical tracts preceding it than to the anti-monarchical tracts that succeed it. Following that bewildering and harrowing moment outside the Banqueting House at Whitehall, January 30, 1649, when the crowd who had come to watch Charles Stuart die groaned as the king was beheaded, Milton sought to prevent the new cult of Charles the Martyr from taking root. He wrote two pamphlets, one of them long enough and detailed enough to be a book. *Eikonoklastes* (1649) was a sustained response to *Eikon Basilike*, a work published after Charles's death, and purportedly of the king's own composition, which was intended to justify the king's actions during his rule and at his disastrous fall. *Eikonoklastes* taxed Charles with intellectual softness: "Kings most commonly, though strong in Legions, are but weak at Arguments; as they who ever have accustom'd from the Cradle to use thir will onley as thir right hand, thir reason alwayes as thir left."[7] Yet all Milton's wit, brilliance, partisanship, and learning could not carry the day for an argument even worse than the argument for King Charles. Whatever its intellectual merits, however effectively it unmasked the propaganda-spectacle quality of *Eikon Basilike* and revealed Charles's hypocrisy, Milton's iconoclasm was no match for the wrenching image of an anointed king judicially murdered after a dubious trial. Parliament, purged of its presbyterian moderates, was no longer the Areopagus of the English nation and not much more than the mail-fist of the New Model Army.

The other pamphlet was three-score pages of overblown rhetoric, a hodgepodge of spurious history lightly reinforced by a stringing together of the most fanatical advocates of insurrection and tyrannicide. The title of the pamphlet is the message: *The Tenure of Kings and Magistrates, Proving that it is Lawfull, and hath been held so through all Ages, for any, who have the Power, to call to account a Tyrant, or wicked KING, and after due conviction, to depose, and put him to death; if the ordinary MAGISTRATE have neglected, or deny'd to doe it. And that they, who of late so much blame Deposing, are the Men that did it themselves*. Most of the authorities whom Milton cited were clerics of the unsettled and unsettling Age of Reformation, minds and souls unworthy of the author's attention and superfluous to the argument of the moment.[8] The tract was not, however, negligible as political theory, for it argued boldly that the power of kings and magistrates is derived from "the People, to the Common good of them all, in whom the power yet remaines fundamentally, and cannot be tak'n from them, without a violation of thir natural birthright."[9] Such an argument would undergird Locke's theory and, indeed, the legal fundamentalism of American constitutionalism.

Milton's specific task—to justify the judicial murder of Charles I—was clearly distasteful to him. The tone of *The Tenure of Kings and Magistrates* is not at all sanguinary. Charles's cadaver is not dishonored. Milton was at pains to advocate a better polity, not simply to decry a worse. *The Tenure* lends credence to John Aubrey's unusually complimentary conclusion that whatever Milton "wrote against Monarchie was out of no animosity to the King's person, or owt of any faction or interest, but out of a pure Zeale to the Liberty of Mankind, which he thought would be greater under a free state than under a Monarchiall government."[10] That same "Zeale to the Liberty of Mankind" drove Milton in 1644 to publish *Areopagitica*.

To understand what compelled a loyal son of the Revolution to challenge a critical policy of the revolutionary regime requires a backward glance beyond the Order for Regulating Printing decreed by both Houses of Parliament on June 14, 1643, which was the immediate object of Milton's attack. The preamble of the Order referred to orders recently made by both Houses pending passage of a bill for an Act of Parliament (which was not now possible because the king's consent could not be obtained). By this bill the Company of Stationers had attempted to suppress

> the late great Abuses and frequent Disorders in printing many false, forged, scandalous, seditious, libellous, and unlicensed Papers, Pamphlets and Books, to the great Defamation of Religion and Government.[11]

Stationers and printers who were not members of the Company had set up printing presses "in corners" and produced works "in such multitudes, that no Industry could be sufficient to discover or bring to Punishment all the several abounding Delinquents." This had infringed the copyright of the Company and had been done for revenge against those Company members who had informed against clandestine publishers, all of which was "to the great Prejudice of the said Company of Stationers and Agents, and to their Discouragement in this Publick Service." Henceforth, no work was to be printed, bound, stitched, or offered for sale unless it was allowed by signature of such as either or both Houses should appoint for licensing and was entered into the register of the Company. The Company's officers and the officials of both Houses of Parliament were given powers of search and seizure for written works, supplies, and presses, as well as the power to arrest unlicensed publishers. Provision was made for the examination and punishment of offenders by either House. A writ of assistance to other officers civil and military was provided. The order concluded with the names or offices of licensers for different types of literature.

In almost all these details, there was nothing novel. The Order reiterated, albeit more briefly, what had long been the provisions of orders of the king in Council and decrees of the High Court of Star Chamber controlling printing by licensing, enforcing the monopoly powers of the Company of Stationers, and maintaining its accustomed practices in registering copyright. For some decades all or most of these provisions had obtained. The state sought to halt dissemination of seditious, schismatic, scandalous, and morally subversive printed matter. Such objectionable materials in fact fell mostly under the category "schismatic," clandestine books on controversial political and religious issues. A few underground presses had operated in England, fitfully and always in peril; most dangerous books were printed in the Continent and smuggled into England, finding their way to a dwindling coterie of Roman Catholic recusants and a sullen, growing crowd of disgruntled Puritans. Most of these printed Puritan pamphlets displayed more vigor against the bishops than other "Romish remnants" in the Anglican Establishment.

The entire apparatus of control was expanded and forcefully tightened during the "Personal Rule" of Charles I in the 1630's. The immediate cause for the crackdown was an agitator, irrepressible in every sense of the word, who suffered from the inimitable distinction of falling afoul of every regime from that against which he published the first of some 200 books and pamphlets in 1627 until his death in 1669, royalist and parliamentary and military and royalist again, and being imprisoned by every one of them save the last: William Prynne, barrister of Lincoln's Inn. The last regime was the monarchy of Charles II, which Prynne had played a large role in restoring in 1660, but under which he was no more able to keep his mouth shut or his inkwell closed than under any of the others. That most astute of Stuart monarchs, deservedly remembered for saying he did not intend to go upon his travels again, appointed Prynne Keeper of the Tower Records, which gave a worthy outlet for his archival passions and moved him to make a substantial contribution to English history instead of simply railing at the regime.[12] Prynne died of old age, a fact remarkable in itself, since he had twice lost his ears for sedition, the second time with enough shock and loss of blood to have killed him, and been imprisoned "in perpetuity" from 1634 to 1640 (latterly in damp and insalubrious prisons) and again from 1650 to 1653.

In 1634, Prynne was tried and sentenced in Star Chamber, along with a binder-bookseller called Sparks and a clerical licenser, the Reverend Thomas Buckner, for publishing a seditious libel against stage plays and masques, *Histrio-Mastix: the Player's Scourge* (1633). This acidulous bombard assailed the king and his queen (the French Roman Catholic, Henrietta Maria) and the royal court for allowing and participating in masques. It seemed to asperse the morality of ladies who performed in masques (which meant the queen), and appeared to threaten the king by making approving references to advocates of tyrannicide. If the Attorney General's case turned more on innuendo than upon explicit sedition, the libel was clear enough and the overall effect of the diatribe was to contemn the State and the Church. Buckner's offense was in having licensed the book without thoroughly reading it, before or after Prynne made additions and changes in manuscript. Sparks was condemned for selling the book despite the fact that he had been

> warned not to goe on to print this booke, least it might cost him his eares. And when it was printed, hee perswades chapmen to buy it. It will sell well; hee shewes the perticular passages that woulde make the booke sell well, and buy it (saith hee) for shortlie it wilbee called in. Where, is to bee noted, that the callinge in of a booke is an excellent profitt to the seller.[13]

Being banned-in-Boston is not a modern phenomenon: and here is a clear indication of how voracious a readership there was for the age's yellow literature. Prynne suffered the loss of his ears, exposure in the pillory, and imprisonment, as well as being assessed a fine of £5,000. The other two offenders were treated more leniently. They were fined, and Sparks saved his ears.

In 1636, having managed even in prison to get hold of books and writing materials, Prynne loosed an attack on bishops, singling out *de innuendo* William Laud, Archbishop of Canterbury, in *A Divine Tragedy Lately Acted*. He was sentenced in Star Chamber for that seditious libel, on June 14, 1637, in company with two other Puritan authors, John Bastwick, M.D., and the Reverend Henry Burton, who had committed the same offense in their works. They were punished with enormous fines (£5,000 each), perpetual imprisonment, in the Channel Islands, without "pen, inke, and paper and to have noe bookes allowed them to read in but bookes of devotion and the Bible," pillory, and the loss of their ears.[14] For Prynne the last punishment meant three mutilating hacks by the hangman, blows that finally removed what was left of his ears, and being branded on the forehead with the letters "S.L." for seditious libeler. Following close on these exemplary punishments came a decree of Star Chamber, on July 11, 1637. This reaffirmed earlier decrees and orders that licensed printing. Containing thirty-three articles and additional explanatory provisions for the licensing procedure, the decree was intended to ensure that every printed work would bear certification that it contained nothing

> contrary to Christian Faith, and the Doctrine and Discipline of the Church of England, nor against the State or Government, nor contrary to good life, or good manners, or otherwise as the nature and subject of the work shall require.[15]

Enforcement and punishment were explicitly confided to Star Chamber and the Court of High Commission for Causes Ecclesiastical, in both of which Archbishop Laud had come to play a leading, sometimes dominant, role. The decree was publicly proclaimed at the last sitting of Star Chamber in Trinity Term, when all the judges of the common law courts, some justices of the peace, and a large crowd of notables were present in court, and it was printed for wide distribution.

So long as the king's Personal Rule maintained civil order from 1629 to 1640, acting with increasing rigor against seditious and criminally libelous publications in Star Chamber and against blasphemous, heterodox, and schismatic works in the Court of High Commission for Causes Ecclesiastical, repression worked. But this changed abruptly with the staggering events of the summer and fall of 1640. A Scots army invaded England in the name of the Covenant, a religious pledge that was equally a political movement. The English militia, the only force the king had to defend his southern kingdom against his northern, disintegrated into mutinous desertion. The king was forced to convene Parliament: first the abortive Short Parliament, in April 1640, and then in November 1640 a parliament that the king could not control: the Long Parliament, which showed an implacable interest in destroying the king's most loyal ministers, reversing the policies of the personal rule, and cleansing the Anglican Church of its "Arminian Prelacy and corrupt Popish remnants."

The licensing system, like almost every other institution in Church and state, simply ceased to function. Indeed, among the first acts of the Parliament was to vacate the sentence against Prynne, Bastwick, and Burton and to bring about their triumphal return from prison exile in the early weeks of the Parliament—in effect, the symbolic crash of licensing. A genuine revolutionary ethos produced a sudden, furious, overwhelming flood of ephemeral literature, at best polemical, in the main inflammatory, treasonous at worst. Peer, squire, philosopher, cleric, lawyer, poet, artisan, autodidact, and madman—all sorts and conditions of men (and a few women, one suspects)—all galloped into print, unhampered, unlicensed, and probably in more cases than the giddy authors would admit, unread. After almost two centuries, the great promise of Gutenberg's movable type was fully realized, and the modern age of print, in all its facets (including journalism), was born. The only comparable cultural revolutions came in the wake of the inventions of the twentieth century, with the work of Guglielmo Marconi and Lee De Forest in the first decades of the century and that of Steve Wozniak, Steve Jobs and those who developed the Internet in the years before the new millennium.

Parliament's fears were those of any regime in the best of times, magnified by self-doubt about its legitimacy, especially after it took up arms against the king in mid-1642. There was a growing recognition that forces beyond Parliament's control had been unleashed and that increasingly radical solutions were being demanded from below. The published literature between 1640 and 1644 reflected this radicalism. Englishmen began talking revolutionary talk even before they had thought revolutionary thoughts. While some would in time recoil from the violence and destruction they had advocated blindly ignorant of the real life (and death) consequences of their chatter and posturing, the damage had been done.

The achievements of the first year of the Long Parliament (1640–1641) in dismantling the "Personal Rule" and beginning what Puritans called a "reform" of the Church of England, under presbyterian auspices—most of these changes made in conjunction with a reluctant but necessarily compliant king—fueled the demand for further radical reform. The political rhetoric of the multiplying ephemeral literature began to reveal programmatic and agenda-driven revolutionary ideas. Much of this stuff was printed sermons, those highly strung, seemingly interminable expositions of meandering scriptural pedanticism given high liturgical function in Reformed Protestantism.

Violence, in tone and advocacy, mounted, not least in those sermons regularly preached before Parliament. On November 5, 1641, the anniversary of the Gunpowder Plot, Cornelius Burges, D.D., preached to the Commons on the text, "Surely the rage of man shall praise thee, the rest of the rage shalt thou restraine" (Psalms 76:10). Dr. Burges, a respectable Puritan divine, not a radical sectarian, was at the time prominent in the Westminster Assembly. Ultimately he would protest the execution of Charles I. Yet his 1641 exhortation concluded with imagery more appropriate to the chariot than the pulpit: "Those unnaturall Rebels that now rage so desperately, should be *but bread for you*; and all your enemies should be compelled to lick the dust of your feet."[16] In the next two years the pamphlet-rattling became more extreme and more temporally political. Incendiary pieces by Edward Bowles, Jeremiah Burroughs, and—no surprise, William Prynne—prefigured the abolition of peerage and monarchy, the deposition of the king and even his destruction, and the social "leveling" in a full and uncompromising revolution. A recent scholar has argued that

> The willingness of English pamphleteers in 1642 to contemplate the destruction of the ancient constitution must be part of any explanation of why there is no parallel to the Putney debates to be found elsewhere in seventeenth century Europe, of why no other contemporary rebellion culminated in the trial and execution of a king. . . .

This ends with the chilling observation, that whoever swung the axe which severed Charles's neck, "Bowles, Burroughs and Prynne (no matter how far their views had changed by 1649) had sharpened it."[17] Having heard Burges's address and other trumpets out of Zion, having read increasingly strident incitements to ever more radical political changes like Prynne's, the majority of the Members of Parliament, by June 1643, were thoroughly alarmed. The result was the licensing order.

Milton's attack on licensing in *Areopagitica* owed something to self-interest, but it was not self-serving. He had made abundant use of the freedom of unhindered publication after 1640, and his five tracts against prelacy enjoyed widespread approval inside and outside the Commons because they echoed Parliament's current condemnation of the bishops. None in authority challenged those exercises, which hurried unlicensed through the press. It was otherwise with *The Doctrine and Discipline of Divorce, Restor'd to the good of both sexes, from the Bondage of Canon Law and other Mistakes, to Christian Freedom, guided by the Rule of Charity; wherein also many places of Scripture have recovered their long-lost Meaning; reasonable to be now thought of in the Reformation intended.* Here again, the title is the message. This remarkable salvo was launched in 1643, at the time Milton's seventeen-year-old bride of a few months went home to her Royalist father upon finding herself unsuited (was it a difference of temperament, intellect, or energy?) to partake in the philosophical life of a man twice her age. This remarkable tract advocated not judicial separation or annulment (the only two forms of "divorce" recognized by canon law, Anglican as well as Roman) but actual dissolution of the marriage, divorce in the modern sense. Very modern indeed were the grounds on which he proposed to freely grant divorce; they were tantamount to the modern doctrine of irreconcilable differences. Whether Milton's doctrine of divorce was good for both sexes or not, it certainly offered a boon for the husband. It relieved him of much responsibility and at the most was only slightly conditioned by concerns for children or disagreement between the spouses. It took little account of practical problems or legal difficulties. If "Christian Freedom" was its end, the "Rule of Charity" was certainly not its means. The work's scriptural exegesis was superficial. Despite the pamphlet's attack on canon law and its advocacy of further reformation, whatever resonance these plaints could be expected to have among the anti-prelatical fell on deaf ears because the tract was accounted scandalous to faith and morals from whatever quarter the Christian approached its idea and its arguments. Hot words from divines, the reprehension of lawyers, a few instances of the work being cited to justify infidelity (in one case by a wife who left her "unsanctified" husband to take up with a preacher, of what degree of sanctification one can only guess), and the application of the undeserved pejorative tag of "Miltonists" to describe a putative but largely chimerical sect of divorce advocates gave Milton a notoriety he did not seek but was, characteristically, too pugnacious to avoid. He produced a second edition, unlicensed still, in early 1644, with additional material, some of it even more scandalous than that in the first, openly addressed under his name to Parliament and the Westminster Assembly. Attacked in debate in the latter and in a sermon preached before the former in the summer of 1644, Milton stood in real danger of punishment by Parliament. Nothing happened. Parliament had more pressing concerns in conducting a strenuous and so far much less than successful war against the king, and Milton was too useful an adherent to be alienated while his propagandistic talents were still sorely needed.

As Sir Leslie Stephen noted, in the case of his marital troubles and his literary reaction to them "Milton's indignation took the form, usual to him, of seeing in his particular case the illustration of a general principle to be enunciated in the most unqualified terms."[18] The same observation is applicable to *Areopagitica*: though it clearly struck a defensive stance for the moment and to a specific end, it was cast in such widespread generalization and universalized rhetoric that it would serve for all seasons and to any end. That is one reason why it has lasted so long and never ceased to attract.

Granted, the attraction depends little on the arrangement or the rhetoric of *Areopagitica*. It is difficult to read. It is loaded with allusions that presume the reader will be familiar with Classical letters, Scripture, patristic commentary, medieval history and contemporary affairs, mixed with labored wit and leaden imagery. Its syntax is even more torturous than would be expected from a work of its genre and era. Its argument is spiral, not linear, making for repetitiousness and circularity. Worse, it also suffers from the shortcomings familiar to any lawyer with a bad case: it introduces every defense possible (plausibility aside) while completing few. A synopsis might help, though it remains uncertain whether a précis would open up all of Milton's arguments or reveal their relative incoherence when taken as a whole. The book is like a grapnel thrown blindly in hopes that it will snag solid ground on the Areopagus. The confusion in argumentation which annoys the tract's ardent admirers and frustrates its casual readers was the product less of a lack of clarity of vision on the author's part than of his uncertainty as to what line would achieve his ends.

Areopagitica begins with a familiar revolutionary Miltonian stance, with a wholesale attack on "Popery" with its Index and Inquisition and on Anglican "Prelacy" and its licensing. Discounting ancient practices of censorship (which the author was at some pains to find more limited and more benign than the evidence would support), Milton identifies the advent of modern censorship as beginning with Pope Martin V's reaction to the threat of heterodoxy raised by John Wyclif and Jan Hus at the turn of the fourteenth century. Milton lauds Protestant city-states abroad for their singular absence of licensing, a point well taken, while overlooking how effectively Geneva, Frankfurt, Amsterdam, Boston and other such theocentric Protestant polities were, able because of their small size, settled limits, and watchful magistrates, to discourage undesirable publication by controlling the number of printers and being certain of their orthodoxy. The warmth of Milton's attack is intended to warn the presbyterians of Parliament and the Westminster Assembly of the company they would keep if they did not rescind the Order of June 14, 1643.

From this point, Milton moves to an argument for the positive virtues of unlicensed printing. Citing examples ranging from Dionysius the Great, the third-century Bishop of Alexandria, to his contemporary and friend, John Selden, Milton argues that even bad books can have good effects, for God, having given man the "gift of reason," trusts man to choose.[19] Bad books can be "read" usefully, though to "practize" them would be pernicious. Milton accepts the fact and the function of Evil, that *Crescit in Orbe dolus*, that Evil grows in the world. As orthodox Christianity had done since the disavowal of the great early Christological heresies, he argues that Evil is necessary in order for one to know Good. Good cannot be chosen if Evil is not seen and known.[20] He tolls Edmund Spenser (playfully, for that worthy had founded the literary circle called "Areopagus" in Elizabeth's reign) to round out his argument. In the second book of *The Faerie Queene*, the Knight of Temperance, Sir Guyon, visits the Cave of Mammon, captures the epitome of Intemperance, Acrasia, and destroys her Bower of Bliss, thereby demonstrating true temperance, as the purpose of his quest and trial had been that "he might see and know, and yet abstain."[21] Harm done by books Milton tackles head on. That books might "spread infection" Milton dispatches with a mass of examples in support of the proposition that all human learning and religious controversy would have to be banned if "infection" was to be stopped. In fact, he argues, books are more dangerous to the learned than the ignorant, and yet, since they are essential to sustain learning, to suppress them for that reason would be "vain and impossible attempts" with nothing gained, for the ignorant would be as readily corrupted by word of mouth by the learned as by the books themselves, which can corrupt the meaner sort only if construed by the learned.[22] And if corruption is so widespread among the learned, then how can Church or state rely on the licenser not to be corrupted? Juvenal's skeptical *Quis custodiet ipsos Custodes?* (Who keeps the keepers?) is not far from Milton' s mind. Neither is the object of the watch in the sixth book of Juvenal's *Satires*, the locked-up wife who seduces the guards. As to the harm that comes from being exposed to temptations without necessity and in misemploying one's time in vain things, Milton answers that such books are not temptations but materials to fashion "effective and strong med'cins," antidotes to vanity.[23] He argues that the "ingenuity of Truth" moves faster than the "pace of method and discours can" to "overtake" it.[24] Truth will out, and Truth can no more be known without Falsehood than Good can be without Evil.

Milton rejects Plato's *Republic* as not of this world and therefore without prescriptive value for its real problems. Plato's lofty seriousness is belied by the philosopher's fondness for Aristophanes and his own "wanton" writings, and if applied would lead to a gross error:

> If we think to regulat Printing, thereby to rectifie manners, we must regulat all recreations and pastimes, all that is delightfull to man. No musick must be heard, no song be set or sung, but what is grave and *Dorick*.[25]

Such would be to deny passions and pleasures, which "rightly temper'd are the very ingredients of vertu."[26] So Virtue, like Truth and like Good (elements of a kind of trinity of worth and worthiness), can only be seen and known by its opposite and denial. Finally, the hopelessness of trying to license printing is evident in the virtual impossibility of finding a censor of the requisite learning and judiciousness to undertake such soul-destroying work, so that the job could be filled only by those "either ignorant, imperious, and remisse, or basely pecuniary."[27]

Most of the remainder of *Areopagitica* is devoted to the harm that licensing will do to learning and letters. First and foremost, Milton asserts, will be the discouragement of learning. The learned man will become the inferior and the victim, lacking intellectual authority "under the tuition, under the corrections of his patriarchal licencer to blot or alter what precisely accords not with the hidebound humor which he calls his judgement."[28] Milton argues that the state constitutes "my governours, but not my criticks," and maintains that the effect of licensing would be to destroy originality and creativity, since the licenser is enjoined "to let passe nothing but what is vulgarly receiv'd already."[29] Milton praises the relative freedom of England, compared to other countries, and not least the Roman States of Italy, where Galileo had been silenced and imprisoned. If licensing be allowed to stand in England, he asserts, it would be a second prelatical tyranny, by which "Bishops and Presbyters are the same to us both name and thing," and the parson of "a small unlearned Parish, on the sudden shall be exalted Archbishop over a large dioces of books, and yet not remove, but keep his other cure too, a mysticall pluralist," which will make "a coventicle of every Christian meeting."[30] A state governed by the rules of justice and fortitude, a Church built on the rock of faith and true knowledge cannot be so fearful. With still no settlement in religion, to restrain writing would cause doubt and discouragement.

Milton pleads earnestly with Parliament to require that the Westminster Assembly chastise no longer the learned and the literate, quoting Bacon to good effect: "The punishing of wits enhaunces their autority, and a forbidd' n writing is thought to be a certain spark of truth that flies up in the faces of them who seeke to tread it out." Licensing might well prove the "nursing mother to sects."[31] The effect of licensing would be to persuade the laity to abandon religion to the clergy, the laity becoming passive and "occasionally" religious, not living the Christian life, and the clergy becoming intellectually lazy because they would be without challenge. The vision of "reforming the Reformation" led by the English nation from London, "the mansion house of liberty," will be lost if the nation gives up the process of "trying all things, assenting to the force of reason and convincement," where through knowledge could be made "a knowing people, a Nation of Prophets, of Sages, and of Worthies."[32] Knowledge comes through "much arguing, much writing, many opinions; for opinion in good men is but knowledge in the making."[33]

Milton's celebrated metaphor of the Church as a building in which its perfection is a "gracefull symmetry" arising "out of many moderat varieties and brotherly dissimilitudes that are not vastly disproportionall," his certainty at the fulfillment of Moses' vision of the entire race become Prophets, and his vision of "a noble and puissant Nation" soaring like an eagle,[34] all lead to a peroration in which the Parliament is warned that if it binds writers it must first become oppressive, arbitrary, and tyrannical, in effect suppressing itself as much as it suppresses authors. Milton restates the strengths of Truth and urges tenderness for those who desire to live in purity by God's Ordinances as conscience directs them, even though not entirely in conformity. And in those words which have become the battle cry of civil libertarians, he declares his own preference and proclaims his own faith: "Give me the liberty to know, to utter, and to argue freely according to conscience, above all liberties."[35]

Milton might have ended here. That he did not is sobering. In the remaining score of pages, he fought a kind of rearguard action, almost as if he were in retreat and was attempting to salvage what he could of his argument. Or perhaps these concluding remarks and exhortations can be read as concessions offered to political opponents in the hope of finding common ground, albeit lower ground than the high terrain he had earlier offered to take and hold. Milton hoped to persuade Parliament that while it could regulate, even suppress, printed publications, it should not do so by prepublication licensing. In modern terms, there should be no prior restraint. From the outset, Milton had claimed no greater objective than this: *Areopagitica, A Speech of Mr. John Milton for the Liberty of Unlicensed Printing, to the Parliament of England*. While his arguments could be extended to advance and support as complete a freedom of speech and press as we enjoy in this country today and beyond—though it is hard to see much distance left to go—Milton had consistently conceded that there were limitations:

> Impunity and remissenes, for certain are the bane of a Commonwealth, but here the great art lyes to discern in what the law is to bid restraint and punishment, and in what things perswasion only is to work.[36]

The perils of publication were not cloaked:

> He who is not trusted with his own actions, his drift not being known to be evill, and STANDING TO THE HAZARD OF LAW AND PENALTY, has no great argument to think himself reputed in the Commonwealth wherein he was born, for other then a fool or a foreiner.[37]

In allowing that "the State shall be my governours but not my criticks," Milton accepted the responsibility of the state to regulate the press. At the end, he was explicit about those tenets and opinions to which he proposed to deny toleration and, implicitly, publication:

> I mean not [to be] tolerated Popery, and open superstition, which as it extirpats all religions and civill supremacies, so it self should be extirpat, . . . that also which is impious or evil absolutely either against faith or maners no law can possibly permit, that intends not to unlaw it self.[38]

Finally, Milton commended Parliament for the order requiring that the name of the author or at least the printer of any book be registered, and graciously if unpersuasively distinguished that order from the licensing requirement of the "Star-chamber decree to that purpose made in those very times when that Court did the rest of those her pious works, for which she is now fall'n from the Starres with *Lucifer*." Milton did not recoil from contemplating the fate of pernicious books:

> Those which otherwise come forth, if they be found mischievous and libellous, the fire and the executioner will be the timeliest and the most effectuall remedy, that mans prevention can use.[39]

The Star Chamber decree referred to was, of course, that of July 11, 1637, following the sentencing of Prynne, Bastwick, and Burton—and the burning of *their* books by the public executioner.

Milton had appealed to the fearfulness, want of imagination, and absence of charity in his "governours," which he hoped might persuade them to grant half a loaf of press freedom. He was too skeptical not to have appreciated the irony of his concessions. He was also too astute an historian to have failed to realize that though, when Truth "and Falshood grapple; who ever knew Truth put to the wors, in a free and open encounter,"[40] it is difficult to ensure that the encounter is genuinely free and open. When fanaticism is open, half-truths will go unchallenged—and fanaticism has seldom been less open than it was during the rule of the New Model Army and the reign of England's "visible saints."

Having served the English Revolution as propagandist, shortly after the execution of Charles I, Milton was appointed by the revolutionary junta, the Council of State, as its Secretary for Foreign Languages. He was responsible for diplomatic exchanges in Latin and other languages and such other services as the Council directed. At least once, those services exacted an extraordinary price, of effort and mind and also of conscience. In 1650, the irrepressible William Prynne, outraged by the execution of the king and refusing to be taxed by a regime he considered illegitimate, broke with the Revolution. The Council arrested him and issued a warrant for searching chambers:

> These are to will and require you forthwith to make your repaire to the studdy and chamber of William Prynne, Esquire, in Lincolns Inne or elsewhere, which you are dilligently to search for all writeings, letters or other papers or recordes belonging to the Commonwealth, and alsoe for all writeings, letters or papers by him written, or in his custody, of dangerous nature against the Commonwealth, all which you are to seize and seale up, and bring or cause to be safely brought to this Councell, that thereupon further order may be given concern-

> ing them; of which you are not to fayle, and for which this shall be your sufficient warrant. Given at the Councell of State at Whitehall, this 25th. day of June 1650.
>
> Signed in the name and by order of the Councell of State appointed by authority of Parliament.
> Jo: Bradshawe, President

The warrant was directed

> To John Milton, Esq.
> Secretary to the Councell
> for forreigne languages.[41]

Milton did not fail to do his duty, as his office and as the revolution demanded. Enough was found to persuade the Council to keep Prynne in prison for three years.

Milton was neither friend nor admirer of Prynne. Having himself written a masque, *Comus*, in the 1630's, he abhorred *Histrio-Mastix*. Although he agreed with Prynne in savaging prelacy, he was not in accord with Prynne's presbyterianism. Prynne had attacked Milton hotly in print over divorce, eliciting an equally uncompromising printed response. By 1650, Milton and Prynne shared no common ground, save a tacit recognition that the English Revolution would probably never succeed in attaining legitimacy and hence not survive.

Nonetheless, Milton's eyes, already clouding from cataracts, would have seen no beauty in a business at which his conscience rebelled. Samson Agonistes? Perhaps. Should Milton have then asked the question, "Doth God exact day-labour, light deny'd?" Certainly, for his courage never failed him. He would, however, have winced at Patience's reply. He had seen already that Revolution's yoke is never mild, that its state is despotic rather than kingly, and that, among the thousands who at its bidding speed, too many who serve will only search and seize.

CHAPTER THIRTEEN

The Laws and Liberties of Massachusetts

Certainly the rarest book of the common law is *The Book of the General Lawes and Libertyes Concerning the Inhabitants of the Massachusets*, published 1648. There is only one known copy extant. Yet the importance of the *Lawes and Libertyes* goes far beyond its rarity. It was the first printed compilation of the laws of any English colony, and served as the model for similar efforts elsewhere and subsequent revisions in Massachusetts. It was the first response of colonial oligarchy—and an effective, lasting response—to a basic, popular agitation that can only be characterized as democratic. It was a document which reflected an English past but promised an American future.

The circumstances surrounding its compiling and publication have an intrinsic interest for the historian of American legal institutions.[1] What requires immediate emphasis is that the *Lawes and Libertyes* was not a code. What it was clearly reflected the constitutional framework within which it developed and the political-legal theory which underlay the promulgation of law in the Massachusetts Bay Colony from its settlement in 1630 to the publication of 1648.

The "City upon a Hill" which the founders of the Bay Colony established has been variously called a Godly Commonwealth, a Bible Commonwealth, and a Puritan Commonwealth. Each term is at least partially correct. However, recent scholarship has stressed the dissimilarity of Massachusetts congregationalism to Old England's puritanism with its strenuously presbyterian polity and has placed in a much-reduced perspective the role of Scripture as a source of law and foundation for political practice in early Massachusetts. Accepting, then, that Godly Commonwealth is the most useful term, nonetheless the emphasis is on the word commonwealth. In seventeenth century usage, *commonwealth* admitted of a number of meanings, some subversive of the strongly monarchical polity which was the accepted mode of European government. At its most innocuous, commonwealth meant a government established to advance the common-weal of a people. This was the literal translation of the Latin *res publicae*, public things. But the word already had the overtones of the direct Latin term, *respublica*, translated into English as republic, connoting a polity without a monarch. Republics in this sense were very few in the early seventeenth century. The most notable was the city-state of Venice; the United Provinces of the Netherlands were already commonly referred to as the Dutch Republic, although technically they owed allegiance to the King of Spain, and would continue to do so until the general peace of 1648 which ended the Thirty Years' War. In an age when monarchy was becoming increasingly absolutist, republicanism was abhorrent to the vast majority of Europeans who found legitimacy only in the crowned head. Republicanism was defended—apologetically—only by the few whose polity was, largely accidentally and even regretfully, not monarchical. Old England would experience a season of republicanism, from 1649 to 1660, but would return to monarchy with outright expressions of relief with the restoration of Charles II after the Cromwellian Interregnum. The founding fathers of Massachusetts intended a commonwealth in its limited sense of advancing the commonweal, but they did not shrink from the practical consequences of their pioneering experiment in government, which was a republic in everything but name.

A recent scholar of early modern European republicanism has given us a succinct definition of it, drawn from his own profound study of Venetian republicanism:

> A true republic was in the first place a particular power, not a participant in a universal system directed by some superior authority; and it claimed the right to determine its own policies simply on the basis of its particular interest. Nor was its internal structure, in the medieval sense, systematic. It was directed not to a single end from above, by a prince, but by a body of citizens, who somehow represented the community and its interests, and who were related to one another by a principle very different from that of hierarchy.[2]

Everything that Professor William Bouwsma says here about Venetian republicanism is equally descriptive of the Massachusetts Bay commonwealth. To be sure, the magistrates, ministers, and elected deputies of the Bay Colony never espoused an avowedly republican theory. Significantly, while they were prepared to make "laws" by act of the General Court, they never called those laws statutes, for the simple reason that for Englishmen only the King in Parliament could make a statute. They recognized that ultimately their powers were derived from the King's letters patent under the Great Seal to the Governor and Assistants of the Massachusetts Bay Company, while strenuously (and until 1684, successfully) resisting all attempts to have the patent returned to England for surrender or revocation. Nonetheless, even though they scrupulously observed the technicalities and the niceties of their constitutional position under the King of England, the Bay Colonists carried their allegiance so lightly, even so quietly, as to leave the impression that it hardly existed. Thus, the official instruments of Bay government studiously avoided regal references, even to the extent that the records of the General Court and other bodies never used the regnal year but only Anno Domini. Only if an instrument was to be used in England or elsewhere outside the Bay would there be a reference to the King and dating by his regnal year.[3]

When the first lawyer to practice in Massachusetts returned to England in 1641 after a three years' sojourn in practice in the colony, he published a penetrating pamphlet on the errors and infirmities of the governors of the colony. He freely conceded that, "wiser men than they, going into a wildernesse to set up another strange government differing from the setled government here [England], might have falne into greater errors then they have done."[4] What worried Thomas Lechford, solicitor, was the patently republican and congregational tone of state and church in New England. As he had written before his departure,

> I thank God, now I understand by experience, that there is no such government for English men, or any Nation, as a Monarchy; nor for Christians, as by a lawfull Ministerie, under godly Diocesan Bishops, deducing their station and calling from Christ and his Apostles, in descent or succession.[5]

Lechford argued that there were four types of civil government paralleling four types of ecclesiastical polity. He spelled them out carefully:

1) "Monarchicall absolute without laws"—tyranny
   "Episcopall absolute"—"Popish" tyranny
2) "Monarchicall bounded by Lawes"—English monarchy
   "Episcopall regulated by just Lawes"—the Church of England
3) "Aristocraticall"—as the Long Parliament seemed to advance
   "Presbyterian"—as the mainline Puritans in England demanded
4) "Democraticall"—as in New England
   "Congregationall"—as in New England.[6]

Lechford's preference was clearly for the second type of civil government. He had had too much of the fourth in Boston, and he was suspicious of the third, seeing it as basically inimical to the second. Events were to prove him right in a matter of only a few years: Aristocraticall-Presbyterian would work the destruction of English monarchy and episcopalianism, and in turn would fall to Democraticall-Congregationall polity. By the 1650's, under Cromwell's rule, Old England would be largely indistinguishable from New.

It should not surprise us, then, that there is not a single reference anywhere in the *Lawes and Libertyes* to the King, monarchy, the realm, or any other term of regality. From title-page to the oath for viewers of pipestaves, there is nothing that would indicate that the Bay colonists were subjects of Charles I. None of the oaths of office bound the officer to any allegiance beyond that to the "Commonwealth" or the "Jurisdiction."[7] Of Indians, the book explains, "divers of them are become subjects to the English"—which is a very strange way to speak of a king's subjects.[8] That royal prerogative of a whale or great fish cast up on shore is saved to such order as the General Court shall make, but without a word that under English law it was the King's trove.[9] The only citation to any institution beyond the Bay is that to the "High Court of Parliament in England" in the Proheme. Such silence is deafening.

The reluctance of the Bay Colony's founders to acknowledge the authority of the King as a matter of style and regularity of usage was potentially dangerous. The risk was not so much that it invited the descent of the King's wrath upon his contemptuous subjects—after 1640, Charles was in no position to do anything about New England—but because by declining to invoke royal authority the founding fathers forbore to rely upon the strongest argument for their own authority to rule. Refusing to claim authority under the crown of England put at risk the Bay Colony government's own legitimacy. Legitimacy was not a concern peculiar to the seventeenth century. However, it received unusual emphasis at a time when it became finally and universally admitted that the old medieval order of knowledge, belief, and authority had disappeared, religious strife had destroyed the unitary religious basis for western political values, and Europe had fallen into chaos from international rivalries and internecine wars. Monarchy was the great beneficiary of the destruction of the medieval system. The recognized monarch, scion of monarchs, ruling by divine right, answerable only to God at the last trump, was the exemplary legitimate authority over civil government (and in England's case, over ecclesiastical government as well). This legitimacy, enjoyed by the monarch, justified his exercise of power and, indeed, sanctioned his expansion of power in the defense of the state. That expansion was increasingly towards absolutism, and in monarchies throughout Europe, save in the England of Charles I, absolutism seemed the wave of the future. It was much more difficult to establish a basis for legitimacy in a state without a monarch. The ultimate appeal to authority conferring legitimacy remained an appeal to God. While the anointed wearer of the crown, an individual, was easily enough conceived of as the instrument of God on earth, a set of unanointed individuals as diverse and as numerous as the freemen of the Bay Colony was much more difficult to appreciate as the instrument of God. The founding magistrates' cutting away from the accepted mode of legitimacy was a very bold stroke.

If not the king, what then was the source of legitimate rule or authority? The magistrates and ministers of the Bay Colony were certainly educated and articulate, but far too occupied with immediate concerns and pressing necessities to devote much time to political theorizing. John Winthrop, Senior, the first governor and the colony's leading light, wrote that "In all their administrations, the Officers of this Bodye Politick have a Rule to walk by . . . which Rule is the *Worde of God*."[10] The Reverend John Cotton, in concluding the body of laws that he proposed in 1636, *Moses his Judicials*, cited Isaiah 33: 22, "The Lord is our Judge, The Lord is our Law-giver, The Lord is our King: He will save us."[11] Both men appealed to God as revealed in Scripture as the fundamental authority for governance. Consequently, we can reasonably expect that the Proheme or dedicatory epistle to the *Lawes and Libertyes*, in which both men had a part, would reflect the reliance upon God for civil authority that both had espoused elsewhere. And that indeed was what was relied upon. The words are John Cotton's:

> So soon as God had set up Politicall Government among his people Israel hee gave them a body of lawes for judgement both in civil and criminal causes. These were breif and fundamental principles, yet withall so full and comprehensive as out of them clear deductions were to be drawne to all particular cases in future times.

In short, positive law—the law of the commonwealth—is deduced from God's Law as revealed in Scripture. But God would not confer legitimacy on government any more than he would confer grace on the individual unless the government was a worthy recipient. If the government was in covenant with God, if it was bound with God to observe His laws, then it was legitimate. This was, of course, a civil parallel to the ecclesiastical covenant that bound the "visible saints" of the church congregation to each other and to God.

This theme of covenant is developed in the first paragraph of the Proheme by John Winthrop. The "peculiar people" of God were the ancient Jews. They had, however, forfeited their favored place, "Because that, when they knew God, they glorified *him* not as God, neither were thankful; but became vain in their imaginations, and their foolish heart was darkened [Romans 1:21]." The Gentiles, though not enjoying any special favor with God, came to stand in contrast to the contempt of the Jews, "For when the Gentiles, which have not the law, do by nature the things contained in the law, these, having not the law, are a law unto themselves [Romans 2:14]." Then God, despite his covenant with the Jews, withdrew his presence from them, chiding them, "Thou therefore which teachest another, teachest thou not thyself? thou that preachest a man should not steal, dost thou steal? [Romans 2:21]." The thrust of Winthrop's argument is clear. The Bay colonists had taken up the covenant of Grace in Christ and so "may injoye the special presence of God in the puritie and native simplicitie of all his Ordinances by which he is so neer to his owne people." The remarkable token of God's grace was that in New England as in Israel in the wilderness, civil and ecclesiastical polities had grown up together "like two twinnes," strengthening each other and avoiding destructive contention. Through the covenant of grace, God's law provided all the legitimating authority necessary to govern his new-favored "visible saints" in New England.

This did not fully solve the problem. What if not everyone was a visible saint, in covenant with God through the covenant taken on entering the Church? There were such in the Bay, and the proportion of non-churchmen (who were also non-freemen) to churchmen (freemen) was growing. This worried the magistrates and ministers, not so much because such reprobates constituted a threat to the good order of the commonwealth or served to introduce sin into it. Rather, the problem was that the legitimacy of the Godly Commonwealth, which depended upon the covenant of grace, could not admit of authority over those *not* covenanted in grace. The government could exercise legitimate authority over the elect because they were bound in the grace that came with election, but it had no claim over the reprobate, the un-covenanted. How dreadful a dilemma this was is made very evident in the third from the last paragraph of the Proheme. To the possible objection of the non-freemen, that they had had no hand in the making of the laws, the magistrates could answer only that because the non-freemen enjoyed the protection of the commonwealth they were bound tacitly to obey its government and abide by its laws. This is not an argument for legitimacy founded upon God's law. Indeed, it is not derived from God's law, but rather from the natural law, as Winthrop admits in citing the maxim *Qui sentit commodum sentire debet et onus*, He who enjoys the benefit ought also to bear the burden. In short, the structure upon which the legitimacy of the colony's government depended was sound only insofar as those who were governed by it were covenanted in grace. For the rest, another authority, and one much less exalted, would have to be summoned in defense of the regime.

Regimes do not rise or fall entirely from the merits or demerits of their legitimacy. Yet the founders of Massachusetts, as far as their legitimacy is concerned, made a very large claim for a very peculiar position. A Godly commonwealth that relied upon natural law as against God's law for justification was no more perfect than, say, the realm of England! That chafed. But then, so too did the presence of so many un-covenanted non-freemen. The history of the first half-century of the Bay was above all the history of the commonwealth's inability to perfect its godliness, and consequently the long, slow but steady erosion of the Godly commonwealth into a merely good civic commonwealth. Realities and necessities, the inability either to survive without the un-covenanted or to enforce exclusivity by immigration only of the covenanted, dictated the historical process of the change that overtook the colony.

Perhaps the Reverend John Cotton, whose reputation for fundamentalist rigorousness might lead us to expect nothing apologetic on the point of the Godly commonwealth, in the last paragraph of the Proheme betrayed anxiety. Cotton roundly condemned any distinction between the laws of God and the laws of men in the matter of civil obedience, so long as the authority was of God: "Let every soul be subject unto the higher powers. For there is no power but of God: the powers that be are ordained of God [Romans 13:1]." Though the administration of the law is deduced from the word of God in Scripture, Cotton was still forced to admit that "the clear light of nature in civil nations" also provided a starting point for deduction. His conclusion, given that admission, does not follow: that a "humane law" tending to the common good according to those principles "is mediately a law of God." It was not, and Cotton knew it. That he would try to make it so and binding even on the reprobate for "conscience sake" by citing Romans 13:5, "Wherefore ye must needs be subject, not only for wrath, but also for conscience' sake," reveals a certain uneasiness, maybe some fear, that the Godly Commonwealth was too narrowly founded on too small a base to survive the challenge of the un-covenanted. So history would prove.

If the founders of the Bay Colony were wanting in theory, in the practice of government and in the implementation of law they were remarkably successful. Pragmatism was their most conspicuous attribute. The *Lawes and Libertyes* was issued to satisfy the inhabitants' "longing expectation, and their frequent complaints for want of such a volume: wherein (upon every occasion) you might readily see the rule which you ought to walk by."[12] The founding magistrates recognized that the laws would change, for "*Crescit in Orbe dolus*," Evil groweth in the world. After all, the English Parliament had taken four centuries to do a work that was still not done. Though they eschewed making the Body of Liberties of 1641 a body of explicitly fundamental guarantees, they still incorporated almost all those "liberties" in the greater compilation, reduced perhaps to mere municipal law, well mixed with more humdrum provisions, but still recognizably far-reaching. The *Lawes and Libertyes* is inimitable in the experience of the English-speaking world precisely because what it contains are not one or the other, but both—laws and liberties.

The *Lawes and Libertyes* was inimitable in another way. Many of its provisions are markedly different from English law, statute and common-law, of the period. The letters patent of March 4, 1629 to the Company, which was the charter of the Bay Colony, gave power to the Company's officers

> to make lawes and ordinances for the good and welfare of the saide Company, and for the government and ordering of the said landes and plantacion, and the people inhabiting and to inhabite the same, as to them from tyme to tyme shalbe thought meete. Soe as such lawes and ordinances be not contrarie or repugnant to the lawes and statutes of this our realme of England.[13]

The *Lawes and Libertyes* constituted an exercise of that power, but the conditioning clause was very much observed in the breach. The "Capital Lawes" were both fewer in number than the English capital felonies and in particular crimes more severe.[14] Witchcraft, murder, manslaughter (anger, or cruelty of passion), murder by poisoning, bestiality, sodomy (buggery), and rape were English felonies punishable by death. Bearing false witness, either as perjury or as conspiracy to indict for treason or felony, was only a misdemeanor in English law. Idolatry, blasphemy, adultery, cursing or smiting one's parents, and the rebelliousness of a son were simply offenses punishable by ecclesiastical courts in England, or, in the case of smiting only, a misdemeanor at common law. Manstealing was not an offense at common or canon law. Conspiracy and Attempt of Invasion might come within the English statute law of treason, and hence be punishable by death. Of course, these Capital Lawes were pre-eminently the Biblical crimes to be repressed most severely in a godly and puritan commonwealth. What were not capital crimes—larceny, burglary, robbery, arson, coin-clipping, etc.—are equally noteworthy. Under its provision for Dowries, while the English common law was followed in the matter of lands, the *Lawes and Libertye*s was, by following the practices of the Roman and canon laws, far more generous to the widow in the matter of goods and chattels.[15] The General Court had as the model before its eyes the High Court of Parliament. Such arrogation, arguably in breach of the provision of the King's letters patent, is not surprising, given the colonists' understanding of what had to be done and how what was done could be justified and made legitimate. The pragmatism and the theory were nicely mixed, the product of sophisticated minds facing stern realities.

There is a tendency to underestimate the colonists' sophistication—a reluctance to credit the depth and the extent of the New England magistrates' experience of government and judicature in Old England. Borough courts and manor courts have persistently been offered as the models which, colonial historians suppose, were looked to for the Bay courts, and the Court of Assistants has been taken to be a replica of an English quarter sessions. But although the wilderness was primeval, Massachusetts society was not primitive. Neither were the instruments for its governance. The acutely observant Thomas Lechford knew what the magistrates were about:

> In the generall Court, or great quarter Courts [of Assistants], before the Civill Magistrates, are tryed all actions and causes civill and criminall, and also Ecclesiasticall, especially touching non-members: And they themselves say, that in the general and quarter Courts, they have the power of Parliament, Kings Bench, Common Pleas, Chancery, High Commission, and Star-chamber, and all other Courts of England, and in divers cases have exercised that power upon the Kings Subjects there, as is not difficult to prove.[16]

Lechford did not exaggerate, for scholarship has demonstrated the equity function that the Court of Assistants exercised, following the Chancery, and its willingness to repress serious misdemeanor with the rigor and the forms of Star Chamber.[17] The founding fathers built all the institutions necessary for the preservation of law, liberty, and order among seventeenth century Englishmen. Therefore, they built more than they suspected they would have to when they first set out upon their mission into the wilderness. The constant development of institutional forms and constructs between the original letters patent of charter carried to the Bay Colony in 1630 and the publication of the *Lawes and Libertyes* in 1648—not even two decades—was phenomenal. Two things never cease to amaze the historian observing this development. The first is how the appropriateness and sufficiency of the institutions that were established testify to the founders' sophistication in experience and understanding of the entire range of English institutions. Nothing was established which was inimical to the larger purposes of the founders; nothing was instituted that was more than was needed for the purpose. There was very little backing and filling. Most institutions survived because they were really needed and were economical to the task. Absent from Massachusetts was any widespread wild experimentation—and equally, any serious bias against necessary change.

The second thing that amazes the historian, is the utter confidence of the magistrates in the rightness, legitimacy, and authority with which they built, without recourse to Old England and without evocation of authority beyond that law of the God Whom they were very sure they served and Whose purposes they were convinced they were to advance on earth. Their theory might be imperfect, but there was no hesitation in acting as if it were not. In this the consensual played an important part. If the freemen (and churchmen) were a diminishing minority proportionate to the rest, they were listened to with increasing respect. The *Lawes and Libertyes* was a respectful response to their demands. Lechford's description of the Bay Colony's polity as "Democraticall and Congregationall" was right on both counts. Herein lay the promise of the American future based on an English past. This small society huddled around the estuary of a half-dozen little rivers was from its very origins and earliest developments a society recognizably different from any to be found in Old England.

Republicanism begins with that society. Independence begins with that society. Thus, two constituents of what will become the American nation were already present in Boston. And a third element, the experience of the rule of law, was also established there, equally early, flourishing in that rocky soil because of the application and the learning that those who cultivated it had brought with them. The *Lawes and Libertyes* is an unmistakably American artifact, but it is not only the first American law book. It is also a monument to English notions of the rule of law, English pragmatism, and the sureness with which Englishmen in the seventeenth century believed that God was with them, even unto a "City upon a Hill."

CHAPTER FOURTEEN

Trial of Charles I

Crown, as noun and verb, appears two-hundred and sixty times across thirty-six of William Shakespeare's works. The incidence is highest in the history plays, of course: two-thirds are found in *King John*, *Richard II*, the two parts of *Henry IV*, *Henry V*, all three parts of *Henry VI*, *Richard III*, and *Henry VIII*, with *Henry VI Part 1*, on its own, accounting for a quarter of the total. The tragedies and the Roman plays and the comedies share the remainder, and even the sonnets provide an entry:

> Incertainties now crown themselves assured,
> And peace proclaims olives of endless age.

This crowning can be dismissed as the tolling of romantic love—seemingly innocent of connotations that are more portentous and political. But to read on through to the end of Sonnet 107 is to feel the chill of those closing lines:

> Now with the drops of this most balmy time
> My love looks fresh, and Death to me subscribes,
> Since, spite of him, I'll live in this poor rime,
> While he insults o'er dull and speechless tribes:
> And thou in this shalt find thy monument,
> When tyrants' crests and tombs of brass are spent.

Tyrants' crests and tombs of brass make the connection. Shakespeare's history plays, true to the mediaeval past of England, are about little else. Witness sleepless Henry IV railing at his insomnia:

> Canst thou, O partial sleep, give thy repose
> To the wet sea-boy in an hour so rude;

And in the calmest and most stillest night,
With all appliances and means to boot,
Deny it to a king? Then, happy low, lie down!
Uneasy lies the head that wears a crown. [*Henry IV Part 2*, III.i]

There was good reason for Henry IV's unease. His crown had been taken from the head of the hapless Richard II, who had been forced to abdicate and then been struck down by one of his jail-keepers (if we credit Shakespeare's version of events) at Pontefract Castle, in the cold of February 1400. Henry IV's grandson, Henry VI, would have the crown wrested from him by Edward IV, and then be murdered in the Tower of London, in 1471. That foul deed was probably the work of Edward's younger brother, Richard Duke of Gloucester. Richard in turn usurped the crown from Edward's infant son, Edward V, who with his younger brother suffered a sudden death, in the Tower of London, *ca.*1483 (crimes that served Richard's interest, though not necessarily executed by his command or with his connivance). Richard, in turn, at Bosworth Field on August 22, 1485, lost his crown and life in battle with Henry, Earl of Richmond, henceforth Henry VII.

The singular, savage eloquence that Shakespeare bestowed on Richard reflects the sinister, savage political conflict between York and Lancaster:

Slave, I have set my life upon a cast,
And I will stand the hazard of the die:
I think there be six Richmonds in the field;
Five have I slain to-day instead of him.
A horse! a horse! my kingdom for a horse! [*Richard III*, V.iv]

Nonetheless, in the sordid and brutal chronicle of English internecine slaughter, the Wars of the Roses were merely an entr'acte. For sixteen decades before Bosworth Field, beginning at Berkeley Castle in 1327, violent ends had routinely been visited upon the rulers of England. At Berkeley, Edward II, dethroned by his estranged wife leading a powerful faction of exiled nobles whom he had turned against him by his promotion of low-born favorites, was first starved near to death, then dispatched by an ingeniously gruesome method that left no external marks on the cadaver.

Yet nowhere in all this sanguinary chronicle of usurpation, deposition, and murder can be found anything approaching the enormity voiced by Oliver Cromwell two days before Charles I stood his trial in Westminster Hall on January 20, 1649. Hearing Algernon Sidney's reasons for refusing to serve as a judge in the matter, Cromwell shot back, "I tell you we will cut off his head with the crown on it."[1] Cromwell and his aiders and abettors were as good as their word. On January 30, 1649, on the scaffold outside the Banqueting House in Whitehall, the king would wear only a cap to secure his locks from the ax—but it was a crowned head that rolled from a regal body that day. Medieval kings had been customarily deposed and murdered furtively (this was the fate that Elizabeth I, in such ways a traditionalist, herself suggested for Mary Queen of Scots), or, more exceptionally, killed in fair battle, helmeted and crownless. Charles I was tried publicly and executed publicly, as king. Never before in English history, and as far as it can be determined in European history generally, had any reigning monarch been murdered judicially. The enormity of it did not escape contemporaries: the four-score out of seven-score men summoned to judge him, who like Sidney refused to have anything to do with it; the many soldiers at the trial who shuffled uneasily and looked shamefaced when they gazed upon their monarch, responding to the sentiments of deference, wonderment, and foreboding evoked by his sorry figure; the hundreds who at the moment the ax fell set up a "dismal universal groan" around the scaffold that none had ever heard before in an age when public executions constituted spectator sport; the thousands of Englishmen who would never accept the slightest claim to legitimacy of the short-lived Commonwealth or its successor the Protectorate that followed the formal abolition of monarchy soon after the king's murder. The Spanish ambassador noted that England had become another Protestant republic (the United Provinces of the Netherlands was the other), and he was apprehensive of more of the same. Other princes feared that the infamous act was a forbidding omen threatening monarchy and the persons of monarchs everywhere.

It required another one and one-half centuries for those fears to materialize, in the Place de la Révolution, on another cold January day (January 21, 1793), when Citoyen Capet, Louis XVI, King of the French, quondam Louis XVI, King of France, was guillotined after a mock trial bearing an uncanny resemblance to that of Charles I in the matters of tribunal, sittings, charges, the king's defense, and the vote to condemn. Again, the ultimate victim would be the new regime, beginning with the First Republic, followed by the Consulate, finally by the Empire of Bonaparte, none of which achieved legitimacy. After the lot crashed, a new attempt at monarchy followed.

A century afterward, Lenin had the cold-bloodedness to go back to the old way of doing things. Czar Nicholas II and the royal family, with their physician and personal servants, were summarily disposed of in a fusillade of small-arms fire in the cellar of the house in Ekaterinburg where they were held captive. For seventy years the Soviet regime survived if not always thrived. But one quality ultimately eluded it: political legitimacy, not merely in Russian eyes, but in the eyes of people all around the world. Now that regime is gone. The bodies of the Romanovs, as they have become identified, have been honorably re-interred in St. Petersburg, among their ancestors and antecedents.

There is no single, simple, uniquely mystical attribute of monarchy that alone affords it legitimacy and thereby denies the regime that succeeds a monarchy the ability to establish a new legitimacy. None, not even monarchs themselves, made any claim that kings are sinless or inerrant. They are human. The institution's most eloquent defender and avid advocate, James VI and I of Scotland and England, in his numerous works on kingship struck a single prevailing note, which was the king's divinely ordained and divinely derived obligation truly to imitate God in justice and righteousness in governing his people and conducting the affairs of his state.[2] James recognized with complete clarity that failure to discharge the obligation placed upon the king by God could constitute tyranny and might well lead not merely to divine retribution in eternity but also to deposition and death in this present world. James reminded his son and heir apparent at the time, Prince Henry, that a tyrannical king's subjects might become his

> burreaux [public executioners]: and although that rebellion be euer vnlawfull on their part, yet is the world so wearied of him, that his fall is little meaned by the rest of his Subjects, and but smiled at by his neighbours.[3]

The prophetic quality of James's vision testifies to the pragmatism that monarchs required in a Europe that was simultaneously suffering the first modern continental war, the first modern revolution, and the last and greatest medieval schism. Regal legitimacy was not defined by the paraphernalia of kingship, Henry IV's "appliances and means to boot," not orb, scepter, and crown, not prerogatives and pre-eminences, not foot and cavalry, not even religious approbation. It had less to do with reverence than with rationality: in the king, his subjects saw the essential safeguard of their lives, liberties, and property. Legitimacy was the authority requisite for the essential and unique role that the king played in the polity in the preservation of justice and the advancement of righteousness. For that reason, and that reason alone, the king was acknowledged to be the fount of justice, maintaining the law and participating in making law to righteous ends by right means.

This understanding of legitimacy was twice voiced at climactic moments when the whole polity of a people and a nation-state stood on the precipice and looked into the black hole of lost legitimacy. Neither speaker had a philosopher's intellect and the character of each was seriously flawed, deeply enough to impeach his credibility. But what each said in the forum that condemned him long survived him and proved all too true, both as analysis and prophecy. On December 26, 1792, with Louis XVI facing a revolutionary Convention that was already committed to his destruction, one of his counsel stunned his judges. Raymond-Romain de Sèze noted that King Louis, shorn of the inviolability accorded him by the Constitution of 1791, as "Citoyen Capet" did not have the rights of an ordinary French citizen:

> I look among you judges and see only accusers; Louis will therefore be the only Frenchman for whom there exists neither law nor legal form. He will have neither the rights of the citizen nor the prerogatives of the king.[4]

The Convention was troubled. Sèze concluded by admitting that if he achieved nothing there, he would rely upon history, warning them to take care in their judgment, for history would judge them over centuries. Then the king himself spoke, simple, direct, compelling words of his clear conscience and his love for the people. It was to no avail. But Sèze's reliance on history was not confounded. Within a year of the king's death the Revolution began consuming its own; within four years' time, most of the king's judges had themselves shared the monarch's fate, at the hands of their brethren.

This drama in Paris played out almost exactly 144 years after Charles I at Westminster uttered the same prophecy even more explicitly. Judgment was delivered:

> For all which treasons and crimes this Court doth adjudge that the said Charles Stuart, as a tyrant, traytor, murtherer and publique enimy to the good people of this nation, shall be put to death by the severing of his heade from his body.
>
> After the sentence reade the *Lo. President* [John Bradshawe] said: This sentence now read and published, it is the act, sentence, judgment and resolution of the whole court.
>
> Whereupon the court stood up and owned it.
>
> *The King*. Will you hear me a word, Sir?
>
> *Bradshawe*. Sir, you are not to be heard after the sentence.
>
> *The King*. No, Sir?
>
> *Bradshawe*. No, Sir, by your favour, Sir. Guard, withdraw your prisoner.
>
> *The King*. I may speak after the sentence—By your favour, Sir, I may speak after the sentence over. By your favour—hold—the sentence, Sir—I say, Sir, I do—
>
> *Bradshawe*. Guard, withdraw your prisoner.
>
> *The King*. I am not suffered for to speak. Expect what Justice other people will have.[5]

The expectation appeared soon enough. Rule by major generals, parliaments summoned by writs and then dispersed by the sword, legislation by executive ordinance, judges sacked for refusing to excuse lawlessness. If less bloody than the Jacobin Terror, the English Revolution of saints-in-arms was hardly less a despotism. At least, it was a regime so despotic and illegitimate that after the death of Cromwell, the only figure capable of controlling the army, it unraveled rapidly. In 1660, King Charles II was restored by a rump of the army marching down from Coldstream on the Scottish border under General Monck and the concurrence of the Rump of the Long Parliament afforced by the members excluded by Colonel Pride on the eve of Charles I's trial.

Only in the last few dramatic moments of the so-called trial of Charles I, in his exchange with Lord President Bradshawe, is to be found a disputation that invokes the law and the matter that supplies a classic quality to this otherwise wholly dolorous event. For here alone was drawn a clear issue to support an adversarial forensic engagement that within our common-law tradition constitutes trial. For four days of hearings Charles Stuart had maintained steadfastly that he was "Charles, King of England, Scotland, France, and Ireland, Defender of the Faith, etc." Therefore, the tribunal that he confronted had no authority to try him, for treason could be committed only by acts in defeasance of the king himself, the only crimes acts of malfeasance by others committed against his peace. English law did not recognize a crime called tyranny—had no true bill, writ, or warrant to direct against malefactors termed "tyrant" or "public enemy." On the first day, pressed by Bradshawe to plead guilty or not guilty, the king enunciated precisely and clearly what he had lived to do and what he was prepared to die for:

> *The King*. I do tell you, Sir, England was never yet an elective kingdom, it was an hereditary kingdom for near this thousand years. Therefore let me know by what authority I am called hither. Your authority raised by an usurped power I will never—I will never betray my trust. I am entrusted with the liberties of my people. I do stand more for the liberties of my people than anyone that is seated here as a judge: therefore show me by what lawful authority I am seated here and I will answer it. Otherwise I will not betray the liberties of my people.[6]

These words echoed those of the king's father pronounced in the House of Commons in 1607 when the House had taken up hue and cry after a Cambridge civilian of much learning and slight sagacity who cast the royal prerogative higher than it could fly, to James I's evident discomfort. James's minister, the Earl of Salisbury, told the House:

> His Majesty said further that for his kingdom he was beholden to no elective power, . . . [and] that, though he did derive his title from the loins of his ancestors, yet the law did set the crown upon his head, and he is a king by the common law of the land.[7]

Indeed, Charles had made the point that the liberties of his people had been entrusted to him by God, by old and lawful descent, and he would not answer to a new unlawful authority.[8] He argued, correctly, that there was no lawful authority in that body, but merely a usurped power threatening the liberty of every subject as much as it did his life. So he did not answer. And at the last, as the guards dragged him away, he drew the clearest contrast between what had occurred there and what went by the name of justice in his realm. If the fount of justice was contaminated by the effusion of its own blood, then there could be no justice.

Who was this man of such tenacity, even obstinacy? Admittedly, during the quarter-century of his rule duplicity and obduracy had seemed far more characteristic of him. In power he appeared myopic and his vision opaque; powerless he was far-seeing and clear-sighted. Most accounts of Charles's rule manage somehow to slight the man and, by invidious comparison, often to overrate the meanest of his associates and his adversaries. Nor has Charles done much better with his biographers. Only now, after generations of meticulous modern historical research on Stuart Britain, are there genuinely scholarly biographies of Charles I, and the best of these demonstrate that much more remains to be done with the subject. His father James I and his heir Charles II, are more familiar and better limned in lifelike hues and true dimensions. Charles's nemesis, who at his trial was the presence which even when absent was always present—Oliver Cromwell—has drawn as much ink in death as he did blood in life. Certainly, Cromwell offers more than Charles, since he delivered himself freely in letters, speeches, and memoranda, carefully preserved and latterly well edited, providing a rich source for his thoughts as well as his acts.[9]

The vast muniment by which Cromwell can be studied was very much a product of his fervent, pious, mystical absorption with God, whereby he was compelled to agonize and soliloquize mightily in recalling His injunctions, assurances, and approbations.[10] There was none of this with Charles. He talked to God only through the elegant and orotund rhetoric, full of imagery and tautology, of Cranmer's Book of Common Prayer, containing the rites and ceremonies of the Church by law established. What God said to Charles, Charles kept to himself. The difference with Cromwell was not one of piety but of theology—in the case of Cromwell, quasi-mystical theology. In routine and temporal intercourse, Charles also stood in marked contrast to his father, James I. Where James had been loquacious, Charles was taciturn, keeping his own counsel, saying little publicly, and even with his ministers and councillors confiding little and nothing with much intimacy. Save with "Steenie" (George Villiers, Duke of Buckingham), and after that companion's murder in 1628, with his queen, Henrietta Maria, Charles was never comfortable speaking frankly and familiarly. James's vulgar and garrulous bonhomie fueled the notion (quite unfounded) that his heart and mind were as open as his mouth. Charles appeared a closed book. His guarded speech seemed to mask a closed mind, perhaps a calculating mind. Listening to Charles was an exercise in fathoming a hidden meaning, a cloaked agenda. Much of his reputation for unreliability and duplicitousness stemmed from his unwillingness to telegraph his intentions, so that others would in the logical course of things think they understood what he meant only to be greatly disabused by events. His enemies thought him a machiavel. In fact, he probably lacked the sagacity to be Machiavellian. He was certainly not eloquent enough to have played the role.

A clue to the king's character and mentality is afforded by his aesthetic sensibilities, artistic taste, and passion for *objets*.[11] He was the greatest collector of art and a principal patron of the best artists of his age. His taste demonstrated a contemplative nature that was withdrawn and all absorbed in the beauty of the thing at hand. While he was fond of the extravagant theatrical productions presented at Court, by the barristers in their Inns, and under noble patronage—especially when he and his queen had roles—his interest in these masques had more to do with the artistry of the staging and the allegorical qualities of the script than with a passion for drama itself. Indeed, one suspects that the cultivation of artistic sensibilities played a larger part in Charles's development than the more avowedly and directly intellectual evolution that characterized his father's upbringing and provided James with analytical capacities that clearly Charles did not have. Rather than an ear for dialectic, Charles had an eye for space and scape, light and shade, and this found its outlet in his steady support of building and even urban renewal. His Court architect, gladly continued from James's reign, was Inigo Jones. Charles, confiding direction to Jones, prosecuted with renewed vigor the hitherto desultory attempts to control slum building in and around London and metropolitan urban sprawl by law and regulation.[12] Charles threw himself into active encouragement of Jones's labors to complete or elaborate the great monuments of that genius: the Queen's House at Greenwich, Lincoln's Inn chapel, Covent Garden, Lincoln's Inn

Fields. And the Banqueting House at Whitehall, which would feel Charles's last footfall as he stepped through its window to the block outside.

The search for Charles begins with pathology. As an infant he suffered from acute rickets: soft bones, and marked deformity caused by an inability to assimilate phosphorous and calcium that resulted from malnutrition and insufficient exposure to ultraviolet rays. In short, he was poorly fed from birth and too long confined in Holyrood Palace, under the Firth of Forth's leaden skies. It was more than a year after James I, Queen Anne, and Prince Henry traded Edinburgh for Westminster that Charles's keepers thought the boy strong enough to make the trip. He was already four years old and had only begun to walk. He remained frail and sickly throughout his youth and, in part because of his disease, had none of his older brother's robust good looks. Charles was given to bouts of melancholy, which is a recognized consequence of rickets. He became an arduous sportsman, though he preferred the chase because mounted he was a match for anyone, his physical weakness overborne by a ferocious courage. His favorite likeness of himself was Van Dyck's bold equestrian oil.

Rickets left on Charles another, even more indelible, mark. The scrawny, deformed infant was barely suffered by his mother. His father's affection was focused upon his older brother, and so Charles went unloved. Even after Prince Henry died of typhoid in 1612, *aet* 18, Charles could not fill his void in the parents' affection. The best he could do was to seek for and find affection in the older youths who moved into James's circle as favorites. It was the last of these who provided a barely adult Charles with the constant companionship and genuine affection he had not found before. When Buckingham was murdered in 1628, Charles plummeted into an abyss of grief and despair from which he was saved only by the love of his volatile and mercurial French bride of four years, Henrietta Maria, sister of Louis XIII of France. Thereafter, his reliance on her became profound; there was never again any other favorite but the queen. He requited her love with a monogamous constancy virtually unknown in princes of the age. That she proved all that a wife should be, during his life and beyond his death, did not make any less perilous the fact that he relied heavily upon her acceptance and affection, as to a lesser extent that of others, for self-justification and self-assurance. He was too yielding and too easily influenced by those surrounding him to be a consistent and capable ruler. That his last favorite was the least selfish and most loyal—probably also the most practical—did not guarantee that Henrietta Maria's contributions to policy were more sound and beneficial than those before supplied by "Steenie."

Much less hard, literary evidence exists (or ever existed) to reflect the king at work *in propria persona* than exists to document others' contributions to the statecraft and governance of the age. Inevitably, Charles's conduct of affairs has generally been underestimated and his actions undervalued. This is true even of the best studies. A beautifully paced and brilliantly executed study of his halcyon days in the last few years of his Personal Rule depicts Charles in full connubial bliss, enjoying the lively company of his four young children, happy among his *objets*, diverted by masques, and oblivious of the worst that was about to be.[13] There is nothing positively wrong about the picture. What is lacking is an attempt to detect and demonstrate what the king might have been doing as prince rather than as partner, parent, patron, and player. The job is a tough one and to a great extent thankless. Tough, because a thoroughly informed and masterful historian must make projections from the known to the unknown (not statistically but, rather, anecdotally), and finally take a Kierkegaardian leap into faith in order to suggest how, by whom, in what ways, and to what extent the king's hand was on the tiller of the ship of state. Thankless, because it is so much simpler and more likely to elicit applause and encomia to write about how the great forces of history—yes, even economic determinism and historical materialism, alive and well still in those citadels of lost causes, universities—shaped events, led inevitably to civil war and revolution, and could only issue in the death of Charles Stuart.

Nonetheless, almost imperceptibly, this has begun to change. If fifty years ago one felt lonely and vulnerable suggesting that the Personal Rule of Charles I really was Charles's, that many of its most important policies bore the mark of his exigency, it is less lonely now.[14] That Charles, even more than his ministers (and possibly with a better sense of generalship though poorer statecraft), vigorously prosecuted war against his rebellious Scots subjects, 1638–1640, is no longer doubted:

> Ultimately, it was Charles I who insisted not once but twice that he should prosecute an ill-advised and badly financed war against Covenanter Scotland. Insufficient counsel and lack of funds were direct results of the king's political decisions.[15]

Moreover, if Charles nowadays suffers blame at the hands of an historian, it is not because of his detachment and frivolousness, but rather because he did so much to deserve it. There is something both right and reassuring about this judgment:

> In explaining the triumph of the Covenanters in Scotland itself, it is necessary to place a very heavy responsibility on the king. He was not, in fact, nearly as

> duplicitous as he is sometimes taken to be, but he did feel a very profound incomprehension and distaste for the religious convictions of large numbers of his subjects.[16]

Another scholar has suggested that the English Revolution might better be called The English Wars of Religion, to distinguish it from the later modern revolutions and tie it more closely to the Reformation. That distinction presents the danger of failing to understand that the English Revolution faced both ways, and as the Reformation's consequences flowed into it so its consequences flowed into the Age of Democratic Revolutions. To reject this suggestion is not to take religion out of the volatile mix of plaints and grievances, not to deny its dominance as a genuine ideological force that made the English Revolution. But religion worked at only one level of authority, and that was not the level under which Charles was put to death. The author's conclusions go too far: Charles's failure to respond to the fear of his subjects that the Protestant religion would be subverted weakened his hold on the affections of his people and raised in them a perception and belief which made civil war necessary and which was ultimately to bring the king to the scaffold.[17] But even to over-emphasize religion as an element in the destruction of the king is not to deny that Charles was a central actor and efficient cause of the war that ended his rule.

Charles's destruction is the strongest evidence of his central importance to the age and its events. Merely to remove his crown did not require taking his head first. The ax was not a tool to chop down a symbol or deface an icon: it was to bisect "Charles Stuart tyrant" for his own misdeeds, not merely those of his ministers, aides, and abettors. The elaborate show trial that the army and its leader determined upon was intended to manifest openly and clearly to the world, the English people, the king's subjects in Scotland and in Ireland, foreign princes and powers, and not least to posterity the "crimes" of Charles I. The trial was also intended to reinforce the judges' belief in the rightness of their actions; this was not the first time that usurpers had whistled shrilly in the graveyard. Thwarted by the king's refusal to play courtroom-courtroom, the tribunal turned to hearing witnesses for the record absent the king, and without possibility of cross-examination. To doubt the sincerity of Charles's accusers and judges, to question whether they really did believe the king a criminal with his hands steeped in the blood of the righteous, to suspect that this was all a charade staged by cynics for a purely Machiavellian purpose is to assign all emotions to the category of neurosis and all beliefs to the category of psychosis.

Were they right, was he a tyrant? The question has never failed to excite debate. Some externals can be peeled off to narrow the issue. First, whatever the Puritans might have suffered, theological heterodoxy was not a charge against Charles. The king's governance of the Church by law established, which was more solidly and legally vested in his sole authority than any secular power he exercised, was not central to the accusations, but his ecclesiastical discipline was trumpeted to aggravate the accusations and allow Bradshawe to strike the posture of answering to a higher authority. Second, beyond the vicious charge against Charles at the trial, that he had connived at the poisoning of his father, James I, few suggested and fewer still believed that this man was a monster of ordinary criminal dimensions. The operable word was "tyrant," his crime tyranny.

Leaving aside the difficulty of tyranny, the argument that Charles's rule constituted tyranny naturally divides into two distinct chronological parts, at 1642. Grievances from the period before 1642, royal trespasses that could be seen as contravening the ancient constitution, the practices of kingship and governance hallowed by more than a century of implementation, had been redressed by the first session of the Long Parliament in 1640–1641. Remedy had been provided by the legislation passed by the king in Parliament and by the punishment of his "evil counsellors," including the legislated murder of Thomas Wentworth, Earl of Strafford. In effect, for crimes prior to 1642, even a tyrant could reasonably plead a general pardon (as was issued at the end of every parliament). For the period after 1642, the charge of tyranny was essentially that Charles had levied war against his subjects. Less turned on who fired the first shot and whether the king was seen in armor taking the field against his subjects than by what authority Parliament had taken control of the militia, the polity's only military force, and by what authority the king could alone control the militia and whether in defense of that authority he could use military force. Whatever the provocations and exigencies, the king's prerogative, accepted and not before so deeply questioned, gave him sole control over the militia, and the king had clear authority to use force to defend his prerogative and his crown. With regard to the period after 1642, to make the charge of tyranny stick required substantial evidence that the king had gone beyond all lawful exercise of the police power. No evidence adduced at the trial, nothing less transparent than the farrago of accusations drummed by the prosecutor and nothing submitted by Bradshawe in his long meander through theorists of tyrannicide, could establish that.

The answer to the question depends ultimately on what was then perceived at the time as constitutionally correct and legally right. It was accepted at the time that there was only one constitution and one system of law governing England. Any theory about the constitution and the law could be tested against the single standard applicable to both. There was no great gulf between the king and his parliamentary adversaries as to the nature of the constitution and the effects of the laws. The most coherent statements included James I's major political writings[18] and countless speeches by members of Parliament on both sides of every issue of grievances that had arisen between 1621 and 1642, creating a rich tradition of parliamentary consensus as to what the ancient constitution was. The summation of the consensus was the work of the actor and analyst who first attempted to make historical sense of the revolution in which he had been caught up: Edward Hyde, later Earl of Clarendon. At the critical juncture, when war was becoming inevitable, Hyde refurbished the late-medieval notion of mixed monarchy and made it Charles's platform from which he responded to Parliament's demands and resisted Parliament's encroachments on his regality. Charles embraced the doctrine on June 18, 1642, in an answer drafted by Hyde to the Nineteen Propositions advanced by Parliament. In this answer, the king firmly declined to accept the Parliament's radical demands for wide executive powers, including appointment of ministers, in defeasance of his regality. Mixed monarchy required consensus based on a symbiotic relationship between the king and the three estates (clergy, nobility, commonalty) in Parliament. The relationship could and should have tensions, but the ties that bound all to common duty for the commonweal were to be maintained untorn and resilient in order to contain the tensions. Thus the mix encompassed monarchy, aristocracy, and democracy in a functional balance that would discourage the preponderance of any one element of the three. Modern constitutional theory—including that made practic at Philadelphia in 1787—owes much to that doctrine. More to the point, mixed monarchy already enjoyed substantial agreement as being the essence of the ancient constitution. But by the summer of 1642, Parliament, which had already embarked on a campaign to gain unitary political hegemony, in the House of Commons and in the field, was already beyond this appeal.

The king acted upon this view of the constitution. He was right to do so, and in any event he would have been derelict not to have done so. He said as much as he denied the tribunal's authority to try him. The actions of Parliament after 1642 and the absence of those MPs who failed to heed the king's summons to his subjects to rally to his colors at Nottingham were in defeasance of his crown and dignity. This constituted treason. The forces of Parliament made war upon the king within his realm. He had no alternative but to resist and to use all effectual but acceptable methods to suppress the treason. This did not constitute tyranny; it was strong and strait governance. How clear was the king's case was admitted implicitly by the Rump of the Long Parliament after it was purged by Colonel Pride on behalf of the army. Recognizing that the House of Lords would not participate in the destruction of the king and that he himself would not consent to go quietly from the scene, on January 4, 1649, the Commons arrogated to themselves alone the "Supreme Authority of this Nation," with full power to enact and declare law "although the consent and concurrence of the king and House of Peers might not be had thereunto."[19] This was more than treason: it was usurpation. It violated every precept and traduced every institution of the ancient constitution. It was not merely a shift to enable the Commons to destroy the king; it was tyranny, full and revealed, unblushing and shameless.

To his honor, perhaps to his glory, Charles was prepared to defend his crown and dignity, and therefore the liberties of his subjects and the rule of law, unto death. It is too much to say that he died for mixed monarchy. Abstract doctrine seldom moves a sacred head sore-wounded to martyrdom. Closer to the truth would be the judgment that he died, by his own confession, for the Church of England, although his religious concerns were clearly secondary to his principal concern for the civil polity and the law. But Charles did not die because he was a fanatic.[20] Rather, he saw with complete clarity that while he had lost the crown he had not lost the sole legitimate right to wear it. At the end, the courageous intensity that was the deepest part of his character persuaded him that he had done all he could.[21] Edward Hyde, retrospectively in deep admiration for the battle Charles had waged, concluded that

> he was the worthiest gentleman, the best master, the best friend, the best husband, the best father, and the best Christian, that the age in which he lived had produced. And if he were not the best king, if he were without some parts and qualities which have made some kings great and happy, no other prince was ever unhappy who was possessed of half his virtues and endowments, and so much without any kind of vice.[22]

Hyde was not blind to the fact that Charles had too often tried to placate when he ought to have stood firm, remained intransigent when he could have stooped to conquer, and reneged when he should have kept faith. Hyde's balanced encomium was neither faint nor damning, but he accepted the truth that Charles I contributed to his own misfortunes.

Perhaps, at the last, we are left with Charles's myopia. Almost alone among Englishmen, he seemed not to have apprehended the gathering storm. An old Somerset justice of the peace, Sir Thomas Wyndham, on his deathbed in 1635, exhorted his sons, one of whom served Charles in his privy chamber, with these words:

> My sons! We have hitherto seen serene and quiet times; but now prepare yourselves for cloudy and troublesome. I command you to honour and obey your sovereign, and in all times to adhere to the Crown; and though the Crown should hang upon a bush, I charge you to forsake it not.[23]

The younger Wyndhams did not forsake the crown. All four were Royalists; three of them died to preserve that crown. The long night of civil war, usurpation, regicide, and authoritarianism was clearly perceived in a portentous Commons debate on July 9, 1642, while Charles still believed that Parliament would blink first. Old Sir Benjamin Rudyard warned the House, "If Blood begins once to touch Blood, we shall presently fall into a *certain Misery*, and must attend an *uncertain Success*, God knows when and God knows what . . . ."[24] Bulstrode Whitelocke, a lawyer, was more direct and more perspicacious:

> We must surrender up our Laws, Liberties, Properties, and Lives, into the Hands of insolent *Mercenaries*, whose Rage and Violence will command us and all we have, and Reason, Honour and Justice will leave our Land, the *Ignoble* will rule the Noble, and *Baseness* will be preferred before Virtue, *Prophaneness* before Piety. . . . What the Issue of it will be, no Man alive can tell: probably few of us now here may live to see the End of it. It hath been said, That *he that draws his sword against his Prince, must throw away the Scabbard*.[25]

Every word proved true.

Why did the king not see the chasm opening between him and his people? The day before he died, Charles's two younger children were permitted to see him; his two older, Charles and James, were on the Continent trying valiantly to raise means to rescue him. He exhorted ten-year-old Henry of Gloucester never to let Parliament make him king, because it would be over the dead bodies of Charles and James, and at the last they would cut off his head, too. Princess Elizabeth, *aet* 13, was told by her father "not to grieve or torment myself for him, for it would be a glorious death that he should die, for the laws and liberties of this land, and for maintaining the true Protestant religion." (Alas, she could only grieve and torment herself, dying of a broken heart two years later.) Charles commended to Elizabeth the sermons of Bishop Lancelot Andrewes (full of light and evangelistic comfort), Richard Hooker's *Laws of Ecclesiastical Polity* (the rock upon which Anglicanism was founded, distinct from Rome and Geneva), and the martyred Archbishop William Laud's book against the English Jesuit John Fisher (a vigorous defense of the validity and orthodoxy of the Church of England).[26] Good, sound words, admirable advice. But one book was missing: *Basilikon Doron*, written by Elizabeth's grandfather, James VI and I, with its clear warning that a tyrant's miserable and infamous life might make his subjects his executioners. Possibly Prince Charles never read *Basilikon Doron*. Perhaps he did and, firm in his own belief that he was not a tyrant, dismissed it as inapplicable to himself. Was he mistaken?

CHAPTER FIFTEEN

Matthew Hale

Among the poignant stanzas of Gray's "Elegy in a Country Churchyard," there is one that might serve as proheme to the most brilliant work of Sir Matthew Hale, *The History and Analysis of the Common Law of England*. It is not the quatrain that evokes Hampden and Milton and Cromwell and the unnamed "little tyrant of his fields." It is the stanza that precedes it:

> Full many a gem of purest ray serene,
> The dark unfathom'd caves of ocean bear;
> Full many a flower is born to blush unseen,
> And waste its sweetness on the desert air.

Hale wrote his legal history in the 1660's and 1670's; Gray penned his lyric during the 1740's; had Hale had his way, the *History* would still have been in manuscript, unprinted, when Gray wrote. The *History* is a tacitly incomplete work and the accompanying *Analysis* explicitly so. Clearly neither was intended by Hale for publication in his lifetime in the form extant. Moreover, in bequeathing his manuscripts to Lincoln's Inn, both collections from others and works of his own, Hale referred to his works as

> a treasure that are not fit for every man's view; nor is every man capable of making use of them: only I would have nothing of these books printed, but entirely preserved together for the use of the industrious learned members of that society.[1]

When, almost forty years after Hale's death, the *History* was published, the anonymous editor felt compelled to preserve the anonymity of the author with the attribution, "Written by a Learned Hand." It was almost as if that ghostly hand reached beyond the grave to maintain the author's privacy.

Sir Matthew Hale (1609–1676), successively serjeant-at-law, Justice of the Common Pleas (1653–1658), Chief Baron of the Exchequer (1660–1671), and Chief Justice of the King's Bench (1671–1676), for a season a Member of Parliament, and an active lawyer much involved in affairs of government and of state, was a public figure during both the Interregnum under Cromwell and in the era following the Restoration of Charles II in 1660. His light could not be hidden under a bushel. He was accounted by his contemporaries the most learned lawyer of the age. His reputation was enhanced by three centuries of subsequent scholarship ranking him one of the greatest jurists of the modern common law: nearly the equal of Coke and the first of that famous triad of Hale, Holt, and Mansfield who ruled over the common law for a century. Hale essayed that synthesis of the law of England brought to full flower by Blackstone, as immediately evident in the Ramist table, the *Analysis* customarily printed with the *History*, which served as the model for Blackstone's methodology.[2]

Hale's contemporary reputation was raised on no significant corpus of juristic writings. All that he published in his lifetime was a brief preface to Henry Rolle's *Abridgment* (1668), commending that worthy enterprise which Hale had seen into print.[3] Shortly after his death, an admirer did him the considerable disservice of publishing *Pleas of the Crown, or a Methodical Summary of the Principal Matters Relating to that Subject* (1678). The subtitle tells all, for it was nothing more than a series of head notes (printed crudely as they stood without revision by the author) for a longer work, *History of Pleas of the Crown*, which would be published six decades after Hale's death in 1676. Hale's subsequent reputation owes most to the *History of Pleas of the Crown* (1736) and our legal classic, the *History of the Common Law* (1713), with some slight reinforcement from shorter tracts published in the course of the eighteenth century. Even so, in 1680 the unpublished *History of Pleas of the Crown* was highly enough regarded that the House of Commons appointed a committee to bring it to the press. Nothing came of it. The project was a victim of the great Exclusion Crisis which saw three Parliaments dissolved by Charles II in almost as many years in order to save the throne for his Catholic brother, James Duke of York, who would become James II in 1685 only to be driven from his throne by the Glorious Revolution of 1688. Even allowing for some circulation in manuscript of parts of his two major works among his friends and colleagues, Hale's contemporary reputation as a scholarly jurist could have owed little to his legal writings.

We are presented with two mysteries, and to understand Hale's work as well as to appreciate his extraordinary scholarly reputation then (and, to some extent, since) we need to solve both. First, why did Hale, who wrote a great deal, publish virtually nothing on the law during his lifetime? Second, absent such a corpus, what was the foundation for his contemporary fame as a scholarly jurist? Beyond the obvious relevance of publication to fame, there appears to have been also a subtle relationship between his motives in not publishing and the awe in which his contemporaries held him. To solve one mystery might go some way towards solving the other.

We begin with the inimitable qualities of Matthew Hale. Much of the best recent scholarship on Hale points to the centralness of two pronounced strains in mind and spirit which constituted distinctive qualities of his being and attributes of his life: his intellectual interest in "natural philosophy" and his spiritual commitment to Christian piety. These set him apart from earlier great jurists, not least Sir Edward Coke, and virtually all of his contemporaries of bench and bar.

As a "natural philosopher" of the epoch, Hale should be classed among those *virtuosi* for whom some form of scientific endeavor, whether observation, experimentation, collection, or merely speculation, constituted avocation rather than vocation, but with an intensity which gave real meaning to the old sense of the word *amateur*—one who loves. *Virtuosi* was an apt name, redolent of the manliness of the Renaissance's *virtu,* of the masterfulness of an accomplished mind, a sure hand, and a wide-ranging and speculative spirit. Though they spread themselves broadly and often thinly over the realm of knowledge, the *virtuosi* were not dilettantes, not amateurs as we use the term. In the last half of the seventeenth century and early decades of the eighteenth, the *virtuosi* everywhere in Europe—but most significantly in England—mounted a brilliant spectacle of intellectual vigor probably unmatched in any other epoch of so short a duration in the history of our civilization. Among the English exemplars were Isaac Newton—the greatest of the order—the luminous theorist John Locke, the chemist Robert Boyle, the biologist John Ray, and a number of others who formed the Royal Society of London for Improving Natural Knowledge in 1662. The underlying principle of the *virtuosi* was that the common search for truth in "natural philosophy" and for natural order was open to all talents without credal, national, social, or ideological tests. The vision was breathtaking:

> It is to be noted that they [the Royal Society] have freely admitted Men of different Religions, Countries, and Professions of Life. . . . For they openly profess, not to lay the Foundation of an English, Scotch, Irish, Popish, or Protestant Philosophy; but a Philosophy of Mankind.[4]

On the rubble of the bare, ruined, choirs of sectarian strife and internecine war, a handful of clerics, lawyers, physicians, academics, country gentlemen, civil servants, merchants, soldiers, sailors, essayed nothing less than a Philosophy of Mankind to be raised by the search for truth. All contributions were gratefully received: no knowledge was negligible, no branch of knowledge out of bounds for the quest, no proffered competencies and skills refused. The assumption of the endeavor was that nature was orderly, that all human action so far as it was consonant with nature could partake of the same orderliness. For a lawyer there was a job to do in the common enterprise, to bring the search for truth to the way men order their conflicts by law.

Though Hale did not belong to the Royal Society, his closest friends were members, and he moved freely in that circle. He himself published two works in the new science: *An Essay touching the Gravitation or Non-gravitation of Fluid Bodies* (1673), and *Difficiles Nugae, or Observations touching the Torricellian Experiment* (1674). A third work, *The Primitive Origination of Mankind Considered and Examined according to the Light of Nature* (1677), was published by Hale's close friends and fellow natural philosophers, the divines John Wilkins and John Tillotson, to Hale's blushing gratification, after he had sent the manuscript anonymously to Wilkins for his opinion of its merit. Hale never claimed any great expertise in natural philosophy. Rather, as he said, he indulged in it to the extent such leisure as his judicial duties and juristic labors allowed in order to "recreate" himself. His modesty was sincere enough, but it was also the accustomed stance of the *virtuoso*, the "amateur" engaged in the common enterprise for truth. Natural philosophy as yet had neither spawned professionalism nor fashioned orthodoxies to be defended to the death. There was a new science but no scientists.

Hale's creative involvement in the new science was not negligible. Besides contributing to the endeavor by his own speculative writings, Hale brought to the search for truth abundant professional experience of the nature of truth as evidence. Barbara Shapiro has suggested that Hale—and the law—gained as much from the search as he brought to it. "Natural philosophic" speculation perceptibly shifted the search for truth from an absolute standard to probability, to truth based upon the degree of certainty obtainable from the evidence. She concluded:

> Again stating the minimum case, the movements toward systematization and evaluation [of evidence] in terms of degrees of certainty are parallel and so nearly identical in law and science that leading lawyers of the day, many of whom

> also engaged in science, certainly found no need to resist the encroachments of science or to assert the autonomy of law. I think it is possible to go one step further and assert that a significant number of lawyers naturally assumed that a court should seek truth in the most scientifically correct way; thus they borrowed much of the doctrine of certainty although they would not have thought of themselves so much as borrowing science as conforming to the best general intellectual practices of the day.[5]

Thus, rather than attributing to the eighteenth century (and Bentham) the origins of a sophisticated law of evidence in the common-law system, it appears that the foundations of it were laid a century earlier, despite the continuation of the rhetoric of medieval legal practice of giving equal and indiscriminate weight to all testimony under oath, etc. That Hale's "virtuosity" made a contribution to this end is evident in the *History*, in his careful weighing of historical evidence in terms of its credibility and his acceptance of probabilities short of moral certainty in constructing a portrait of the law's past. The full extent of Hale's direct contribution to the development of probability in legal evidence awaits the scholar who will actually assess in detail Hale's career on the bench.

The other distinctive quality of Hale was a highly orthodox but non-sectarian Christian piety. Two of his works bare his soul, but in strikingly different ways. *Contemplations Moral and Divine* (1676) was published shortly before Hale's death, against his express will, by an overzealous chaplain to the Archbishop of Canterbury. The book was essentially a work of eschatology and soteriology, centered on the twin themes of contemplation of death and the accountability exacted of the soul by God for the use of one's life and works on earth. It breathed strongly that characteristic exhortatory moral theology which had been a constant in Hale's correspondence with his children and much evident in his conversation with his friends. Its message could not be lost on even the worst sinner or most obdurate skeptic, and its clear witness to the faith constituted a discharge of Hale's duty to God and man, as well as offering a source of comfort to the old judge in the twilight of his own life. *Lord Chief Justice Matthew Hale on the Nature of True Religion, the Causes of its Corruption, and the Church's Calamity by Men's Additions and Violence, with the Desired Cure* (1684) was published in homage to the memory of its author by the great Presbyterian divine, Richard Baxter, a dear friend of Hale by virtue of their common intellectual interests, piety, Christian charitableness, and—it must be emphatically said—visible saintliness. No less pronounced in its moral content, The *Nature of True Religion* is irenic, tolerant, and latitudinarian in its reflections on the religious controversies of the preceding half-century. Affirming episcopalianism as the most suitable ecclesiastical polity while denying that polity is the essence of religion, accepting modest ceremonies as good but that the observance of religion lies in fear of God and not in ceremonies, and that moderation, temperance, and prudence should direct Christian men as they dispute non-essentials, Hale likened the sectarianism of his day to boys blowing bubbles, chasing each his own and calling it religion.

Charles Gray has suggested that Hale wrote for himself rather than for others, that he wrote in order to clarify and gain perspective on things so that he could better cope with a world in which sin increases, and that one should expect such "privatization of intellectual life" in a "psychological Puritan, which Hale plainly was."[6] The Puritan tendency was for "publicization" of intellectual (and spiritual) life: witness the many fervent and perfervid Puritan tracts the age produced relating the never-ending struggle of the visible saint strenuously wrestling Satan to ultimate but never final defeat. To make one's faith a private matter seems more of a piece with the contemplative and meditative tradition in Anglicanism. Still, Professor Gray has a point. Clearly, Hale sought to order his experience—both intellectual and spiritual—by recording his contemplations and speculations. Publication of such reflections was not requisite to this purpose.

That Hale was loath to publish for that reason goes only so far toward explaining why he eschewed publication of his legal work. There is a danger in allowing the notion of "privatization" to substitute for more cogent reasons. Whether Puritan or mainstream Anglican, the urge to "privatization" might have had a more profound motivation and one dictated by something beyond idiosyncrasy. The contrast between the large corpus of legal and religious writings which he declined to publish and the considerable corpus of scientific papers that he chose to publish is arresting. His motives in publishing each of the three scientific works that appeared during his life are clear, and in the case of two of them because he was quite explicit in his reasons. In *Difficiles Nugae*, Hale maintained anonymity, but only, said he, because if his views were wrong, anonymity would make it easier for him to retract his error. In the earlier book on gravitation, Hale explained that though his propositions could be wrong, publishing them might encourage better minds than his to deal with the subject. And Wilkins and Tillotson had had no trouble overcoming Hale's genuine modesty in obtaining his consent to let them publish *The Primitive Origination of Mankind*.

The uncharitable might say that Hale the "natural philosopher" fell under the stricture of William Hudson, advanced a half-century before, as an example of

> this cracking age, when all men in all professions . . . for fear of burying their talent, post to the press to publish to others that which they well understand not themselves.[7]

The same charge certainly cannot be leveled at Hale the jurist, for he well understood the law and that better than all others. But Hale the jurist and the pious Christian was reluctant to publish in law or religion precisely because, whether or not he was aware of Hudson's criticism and dire warning, he acted on its premise. Natural philosophy was a neutral realm of endeavor; if too new to create orthodoxy also too new to be a heterodoxy challenging orthodoxy. It offered an area for debate but not dispute, enquiry that operated on a plane above and beyond the controversial and divisive issues that rent asunder seventeenth century England. It was otherwise with law and religion. None was more sensitive than Hale to the explosiveness of those issues, their latent capacity to do mischief to the polity and to bring back misery to the people. Hale had not only experienced the English revolution at first hand and at a high level. However reluctantly, and despite his scruples and his sentiments, he had served the revolutionary regime.

The English revolution of the mid-seventeenth century has two noteworthy distinctions. It was the first modern revolution fueled by an ideology of such potency as to create a national revolutionary ethos and to provide a continuum of democratic revolutionary change sweeping away virtually all political institutions and radically changing the social structure of the society. In this, it was at least the precursor if not the fount of the later revolutions, the American in 1775, the French in 1789, and the Russian in 1917.

Its second distinction is that it was a failed revolution. It failed to attain and to sustain the quantum of power requisite to effect lasting change undertaken by violent force, to create the force-that-succeeds in making a revolution. It failed to legitimize the force-that-succeeds by institutionalizing the changes accomplished by that force before the power created in the revolutionary ethos disappeared. It failed to sustain the revolutionary dynamic. The failure was as much symbolic as real. The English revolution judicially murdered a king but it could not fashion an acceptable substitute. "Lord Protector" Oliver Cromwell, a mere country squire, was to be guardian of England's liberties. His only success in protecting those liberties from a revolutionary army in which the sergeants and corporals were drawn from the most radical stratum in society grew from his singular capacity to check the army's excesses and play off its republican believers against its millenarian fanatics. Except for Cromwell it would have been worse. But he could not pay off and dismiss the army, and he lacked sufficient legitimacy to govern without its pikes. *Ould rednosed Noll that Grand Tirant*—that scurrilous epitaph may be the most revealing description of Oliver, Lord Protector and his less-than-regal style.[8] The nose fitted. So too did the job description, for Cromwell was indeed the wielder of the power of a despot. Perhaps he was a benign despot. He was certainly not a legitimate one, and Englishmen knew it.

Probably no Englishman was more aware of how profoundly legitimacy had eluded Cromwell than was Matthew Hale. The quintessential lawyer in an age when politics used lawyers as handmaidens, Hale knew what was legitimate and what was not. He was also Royalist at least in his sympathies and a loyal adherent of the Church by law established. The beheading of Charles I and the abolition of episcopacy were profoundly illegitimate acts in his eyes. Hale had entered the Parliament's Solemn League and Covenant as much from a conscientious concern to maintain religion as in order to continue a growing and lucrative practice at the bar. He accepted as just and necessary the early demand for reform of grievances by the Parliament, but when the Commons moved to the radical suppression of all the old institutions, much of the old ways, and at least some of the old law, Hale parted company with Parliament. By accident as well as by sentiment, he moved in Royalist circles. When he was admitted to Lincoln's Inn in 1628, it was to the chambers of William Noy, a leading member of the Commons' opposition in the 1620's who finished his career in 1634 as Charles I's Attorney-General, the author of that Stuart financial expedient of all financial expedients, ship money. Hale succeeded to much of Noye's clientele, including Archbishop William Laud, who mourned Noye as the Church of England's best friend among the laity. Hale would be among Laud's counsel at his treason trial in the Lords in 1643. In the course of the civil wars and their aftermath, Hale defended Royalists (impeached bishops, the Duke of Hamilton, Irish conspirator Connor Maguire, Presbyterian conspirator Christopher Love). Indeed, tradition has it that Hale suggested to Charles I that he found his defense in 1649 on refusal to acknowledge the jurisdiction of Parliament to try him. Hale's courage, scrupulousness, and learning attracted the favorable attention of his adversaries in court, and as Charles I had co-opted Noye twenty years before, so the victorious Parliament and Cromwell sought to bring Hale into the revolutionary camp. Hale was prominent in a commission appointed in 1652 by the Parliament (or what was left of it, the Rump, after purges of the crypto-Royalists in the Commons and the entire House of Lords) for the reform of the law, chairing it during its early deliberations. There he was a voice of moderation and even of tradition against the radical calls to change the English nation's entire judicial and legal structure. Little came of the commission's labors, for the Rump was soon purged by Cromwell, and the Protectorship set up under his dictate. In 1653, Cromwell offered Hale an appointment as puisne justice of the Common Pleas. Hale initially refused the office: with accustomed candor and remarkable courage, he told Cromwell to his face that he was not satisfied as to his authority to appoint the judiciary. This elicited from Cromwell a retort that if probably apocryphal was nonetheless revealing:

> I will not . . . be argued out of it—It is my desire to rule according to the laws of the land, for which purpose I have pitched upon you; but if you won't let me govern by red gowns, I am resolved to govern by red coats.[9]

Cromwell's threat had its own persuasiveness, and so too did the counsel of his Royalist friends, who urged Hale to serve in order to maintain the integrity of the law and the administration of justice. Even after accepting and taking his seat on the bench which tried only civil cases, he was reluctant to try criminal cases when on the assize circuit on the grounds that to pass sentence, not least of death, under an authority derived only from usurpation was wrong—a position which reinforced his compassion founded on religion and his professional sensitivity to a criminal law that punished so many minor offenses with death. Even in his civil work, Hale found occasion to question Cromwell's dedication to establishing justice, and he regretted his decision to serve a regime with such tenuous legitimacy. With Cromwell's death in 1658, Hale resigned the office, refusing to serve under Cromwell's son and successor, Richard, for whose rule there was not even a scintilla of legitimacy.

The Restoration of Charles II in 1660 in the twelfth year of the new king's reign—though not his rule, for save for an abortive filibustering expedition to take his throne early in the 1650's, Charles had been in exile on the Continent—restored legitimate government and legitimacy to government. It did so by a settlement that at least theoretically consigned nineteen years of England's history to oblivion. The Restoration was raised on the tacit understanding that none of the great politico-constitutional and religious issues which had provoked the revolution would be settled categorically and emphatically. Held valid were those acts of the Long Parliament which in 1641 had received the royal assent (and which had abolished the most egregious grievances of the previous four decades of Stuart rule), but all the "ordinances" of the Interregnum between 1641 and 1660 were declared null and void. The old institutions of King, Lords, and Commons were re-erected, but the invitation to Charles to take his throne and the convoking of the Lords to participate in the process came from a "Convention" called into being by the last surviving Members of the Long Parliament which had made the revolution. There was no White Terror of revenge: the new king had spoken of excepting from mercy only those who had signed his father's death-warrant, and those who were executed or jailed came almost exclusively from this small group of regicides. The crown, the Church, and those who had remained faithful to both were reendowed for realty confiscated in the revolution, but there was no wholesale expropriation from those who had benefited by the revolution. The Church of England by law established was reestablished by law, with bishops and convocations and ecclesiastical courts, but its old comprehensiveness and singularity were not assured. A revolution which had been done in the whole was dismantled by half. An eminent scholar of Stuart politics summed up the Restoration as Charles II returning to England

> to take over the constitution of 1641, the ancient constitution the parliamentarian gentry had always wanted to preserve. . . . King and gentry resumed their partnership, and resumed the attempt to secure an unattainable unity in religion, and to work an outdated constitution.[10]

None was more skeptical than Hale that the Restoration of Charles II signaled the end of the most profound disruption in England's history. None was less convinced than he that a revolutionary epoch of twenty years' duration could be considered no more than a bitter memory, buried and unrepeatable. Charles might joke that he had no intention of "going upon his travels again," but Hale would not have found humor in that witticism which raised for him and many others a possibility of enormous dreadfulness.

Hale had special reason to be apprehensive. Pious Anglican and learned jurist, he recognized how far unity in religion was unattainable and the constitution outdated. It had taken only a few months for the hope of religious unity to be wrecked. The vengeful intransigence of the restored episcopate proved to be balanced perfectly by the inordinate expectations and unremorseful justification of the Presbyterians, the most numerous group of dissenters, whose national conference in 1661, despite the best efforts of the Presbyterian divine Richard Baxter, broke up without reuniting with the Church. It took longer for the unresolved issues surrounding how England should be governed and what the relation between King and Parliament should be to surface. But by the 1670's, when the fall of the Earl of Clarendon removed a chief minister who had adeptly maintained the political balance, hostile factions readily moved into the open, playing ideological cards for political ends, raising the specter of another breakdown in the polity. That the King's heir was his devoutly Roman Catholic brother James, that the King himself inclined increasingly to ally with the principal Catholic power, the France of Louis XIV, and that the King ultimately became a fiscal client of France presented even the most loyal Parliament with a constant dilemma for which the outdated constitution could suggest no practical solution, other than a proto-revolutionary attempt to exclude James from the throne when Charles would die. Hale did not live long enough to witness that parlous spectacle raised in the three Exclusion Parliaments of 1679 to 1681, but his political acuity was too sharp for him to have found much comfort in the political developments of the last decade of his life.

The tacit understanding upon which the Restoration settlement was worked, that none of the old issues would be settled, had a tacit corollary: those issues would not be raised, at least not as polemical theories to be threshed out in public. The Restoration was, until the Exclusion Crisis, strangely barren of political theory, or at least political theorizing in print. The best efforts of many of the best minds went into the new science, lawyers produced careful and increasingly sophisticated reports and practice books, and clerics (Anglicans and Dissenters alike) avoided dogmatic theology and ecclesiology in favor of moral theology and Scriptural exegesis. Hale exemplified this phenomenon. Yet, as a jurist he could not avoid reflecting on the issues or eschew dealing with them in theoretical context. And he was too perspicacious, too keen in observation, and too long of memory not to realize that the old issues as new theory could surface at any time. He had a professional responsibility to be able to deal with them should circumstances demand. If he wrote merely for himself, he still prepared himself for the day when he might be obliged to deliver himself publicly and in print on disputed matters from which professionally he could not escape and upon which civic duty demanded his voice be heard.

In greatest part and beyond perfectionism and natural modesty, Hale did not publish his juristic work because he feared it would unnecessarily fuel the flames of political contentiousness. He was not wrong—his tenderness not misplaced, his apprehensiveness not unfounded—and especially so in the case of *The History of the Common Law*. For this classic is not quite what it appears to be, what subsequent scholarship has accepted it as being, or even what perhaps Hale really supposed it was.

No serious recent scholar has argued that *The History of the Common Law* was an objective, modern, historiographical effort, an essay in positivist history. That has not prevented serious recent scholars from justifiably finding considerable historical merit in the work, that it is "good history within the limits of evidence and scholarship available to anyone in the seventeenth century," as Charles Gray noted.[11] Barbara Shapiro saw the work as "the first attempt at a true history of English law."[12] D. E. C. Yale, who commands the legal historical scholarship of the late seventeenth century as no other scholar has, provided a brilliant, critical, and favorable analysis of Hale as "legal historian."[13] Even older generations of legal historians assessed the work in terms of its accuracy and usefulness. Frederic William Maitland praised it with faint damnation and William Searle Holdsworth lauded it as the best work on medieval English legal history prior to Pollock and Maitland![14] But while this is interesting and important, it misses the point. Matthew Hale was less concerned with writing the history of the common law (however *history* may be defined) as an exercise in jurisprudential scholarship than in uncovering the politico-constitutional origins and extent of the common law. *The History of the Common Law* was a tract of the times, if not entirely for the times. It was a book that Hale correctly understood to be too controversial and too dangerously unsettling to be published until the uncertain present had become such a remote past that the lamb of stability could lie down with the lion of change. Or, until the lion threatening to eat the lamb, Chief Justice Matthew Hale could no longer in good conscience remain silent.

If the *History* was a tract, then who was the enemy? There were in fact two enemies, together the most persistent and the most credible political theories produced by the revolution, each commanding the highest ground at their respective political extremes. Most venerable and most popular, the lowest common denominator of pro-Parliamentarian and ultimately revolutionary theory was that of the Norman Yoke. As this version of history had it, Anglo-Saxon liberties had flourished, thanks to the common law and to Parliament (both were believed to be so old) until the Norman Conquest of William I in 1066 placed upon the English a "Norman Yoke." For centuries thereafter, the Normans and their successors on the throne had subverted their subjects' liberties, turned the common law to regal ends, and threatened the erosion of the authority of Parliament. Sir Edward Coke had been a consistent, intemperate, and remarkably convincing (for want of evidence and despite the evidence), proponent of this theory. The theory was widely shared and Coke was often little more than first among equals, but his reputation as a jurist lent considerable cachet. The thrust of Coke's politico-constitutional theory was conservative and preservative: to restore and maintain the pre-Conquest liberties and institutions of the English nation and people by countering the threat posed by Stuart "despotism." The idea of the Norman Yoke assumed a past golden age that might yet be recovered by cutting away the degenerative innovations of post-Conquest kingship. Usages which grew from time immemorial (that is, before 1066) carried more than merely the authority of the past; they were the touchstone for the melioration of present discontents and the assurance of a better future.

The other theory was more pernicious because it was uncompromisingly radical, making no appeal to the past, providing nothing to conserve, and breaking explicitly with any prior usage or tradition that did not correspond to its uncompromising proposition:

> In all cities or bodies politic not subordinate but independent, that one man or one council, to whom the particular members have given that common power, is called their sovereign, and his power the sovereign power; which consisteth in the power and strength that every of the members have transferred to him from themselves, by covenant.[15]

Thomas Hobbes's tract clearly went to the support of an absolute monarchy, unrestrained and unrestrainable by instruments, institutions, or customs. Hobbes elicited from Hale a counterblast which showed none of the respectful and almost shamefacedly apologetic disagreement which was Hale's wont in differing with Coke.[16] To Hale, Hobbes's notions were especially mischievous because they were likely to tar the restored monarch, once Hobbes's pupil, with tyranny-by-association. Even more fundamentally, what Hobbes sought was diametrically opposed to Hale's understanding of the constitution and the role of the common law in it.[17]

The History of the Common Law of England dealt exactly, learnedly, and candidly, though not explicitly, with both of the current politico-constitutional theories which Hale sought to counter. The Norman Yoke received short shrift in Chapters V-VI: William I took England as lawful claimant to be the successor to Edward the Confessor, Harold was the usurper, and there was no general alteration of the laws or the constitutional construct of the nation, and neither did William intend any. The dismal tableau of the law's steady degeneration fared no better at Hale's hands. The *History* was a sustained treatment of the crucial contributions of a long line of great and able monarchs to the development of the common law. Where Coke had come to bury Caesar—even the English Justinian, Edward I—Hale praised him. Toward legislation, Coke was cool at best, willing to believe the worst. While he worked routinely and matter-of-factly with statutes, the law he loved and trusted was law as discovered by the judges. In his eyes, much statute law was either unnecessary or corrosive of the good law already existing and declared by those lions under the throne, the judges. The best example is Coke's animus, bordering on the apoplectic, towards the statute *De Donis Conditionalibus* and the entails that this modification of common-law rules had made possible. Hale recognized the role of legislation in the maintenance of a responsive legal system able to deal with novel situations by innovative legislative creation. Hale was highly skeptical of the law as history, of the remote past as mechanically determinative of the present, especially in politically and constitutionally charged situations. One function of the *History of the Common Law* was in fact to rid the lawyer of the Cokeian imperative of waiting upon Clio as not only the muse of history but also as the oracle of the law.

As for Hobbes, the *History* provides the detail supportive of Hale's briefer criticism of Hobbes's *Dialogue*. The law as Hale demonstrated its development was experiential and pragmatic, not victimized by mere "reason" (upon which Hobbes relied as justification for his great whale of sovereignty) and better than the arbitrariness and uncertainty of the sovereign's exercise of reason. The law as settled institution in the English experience stood as the buttress of mixed-monarchy, by which the King and the Estates in harmony and cooperation provided for exigencies by legislation and responded positively and melioratively to grievances. The proof of Hale's brilliant point in his response to Hobbes's *Dialogue*—that the falsity of the Hobbesian argument that there can be no qualification to the power of the sovereign is demonstrated by the laws and customs of England as facts which exist—is abundantly provided in the *History* (and it should warm the heart of every surviving Legal Realist). Indeed, the overall impact of Hale's *History*, insofar as it addressed the Hobbesian construct, was to point toward rights assured by law stronger and more fundamental than John Locke would admit or any polity would be prepared to accept until the debates at Philadelphia in the hot summer of 1787.

We have solved one mystery: why Hale did not publish. We are presented with another. Would Hale ever have published his juristic writings, given his clear sensitivity to starting hares that might not be stopped short of another revolution? The answer, which can at best be an informed guess, is yes. The stances taken by Hale in many of his juristic writings, most notably in *The History of the Common Law*, were directly relevant to the great outburst of political theorizing unleashed after 1680 by the Exclusion Crisis. The flood included publication of a work written a half-century before and the reply to it written during the crisis but not published until after the Glorious Revolution of 1688: Robert Filmer's *Patriarcha* and John Locke's *Two Treatises on Civil Government*, respectively. If that great intellectual confrontation dominates the constitutional theory of the era because Locke's work was pressed into service, after the fact, as an apology for the events of 1688, the questions raised by Hobbes in the *Dialogue* published in 1680 were no less pressing, and had Hale been alive would undoubtedly have been addressed by him in the forms of those works that he had written earlier and kept in waiting against such an unhappy event. Indeed, the Commons' attempt to publish the *History of the Pleas of the Crown* in 1680 grew from the MPs' correct apprehension that Hale had something of great importance to say about the Crisis and would have contributed to the constitutional debate, if not weighed into the political fray, were he alive.

We must still solve one other mystery: absent a corpus of published juristic works, what was the foundation for Hale's contemporary fame as a scholarly jurist? The leading clue is to be found in Hale's silence during the Restoration period. By his manifest learning and impartial conduct on the bench, by his "natural philosophic" speculations published and conveyed by discourse among the intellectuals of his day, and by his exemplary demeanor as a pious and devoted Churchman, Hale was held to be a man above partisanship and beyond the corruption of power. These were the qualities lauded by Gilbert Burnet, his younger contemporary and admiring first biographer, and they clearly reflected contemporary opinion about the Lord Chief Justice.[18] Hale was unwilling to deliver himself upon questions the discussion of which would breach the tacit political agreement of the Restoration that they be left in silence. This was taken as a token of his respect for the constitution and the common law and as a sign of his respect for the political balance and restraint that alone could avoid the horrors of the mid-century. Hale was very much the new-style judge, above the arena of politics, a servant of the law not of men, the judge whose unexceptionable conduct during an exceptional career on all three of the great courts under two regimes at the poles of legitimacy would serve as the model for a judiciary which was finally guaranteed its independence from politics in 1701. The Act of Settlement, in the last year of the reign of William III, was the tombstone on the grave of a century of revolution. It assured a Protestant succession to the throne, went a long way toward making the King's ministers responsible to Parliament, and gave life tenure to judges who could only be removed for misconduct by the action of the King and Parliament together. Here was recognition that *Justitia*, blindfolded and holding the scales of judiciousness and the sword of justice, was the most notable victim of internecine strife and revolution, that if the law is silent among arms it is strangled by civil war. Hale's contemporaries understood that to his voice they should hearken because he said so little.

In the event, Hale would not say it to them, only to their heirs and to us in the posthumous publication of his works. He, who loved the symmetry of Newton's celestial orbs, had the rare good fortune of being born and having died in equal symmetry, on two of the great feasts dear to the Anglican's heart (if not his soul): born on the Feast of All Saints, November 1, 1609, he died on the Feast of the Nativity, December 25, 1676. With the pious modesty displayed over his entire life, Hale refused the offer to have the Sacrament brought to him at home, received it in the parish church on the Sunday before his death, and was buried in the churchyard at Alderly, Gloucestershire, rather than in the church. He had said "churches are for the living and church-yards for the dead."[19] Sir Matthew Hale was not a village Hampden, or a mute inglorious Milton—certainly not a Cromwell, even one guiltless of his country's blood. Yet Gray's "Elegy" can be as well Hale's epitaph as that of his more humble neighbors,

> Far from the madding crowd's ignoble strife,
> Their sober wishes never learn'd to stray;
> Along the cool sequester'd vale of life,
> They kept the noiseless tenor of their way.

REFERENCE MATTER

Notes

EDITOR'S INTRODUCTION

1. Sir William Holdsworth, "Glanvil and Bracton," in Holdsworth, *Some Makers of English Law* (Cambridge, 1938) p. 8; *see also* Paul Brand, "Time Out of Mind": The Knowledge and Use of the Eleventh- and Twelfth-Century Past in Thirteenth-Century Litigation," *Anglo-Norman Studies* 16 (1994) pp. 37–54.

2. Bracton, *De Legibus et Consuetudibus Angliae* IV.6, T. Twiss, ed. (London, 1883), quoted in W. L. Warren, *Henry II* (Berkeley, California, 1977) p. 340.

3. A. W. B. Simpson, "The Common Law and Legal Theory," in A. W. B. Simpson, *Legal History and Legal Theory: Essays on the Common Law* (London, 1987) pp. 359–382, 364.

4. S. B. Chrimes, Introduction, to Sir John Fortescue, *De Laudibus Legum Angliae* (Cambridge, 1942) p. xcv.

5. Simpson, "The Common Law and Legal Theory" pp. 367–368.

6. *Ibid.*, at 376.

7. T. S. Eliot, "Tradition and the Individual Talent," in T. S. Eliot, *The Sacred Wood* (1942) pp. 47–59, 49–50 (emphasis in original).

CHAPTER I: GLANVILL

The Treatise on the Laws and Customs of the Realm of England Commonly Called Glanvil, Edited with Introduction, Notes and Translation by G. D. G. Hall, Thomas Nelson and Sons Ltd., Edinburgh, 1965; The Legal Classics Library, 1990.

1. John Cowell, *The Interpreter* (London, 1701), *sub* "Glanvill."

2. William Blackstone, *Commentaries on the Laws of England*, I, Legal Classics Library Edition (1983) p. 72.

3. Pollock and Maitland, *The History of English Law*, I, Legal Classics Library Edition (1983) p. 166.

4. *Ibid.*, p. 167.

5. T. F. T. Plucknett, *Early English Legal Literature* (Cambridge, 1958) pp. 37–38.

6. *Royal Writs in England from the Conquest to Glanvill*, R. C. van Caenegem, ed., 77 Selden Society (London, 1959) p. 355.

7. Glanvill, Introduction, p. xxix.

8. Glanvill, Introduction, p. xxxi.

9. Pollock and Maitland, I, p. 165.

10. W. L. Warren, *Henry II* (Berkeley, 1973) p. 237.

11. R. C. van Caenegem, *The Birth of the English Common Law* (Cambridge, 1973), p. 104.

12. Glanvill, p. 1.

13. Compare with the Proemium in Justinian's *Institutes*: "Imperial majesty should be armed with laws as well as glorified with arms, that there may be good government in times both of war and of peace, and the ruler of Rome may not only be victorious over his enemies, but may show himself as scrupulously regardful of justice as triumphant over his conquered foes."

14. *Royal Writs*, van Caenegem, p. 89.

15. Glanvill, Introduction, p. xxviii.

CHAPTER 2: MAGNA CARTA

Richard Thomson, *An Historical Essay on the Magna Charta of King John: to which are added, the Great Charter in Latin and English; the Charters of Liberties and Confirmations, granted by Henry III. and Edward I; the Original Charter of the Forests; and Various Authentic Instrument connected with Them*, John Major and Robert Jennings, London, 1829; The Legal Classics Library, 1982.

1. W. C. Sellar (Aegrot: Oxon.) and R. J. Yeatman (Failed M.A., etc., Oxon.), *1066 and All That* (London, 1930) p. 34.

2. Doris Mary Stenton, *After Runnymede: Magna Carta in the Middle Ages* (Charlottesville, Virginia, 1965) p. 33.

3. 42 Edward III, c. 1.

4. 42 Edward III, c. 3 (author's translation).

5. T. F. T. Plucknett, *Statutes and Their Interpretation in the First Half of the Fourteenth Century* (Cambridge, 1922) p. 135.

6. Stenton, *After Runnymede*, p. 54 (not good theatre); A. F. Pollard, *Henry VIII* (London, 1905) pp. 27–28 (forgotten); Lily B. Campbell, *Shakespeare's "Histories"* (San Marino, 1968) p. 142 (Elizabeth not bothered).

7. John Winthrop, *Winthrop's Journal "History of New England" 1630–1649*, vol. I, J. K. Hosmer, ed. (New York, 1908) p. 151.

8. *Lawes and Libertyes*, Thomas G. Barnes, ed. (San Marino, California 1975), Introduction, pp. 7–8.

9. *Records of the Governor and Company of the Masschusetts Bay in New England*, II, N. B. Shurtleff, ed. (Boston, 1853) p. 212. Besides Coke's *Second Institutes*, two copies of his *First Institutes* ("Coke upon Littleton," on real property) and two copies of his *Reports* (the First through Eleventh Parts were in print at the time) were to be bought, along with other books.

10. *Legal Papers of John Adams*, vol. II, L. K. Wroth and H. B. Zobel, eds. (Cambridge, Massachusetts, 1965) pp. 200–201, 207, in the case of *Sewall v. Hancock*. The

defendant was, of course, *the* signer of the Declaration of Independence—and this case was, politically, Adams's most important until the Boston Massacre trials. Adams's defense of Hancock fuelled colonial opposition to imperial customs and the vice-admiralty courts.

CHAPTER 3: THOMAS LITTLETON

Edward Coke, *The First Part of the Institutes of the Laws of England; or a Commentary upon Littleton. Not the Name of the Author Only, but of the Law Itself*, vol. I, with additions of notes, reference, and proper tables by Francis Hargrave and Charles Butler, Esqrs. of Lincoln's Inn, including also the notes of Lord Chief Justice Hale and Lord Chancellor Nottingham; and an analysis of Littleton, written by an unknown Hand in 1658–1659, Charles Butler, ed., 18th edition corrected, London, 1823; The Legal Classics Library, 1985.

1. The will is given, in extenso, in Eugene Wambaugh's *Littleton's Tenures in English* (Washington, 1903) pp. xlvii–lvii.

2. John Fortescue, *De Laudibus Legum Angliae*, The Legal Classics Library (1984) pp. xvii–xviii.

3. Littleton's *Tenures* were known by many titles, and for the first five editions (to 1510?) there was no title page, only the printer's colophon. The title used here is that of the 1540 edition.

4. John Lettou and William de Machlinia were the printers, probably both Low Countrymen, William's name indicating an origin in Mechelen (Malines) near Antwerp.

5. Joseph Henry Beale, *A Bibliography of Early English Law Books* [to 1600] (Cambridge, Massachusetts, 1926); R. B. Anderson, *A Supplement to Beale's Bibliography* (Cambridge, Massachusetts, 1943); A. W. Pollard & G. R. Redgrave, *A Short-Title Catalogue of Books Printed in England, Scotland, & Ireland, 1475–1640* (London, 1956); Donald Wing, *Short-Title Catalogue . . . 1641–1700*, 3 vols. (New York, 1945–1951).

6. Thomas G. Barnes, "Star Chamber Litigants and their Counsel 1596–1641," *Legal Records and the Historian*, J. H. Baker, ed. (London, 1978) p. 23.

7. A modest upturn began in 1645–1649 and carried on in into the Restoration, at about 270 admissions per year. These figures are based upon the author's own compilations and those of Wilfrid R. Prest in his pioneering study, *The Inns of Court under Elizabeth I and the Early Stuarts* (Totowa, New Jersey, 1972).

8. Prest, p. 52; Barnes, pp. 25–26.

9. *A Catalogue of the Library of Sir Edward Coke*, W. O. Hassall, ed. (New Haven, 1950) nos. 369, 305, 405. "Littleton mixed" (no. 869) is still extant, in the British Library: Harleian MS. 6687. The early editions of Littleton, all in octavo like this one of Coke's, had fairly wide margins, which facilitated noting-up.

10. The Twelfth and Thirteenth Parts of Coke's Reports were published posthumously in 1656 and 1658, respectively. Many of the cases reported in these volumes are in fragmentary or inferior form.

11. *See* Thomas G. Barnes, "A Cheshire Seductress, Precedent, and a 'Sore Blow' to Star Chamber," *On the Laws and Customes of England: Essays in Honor of Samuel E. Thorne*, M. S. Arnold et al., eds. (Chapel Hill, 1981) pp. 59–82; and J. H. Baker,

"New Light on Slade's Case," *Cambridge Law Journal* 29 (1971) pp. 51–76 and 213–236.

12. *Tenures,* vol. I, pp. lxi–cxxviii.

13. *Ibid.,* p. xxx.

14. Allen D. Boyer, "Coke, Sir Edward (1552–1634)," *Oxford Dictionary of National Biography* (Oxford, 2004).

15. J. F. Stephen, *History of the Criminal Law*, vol. II (London, 1883) p. 206.

16. W. S. Holdsworth, *A History of English Law*, vol. V (London, 1945) p. 467.

17. T. F. T. Plucknett, *A Concise History of the Common Law* (Boston, 1956) p. 278.

18. P. H. Winfield, *The Chief Sources of English Legal History* (Cambridge, Massachusetts, 1925) p. 334.

19. J. H. Baker, *An Introduction to English Legal History* (London, 1979) p. 65.

20. In Book One, Chapter I, of the eighteenth edition (which may be taken to set the standard), only about 2.5 percent of the text is Littleton—but in this, the first Chapter, Coke dilated mightily, on every subject under the sun (and not in Littleton) so it is atypical. However, Book Two, Chapters 3–4, on Escuage and Knight Service, is somewhat more typical, and still only 9 percent of the text is Littleton's.

21. Preface to the *Tenures,* vol. I, p. xlii.

22. 3 Coke's Reports 59.

23. Holdsworth, vol. II, p. 572. Littleton's reading is still extant in manuscript.

24. *Tenures,* fols. 393b–394b. The foliation—not pagination—of the text in our edition is the established foliation for Coke upon Littleton from the first edition onwards. It makes reference less confusing than would otherwise be the case, but with so much later intruded material it makes exact citation to material, especially later notes, difficult.

25. *A Calendar of the Inner Temple Records*, vol. I, F. A. Inderwick, ed. (London, 1896) p. 1.

26. *Tenures*, fol. 394a.

27. T. F. T. Plucknett, *Early English Legal Literature* (Cambridge, 1958) p. 113.

28. *Tenures*, fol. 394a.

29. It was William West of the Inner Temple who, in 1581, divided Littleton's text into sections, an arrangement preserved beginning with Tottell's French edition of that year (Beale, T.30). However, West in essence only imposed enumeration on what was already a logically structured series of propositions.

30. Holdsworth, vol. II, p. 574.

31. For the best concise recent treatment of *Taltarum's Case*, see A. W. B. Simpson, *An Introduction to the History of the Land Law* (Oxford, 1961) pp. 122–123; *see also* S. F. C. Milsom, *Historical Foundations of the Common Law* (London, 1969) pp. 156, 394 (explanatory note to p. 156).

32. *Tenures*, fol. 379b. The case that finally admitted the contingent remainder in all its unsettling grandeur was *Colthirst v. Bejushin*, 1 Plowden's Commentaries 21 (1550); *see* Milsom, pp. 165, 397 (explanatory note to p. 165).

33. Wambaugh, pp. xlix, liii.

34. Wambaugh, pp. xlix, liii.

35. A large step taken to close the gap is Joseph Biancalana, *The Fee Tail and the Common Recovery in Medieval England: 1176–1502* (Cambridge, 2001).

36. 4 Coke's Reports 7b.

37. *Tenures,* p. xxxvi.

CHAPTER 4: JOHN FORTESCUE

De Laudibus Legum Angliae: A Treatise in Commendation of the Laws of England by Chancellor Sir John Fortescue, Francis Gregor trans., Andrew Amos, ed., and a life of the author by Thomas (Fortescue) Lord Clermont, Robert Clarke & Co., Cincinnati, 1874; The Legal Classics Library, 1984.

1. *Henry VI Part 3*, Act V, sc. v.

2. John Rastell in 1513 had referred descriptively to Fortescue's work as "de laudibus legum Anglie"; it fell to Selden to give it that title which it has borne since.

3. Raleigh's *History of the World*, vol. 1, p. 247, quoted in S. B. Chrimes's Introduction to Fortescue, *De Laudibus Legum Anglie* (Cambridge, 1942) p. civ.

4. 8 Coke Reports, Preface, quoted in Chrimes, p. cvii, n, l.

5. Professor Chrimes provides a chronology of Fortescue's life containing more than 150 entries, drawn largely from the Public Records, in Chrimes, pp. lix–lxvii.

6. *Paston Letters and Papers of the Fifteenth Century,* 3 Parts, Early English Text Society (Oxford, 1971–2006); *The Stonor Letters and Papers, 1290–1483*, 2 vols., C. L. Kingsford, ed., Camden Society Third Series 29 and 30 (London, 1919) and *Camden Miscellany XIII*, Third Series 34 (London, 1924).

7. The introduction to The Legal Classics Library edition of *De Laudibus* was written by Clermont, whose biography, *Sir John Fortescue, Knight: His Life, Works, and Family History*, 2 vols. (London, 1869), long dominated the study of Fortescue.

8. Chrimes, p. lxix, n. 2.

9. Chrimes, p. 195, note to 116, 4.

10. Chrimes, p. xcii, n. 2. Ewart Lewis, *Medieval Political Ideas*, 2 vols. (London, 1954) provides a sound translation of *De Natura Legis Naturae*. Bar was a ducal territory of René of Anjou, Queen Margaret's father. St-Mihiel, on the right bank of the Meuse, was the site of the AEF's notable victory in September 1918 against the Germans.

11. Charles Plummer, ed., Fortescue's *The Governance of England* (Oxford, 1885). This work comprises only some twenty-five pages of text.

12. Percy H. Winfield, *The Chief Sources of English Legal History* (Cambridge Massachusetts, 1925) p. 317.

13. This changed perspective owes a great deal to B. P. Wolfe's work. This convincing revisionism is reflected in the substance and the title of the best one-volume treatment of early modern Britain, Roger Lockyer's *Tudor and Stuart Britain 1471–1714* (London, 1964)—the beginning date tells the story, and a far cry it is from the traditional great divide of 1485 and Henry VII's accession!

14. Chrimes, pp. lxxxvi–lxxxviii.

15. *De Laudibus,* pp. 61, 241. Incidentally, Fortescue appears to have been an early user if not the originator of the phrase, "comparisons are odious," so popular

in the next couple of centuries, appearing in one form or another in Cervantes, Marlowe, Shakespeare, Burton, Heywood, Donne, and Herbert.

16. *De Laudibus,* p. 27.

17. Compare Chrimes's *English Constitutional Ideas in the Fifteenth Century* (Cambridge, 1936) pp. 314–318 with Chrimes, pp. xciii–xcv.

18. For recent scholarship on the expanded activity of the Council as a judicial body under Henry VII (with glances backward), see *Select Cases in the Council of Henry VII*, C. G. Bayne & W. H. Dunham Jr., eds., Selden Society 75 (London, 1958), reviewed by Thomas G. Barnes in *Speculum,* vol. 34 (1959) pp. 649–651.

19. John Foxe, *Actes and Monuments* (London, 1563) [STC 11222].

20. H. D. Hazeltine's "General Preface" in Chrimes, p. xix.

21. *The Stuart Constitution 1603–1688*, J. P. Kenyon, ed. (Cambridge, 1969) p. 10.

22. *Ibid.*, p. 21.

CHAPTER 5: RICHARD HOOKER

Of the Laws of Ecclesiastical Polity by Richard Hooker, Books 1 to 4, Introduction by Ronald Bayne, J. M. Dent & Co., London, &E. P. Dutton, New York, 1907; The Legal Classics Library, 1998.

1. Richard Hooker, *Laws of Ecclesiastical Polity*, 4. 14. 1, pp. 421–422.

2. 26 Henry VIII, c. 1 (1534).

3. Thomas Hobbes, *Leviathan*, vol. I, 13.

4. *Eccles. Polity,* 3, 2.1, p. 297. In a more limited sense, Hooker used polity to indicate a particular form of civil organization, a specific form of government—as he indicated, perhaps somewhat surprisingly, in preferring the "polity" of Sparta to that of Athens. *Eccles. Polity*, 5. 79. 3; a statement perhaps not so surprising when one realizes Hooker's deep suspicion of the viability of democracy.

5. Matthew 5:17–18. The Gospel of Matthew, chapters 5–7, recording the Sermon on the Mount, begins with the Beatitudes and ends with the parable of the wise man who built his house upon a rock. That sermon was the Christly amendment to the Judaic Law, which astonished the multitude, "For he taught them as *one* having authority, and not as the scribes," Matthew 7:29—a promulgation of God's law to the believer.

6. A precise illustration of this point is to be found in Pope Pius V's excommunication of Elizabeth in 1570. Before publishing his bull *Regnans in excelsis*, the Pope had directed the trial of Elizabeth—in absentia—before the Roman Curia for usurpation and heresy. A number of English Roman Catholic exiles testified to her heterodoxy, resulting in her condemnation. Due process was meticulously observed, insofar as that was possible where the defendant was not amenable to the jurisdiction.

7. See generally G. R. M. Ward, *The Foundation Statutes of Bishop Fox and Corpus Christi College* (London, 1843) p. xv.

8. J. G. Milne, *The Early History of Corpus Christi College Oxford* (Oxford, 1946) pp. 37–39. The library remains very much as it was in Hooker's day, little changed in outward appearance, the ancient books still shelved in desked presses (although no longer chained).

9. Thomas Fuller, quoted in Wilfrid R. Prest, *The Inns of Court under Elizabeth I and the Early Stuarts, 1590–1640* (Totowa, New Jersey, 1972) p. 194.

10. Quoted *ibid.*, p. 195. In 1595 Travers became the first Provost of Trinity College, Dublin, which put him beyond Whitgift's reach. He died in 1643, aetat 95, having witnessed for a season the triumph of presbyterianism in England.

11. Hooker, "The Certainty and Perpetuity of Faith in the Elect," *Eccles. Polity,* pp. 1–13 and "Justification, Works, and how the Foundation of Faith is Overthrown," *Eccles. Polity,* pp. 14–76, respectively.

12. *Eccles. Polity,* p. 2.

13. *Ibid.*, pp. 47–48 (emphasis supplied).

14. *Ibid.*, II, 7, pp. 264–276.

15. *Ibid.*, II. 8, pp. 276–282.

16. *Ibid.*, II. 8, pp. 276–282.

17. Horton Davies, *Worship and Theology in England: From Cranmer to Hooker, 1534–1603* (Princeton, 1970) p. xv.

18. Scriptural moral criteria for bishops and deacons are set forth in I Timothy 3; "bishoppe" in verse 1 in the English Calvinists' Bible of Hooker's time, the Geneva Bible, is marginally noted: "Whether he be Pastor or Elder." "Bishop" was an Anglo-Saxon corruption of Latin *episcopus*, from the Greek word for overseer. It was the development of the office beginning in the primitive Church that gave to the later "overseer" the particular responsibilities and powers, temporal and spiritual—particularly the Sacraments of Ordination and Confirmation—that those called bishop came to have and those called presbyter did not.

19. Respectively, *Reason is the soul of the law, The law always intends what agrees with reason, Nothing is licit which is contrary to reason.* 7 Co. Rep. 7; Co. Litt. 78b; Co. Litt. 97b. See J. U. Lewis, "Coke's Theory of Artificial Reason," 84 *Law Quarterly Review* (1968) pp. 330–340 for a full and sensible discussion of Coke's concept.

20. Original essays demonstrating such connections are collected in Constance Jordan & Karen Cunningham, eds., *The Law in Shakespeare* (Palgrave Macmillan, 2006).

21. The best treatment of New England covenant theology remains Perry Miller, *The New England Mind* (Boston, 1939).

22. *Eccles. Polity*, I. 1.2, p. 150.

23. *Ibid.*, I. 8. 8, pp. 181–182.

24. *Ibid.,* I. 10. 1, p. 188.

25. *Ibid.*, I. 10. 4, p. 191.

26. 1 Elizabeth I, c. 1 and c. 2, respectively. Both acts remain largely in force, and the Book of Common Prayer was virtually unchanged until 1980 when the Church of England contracted the New Age itch to modernize, euphemize, and sterilize liturgical rites.

27. Thomas Erastus (1524–1583) was a Swiss-German Reformed Protestant, of the persuasion of Zwingli rather than Calvin, who in fact did *not* posit the "Erastian" notion of monarchical supremacy over the Church.

28. *Eccles. Polity*, IV. 24.7, p. 429.

29. *Eccles. Polity*, V. 6. 2.

CHAPTER 6: JAMES VI AND I

The Political Works of James I Reprinted from the Edition of 1616, Charles Howard McIlwain, ed. & intro., Harvard University Press, Cambridge, 1918; The Legal Classics Library, 1994.

1. *Letters of King James VI & I*, G. P. V. Akrigg, ed. (Berkeley, 1984) pp. 336–337 (early 1615). Carr fell in 1615 on discovery that his wife had collaborated in poisoning his former mentor, Sir Thomas Overbury, while Overbury was a prisoner in the Tower. The schoolmaster alluded to was the formidable George Buchanan.

2. *Scottish Diaries and Memoirs 1550–1746*, J. G. Fyfe, ed. (Stirling, n.d.) pp. 109–111.

3. Quoted in Antonia Fraser, *King James VI of Scotland, I of England* (New York, 1975) p. 104.

4. Quoted in Antonia Fraser, *King James VI of Scotland, I of England* (New York, 1975) p. 104.

5. David H. Willson, *James VI and I* (London, 1956) p. 36.

6. *Ibid.*, p. 71.

7. *Historical Collections*, vol. I, John Rushworth, ed. (London, 1721) pp. 155–156.

8. *Ibid.*, pp. 157–158.

9. *Ibid.*, p. 160.

10. Bodleian Library, University of Oxford: MS Add. C. 302, fo. 18; *AG ore tenus v. Moseley, Markehall, and Greene* (Oct. 17, 1627), reported in BL Lansdowne MS 620, fos. 50–51. The minstrels testified they were not the author of the song, but had received copies from others.

11. A. Weldon, *The Court and Character of King James* (London, 1650).

12. The current consensus is that James's relationship with Villiers was actively homosexual; Villiers's biographer argues that it began in August 1615, well before the fall of Somerset. Roger Lockyer, *Buckingham* (London, 1981) p. 22.

13. Akrigg, p. 431, James to Buckingham [December 1623?].

14. Thomas G. Barnes, "Deputies not Principals, Lieutenants not Captains: the Institutional Failure of Lieutenancy in the 1620s," *War and Government in Britain, 1598–1650*, M. C. Fissel, ed. (Manchester, 1991) pp. 82–83.

15. Ida Macalpine & R. A. Hunter, *George III and the Mad Business* (London, 1969) pp. 201–209.

16. Based on James's style of delivery—deliberate and not strongly emphasized, smartly paced rather than languid—each page of a speech to Parliament in the *Political Works* would require four to five minutes.

17. Wallace Notestein, "The Winning of the Initiative by the House of Commons," British Academy Ralegh Lecture (London, 1924).

18. James followed the contemporary practice of beginning the new year on the Feast of the Annunciation, March 25, so that the period from January 1 to March 24 would be given as the previous year, hence the date in the title, *Political Works*, p. 269.

19. *Political Works*, p. 269.

20. *Ibid.*, p. 274.

21. *Ibid.*, p. 278.

22. *Ibid.*, p. 280.

23. *Ibid.*, p. 284.

24. *Ibid.*, pp. 287, 289.

25. The point is discussed in the chapter on Sir John Fortescue, *supra*.

26. *Political Works,* pp. 290–291.

27. STC 5900. Despite its immediate fate, it went to subsequent editions, in 1637 and as late as 1701.

28. *The Stuart Constitution*, J. P. Kenyon, ed. (Cambridge, 1966) p. 12.

29. James's vivid disclaimer came back to haunt his heir. In the debates on supply in the Parliament of 1628, the opposition leader, Sir Robert Phelips, quoted it to withhold supply, 2 April 1628, *Commons Debates 1628*, vol. II, R. C. Johnson & M. J. Cole, eds. (New Haven, 1977) p. 251.

30. *Political Works*, pp. 310–311.

31. *Ibid.*, p. 318.

32. *AG ex rel. Sir Richard Egerton v. Richard Brereton et al* (June 29, 1614), two years before. The issue was whether Star Chamber could award damages; six voices said yes, four no. T. G. Barnes, "A Cheshire Seductress, Precedent, and a 'sore Blow' to Star Chamber," *On the Laws and Customs of England: Essays in Honor of Samuel E. Thorne,* Morris S. Arnold et al., eds.(Chapel Hill, 1981) pp. 359–382.

33. *See* the essay on Sir Edward Coke, *infra*.

34. Quoted in Akrigg, p. 6.

35. *Political Works*, p. liii.

36. *Scottish Diaries and Memoirs 1550–1746*, pp. 109–111.

37. Jennifer M. Brown, "Scottish Politics 1567–1625," *The Reign of James VI and I*, A. G. R Smith, ed. (London, 1973) p. 25.

38. *Political Works,* p. xlv.

39. *Ibid.*, p. 19.

CHAPTER 7: FRANCIS BACON

The Elements of the Common Lawes of England, Branched into a Double Tract: The one Contayning a Collection of some principall Rules and Maximes of the Common Lawe, with their Latitude and Extent. Explicated for the more facile Introduction of such as are studiously addicted to that noble Profession. The Other the Vse of the Common Law, for preseruation of our Persons, Goods, and good Names. According to the Lawes and Customes of this Land, By the late Sir Francis Bacon Knight, Lord Verulam and Viscount S. Alban, Assignes of I. [John] More Esq., London, 1630 [STC 1134]; The Legal Classics Library, 1997.

1. Bacon, *Elements of the Common Lawes*, Preface.

2. Quoted in Catherine Drinker Bowen, *Francis Bacon: The Temper of a Man* (Boston, 1963) p. 194.

3. The last word to date is Judge Noonan's treatment of Bacon's receiving of gifts as Lord Chancellor, in John T. Noonan Jr., *Bribes* (New York, 1988).

4. Francis Bacon, *Apophthegms*, in *The Moral and Historical Works of Lord Bacon*, Joseph Devey, ed. (London, 1852) p. 172.

5. W. S. Holdsworth, *A History of English Law*, vol. V (London, 1945) pp. 395–396. The reading is most easily obtainable in James Spedding, R. L. Ellis, and D. D. Heath, eds., *The Works of Francis Bacon*, vol. VII (London, 1864) pp. 391–450.

6. Douglas Denon Heath, redactor of Bacon's legal writings in *Works*, had strong reservations about Bacon's authorship of *The Use of the Law*; see *Works*, XIV, pp. 363–368.

7. Bacon's own explanation of his vigor in the prosecution of Essex for his treason was published in 1604, and all of his biographers go into the incident in some detail. Whether seen as base betrayal of a friend and mentor or as the reluctant duty of the Queen's loyal servant, Bacon's advocacy was quite extraordinary. *Brereton's Case* saw Bacon as Attorney General in Star Chamber casting the prerogative so high on the basis of so few precedents as to be breathtaking—and nearly disastrous. Thomas G. Barnes, "A Cheshire Seductress, Precedent, and a 'Sore Blow' to Star Chamber," *On the Laws and Customs of England: Essays in Honor of Samuel E. Thorne*, M. S. Arnold et al., eds. (Chapel Hill, 1981) pp. 359–382.

8. See Daniel R. Coquillette, *Francis Bacon* (Stanford, 1992).

9. Moore's Reports, 817.

10. Bracton, Bk. I, ch. 8.

11. *Latin for Lawyers*, 3d ed. (London, 1960).

12. Samuel E. Thorne, *Sir Edward Coke, 1552–1952* (Selden Society Lecture, London, 1957) p. 7. The reference to books means the Year Books, in which Coke supposedly found his ancient authorities.

13. These notes, along with a large collection of his own notes of trials in the Star Chamber, are numerous among Ellesmere's large manuscript corpus preserved in the Huntington Library, San Marino, California.

14. Bacon, *Maximes*, pp. 1–6.

15. *Scott v. Shepherd* (1773), 2 W. Bl. 892 [96 ER 525].

16. Bacon, *Maximes*, Preface.

17. *Ibid.*, Preface.

18. Bacon, *De Augmentis,* Aphorism 85, quoted in Holdsworth, p. 240 (Spedding's translation).

19. Bacon, *Maximes*, Preface.

20. "Touching the Compiling and Amendment of the Laws of England," *The Life and Letters of Francis Bacon*, vol. VI, James Spedding, ed. (London, 1872) p. 67.

21. Bacon, *De Augmentis*, Aphorism 86.

22. *Ibid.*, Aphorism 82.

23. Allen D. Boyer, *Sir Edward Coke and the Elizabethan Age* (Stanford, 2003) p. 291. Sir Nicholas Bacon, Francis's father, was Lord Keeper, 1558–1579, and one of Elizabeth's most trusted advisors. In rural Norfolk, where he was a powerful landlord, Sir Nicholas had done business with Coke's stepfather Robert Bozoun. Coke knew Sir Nicholas's other sons, Francis's half-brothers, as friends, political allies, and valued clients.

24. Catherine D. Bowen, *The Lion and the Throne* (Boston, 1956), on Coke, is a more ambitious and searching book than her *Francis Bacon: The Temper of a Man* (Boston, 1963), but the latter is by virtue of greater accuracy and a modicum of historical command a more valuable work.

25. *Life and Letters*, VI, p. 70.

CHAPTER 8: SIR EDWARD COKE

Edward Coke, *The First Part of the Institutes of the Laws of England; or a Commentary upon Littleton. Note the Names of the Author Only, but of the Law Itself*, Vol. II, with additions of notes, reference, and proper tables by Francis Hargrave and Charles Butler, Esqrs. Of Lincoln's Inn, including also the notes of Lord Chief Justice Hale and Lord Chancellor Nottingham; and an analysis of Littleton, written by an unknown Hand in 1658–1659, Charles Butler, ed., 18th edition corrected, London, 1823; The Legal Classics Library, 1985.

1. Catherine Drinker Bowen, *The Lion and the Throne* (Boston, 1956) p. 535.

2. *Ibid*., p. 280. Mrs. Bowen translated *cassis* as *shield*, which is much too free a rendering; this is not the worst bit of literary license in the book.

3. 1 *Institutes*, fo. 280b.

4. The Lyon's Inn reading, which is extant, was on 27 Edw. I, *De Finibus* (1299). The Inner Temple reading, which was discontinued after the fifth lecture because of the plague, was on the Statute of Uses.

5. *Calendar of Inner Temple Records*, vol. I, F. A. Inderwick, ed. (London, 1896).

6. 1 Plowden, 21.

7. 1 Coke Rep., 88b (1579). *Shelley* is reported, in printed versions, by Dyer, Moore, and Anderson. Of the four reports, Coke's is patently the least reliable but the most frequently cited.

8. 1 Coke Rep., 113b.

9. J.H., *The Compleat Clerk*, 5th ed. (London, 1683) pp. 369–386. From the names of the counsel and other internal evidence the date of this settlement and its provenance can be established.

10. 3 Chan. Car. and 1–2 Swanson, 454. Strict settlement can still be used both to settle land consensually and to settle the profits from the alienation of the land. The great agricultural depression of the 1870's gutted many large estates, and what the free market did not do then death duties have done since to destroy the landed estate and hence render obsolete strict settlement.

11. BL Harleian MS 7193, fo. 16.

12. Coke, CJKB, and Hobart, CJCP, on reference from Star Chamber in *Proctor's Case* (1614), rendered opinion that the question posed "must be determined by the precedents of the Court of Star-Chamber," 12 Coke Rep. 118. For a treatment of precedent in this sense, see Thomas G. Barnes, "A Cheshire Seductress, Precedent, and a 'Sore Blow' to Star Chamber," *On the Laws and Customs of England: Essays in Honor of Samuel, E. Thorne*, M. S. Arnold et al., eds. (Chapel Hill, 1981) pp. 363–379.

13. Thomas G. Barnes, "Star Chamber Litigants and Their Counsel, 1596–1641," *Legal Records and the Historian*, J. H. Baker, ed. (London, 1978) pp. 11–12.

14. *Novum judicium non dat jus novum, sed declarat antiquum, judicium est juris dictum et per judicium jus est noviter revelatum quod diu fuit velatum*, 12 Coke Rep., 42 (author's translation).

15. Inner Temple Library, Petyt MS 511, vol. 13, fo. 131v.

16. The confrontations between Coke and the King are succinctly treated in

Allen D. Boyer, "Coke, Sir Edward (1552–1634)," *Oxford Dictionary of National Biography* (Oxford, 2004), sub. "Kings bench and chancery."

17. Huntington Library, Ellesmere MS 1763, "*Pro Marchiis Walliae*," 3 Nov. 1608.

18. Boyer, "Coke," *Oxford DNB* for the issues raised by Coke's resistance.

19. Barnes, "Cheshire Seductress," pp. 379–382.

20. *Ibid.* See also Sir John Baker, "The Common Lawyers and the Chancery: 1616," *Law, Liberty, and Parliament: Selected Essays on the Writings of Sir Edward Coke*, Allen D. Boyer, ed. (Indianapolis, 2004) pp. 254–281, and W. J. Jones, "The Crown and the Courts in England, 1603–1625," *ibid.*, pp. 282–301.

21. See J. A. Guy, "The Origins of the Petition of Right Reconsidered," *Ibid.*, pp. 328–356.

22. Thomas Fuller, *The Worthies of England*, vol. II (London, 1682) p. 452.

23. The first volume of Allen D. Boyer's biographic and historiographical study of Coke has already set the early story straight. Allen D. Boyer, *Sir Edward Coke and the Elizabethan Age* (Stanford, 2003).

24. Donald O. Wagner, "Coke and the Rise of Economic Liberalism," *Economic History Review*, 1st series, vol. 6 (1935) pp. 30–44, and "The Common Law and Free Enterprise: An Early Case of Monopoly," *Econ. Hist. Rev.* 1st. series, vol. 7 (1937), pp. 217–220. Barbara Malament, "The 'Economic Liberalism' of Sir Edward Coke," 76 *Yale Law Journal* (1967) pp. 1321–1358, convincingly demolishes Wagner's thesis.

25. Jean Beauté, *Un Grand Juriste Anglais: Sir Edward Coke, 1552–1634, ses Idées Politiques et Constitutionelles* (Paris, 1975).

26. Stephen D. White, *Sir Edward Coke and the "Grievances of the Commonwealth," 1621–1628* (Chapel Hill, 1979) p. 23.

27. *Parliamentary History*, vol. II (London, 1807) col. 357.

28. *Latin for Lawyers*, 3rd ed. (London, 1960).

29. *See* the chapter on Francis Bacon, *supra.*

30. Records of the Governor and Company of the Massachusetts Bay in New England, vol. II, N. B. Shurtleff, ed. (Boston, 1853) p. 212.

31. 8 Coke Rep. 121a (1610). See T. F. T. Plucknett, "*Bonham's Case* and Judicial Review," *Law, Liberty, and Parliament*, pp. 150–185.

32. Quoted in H. T. Colbourn, *The Lamp of Experience* (New York, 1965) p. 75.

CHAPTER 9: MICHAEL DALTON

The Countrey Justice, Containing the Practice of Justices of the Peace out of their Sessions: Gathered for the better Help of such Justices of Peace as have not been much conversant in the study of the Laws of this Realm: Now again enlarged, with many Precedents and Resolutions of the Quaere's contained in the former impressions. By Michael Dalton of Lincolns Inne Esquire, and one of the Masters of the Chancery. Whereunto is also added by way of Appendix under their proper heads all such Acts and Ordinances as are necessary to be known and put in execution by the Iustices of the peace made and published before the yeer 1655, Company of Stationers, London, 1655 [Wing STC D144]; The Legal Classics Library, 1996.

1. Nikolaus Pevsner, *An Outline of European Architecture* (Harmondsworth, 1952) p. 19.

2. Unpublished; a copy in his hand is in the Houghton Rare Book Library at Harvard; a later rescission, also holograph, is in the All Souls Library.

3. Pollard and Redgrave STC 6205–6211, Wing STC DI43-DI50; Norma Landau, *The Justices of the Peace, 1679–1760* (Berkeley, 1984) p. 334.

4. *The Countrey Justice, Containing the Practice of the Justices of the Peace Out of their Sessions* (London, 1655) Wing STC D144 (author's copy).

5. *Records of Lincoln's Inn, The Black Books*, vol. II (London, 1898) p. 128.

6. Thomas G. Barnes, "Star Chamber Litigants and their Counsel," *Legal Records and the Historian*, J. H. Baker, ed. (London, 1978) pp. 7–28.

7. *Records of Lincoln's Inn*, p. 236.

8. Public Record Office: SP16/212, Liber pacis, Jan.–Feb. 1632, lists Dalton as JP for Cambridgeshire and as "*unus magisteros Canc.*" On three extant lists of commissions of the peace, 1621 and 1626, Dalton is listed as a JP but not as a Master of Chancery. For Masters, see W. J. Jones, *The Elizabethan Court of Chancery* (Oxford, 1967) pp. 103–117.

9. Wilfrid R. Prest, *The Rise of the Barristers: A Social History of the English Bar 1590–1640* (Oxford, 1986) p. 354.

10. *Ibid.*, p. 354.

11. PRO: SP14/33, Liber pacis, April 1608.

12. PRO: C193/13/1, Crown Office entry book, Nov. 1621; he was also seventh Esquire JP. Lists between 1608 and 1621 are not extant.

13. PRO SP16/212, Liber pacis, July 1636.

14. STC 6212 (1623), 6213 (abridged, 1628), Wing D151–D154 (1662–1700).

15. British Library: Sloane MS. 4359.

16. *Reports of Cases in the Courts of Star Chamber and High Commission*, S. R. Gardiner, ed., Camden Society NS, vol. 39 (London, 1886) p. 273; *The Court and Times of Charles the First*, vol. II, T. Birch, ed. (London, 1849) pp. 111–117.

17. PRO: C191/13/3, Liber pacis, Jan.–Feb. 1650; C193/13/4, Liber pacis, May 1652.

18. *Countrey Justice*, p. 183.

19. *Ibid.*, p. 370.

20. *Ibid.*, p. 33.

21. *Ibid.*, p. 213.

22. *Ibid.*, p. 214.

23. *Ibid.*, p. 352.

24. *Ibid.*, p. 400.

25. See J. H. Beale, *A Bibliography of Early English Law Books* (Cambridge, Massachusetts, 1926) pp. 125–129.

26. STC 10969–10977.

27. STC 15163–15174. Lambarde's *Perambulation of Kent* (1576) is the consummate masterpiece of late Tudor county topography and historical geography.

28. William Lambarde, *Eirenarcha* (London, 1619), p. 34. The present author's 1619 copy of *Eirenarcha* is wormed, dog-eared, torn, scribbled in, etc., a *vade mecum* well used over many decades.

29. *Countrey Justice*, p. 22.

30. Thomas G. Barnes, *Somerset 1625–1640: A County's Government during the "Personal Rule"* (Cambridge, Massachusetts, 1961) p. 58.

31. *Countrey Justice*, p. 89.
32. *Ibid.*, pp. 415–418, variously and incorrectly headed.
33. *Ibid.*, p. 417.
34. *Ibid.*, p. 418 (author's translation).
35. *Ibid.*, pp. 113–119.
36. For the Star Chamber case behind it, Thomas G. Barnes, "A Cheshire Seductress, Precedent, and a 'Sore Blow' to Star Chamber," *On the Laws and Customs of England: Essays in Honor of Samuel E. Thorne*, M. S. Arnold et al., eds. (Chapel Hill, 1981), pp. 359–382.
37. Thomas G. Barnes, "A Charge to the Judges of Assize, 1627/8," *Huntington Library Quarterly*, vol. 24 (1961) pp. 251–256; for more routine charges, see *Somerset Assize Orders, 1629–1640*, Thomas G. Barnes, ed., Somerset Record Society, vol. 65 (Frome, 1959), appendix of documents related to assizes.
38. Thomas G. Barnes, "County Politics and a Puritan Cause Célèbre: Somerset Churchales, 1633," *Transactions of the Royal Historical Society*, 5th series, vol. 9 (1959) pp. 103–122.
39. *Countrey Justice,* pp. 58–62.
40. Ferdinando Pulton, *De Pacis Regis et Regni*, 4th ed. (1623) fo. 42v.
41. *Somerset Assize Orders, 1629–1640*, no. 142; see also Thomas G. Barnes, "Star Chamber and the Sophistication of the Criminal Law," *The Criminal Law Review* (London, June 1977) pp. 316–326.
42. See John H. Langbein, *Prosecuting Crime in the Renaissance: England, Germany, France* (Cambridge, Massachusetts, 1974) pp. 6–43, 94–125. Professor Langbein finds pre-Marian statutory authority for magistrates' examinations in arrests involving lesser offenses. The author does not dispute that but argues that its continuation after the Marian statutes in the elaborate form mandated by the Marian statutes for felony was supererogatory.
43. *History of the Criminal Law of England*, vol. II (London, 1883) p. 206.
44. This was the case with Sir Robert Heath, Chief Justice of the Common Pleas, who was dismissed for purely precautionary, even judicially prophylactic reasons in 1634. Thomas G. Barnes, "Cropping the Heath: The Fall of a Chief Justice 1634," *Historical Research* 64 (1991) pp. 331–343.
45. Dr. Penny Darbyshire, Faculty of Law, Kingston University, personal letter to the author, 14 May 1996.
46. Thomas G. Barnes, "Law and Liberty (and Order) in Early Massachusetts," *The English Legal System: Carryover to the Colonies*, William Andrews Clark Memorial Library Seminar (Los Angeles, 1973) pp. 69–70.

CHAPTER 10: WILLIAM HUDSON

[William Hudson] "A Treatise of the Court of Star Chamber," *Collectanea Juridica. Consisting of Tracts relative to the Law and Constitution of England*, Vol. 2 [Francis Hargrave, ed.] E. & R. Brooke, London, 1792; The Legal Classics Library, 1986.

1. *Statutes of the Realm*, 16 Car. I, c. 10.
2. *Somerset Assize Orders, 1629–1640*, Thomas G. Barnes, ed., Somerset Record Soc., vol. 65 (Frome, 1959) pp. xviii–xx, for a description of criminal jury trial at assizes.

3. See *Select Cases in the Council of Henry VII*, C. G. Bayne & W. H. Dunham Jr., eds., Selden Soc., vol. 75 (London, 1958), reviewed by G. R. Elton in *English Historical Review*, vol. 74 (1959) pp. 686–690, and Thomas G. Barnes in *Speculum*, vol. 34 (1959) at p. 650.

4. Compiled from *List & Index to the Proceedings in Star Chamber for the Reign of James I (1603–1625)*, 3 vols., Thomas G. Barnes, ed. (ABF, Chicago, 1975).

5. Thomas G. Barnes, "Mr. Hudson's Star Chamber," *Tudor Rule and Revolution: Essays for G. R. Elton from his American Friends*, DeLloyd J. Guth & J. W. McKenna, eds. (Cambridge, Massachusetts, 1982) pp. 285–308 provides the evidence for this argument, and a fuller description of the treatise itself as well as Hudson's career.

6. Ferdinando Pulton, *De Pacis Regis et Regni*, 4th ed. (London. 1623) fo. 42v.

7. 9 Coke Rep. 55b.

8. BL Lansdowne MS 639, fo. 77; Folger Library MS V.a.133, fo. 72v; Popham's Reports, 129; Public Record Office, STAC8/284/4.

9. See Thomas G. Barnes, "Star Chamber Litigants and their Counsel, 1596–1641," *Legal Records and the Historian*, J. H. Baker, ed. (London, 1978) pp. 14–22 for a treatment of these Star Chamber litigation practices.

10. Hudson, *Treatise*, p. 226.

11. Thomas G. Barnes, "Due Process and Slow Process in the Late Elizabethan-Early Stuart Star Chamber," *American Journal of Legal History*, vol. 6 (1962) pp. 221–249 and 315–346.

12. Hudson, *Treatise*, p. 239.

CHAPTER 11: JOHN SELDEN

The Table-Talk of John Selden Esq with a biographical preface and notes by S. W. Singer Esq. William Pickering, London, 1847; The Legal Classics Library 1989.

1. David C. Douglas, *English Scholars, 1660–1730* (London, 1951) p. 136.

2. *The Oxford Dictionary of the Christian Church*, F. L. Cross, ed. (London, 1958) p. 1362.

3. This claim was asserted first in 1925; Canada is the only Arctic nation that has posited and consistently maintained a sectoral claim to the Pole. See Thomas G. Barnes, "'Canada, True North,' A Here There or a Boreal Myth?" *The American Review of Canadian Studies* 19 (1989) pp. 369–379.

4. *Table Talk*, p. 146.

5. Quoted in *The Stuart Constitution: Documents and Commentary*, J. P. Kenyon, ed. (Cambridge, 1966) p. 107.

6. *Ibid.*, p. 109.

7. *Commons Debates 1628*, vol. II, R. C. Johnson & M. J. Cole, eds. (New Haven, 1977) pp. 154–155.

8. *Aubrey's Brief Lives*, O. L. Dick, ed. (London, 1960) p. 271. Selden was one of the more than 1,200 lawyers who practiced in Star Chamber between 1603 and 1625. He signed pleadings in two cases, neither of them remarkable. This incidence in a court where virtually all barristers pleaded at one time or another and the vast majority no more than once or twice is revelatory.

9. *Table Talk*, p. 228.

CHAPTER 12: JOHN MILTON

Areopagitica, A Speech of Mr. John Milton for the Liberty of Unlicensed Printing, to the Parliament of England, James Russell Lowell intro., The Grolier Club, New York, 1890; The Legal Classics Library, 1992.

1. Eric Hoffer, *The True Believer* (New York, 1951) p. 140. In fact, Milton did not quite have a "draft in pocket," but rather only a notional scheme that can be dated about 1642.
2. Milton, *Samson Agonistes*, line 1745.
3. Milton, Sonnet XVI, On His Blindness.
4. David Loewenstein, *Milton and the Drama of History: Historical Vision, Iconoclasm, and the Literary Imagination* (Cambridge, 1990) p. 49.
5. Milton, *An Apology against a Pamphlet called a Modest Confutation* (London, 1642) pp. 58–59 [Wing STC M2090].
6. *Areopagitica*, p. 175.
7. Milton, *Eikonoklastes* (London, 1650) Preface [Wing STC M2114].
8. Milton, *The Tenure of Kings and Magistrates* (London, 1650) [Wing STAC M2183].
9. *Ibid.*, p. 11.
10. *Aubrey's Brief Lives*, O. L. Dick, ed. (London, 1960) p. 203. Aubrey's vignettes date from the 1670's to the 1690's.
11. *Historical Collections*, Pt. III, vol. ii, John Rushworth, ed. (London, 1721) p. 335.
12. The public records of the age bear Prynne's hand—mostly in excisions. From an assize order book he cut out an order to use in preparing the impeachment trial of Archbishop Laud in 1645 and from the Protectorate Council's order book he sliced the order readmitting Jews to England in order to prepare his attack on that action; *Somerset Assize Orders 1629–1640*, Thomas G. Barnes, ed., Somerset Record Society, vol 65 (Frome 1959) pp. x–xi. In 1662, Prynne published a sterling study of the history of Parliament, *Brevia Parliamentaria Rediviva*. See W. M. Lamont, *Marginal Prynne* (London, 1963) for Prynne's extraordinary career.
13. Houghton Library Harvard: Eng.MS.1359, fo. 58, *AG v. Prynne et al.*, hearing, 13 Feb. 1634. The author has transcribed and edited this unique manuscript report, which will shortly be published with introduction by the Ames Foundation.
14. Bodleian Library, MS Rawlinson D. 720, fo. 48v.
15. A Decree of Starre-Chamber concerning Printing (London, 1637) Art. IV. [STC 7757].
16. Cornelius Burges, *Another Sermon Preached to the Honorable House of Commons November the fifth, 1641* (London, 1641) p. 65. [Wing STC B5668].
17. David Wootton, "From Rebellion to Revolution: The Crisis of the Winters of 1642/3 and the Origins of Civil War Radicalism," *English Historical Review*, 105 (1990) pp. 668–669. The Putney Debates took place among the junior officers and rank-and-file of Cromwell's army in 1648, and produced the radical republican manifestos and avowedly democratic arid populist political movements to implement them epitomized by the Levelers, so-called because they would level down society.
18. *Dictionary of National Biography*, vol. XIII (London, 1921–1922) p. 476.

19. *Areopagitica*, p. 53.
20. *Ibid.*, pp. 55–56.
21. *Ibid.*, p. 58.
22. *Ibid.*, pp. 64–66.
23. *Ibid.*, p. 69.
24. *Ibid.*, p. 70.
25. *Ibid.*, pp. 74–75.
26. *Ibid.*, p. 81.
27. *Ibid.*, p. 93.
28. *Ibid.*, p. 101.
29. *Ibid.*, pp. 102–103.
30. *Ibid.*, pp. 118–120.
31. *Ibid.*, p. 123.
32. *Ibid.*, pp. 147–149.
33. *Ibid.*, p. 149.
34. *Ibid.*, pp. 150–159.
35. *Ibid.*, p. 163.
36. *Ibid.*, pp. 79–80.
37. *Ibid.*, pp. 96–97 (emphasis supplied).
38. *Ibid.*, pp. 174–175.
39. *Ibid.*, pp. 185–186.
40. *Ibid.*, p. 167.
41. Library, University of Illinois, Champaign-Urbana, Pre-1650 MS. 168; given in extenso here.

CHAPTER 13: LAWS AND LIBERTIES

The Book of the General Lauues and Libertyes concerning the Inhabitants of the Masschusets Collected out of the Records of the General Court for the Several Years wherein they were Made and Established, And now revised by the same Court and disposed into an Alphabetical order and published by the same Authoritie in the General Court held at Boston the fourteenth of the first month Anno 1647, Cambridge, Massachusetts, 1648. Reprinted from the Copy of the 1648 Edition in the Henry E. Huntington Library, Harvard University Press, Cambridge, Massachusetts, 1929; The Legal Classics Library, 1982.

1. Thomas G. Barnes, "Law and Liberty (and Order) in Early Massachusetts," *The English Legal System: Carryover to the Colonies* (Clark Library, Los Angeles, 1975) pp. 63–89. This essay served as the Introduction to The Legal Classics Library edition of *The Lawes and Libertyes*.
2. William J. Bouwsma, *Venice and the Defense of Republican Liberty* (Berkeley, 1968) p. 11.
3. A license and passport in Latin for the vessel *Sparrow*, issued to John Winthrop, Jr., for a voyage to Bermuda, by the governor, John Winthrop, Sr., began properly enough, "By virtue of letters patent of our most serene lord Charles, King of England, etc., I John Winthrop, Esquire, Governor of the colony of Massachusetts in New England. . . ." Yet the patent ended not with the regnal date, but mere-

ly "Dated twentieth day of December Anno Domini 1638." This is about the most royalist document to be found in the early records of the Bay Colony, and since it was for use in international commerce it could not help but invoke the authority by which it was issued and which alone would give it any weight, either in Bermuda or on the high seas. American Antiquarian Society (Worcester, Massachusetts): manuscript scrivener's book of Thomas Lechford, 1638–1641, p. 29 (author's translation).

4. Thomas Lechford, *Plain Dealing: or Newes from New-England* (London, 1642) Proheme [Wing STC L810].

5. *Ibid.*, p. 68.

6. *Ibid.*, pp. 78–80.

7. *Lawes & Libertyes*, pp. 56–59.

8. *Ibid.*, p. 29.

9. *Ibid.*, p. 55.

10. Quoted in G. L. Haskins, *Law and Authority in Early Massachusetts* (New York, 1960) p. 141.

11. *Collections of the Massachusetts Historical Society for 1798* (Boston, 1798) p. 187.

12. *Lawes & Libertyes*, Proheme.

13. *Records of the Governor and Company of the Massachusetts Bay*, vol. I, N. B. Shurtleff, ed. (Boston, 1853) p. 12.

14. *Lawes & Libertyes,* pp. 5–6. The provision for Man-slaughter relates to homicide *se defendendo*, in self-defense, rather than for the traditional felony of that name, which is provided for under Capital Lawes.

15. *Ibid.*, pp. 17–18.

16. Lechford, *Plain Dealing*, p. 25.

17. See Barnes, "Law and Liberty (and Order) in Early Massachusetts"; also the author's introduction to the Huntington Library's facsimile edition of the *Lawes and Libertyes* (San Marino, 1975).

CHAPTER 14: TRIAL OF CHARLES I

Trial of King Charles the First, J. G. Muddiman, ed., foreword by the Earl of Birkenhead, William Hodge & Co., Edinburgh and London, [1928]; The Legal Classics Library, 1990.

1. *Trial of Charles I*, p. 70.

2. See the chapter on James I, *supra.*

3. *Ibid.*, quoting *Basilikon Doron* (1599).

4. *Chronique de La Révolution, 1788–1799*, Jean Favier et al., eds. (Paris, 1989), p. 313 (the author's translation). See especially the trial in extenso in David P. Jordan, *The King's Trial: The French Revolution vs. Louis XVI*, The Notable Trials Library, Gryphon (New York, 1993).

5. *Trial of Charles I*, p. 129.

6. *Ibid.*, pp. 82–83.

7. See the discussion of James I, *supra.*

8. *Trial of Charles I*, p. 82.

9. A case in point is Maurice Ashley, *Charles I and Oliver Cromwell: A Study in*

Contrasts and Comparisons (London, 1987). Ashley, despite a stout bias in favor of Cromwell, tried hard to do equal justice to Charles, and failed not from prejudice but from an ignorance not of his own making.

10. *Writings and Speeches of Oliver Cromwell*, 4 vols., Wilbur Cortez Abbott, ed. (Cambridge, Massachusetts, 1937–1947) is the essential source. But Thomas Carlyle's *Oliver Cromwell's Letters and Speeches*, 3 vols. (London, 1857) provided plenty of raw material for previous studies.

11. A broad and thoughtful study of Charles as patron is Jerry Brotton, *The Sale of the Late King's Goods: Charles I and His Art Collection* (London, 2006).

12. Thomas G. Barnes, "Prerogative and Environmental Control of London Building in the Early Seventeeth Century: The Lost Opportunity," 58 *California Law Review* (1970) pp. 1332–1362. The bold attempt did not survive the Revolution.

13. Cicely Veronica Wedgwood, *The King's Peace, 1637–1641* (London, 1955).

14. Compare Thomas G. Barnes, *Somerset 1625–1640: A County's Government during the Personal Rule* (Cambridge, Massachusetts, 1961) with L. J. Reeve, *Charles I and the Road to Personal Rule* (Cambridge, 1989) and Conrad Russell, *The Causes of the English Civil War* (Oxford, 1990). What the author saw only through a glass darkly from Somerset, Reeve and Russell see clearly from the perspective of Whitehall.

15. Mark Charles Fissell, *The Bishops' Wars: Charles I's Campaigns against Scotland, 1638–1640* (Cambridge, 1994), pp. 1–2.

16. Conrad Russell, *The Fall of the British Monarchies, 1637–1642* (Oxford, 1991) p. 530.

17. John Morrill, "Charles I, Tyranny and the English Civil War," *The Nature of the English Revolution* (London, 1993) p. 306.

18. *The Political Works of James I*, especially *The Trew Law of Free Monarchies* and *Basilikon Doron*.

19. John Rushworth, *Historical Collections,* vol. VII (London, 1721) pp. 1383–1384.

20. C. V. Wedgwood, "The Trial of Charles I," *The English Civil War and After, 1642–1658*, R. H. Parry, ed. (Berkeley, 1970) p. 42.

21. He never conceded that he had rendered less than the fullest effort, even when at the very last he observed that had he to do what he had done over again, he would do it differently. *Trial of Charles I*, Appendix D, Charles's speech on the scaffold.

22. Clarendon, *History of the Rebellion and Civil War in England*, vol. II (Oxford, 1704) p. 243.

23. Quoted in Barnes, *Somerset 1625–1640*, p. 304.

24. John Rushworth, *Historical Collections,* vol. IV (London, 1721) p. 754.

25. *Ibid*., pp. 754–755. Whitelocke, one of the managers of Strafford's impeachment in 1641 and a Parliamentarian stalwart who served the Commonwealth and Protectorate in high office, would have no part of Charles's trial. He died of old age in 1675.

26. John Buchan, *Oliver Cromwell* (London, 1934) p. 313.

CHAPTER 15: MATTHEW HALE

[Sir Matthew Hale] *The History and Analysis of the Common Law of England, Written by a Learned Hand*, J. Nutt printer. In the Savoy, London, 1713; The Legal Classics Library, 1987.

1. Quoted in "The Life of Matthew Hale," in *The History of the Common Law of England*, Charles Runnington, ed., 6th ed. (London, 1820) p. xlvi.

2. Pierre de la Ramée (Petrus Ramus), 1515–1572, was a French logician whose attack on Aristotelian logic and adherence to Reformed Protestantism made him a walking pincushion of persecution (he would die during the Massacre of St. Bartholomew's Day). Ramist logic, essentially rhetorical, can work both deductively and inductively, allowing analysis of a system to start with either end, the greatest or the least. Ramus's little treatise published in English in 1574 [STC 15246] with subsequent editions to 1632 had enormous intellectual influence in English theological and legal writing. Even Milton wrote a little treatise on Ramus. For an appreciation of the thought of the rhetoricians of early modern England—in particular, the poets, the philosophers, and the lawyers—the essential source remains Walter J. Ong, *Ramus, Method, and the Decay of Dialogue: From the Art of Discourse to the Art of Reason* (Cambridge, Massachusetts, 1958).

3. Rolle's *Abridgment* of Year Book cases and later reports, systematic, intelligently arranged, copious, and accurate, has been termed "one of the lighthouses in the history of our law," Percy Winfield, *The Chief Sources of English Legal History* (Cambridge, Massachsetts, 1925) p. 239. Rolle was a Parliamentarian Justice of King's Bench, 1648–1655, who had resigned his office because of Cromwell's interference with justice; the parallel to Hale's own career and his scrupulosity commended Rolle to him. Hale's preface lauded not only Rolle's learning and the usefulness of his collection, but also his integrity and judiciousness.

4. Thomas Sprat, founder-member and historian of the Royal Society, quoted in J. Blum, R. Cameron, Thomas G. Barnes, *The European World, A History* (Boston, 1977) p. 405.

5. Barbara Shapiro, "Law and Science in Seventeenth-Century England," *Stanford Law Review* 21 (1969) pp. 761–762. This insight is developed at greater length and over a wider front in her book, *Probability and Certainty in Seventeenth Century England: A Study of the Relations between Natural Science, Religion, History, Law, and Literature* (Princeton, 1983).

6. Editor's introduction to Sir Matthew Hale, *The History of the Common Law*, Charles M. Gray, ed. (Chicago, 1971) p. xvi.

7. William Hudson, *A Treatise of the Court of Star Chamber*, The Legal Classics Library (1986) p. 1.

8. See the discussion in the chapter dealing with Michael Dalton, p. 149.

9. Runnington, p. xiv.

10. Conrad Russell, *The Crisis of Parliaments: English History 1509–1660* (London, 1971) p. 397.

11. Gray, p. xxxvi.

12. Shapiro, "Law and Science," p. 746. Prof. Shapiro lumps the *History* with the *Analysis* for her purposes—that yoking, the work of the 1713 editor and not

Hale, obscures the fact that Hale undertook them to very different ends, and clearly intended to publish the *Analysis* when he had completed it (which he never did).

13. D. E. C. Yale, *Hale as Legal Historian*, Selden Society Lecture (London, 1976).

14. F. W. Maitland, *Collected Papers*, vol. II, H. A. L. Fisher, ed. (Cambridge, 1911) p. 5; W. S. Holdsworth, *A History of English Law*, vol. VI (London, 1924) p. 586.

15. Thomas Hobbes, *The Elements of Law Natural and Political*, Ferdinand Tönnies, ed. (Cambridge, 1928) p. 81.

16. "Reflections by the Lrd. Cheife Justice Hale on Mr. Hobbes His Dialogue of the Law," Appendix III, in Sir William Holdsworth, *A History of English Law*, vol. V (London, 1924) p. 500. Hobbes's tract, very much of a piece with *Leviathan* in its specific premise (1651), was published in 1681, two years after his death, a contribution to the Exclusion Crisis. However, it appears to have circulated earlier in learned circles, which would account for Hale's critique of it.

17. Gray, p. xxxvi.

18. Gilbert Burnet, *Lives of Sir Matthew Hale and John Earl of Rochester* (London, 1829)—the Hale life was first published in 1682. See also Burnet's *History of His Own Time*, vol. I, Osmund Airy, ed. (Oxford, 1897).

19. Runnington, p. xl.

Further Reading

This is not a comprehensive bibliography. It is a list of suggested reading reflecting the principal sources from which the relevant essay was drawn. Certain recent works not available when the essay was originally written have been noted or used. Each of the subject-persons, with the exception of Michael Dalton, has been vignetted in the *Oxford Dictionary of National Biography* (Oxford, 2004).

A succinct overview of English legal history, very useful to supply broader context, is Sir John Baker's *An Introduction to English Legal History*, 4th ed. (London, 2002).

GLANVILL

The best succinct commentary on Glanvill is G. D. G. Hall's introduction to his edition of Glanvill, the edition reprinted by the Legal Classics Library. The last word on Henry II must be W. L. Warren's *Henry II* (Berkeley, 1973). Other, wider commentaries are T. F. T. Plucknett, *Early English Legal Literature* (Cambridge, 1958), and the two works by Raoul C. van Caenegem, his revolutionary introduction to *Royal Writs in England from the Conquest to Glanvill*, 77 Selden Society (London, 1959) and a luminous series of lectures on *The Birth of the English Common Law* (Cambridge, 1973). S. F. C. Milsom, *Historical Foundations of the Common Law* (London, 1969), particularly the first two chapters, bears close reading. Most of the legislation of Henry II can be found in David C. Douglas's edited series volume, *English Historical Documents, II: 1042–1189* (London, 1953). Two works by H. G. Richardson and G. O. Sayles, *Law and Legislation from Aethelbert to Magna Carta* (Edinburgh, 1966) and *The Governance of Medieval England from the Conquest to Magna Carta* (Edinburgh, 1963) are essential reading, as are Frank Barlow, *The Feudal Kingdom of England* (London, 1963), D. C. Douglas, *William the Conqueror: The Norman Impact upon England* (London, 1964), Frank Stenton, *The First Century of English Feudalism* (2d ed., Oxford, 1961), and Austin Lane Poole, *From Domesday Book to Magna Carta* (Oxford, 1951). The other two great works of Anglo-Norman authorship in the Age of Henry II are also available: Charles Johnson's translation of the *Dialogus de Scaccario: The Course of the Exchequer by Richard son of Nigel* (London, 1950) and the complete text in authoritative translation of *John of Salisbury: Policraticus*, Cary J. Nederman, ed. (Cambridge, 1990).

MAGNA CARTA

The literature on Magna Carta is vast. The texts of the various versions of the Charters have been reprinted on numerous occasions, in virtually every work of commentary on Magna Carta, quite aside from its appearance in collections of statutes. The first great commentary is, of course, that of Edward Coke, *The Second Institutes* (London, 1642). Modern scholarship is generally taken to have begun with William Blackstone's *The Great Charter and Charter of the Forest* (Oxford, 1759). Systematic study of the Great Charter's origins and subsequent history began with the twentieth century. W. S. McKechnie, *Magna Carta* (1905, amended 1914), however badly its history has dated, remains the fullest clause-by-clause exposition of the Charter.

The 700th anniversary of Runnymede produced *Magna Carta Commemoration Essays,* H. E. Malden, ed. (London, 1917)—another casualty of the Great War, because it lacked the intended contributions of German scholars that had been planned for it, much of whose work was seminal. The essays by G. B. Adams, F. M. Powicke, and particularly H. D. Hazeltine and Paul Vinogradoff (this last on Clause 39) are still very useful. The 750th anniversary of Runnymde, under more auspicious circumstances, provided sparkling essays by S. E. Thorne, P. B. Kurland, W. H. Dunham Jr., and Ivor Jennings published by the American Council of Learned Societies, in *The Great Charter* (New York, 1966). The great English medievalist, Helen Maud Cam, gave a Selden Society lecture in 1965 entitled "Magna Carta—Event or Document," which is brilliant in its insights and extraordinary in its sweep. Virginia established a Magna Carta Commission for the occasion, which published *via* the University Press of Virginia, Charlottesville, a number of "Magna Carta Essays": notably A. E. Dick Howard, *Magna Carta, Text and Commentary* (1964) is an excellent corrective to McKechnie, Doris Mary Stenton, *After Runnymede: Magna Carta in the Middle Ages* (1965) is first-rate, and Maurice Ashley, *Magna Carta in the Seventeenth Century* (1965) makes sense of a very tangled tale. More topical essays were John E. Bebout, *An Ancient Partnership: Local Government, Magna Carta, and the National Interest* (1966), Daniel J. Meador, *Habeas Corpus and Magna Carta* (1966), and Gottfried Dietze, *Magna Carta and Property* (1965).

J. C. Holt, *Magna Carta* (Cambridge, 1965) is the sun in the firmament of the 750th anniversary, to be read with his *The Northerners* (Oxford, 1961), on the leading rebels against John. All subsequent Magna Carta research begins with Holt, who also pioneered the comparative study of the Great Charter from Continental counterparts.

The later history of Magna Carta is still dominated by Faith Thompson, whose *The First Century of Magna Carta* (Milwaukee, 1925) and *Magna Carta: Its Role in the Making of the English Constitution, 1300–1629* (Milwaukee, 1948) have been superseded to the extent that the idea of an "English constitution" has been questioned in J. G. A. Pocock, *The Ancient Constitution and the Feudal Law* (Cambridge,

1957) and J. W. Gough, *Fundamental Law in English Constitutional History* (Oxford, 1961). Other useful works on the reception and history of Magna Carta are *The Roots of Liberty: Magna Carta, Ancient Constitution, and the Anglo-American Tradition of Rule of Law*, Ellis Sandoz, ed. (Columbia, Missouri, 1993), which focuses on the early modern era, and Anthony Musson, *Medieval Law in Context: The Growth of Liberty from Magna Carta to the Peasants' Revolt* (Manchester, 2001). A useful introduction to the textual history of the Charter is offered by a British Library pamphlet, *Magna Carta: Manuscripts and Myths*, by Claire Breay (London, 2002).

LITTLETON

The fate of Thomas Littleton and his *Tenures* argues that admirers are more dangerous than detractors to an author's posthumous reputation. Coke did Littleton scant favor in commending him to posterity, submerging both text and man. For Littleton's life we must still rely almost entirely on Eugene Wambaugh's introduction to his *Littleton's "Tenures" in English* (Washington, 1903). Wambaugh's text likewise remains the most recent attempt at scholarly redaction. The serious student must begin (and end) with the twenty pages in Sir William Holdsworth, *A History of English Law*, III (London, 1909) pp. 571–591, along with Holdsworth's reflections in *Some Makers of English Law* (Cambridge, 1938) pp. 46–68. The Selden Society should take note: a new, critical edition of the *Tenures* would fill a genuine gap in English legal history.

FORTESCUE

One begins with the first volume of *Sir John Fortescue: His Life, Works, and Family History,* compiled and edited by Thomas Fortescue, Lord Clermont and privately printed in 1869 in London. This contains the only edition of *De Natura Legis Naturae. The Governance of England* was edited by Charles Plummer (Oxford, 1885), with a very scholarly though somewhat dated biography in the introduction. The most up-to-date edition and translation of *De Laudibus* is that of S. B. Chrimes, *Sir John Fortescue, De Laudibus Legum Angliae* (Cambridge, 1942). Chrimes's edition and collation of the various texts represented an enormous improvement, and his scholarly apparatus is essential to understanding the text. Shelley Lockwood's new edition of both *De Laudibus* and *The Governance of England*, in the Cambridge Texts in the History of Political Thought series, entitled *Sir John Fortescue: On the Laws and Governance of England* (Cambridge, 1997), provides the most convenient access to the texts and her introduction adds much to our sparse knowledge of the man.

Fortescue's works of political theory (as opposed to his work as a judge), have received much attention since Charles H. McIlwain's *The Growth of Political Thought In the West* (Cambridge, Massachusetts, 1932) first paid proper attention to Fortescue's ideas. A number of European scholars published on Fortescue's political theory before World War II. The more readily available works essential to an appreciation of Fortescue's theory are Chrimes; *English Constitutional Ideas in the Fifteenth Century* (Cambridge, 1936), Max A. Shepard, "The Political and Constitutional Theory of Sir John Fortescue," *Essays in Honor of Charles Howard McIlwain* (Cambridge,

Massachusetts, 1936), and E. F. Jacob, "Sir John Fortescue and the Law of Nature," *Bulletin of the John Rylands Library* (1934).

HOOKER

There have been many editions of Hooker's *Of the Laws of Ecclesiastical Polity*. The gold standard today is the six-volume *Folger Library Edition of the Works of Richard Hooker* (Cambridge, Massachusetts, 1977–1981), for which W. S. Hill was general editor. A thorough bibliography may be found in *Studies in Richard Hooker: Essays Preliminary to an Edition of His Works*, W. S. Hill, ed. (Cleveland, 1972).

Hooker's biography, published in 1665, was written by Izaak Walton, the author of *The Compleat Angler*—a charming piece, though not without considerable critical edge. C. J. Sisson, *The Judicious Marriage of Mr. Hooker and the Birth of the Laws of Ecclesiastical Polity* (Cambridge, Massachusetts, 1940) remains the most thoroughgoing modern study of Hooker. The introductions to the Folger volumes, by Georges Edelen, W. S. Hill, P. G. Stanwood, J. E. Booty, and Laetitia Yeandle and Egil Grislis, are good and informative reading. Books I and VIII of Hooker's *Laws* were published among the Cambridge Texts in the History of Political Thought (Cambridge, 1989), with a short, helpful introduction by A. S. McGrade. For Hooker's continuing influence see H. R. Trevor-Roper, *Catholics, Anglicans, and Puritans* (London, 1987). R. K. Faulkner, *Richard Hooker and the Politics of a Christian England* (Berkeley, California, 1981) is a work of considerable exegesis. Paul E. Forte has contributed "Richard Hooker's Theory of Law," *Journal of Medieval and Renaissance Studies* 12 (1982) pp. 135–141, and further aspects of Hooker's work and role are explored in *Richard Hooker and the Construction of Christian Community*, A. S. McGrade, ed. (Tempe, Arizona, 1997)

Horton Davies, *Worship and Theology in England: From Cranmer to Hooker, 1534–1603* (Princeton, 1970) and *From Andrewes to Baxter and Fox, 1603–1690* (Princeton, 1975) provide brilliant insights. The best studies of Hooker's Puritan challengers are two books by Patrick Collinson, *The Elizabethan Puritan Movement* (London 1967) and *The Religion of Protestants* (Oxford, 1982).

JAMES VI & I

The Workes of James, King of Great Britain, France, and Ireland (London, 1616), STC 14344, second issue with supplement STC 14345, provided the basis for C. H. McIlwain's *The Political Works of James I Reprinted from the Edition of 1616* (Cambridge, Massachusetts, 1918). This was the edition returned to print by the Legal Classics Library. McIlwain provided the major political works but not all of the polemical pieces aimed at Roman Catholic apologists, and none of the writings on witchcraft. More recently, J. P. Sommerville has edited, for the series of Cambridge Texts in the History of Political Thought, *King James VI and I: Political Writings* (Cambridge, 1994).

There are many older biographies of James. Most of them are highly critical, and inevitably look back on James through the prism of the English Civil War. David Harris Willson's *James VI and I* (London, 1956), at best shows scant sympathy for its subject. Jenny Wormald, particularly in her *Oxford DNB* biography of James, treats much more positively and clearly the king's abilities and successes. Robert Ashton's collection, *James I by His Contemporaries* (London, 1969), is especially useful in seeing James as others saw him, while *Letters of King James VI & I*, G. P. V. Akrigg, ed. (Berkeley, 1984) shows James as the king presented himself. Two very useful collections of original essays on the king's career are *The Reign of James VI and I*, ed. A. G. R. Smith (London, 1973), and *The Reign of James VI*, Julian Goodare & Michael Lynch, eds. (East Linton, Scotland, 2000). Conrad Russell revised the portrait of James and his era in *The Crisis of Parliaments: English History 1509–1660* (Oxford, 1971) and James's parliamentary troubles in *Parliaments and English Politics 1621–1629* (Oxford, 1979). Recent scholarship by Leeds Barroll, Helen Payne, and Clare McManus gives life and some importance to James's queen, Anne of Denmark.

BACON

Bacon's own writings, including much of his correspondence, are readily available in the splendid edition devotedly overseen by James Spedding: *The Works of Francis Bacon* (London, 1857–1859); his *The Life and Letters of Francis Bacon* (London, 1861–1874)is still the place to begin biographical study. Catherine Drinker Bowen, *Francis Bacon: The Temper of a Man* (Boston, 1963) must be read judiciously; Dame Daphne Du Maurier, *The Winding Stair: Francis Bacon, His Rise and Fall* (Garden City, New York 1977) illustrates the "gothick" Bacon; Lisa Jardine & Alan Stewart, *Hostage to Fortune: The Troubled Life of Francis Bacon* (New York 1998) ties the narrative to the sources.

Recent excellent scholarly studies of Bacon as lawyer and politician are Daniel R. Coquillette, *Francis Bacon* (Stanford, 1992), Joel J. Epstein, *Francis Bacon: A Political Biography* (Athens, Ohio, 1977), and John T. Noonan's *Bribes* (New York, 1984)—the latter dashing Bacon's defense to the charges of corruption that brought him down.

Bacon the natural philosopher has excited continuous attention. A. R. Hall, *The Scientific Revolution, 1500–1800: The Formation of the Modern Scientific Attitude* (Boston, 1954) remains worthwhile. Julian Martin's *Francis Bacon—The State and the Reform of Natural Philosophy* (Cambridge, 1992) is now the place to start.

Legal maxims are discussed, in broad purview, in Peter Stein's luminous *Regulae Iuris: From Juristic Rules to Legal Maxims* (Edinburgh, 1966). *Latin for Lawyers* (London, 1960), a useful introductory grammar for Latin, provides over eleven hundred maxims with which a lawyer may dress almost any argument.

COKE

Sir Edward Coke has had no shortage of biographers. Short sketches by John Aubrey and Thomas Fuller were followed by Humphrey W. Woolrych, *The Life of the Right Honourable Sir Edward Coke Knt.* (London, 1826) and Cuthbert W. Johnson, *The Life of Sir Edward Coke* (London, 1837). Catherine Drinker Bowen's *The Lion and the Throne* (Boston, 1956) caught Coke's personality and character, albeit marred by breathless admiration and her unfamiliarity with the law. Allen D. Boyer's

Sir Edward Coke and the Elizabethan Age (Stanford, 2003), the first of two volumes that will cover Coke's career, is a brilliant work founded on painstaking research and a practicing lawyer's understanding of law, lawyers, and litigants.

Works on various aspects of Coke's political career and thought are numerous. Jean Beauté, *Un Grand Juriste Anglais: Sir Edward Coke, 1552–1634, ses Idées Politiques et Constitutionelles* (Paris, 1975) sees Coke from a position outside the English historical tradition and its monochromatic Whiggish tint. William J. Jones's introductory monograph, *Politics and the Bench: The Judges and the Origins of the English Civil War* (London, 1971), is a careful study of Coke and the other early Stuart judges confronting the falling-out between King and Parliament. Coke figures large—perhaps too large—in J. W. Gough, *Fundamental Law in English Constitutional History* (Oxford, 1961). On Coke's historical perspective and political theory, much useful work has been done by George L. Mosse, J. G. A. Pocock, J. P. Somerville, and Glenn Burgess. Scholarship on Parliament in the 1620's has not failed to give Coke his due. The serious student of Coke as parliamentarian must consult D. H. Willson, *The Privy Councillors in the House of Commons, 1604–1629* (Minneapolis, 1940); Margaret Judson, *The Crisis of the Constitution* (New Brunswick, 1949); Robert Zaller, *The Parliament of 1621: A Study in Constitutional Conflict* (Berkeley, 1971); Robert E. Ruigh, *The Parliament of 1624: Politics and Foreign Policy* (Cambridge, Massachusetts, 1971); Conrad Russell, *Parliaments and English Politics, 1621–1629* (Oxford, 1979); and Stephen D. White, *Sir Edward Coke and the "Grievances of the Commonwealth," 1621–1628* (Chapel Hill, 1979). Much good new work is being done by Chris Kyle, and the History of Parliament Trust has pushed through nearly to publication with its biographies and essays on the Parliaments of the 1620's.

American preoccupation with *Dr. Bonham's Case* as a putative source for judicial review produced a spate of articles on Coke as jurist. Over eight decades, these have included law-review pieces by T. F. T. Plucknett, L. B. Boudin, Samuel Thorne, Raoul Berger, Charles M. Gray, Allen D. Boyer, Richard Helmholz, and Mary Sarah Bilder. Coke's contribution to the development of contract is limned in A. W. B. Simpson, *A History of the Common Law of Contract: The Rise of the Action of Assumpsit* (Oxford, 1975). Other essential reading includes J. U. Lewis, "Coke's Theory of Artificial Reason," *Law Quarterly Review* 84 (1968) pp. 330–342 and a set of articles by Sir John H. Baker, "New Light on *Slade's Case*," *Cambridge Law Journal* 29 (1971) pp. 51–67 and 213–236 and "Coke's Note-Books and the Sources of his Reports," *Cambridge Law Journal* 30 (1972) pp. 59–86. These latter pieces are collected in Baker's *The Legal Profession and the Common Law* (London, 1986). W. S. Holdsworth devoted much attention to Coke, and on many points what he said remains the only word: see *A History of English Law*, vol. 5 (London, 1924) pp. 423–493, and *Some Makers of English Law* (Cambridge, 1938) pp. 111–132. The Liberty Foundation of Indianapolis has published two useful new works on the Lord Chief Justice: the three-volume *Selected Writings of Sir Edward Coke*, edited by Steve Sheppard (2003), which makes accessible much important material from the *Reports*, the *Institutes*, and Coke's parliamentary speeches, as well as providing a very full bibliography; and *Law, Liberty, and Parliament: Selected Essays on Sir Edward Coke*, edited by Allen Boyer (2004).

DALTON

Modern scholarship on Tudor-Stuart local government, particularly magistracy, began with William B. Willcox, *Gloucestershire: A Study in Local Government, 1590–1640* (New Haven, 1940) and expanded with Thomas G. Barnes's *Somerset 1625–1640: A County's Government during the "Personal Rule"* (Cambridge, Massachusetts, 1961). An explosion of excellent monographs followed, all fitting local developments into a national context and inevitably taking account of the mid-seventeenth-century English revolution. These include J. H. Betley on Dorset, Peter Clark and Alan Everitt on Kent, Anthony Fletcher on Sussex; Clive Holmes on East Anglia and R. W. Ketton-Cremer and A. Hassell Smith on Norfolk; John Morrill on Cheshire, and David Underdown on Somerset post-1640. John H. Gleason's evocative *The Justices of the Peace in England 1559 to 1640* (Oxford, 1969) studies the JPs of six counties, and Norma Landau, *The Justices of the Peace, 1679–1760* (Berkeley, 1984) opens up the subsequent history of magistracy. J. S. Cockburn, *A History of English Assizes, 1558–1714* (Cambridge, 1972) provides a useful overview of that institution so critical to the functioning of magistracy. John H. Langbein's *Prosecuting Crime in the Renaissance: England, Germany, France* (Cambridge, Massachusetts, 1974) is a provocative comparative essay that serves to illustrate how closely Tudor absolutism paralleled (if it did not imitate) continental absolutism. John P. Dawson's *A History of Lay Judges* (Cambridge, Massachusetts, 1960) provides the bond between customary and communal justice and royal justice confided to lay elites. Keith Wrightson and Steve Hindle have done valuable work on self-government by the "middling men" and vestries of England in this same period.

HUDSON

Considering its importance both to law and politics in the sixteenth and seventeenth centuries, it is remarkable that the historiography of Star Chamber is so underdeveloped. Older narrative histories accorded attention to it, less to understand it than to condemn it. Compilations of Star Chamber cases, including three volumes in the Selden Society, have added to the printed primary sources on the court. These constitute only a fraction of more than a thousand cases reported in manuscript.

The early history of the court is treated in the splendid monograph of John A. Guy, *The Cardinal's Court: The Impact of Thomas Wolsey in Star Chamber* (Hassocks, Sussex, 1977). An excellent introduction to the procedure of Star Chamber to the mid-sixteenth century is Dr. Guy's *The Court of Star Chamber and its Records to the Reign of Elizabeth I,* Public Record Office Handbooks No. 21 (HMSO, London, 1985). For the work of the later Star Chamber, the reader may consult the following works by the author: "Star Chamber Mythology," *American Journal of Legal History* 5 (1961) pp. 1–11; "Due Process and Slow Process in the Late Elizabethan–Early Stuart Star Chamber," *American Journal of Legal History* 6 (1962) pp. 221- 249 and 315–356; "Star Chamber and the Sophistication of the Criminal Law," *Criminal Law Review* (London, June, 1977) pp. 316–326; "The Archives and Archival Problems of the Elizabethan and Early Stuart Star Chamber," *Prisca Munimenta: Studies in Ar-*

chival and Administrative History Presented to Dr. A. E. J. Hollaender, Felicity Ranger, ed. (London, 1973) pp. 130–149; "The Prerogative and Environmental Control of London Building in the Early Seventeenth Century: The Lost Opportunity," 58 *California Law Review* (1970) pp. 1332–1363. The late sixteenth-century court of Chancery, Star Chamber's twin, has been thoroughly and authoritatively studied by William J. Jones, *The Elizabethan Court of Chancery* (Oxford, 1967).

SELDEN

John Selden's works were published in three volumes by David Wilkins (London, 1726). A critical modern edition is in order. *Table Talk* has received the bulk of modern scholars' attention, being published by the Selden Society (London, 1927) from the Lincoln's Inn manuscript by Sir Frederick Pollock, Bt., which falls short of the best of present-day editorial work.

Despite the destruction of his notes by fire and a long and painful battle against cancer, David Sandler Berkowitz completed the bulk of his large undertaking on Selden, published posthumously as *John Selden's Formative Years: Politics and Society in Early Seventeenth-Century England* (London, 1989). Equally useful and informative are Paul Christianson's *Discourse on History, Law and Governance in the Later Career of John Selden* (Toronto, 1996), and Reid Barbour's *John Selden: Measures of the Holy Commonwealth in Seventeenth Century England* (Toronto, 2003). George W. Johnson's *Memoirs of John Selden* (London, 1835) still offers useful information.

MILTON

Milton scholarship is industrial-grade. The most distinguished biography of Milton may be William Riley Parker's *Milton: A Biography* (Oxford, 1968). Two outstanding studies by C. A. Patrides, *Milton and the Christian Tradition* (Oxford, 1966) and *The Grand Design of God: The Literary Form of the Christian View of History* (London, 1972), establish the theological foundations (in patristic roots) of Milton, and serve as a counterpoise to more secularist views of him as a political radical. Christopher Hill's two books, *Milton and the English Revolution* (New York, 1978) and *The Experience of Defeat: Milton and Some Contemporaries* (London, 1984), advance the latter perspective, although the Methodist-turned-Marxist may have undervalued the Christological orthodoxy of Milton's ideas. An essay by H. R. Trevor-Roper, "Milton in Politics," *Catholics, Anglicans and Puritans* (Chicago, 1988) sees Milton as both political animal and troubled orthodox believer. On the border between literary criticism and political theory are Keith W. Stavely, *The Politics of Milton's Prose Style* (New Haven, 1975) and Charles R. Geisst, *The Political Thought of John Milton* (London, 1984). Both overemphasize the social consciousness of Milton and his age. Andrew Milner, *John Milton and the English Revolution: A Study in the Sociology of Literature* (London, 1981)treats Milton's development as a social observer and political theorist. Michael Wilding's article, "Milton's Areopagitica: Liberty for the Sects," in *Prose Studies* 9 (1986) pp. 7–38, suggests the connection between Milton's concern with licensing and the notable victims of its practice in the "Personal Rule," Prynne, Bastwick, and Burton, while missing some of its larger ramifications. For the historiographical dimension of Milton, so important to understanding both polemical and poetic works, see Mary Ann Radzinowicz, *Toward Samson Agonistes: The Growth of Milton's Mind* (Princeton, 1978), and the splendid study by David Loewenstein, *Milton and the Drama of History: Historical Vision, Iconoclasm, and the Literary Imagination* (Cambridge, 1990).

LAWS AND LIBERTIES

The first editor of the early laws of Massachusetts, William H. Whitmore in *The Colonial Laws of Massachusetts* (Boston, 1889) despaired at the loss of the *Laws and Liberties*. The 1929 publication (with introduction by Max Farrand) of the Huntington's unique copy spurred observation of its 300th anniversary by two sterling essays: Thorp L. Wolford, "The Laws and Liberties of 1648," *Boston University Law Review* 28 (1948) pp. 426–463 (reprinted in *Essays in the History of Early American Law*, D. H. Flaherty, ed., Chapel Hill, 1969) and Stefan A. Riesenfeld, "Law-Making and Legislative Precedent in American Legal History," *Minnesota Law Review* 33 (1949) pp. 103–134. Subsequent pieces include George L. Haskins, "Codification of the Law in Colonial Massachusetts: A Study in Comparative Law," *Indiana Law Journal* 30 (1954) pp. 1–17, and G. L. Haskins and S. E. Ewing, "The Spread of Massachusetts Law in the Seventeenth Century," *University of Pennsylvania Law Review* 106 (1958) pp. 413–418.

A remarkable increase of interest in early Massachusetts legal history began with the pathfinding George L. Haskins's *Law and Authority in Early Massachusetts: A Study in Tradition and Design* (New York, 1960). *Colonial Justice in Western Massachusetts, 1639–1702: The Pynchon Court Record*, Joseph H. Smith, ed. (Cambridge, Massachusetts, 1961); David T. Konig, *Law and Society in Puritan Massachusetts: Essex County, 1629–1692* (Chapel Hill, 1979); and David Grayson Allen, *In English Ways: The Movement of Societies and the Transferal of English Local Law and Custom to Massachusetts Bay in the Seventeenth Century* (Chapel Hill, 1981) followed. See also M. D. Howe, "The Sources of Law in Colonial Massachusetts," in *Law and Authority in Colonial America*, G. A. Billias, ed. (Barre, Massachusetts, 1965). In 1981, Daniel Coquillette edited for publication a collection of conference papers, published as *Law in Colonial Massachusetts, 1630–1800* (published by the University Press of Virginia for the Colonial Society of Massachusetts, 1984). The *Laws and Liberties* figures prominently in Thomas G. Barnes, "Law and Liberty (and Order) in Early Massachusetts," in *The English Legal System: Carryover to the Colonies* (Clark Library, Los Angeles, 1975) pp. 63–89. More recent explorations include Mark D. Cahn, "Punishment, Discretion, and the Codification of Prescribed Penalties in Colonial Massachusetts," *American Journal of Legal History* 33 (1989) pp. 107–136; G. B. Warden, "Law Reform in England and New England, 1620 to 1660," *William and Mary Quarterly* 35 (1978) pp. 668–690; and Daniel R. Coquillette, "Radical Lawmakers in Colonial Massachusetts: The 'Countenance of Authoritie' and the *Lawes and Libertyes*," *New England Quarterly* 67 (1994) pp. 179–211. Continuing the tradition is Angela Fernandez, "Record-Keeping and Other Trouble-Making: Thomas Lechford and Law Reform in Colonial Massachusetts," *Law and History Review* 23 (2005) pp. 235–278.

A new photo-facsimile edition of *Lawes and Libertyes* was published by the Huntington Library (San Marino, 1975) with introduction and table of sources for the laws by Thomas G. Barnes.

TRIAL OF CHARLES I

The best account of the trial of Charles I is that of Cicely Veronica Wedgwood, *The Trial of Charles I* (London, 1964). A summation of it is to be found in *The English Civil War and After, 1642–1658*, R. H. Parry, ed. (Berkeley, 1970), pp. 41–58. To see Charles I in the larger context of the critical decade 1637–1647, start with Dame Veronica's two admirable narratives, *The King's Peace, 1637–1641* (London, 1955) and *The King's War, 1641–1647* (London, 1958). Among the numerous studies of Charles's nemesis is Lady Antonia Fraser's *Cromwell, The Lord Protector* (New York, 1973). Her account of Cromwell's role in the King's "trial" is authoritative. For the Parliament (so-called) that tried Charles, see Blair Worden, *The Rump Parliament* (Oxford, 1974). Richard Ollard, *This War without an Enemy: A History of the English Civil Wars* (New York, 1976) is both succinct and comprehensive. Conrad Russell's *The Fall of the British Monarchies, 1637–1642* (Oxford, 1991) has returned the search for the immediate causes for revolution—and responsibility for the failure of the regime—to Charles and his ministers. Samuel Rawson Gardiner's two classics, *History of England from the Accession of James I to the Outbreak of the Civil War, 1603–1642*, 10 vol. (London, 1883–1884), and *History of the Great Civil War*, 4 vol. (London, 1893), remain valuable.

Perhaps the best biography of Charles I is Pauline Gregg, *King Charles I* (Berkeley & Los Angeles, 1984), although the customary thoughtfulness of Richard Ollard, in the *Image of the King: Charles I and Charles II* (London, 1979) may be remarked. Charles Carlton, *Charles I, The Personal Monarch* (London, 1983) is psychobiography. John Bowie, *Charles the First* (Boston, 1975) is reliable. L. J. Reeve, *Charles I and the Road to Personal Rule* (Cambridge, 1989) and Brian Quintrell, *Charles I, 1625–1640* (London, 1993) are useful.

MATTHEW HALE

Besides Hale's juristic, scientific, and religious works, referenced in the essay above, three extensive pieces by the Lord Chief Justice, published by that indefatigable legal antiquarian of the eighteenth century, Francis Hargrave, are worth study: "A Treatise in Three Parts on Rivers, Ports, and Concerning the Custom of Goods Imported and Exported"; "Considerations Touching the Amendment or Alteration of Laws"; and "Discourse Concerning the Courts of King's Bench and Common Pleas." These are included in the first volume of *A Collection of Tracts Relating to the Law of England*, F. Hargrave, ed. (London, 1787). Hale's brilliant historical and analytical essay on the legal jurisdiction of the House of Lords, addressing a long-running controversy between the two Houses of Parliament following *Skinner's Case* (1657), was also edited by Hargrave, *The Jurisdiction of the Lords' House, or Parliament Considered according to Ancient Records* (London, 1796). Later editions of Coke's *First Institutes* were published with Hale's commentary on Coke's commentary on Littleton. Finally, Sollom Emlyn edited two volumes of Hale's *History of Pleas of the Crown* (London, 1736).

Alan Cromartie has contributed a provocative assessment of Hale in *Sir Matthew Hale: Law, Religion and Natural Philosophy*, in the Cambridge Studies in Early Modern British History series (Cambridge, 1995). The best prior assessment of Hale's legal and constitutional thought and *The History of the Common Law* is the introduction to that work by Charles M. Gray in the University of Chicago Press Classics of British Historical Literature (Chicago, 1971). David E. C. Yale's Selden Society Lecture, *Hale as Legal Historian* (London, 1976) is erudite. Hale's interaction with the scientific enterprise of the late seventeenth century is weighed by Barbara J. Shapiro in *Probability and Certainty in Seventeenth-Century England: A Study of the Relations between Natural Science, Religion, History, Law, and Literature* (Princeton, 1983). Edmund Heward, *Matthew Hale* (London, 1972) supplies biographical detail and describes Hale's juristic works, but is short on historical context. *An Instance of the Fingerpost*, a remarkable novel by Iain Pears (London, 1997), draws its title from Francis Bacon, and conveys unforgettably the political nastiness of the era in which Hale worked. See Gilbert Burnet's *Life of Sir Matthew Hale* (1682) for contemporary testimony as to Hale's remarkable qualities.

Index

Absolute monarchy, 9, 131, 148–49, 197, 233
Act of Settlement, 10, 235–36
Act of Supremacy, 75–76
Act of Uniformity, 75–76
Adams, John, 31, 135
Adams, Sam, 135
Adiaphora (things indifferent), 61–62, 63, 77, 180
Adrian IV, Pope, 20
Aeropagitica, *see* Milton, John, *Aeropagitica*
Alfred the Great, King, 18–19
Allington, Sir Giles, 140
American Bar Association, 31
Anderson, Edmund, 120
Andrewes, Lancelot, 77, 219
Anglican Church, *see* Church of England
Aphorisms: of Bacon, 103–4; Latin, 104; of Selden, 176. *See also* Maxims
Architecture: analogies, 136; Gothic, 19, 20; of Inigo Jones, 212–13
Aristotle, 99
Arminius, Jacobus, 85
Assizes, 144–46; Cambridge, 140, 141, 145; jurisdiction, 146, 162
Attorneys-General, 153, 157, 159, 165, 228; Bacon as, 248n7; Coke as, 119–20, 122, 124, 125, 162; duties, 119
Aubrey, John, 175, 181–82
Austin, John, 22

Bacon, Sir Francis: *The Apophthegms*, 100; on censorship, 191; common law reform proposals, 107–9, 113; *De Augmentis Scientarum*, 103–4, 106, 107, 110; impeachment for bribery, 98, 112, 128; legal career, 98, 101, 102, 108, 248n7; legal writings, 100–101, 110; life, 98; logic, 99, 102; as Lord Chancellor, 98, 112, 128, 168, 171–72; *Novum Organum*, 99; rivalry with Coke, 111–12, 113, 117, 120–21, 126; Selden and, 168, 171–72; will, 98–99; writings, 99–100
Bacon, Sir Francis, *The Elements of the Common Laws of England*, 8, 98; dedicatory epistle, 101; influence, 111; *Maximes*, 101–4, 106–11; publication, 101–2
Bacon, Sir Nicholas, 248n23
Baker, Sir John, 37
Baronage: feudal, 16; House of Lords, 170; privileges, 170. *See also* Magna Carta
Bastwick, John, 184, 185, 193
Baxter, Richard, 225, 230
Beale, Robert, 27
Becket (film), 14
Becket, Thomas à, 14, 20
Beza, Theodore, 68
Bill of Rights (1689), 24, 28, 29
Bill of Rights, U.S., 27, 31, 161
Blackmail, 161
Blackstone, Sir William, 12, 106, 136, 222–23
Bodin, Jean, 60, 94
Boke of Justices of Peas, The Charge with All the Processe of the Cessions, 141
Bonham's Case, 135
Book of Common Prayer, 75, 77, 81, 144, 211
Book of Orders, 143–44

The Book of the General Laws and Libertyes Concerning the Inhabitants of the Massachusets, see *Laws and Liberties of Massachusetts*
Botero, Giovanni, 94
Bouwsma, William J., 196
Bowen, Catherine Drinker, 112
Bowles, Edward, 186, 187
Boyle, Robert, 223
Bracton, Henry de, 12, 58, 104–5, 124, 156, 166, 170
Bradshawe, John, 209, 210, 216
Bribery, 98, 112, 128, 160
Bridgman, Orlando, 118
Brooke, George, 81
Buchanan, George, 96, 97
Buckingham, George Villiers, Duke of, 82–84, 127, 128, 172, 212, 213
Buckner, Thomas, 183, 184
Burges, Cornelius, 186, 187
Burnet, Gilbert, 235
Burns, Richard, *The Office of Justice of the Peace and Parish Officer*, 137
Burroughs, Jeremiah, 186, 187
Burton, Henry, 184, 185, 193
Butler, Charles, 37

Caesar, Sir Julius, 130
Calvin, Jean, 4, 62, 63, 68, 70; *Institutes of the Christian Religion*, 65, 71–72
Cambridge assizes, 140, 141, 145
Cambridge University, 20, 115, 138
Canon law, 19, 64–65, 140
Capital crimes, 202–3
Carr, Robert, Earl of Somerset, 79
Censorship: licensing of printing, 182–85, 187; Milton on, 191, 192–93
Chancery: Bacon and, 98, 105; Coke and, 119, 126; history, 157; Masters, 138, 141; procedures, 156; writs of prohibition, 90, 123
Charles I, King of England: accession, 83; artistic sensibilities, 212–13; beheading, 96, 180–81, 206–7, 218, 219–20, 228; Buckingham and, 128, 172, 212, 213; character, 5, 211–13, 218–19; children, 219; court cases, 165; *Eikon Basilike*, 181; Five Knights' Case, 8–9, 172–74; Forced Loan, 172; health in childhood, 213; historians' views of, 214–16; judges and, 126, 163; marriage, 84, 212, 213; Personal Rule, 148, 149, 163, 165, 174, 183–85, 214; portraits, 213; Privy Council, 143, 145; relations with Parliament, 93–94, 129, 171, 172, 173–74, 185, 217–18; Selden and, 169; trial, 5, 181, 206–7, 209, 210–11, 215–18; tyranny charges against, 215–18; wars, 84, 128, 172, 185, 214–15, 216; weaknesses as ruler, 213, 218–19
Charles II, King of England: Exclusion Crisis, 222, 231, 235; father's death, 219; marriage, 183; Prynne and, 183; relations with Parliament, 230–31; restoration, 29, 183, 196, 210, 229–31, 235
Chrimes, S. B., 3–4, 48, 49, 51, 53
Chronicles of England, Scotlande, and Irelande (Holinshed), 26–27, 65
Chudleigh's Case, 118
Church of England: adiaphorists, 62, 180; Book of Common Prayer, 75, 77, 81, 144, 211; establishment by law, 73, 75–76, 230; Hampton Court conference, 80, 81, 86; Hooker's description, 64; polity of, 73; royal supremacy, 62, 63–64, 75–76, 86. *See also* Ecclesiastical courts; Reformation
Civil government, types, 197
Civil law, 53; Fortescue on, 54–55, 56; in France, 56, 148
Civil War, English: effects on judiciary, 163; failure of revolution, 227–28; Hooker's influence on Puritans, 77; republicanism, 28–29; rhetoric, 58–59; role of religion, 215; social effects, 227. *See also* Protectorate
Clermont, Thomas Fortescue, Lord, 48
Clifford's Inn, 116
Cobbam, A. B., 72
Coke, Sir Edward: Bacon family and, 248n23; character, 114–15; contemporary views of, 129–30, 132; death, 129; downfall, 126–27; education, 36, 115–17; enemies, 123; on Fortescue, 47; *Fourth Institutes*, 128, 134; historians' views of, 130–31; influence, 7, 132, 134–35; James I and, 91, 92, 115, 120, 121, 123, 124–26, 127, 145; judicial activism, 122–24, 127; legal career, 91, 108, 110, 112, 115, 117–26, 134, 140–41, 162; on legal history, 232–34; legal outlook, 112; on Magna Carta, 27, 28, 31; marriages, 120, 121; maxims, 45, 71, 105, 112–13, 115, 122, 133; as member of

Parliament, 112, 118, 127–29, 132, 172; motto, 114–15; on precedent, 122; rivalry with Bacon, 111–12, 113, 117, 120–21, 126; *Second Institutes*, 27, 133–34, 135; *Third Institutes*, 133–34, 147; tomb inscription, 114
Coke, Sir Edward, *Reports*, 114, 121, 126; on conspiracy, 162; importance, 35–36, 112–13, 134; influence in New England, 134–35; maxims, 105; praise of Glanvill, 11; publication, 35
Coke on Littleton (*The First Part of the Institutes of the Laws of England: or a Commentary upon Littleton*), 7, 35–37, 39, 45, 58, 112, 128; on contingent remainders, 41; disorganization, 36–37; eclecticism, 136; influence, 133, 135; later editions, 36, 37; Preface, 36, 37
Colthirst v. Bejushin, 117, 242n32
Commendams, Case of, 126
Common law: Bacon's reform proposals, 107–9, 113; evidence, 224–25; evolution, 6–7, 156; origins, 155–56; resistance to absolutism, 148–49; role of legislations, 234; rules, 6; seen as ancient, 28, 171
Common Pleas, court of: chief justices, 140–41, 153; Coke as Chief Justice, 91, 110, 115, 120, 121–25, 140–41, 145, 162; Hale as justice, 222, 229; Littleton as justice, 32; Magna Carta provision on, 16; writ of prohibition, 90
Company of Stationers, 182
Conspiracy, 160, 161–62, 202–3
Constitution, ancient, 171, 216–17
Constitution, U.S., *see* United States Constitution
Contingent remainders, 41–42, 117–18, 242n32
Corporal punishment, 155, 184
Corpus Christi College, Oxford University, 66–68
Cotton, John, 199, 201–2
Cotton, Sir Robert, 170, 174
The Countrey Justice, *see* Dalton, Michael, *The Countrey Justice*
Court of High Commission for Causes Ecclesiastical, 27, 139–40, 169, 185. *See also* Ecclesiastical courts
Courts: expansion in Tudor era, 72; in Massachusetts Bay Colony, 203; nineteenth-century reforms, 157; royal referrals to, 110, 124–25; in twentieth century, 150–51. *See also* Common Pleas; King's Bench; Star Chamber
Courts Act of 1971, 150
Cowell, John, 11–12, 90
Crewe, Ranulf, 141
Criminal law: Coke's *Third Institutes*, 133–34, 147; development, 146; felonies and misdemeanors, 146–47, 159; handbooks for justices of the peace, 137; jury trials, 154–55; in Massachusetts Bay Colony, 202–3; sophisticated crimes, 5, 146, 158–62; Star Chamber jurisdiction, 122, 157, 159
Cromwell, Oliver: comparison to Charles I, 211–12; death, 229; Hale and, 228; legitimacy, 228; as Protector, 29, 149, 196, 210, 227–28, 229; trial of Charles I, 206–7
Cromwell, Richard, 229
Crusades, 2, 19
Culpepper, John, 59

Dalton, Michael: legal career, 137–39; life, 137–40; *Officium Vicecomitum: The Office and Authoritie of Sherifs*, 139; religious views, 139–40
Dalton, Michael, *The Countrey Justice*, 5–6; on assizes, 144; author's experience as basis, 140–41; changing roles of justices, 142–43; felonies, 146; format, 142; influence in New England, 135, 137, 151; popularity, 137, 141; publication and reprintings, 137, 143; usefulness, 136–37, 142, 147, 150
Darnley, Henry Stuart, Lord, 79, 87
Davies, Horton, 70
Death penalty, 155, 202–3
De Dominion Regali et Politico (*The Governance of England*; Fortescue), 49–50
De Laudibus Legum Angliae, *see* Fortescue, Sir John, *De Laudibus Legum Angliae*
Democracy, 197, 204
De Natura Legis Naturae (Fortescue), 49, 50, 51, 56
Dickens, Charles, 43
Divorce, 187–88, 194
Doddridge, John, 111, 141
Donne, John, 77, 85
Duchy Chamber of Lancaster, 55
Duke of Norfolk's Case, 118

Eadmer, *Historia Novorum*, 167–68
Ecclesiastical courts: Court of High Com-

mission for Causes Ecclesiastical, 27, 139–40, 169, 185; Dalton on, 139–40; Laud's role, 185; regulation of printing, 185; Selden and, 169; slander cases, 161; writs of prohibition, 90, 123
Education, 20; of gentry, 33–35; of lawyers, 33–35, 56
Edward, Prince of Wales, 46, 47, 49, 50–52
Edward the Confessor, 19, 233
Edward II, King of England, 25, 206
Edward IV, King of England, 32, 46, 49–50, 206
Edward VI, King of England, 62, 73
Eikon Basilike, 181
Eikonoklastes (Milton), 181
"Elegy in a Country Churchyard" (Gray), 221, 236
The Elements of the Common Laws of England (Bacon), 8, 98, 101–4, 106–11
Eliot, Sir John, 172, 174
Eliot, T. S., 7
Elizabeth I, Queen of England: Coke and, 118–20; common law reforms, 108; excommunication, 244n6; Reformation and, 62–63, 73, 76; as Supreme Governor of Church, 62, 64, 75
Ellesmere, Sir Thomas Egerton, Lord, 105–6, 108, 123, 126
English Revolution, *see* Civil War, English
Entails, unbarrable, 40–41
Equity, 34, 43, 55, 156, 203. *See also* Chancery
Erasmus, Desiderius, 67
Essex, Earl of, 102, 120, 248n7
Evidence, law of, 224–25
Exclusion Crisis, 222, 231, 235

Fawkes, Guy, plot of, 86–87, 91, 120
Feudalism, 18
Fifth Amendment, United States Constitution, 27
Filmer, Robert, *Patriarcha*, 235
Finch, Henry, *Nomotechnia*, 111
First Amendment, United States Constitution, 161
Fisher, John, 219–20
Fitzherbert, Anthony, 141
Five Knights' Case, 8–9, 172–74
Fleming, Thomas, 108, 125
Forgery and fraud, 160
Fortescue, Sir John: *De Dominion Regali et Politico* (*The Governance of England*), 49–50; *De Natura Legis Naturae*, 49, 50, 51, 56; Edward, Prince of Wales and, 47, 50–52; Henry VI and, 46; legal career, 3, 32, 47–48; life, 46–48, 49; support of Lancasters, 32, 46, 49, 51, 55–56; writings, 48–51
Fortescue, Sir John, *De Laudibus Legum Angliae*, 39; citations, 57; Coke on, 47; dating, 47, 51; editions, 167; essay on kingship, 52–54; importance, 3–4, 47; influence, 57–60; on jury, 47, 48, 54, 55; on mixed monarchy, 47, 49, 50, 52–53, 59; popularity, 58; treatment of law, 54–57; written for Edward, Prince of Wales, 46, 47, 49, 50–52, 57
Fox, Richard, 66, 67
France: civil law, 56, 148; feudalism, 18; monarchy, 49, 52, 55, 148; police, 148
French Revolution, 148, 207, 209
Fuller, Thomas, 130

Galileo, 180, 191
Gawdy, Francis, 120
Gentry, education of sons at Inns of Court, 33–35, 72, 116
Geoffrey fitz Peter, 13
Germany, feudalism, 18
Glanvill, Ranulf de, 1, 2, 13, 21
Glanvill, *Tractatus de Legibus et Consuetudinibus Regni Anglie qui Glanvilla Vocatur*, 1–2; aphorisms, 104; authorship, 13; dating, 13; jury, 18; praise of, 11–13, 21; preconditions, 18–21; Prologue, 16–17; significance, 11–13, 21–22; writs, 2, 17–18, 22, 156
Glorious Revolution (1688), 59, 222, 235
Gothic architecture, 19, 20
Gray, Charles, 226, 232
Gray, John Chipman, 22
Gray, Thomas, "Elegy in a Country Churchyard," 221, 236
Gray's Inn, 10, 100
Grotius, Hugo: *Mare Liberum*, 169; Milton and, 180
Gunpowder Plot, 86–87, 91, 120

Habeas Corpus Act (1679), 29
Hale, Sir Matthew: character, 9–10; contributions to *Coke on Littleton*, 37; *History of Pleas of the Crown*, 222, 235; legal career, 222, 228–29, 235; legal reform commis-

sion, 228–29; legal writings, 222–23, 258n13; life, 236; natural philosophy interest, 223, 224–25, 226–27, 235; *Nature of True Religion*, 225–26; *Pleas of the Crown*, 222; religious writings, 225–26; reputation, 222–23, 235; Restoration and, 230, 231–32, 235; royalism, 228

Hale, Sir Matthew, *History and Analysis of the Common Law in England*, 9–10, 221, 231–34; critique of Hobbes, 233, 234; decision not to publish, 9, 226, 231, 234–35; historical evidence, 225; influence, 222, 234; publication, 221; purpose, 232

Hall, G. D. G., 13, 21

Hammurabi, 11

Hampton Court conference, 80, 81, 86

Hargrave, Francis, 37, 158

Harvy, Francis, 141

Haskins, Charles Homer, 19

Hatton, Lady Elizabeth, 120, 121, 127

Henrietta Maria, Queen, 183, 212, 213

Henri IV, King of France, 79

Henry, Prince of Wales, 83, 84, 96, 97, 208

Henry I, King of England, 18

Henry II, King of England: appeal, 14–15; character, 14; Glanvill as justiciar, 1, 13, 14; king's court, 16; legal and judicial reforms, 16–18, 21–22, 155–56; life, 13–14; rule of, 15–18, 20–21

Henry III, King of England, 24

Henry IV, King of England, 50, 205–6, 208

Henry VI, King of England, 46–47; death, 206; Fortescue and, 46, 49; Littleton and, 32; restoration, 49, 51

Henry VII, King of England, 26, 206

Henry VIII, King of England, 14, 62, 72, 73, 126

High Court of Parliament, 112, 128, 129, 203

History and Analysis of the Common Law in England, *see* Hale, Sir Matthew, *History and Analysis of the Common Law in England*

History of Tithes (Selden), 169

Hobbes, Thomas: on absolute monarchy, 9, 233; on Coke, 130; *Dialogue*, 234, 235; *Leviathan*, 59, 63–64, 94

Hoffer, Eric, 178

Holbrook, Hal, 153

Holdsworth, Sir William, 7, 36, 40, 43, 100–101, 232

Holinshed, Raphael, *Chronicles of England, Scotlande, and Irelande*, 26–27, 65

Holmes, Oliver Wendell, 22

Holy Roman Empire, 53

Hooker, Richard: life, 65–69, 76; pragmatism, 61, 62

Hooker, Richard, *The Laws of Ecclesiastical Polity*, 4, 69–71; "Certainty and Perpetuity of Faith in the Elect," 69; Charles I on, 219; contributions, 73–75; definition of law, 73–74; influence, 77; "Justification," 69; language, 67; meaning of polity, 63–64; objective, 64, 69, 75, 76; publication, 76–77

House of Commons, *see* Parliament

House of Lords, 170. *See also* Parliament

Hudson, William: death, 166; legal practice, 157–58; *A Treatise of the Court of Star Chamber*, 5, 6, 157–58, 164, 166; on writers, 226–27

Hume, David, 135

Hus, Jan, 189

Hyams, Peter, 153

Hyde, Edward, 217, 218

Hyde, Nicholas, 141, 173

Inner Temple, 35, 38, 68, 116–17, 118, 175

Inns of Chancery, 115–16

Inns of Court: benchers, 116, 118, 157, 175; masters, 68; readerships, 117, 118, 157; readings, 100; students, 33–35, 36, 72, 116–17, 153; training of lawyers, 56, 100, 115

International law, control of seas, 169–70

James I of England and VI of Scotland: Buckingham and, 82–84, 127, 213; character, 212; charge to judges of assize, 91–92, 145; contemporary views of, 79–80, 81–82; death, 81, 216; father, 79, 87; favorites, 82–84, 213; fear of assassination, 87, 97; on king's obligations, 96, 97, 208; legitimacy of rule, 210–11; life, 80–81, 84–85, 96; poetry, 92; relations with courts, 102, 110, 124–25, 126; relations with Parliament, 93–94, 171–72; seen as despot, 81, 85, 92; Selden and, 169; transparency, 92–93; union of Scotland and England, 88–89; war against Spain, 93

James I of England and VI of Scotland, *The Political Works of James I*, 80; "An Apolo-

gie for the Oath of Allegiance," 91, 94; "Basilikon Doron," 4, 95–96, 97, 220; "A Defence of the Right of Kings, against Cardinali Perron," 94; "A Premonition to all Christian Monarches, Free Princes and States," 94; speeches to Parliament, 4–5, 85–91, 92; "The Trew Law of Free Monarchies," 4, 95
James II, King of England, 24, 59, 219, 222, 231
Jefferson, Thomas, 135
Jewel, John, 66
John, King, Magna Carta and, 16, 23
John of Salisbury, *Policraticus*, 20, 21
Jones, Inigo, 212–13
Jordan, W. K., 84
Judges: impeachments, 163; independence from politics, 10, 163, 235–36; political roles, 163; resistance to absolutism, 148–49; roles, 2–3. *See also* Justices of the peace
Judicial activism, 122–24, 127, 160
Judicial review, 163
Juries, 2, 156; criminal trials, 154–55; Dalton on, 140; Fortescue on, 47, 48, 54, 55; Glanvill on, 18; right to trial by, 31
Justices of the peace: changing roles, 142–44, 146, 149; criminal cases, 146–47; handbooks, 137, 141–42; oversight of, 144–46, 147–48; power, 149; in twentieth century, 150–51. *See also* Dalton, Michael
Justinian, 11, 19, 104, 109, 156; *Institutes*, 17, 110

Kent, Henry Grey, Earl of, 172, 175
King's Bench: barristers, 157; chief justices, 153, 222; Coke as Chief Justice, 110, 125–26, 162; jurisdiction, 72, 122, 146, 162, 164
King's Council, 55
Knox, John, 66

Lambarde, William, 5–6, 141–42
Lancaster, house of, *see* Wars of the Roses
Laud, William: books, 219–20; death, 77, 149; ecclesiastical courts and, 139–40, 185; memorial to James I, 81; Prynne's attack on, 184; Puritans and, 77, 145–46; Scots rebellion against, 180; trial, 228, 254n12
Law books: in Massachusetts, 151; printed, 33
Laws and Liberties of Massachusetts: absence of references to king, 9, 198; compared to *The Countrey Justice*, 151; differences from English law, 9, 202–3; importance, 195, 204; liberties protected, 30–31; Proheme (dedicatory epistle), 199–202; purpose, 202
The Laws of Ecclesiastical Polity, *see* Hooker, Richard, *The Laws of Ecclesiastical Polity*
Lawyers: social status, 116; in Star Chamber, 138, 157, 253n8; training, 56, 100, 115
Lechford, Thomas, 197–98, 203, 204
Legal history, English, 232–34. *See also* Hale, Sir Matthew, *History and Analysis of the Common Law in England*
Legal reasoning, 100, 102
Legitimacy: of Cromwell's rule, 228; of James I, 210–11; of Massachusetts Bay Colony rulers, 199–202; of monarchy, 198–99, 208–9; sources, 199–202, 204
Lenin, Vladimir, 207
LeStrange, Sir Hammond, 82
Ley, James, 140–41
Libel, 161, 183–84, 193
Lincoln's Inn, 137, 139, 221, 228
Littleton, Sir Thomas: life, 32, 37–38; motto, 32, 114
Littleton, Sir Thomas, *Tenures*, 3, 57; on contingent remainders, 41–42; didactic purpose, 38–40; epilogue, 38–39, 40; manuscript copies, 38; obsolescence, 34, 57; popularity, 4, 34, 58; printings, 33; property law topics, 40–44; significance, 32–33, 39–40, 45, 58; on unbarrable entails, 40–41; use as textbook, 34; on uses, 42–44. *See also Coke on Littleton*
Locke, John, 223; Coke as precursor, 131; on Hooker, 4; Milton and, 181; *Two Treatises on Civil Government*, 28, 59–60, 75, 177, 235
Logic, 99, 102
Long Parliament, 148, 185–87; demands on king, 217; leaders, 163; legal reform commission, 228–29; legislation, 29, 149–50, 216, 229; members, 174; Rump, 218, 228; sermons preached before, 186
Louis XIII, King of France, 148, 213
Louis XIV, King of France, 16, 231
Louis XV, King of France, 72
Louis XVI, King of France, 148, 207, 209
Luther, Martin, 70
Lyon's Inn, 116, 117

Machiavelli, Niccolo, 94
Magna Carta: Coke on, 132, 133; confirmations, 24, 25; court reforms, 16; implementation as law, 24–25; influence of language, 25; invoked in Five Knights' Case, 173; monument at Runnymede, 31; Petition of Right and, 24, 129, 174; printed with statutes, 24, 27; promulgation, 23–24; revival, 26, 27; role in America, 23, 28–29, 30–31, 135; seventeenth-century views of, 26–27, 28, 29; significance, 3; uniqueness, 23–24; use against Stuart monarchs, 28
Maitland, Frederic William, 12, 13, 232
Margaret of Anjou, Queen, 46, 47, 49, 51
Marlowe, Christopher, *Doctor Faustus*, 8
Marshall, John, 163
Martin V, Pope, 189
Mary, Queen of England, 62, 73, 147
Mary Queen of Scots, 79, 87
Massachusetts Bay Colony: Coke's influence, 134–35; as commonwealth, 195–97, 201; courts, 203; General Court, 31, 134–35, 151, 197, 203; law books, 151; leaders, 197–99, 203, 204; legal institutions, 203–4; legitimacy of rulers, 199–202; letters patent of charter, 197, 202, 203–4; non-freemen, 200–201; relationship with English king, 197, 198–99, 255–56n13; scripture's role, 195–96, 199–200, 201–2, 204. *See also Laws and Liberties of Massachusetts*
Matilda, Queen, 13–14, 15
Maurice of Nassau, 79
Maxims: of Bacon, 103–4, 106–11; of Coke, 45, 71, 105, 112–13, 115, 122, 133; in legal literature, 104–6, 111. *See also* Aphorisms
McIlwain, Charles H., 80, 95, 97
Melville, Andrew, 80, 95
Middle Temple, 68, 116
Milsom, S. F. C., 44
Milton, John: *The Doctrine and Discipline of Divorce*, 187–88; *Eikonoklastes*, 181; life, 8, 179–80, 193–94; marriage, 187; *Paradise Lost*, 178; *Paradise Regained*, 178; poetry, 178–79; political tracts, 179, 180–82; religious views, 180; *Samson Agonistes*, 178; *The Tenure of Kings and Magistrates*, 8, 181–82; tracts against prelacy, 180
Milton, John, *Aeropagitica*, 8, 179; arguments, 188–92; attack on licensing, 187, 189–92; historical context, 182–87; influence, 177, 188–93
Mixed monarchy: Coke on, 131–32; consensus on, 59; contrast to absolute monarchy, 148; Fortescue on, 47, 49, 50, 52–53, 59; James I on, 87–88, 96; legal institutions and, 234; parliamentary role, 94, 217–18; Protectorate, 29
Monarchy: absolute, 9, 131, 148–49, 197, 233; female succession, 55–56; French, 49, 52, 55, 148; legitimacy, 198–99, 208–9; murders of kings, 206, 207–8; relations with Parliament, 29; supremacy over Church of England, 62, 63–64, 75–76, 86. *See also* Mixed monarchy
Montesquieu, 60, 131
Moore, John, 101, 107
Morice, James, 27
Mountagu, Henry, 140–41
Mulcaster, Robert, 47

Natural law, 50, 168, 201
Natural philosophy, 223–25, 226–27, 235
Nature, state of, 63–64
Netherlands, 196, 207
New England colonies, charters, 29–30. *See also* Massachusetts Bay Colony
Newton, Isaac, 223, 236
Nicholas II, Czar, 207–8
Norman conquest, 16, 18, 232, 233
Nottingham, Heneage Finch, Earl of, 37
Noy, William, 228; *Principal Grounds and Maximes of the Lawes of the Kingdome*, 111

Otis, James, 135
Oxford University, 20, 66–68, 96

Paris, Matthew, *Angli Historia Maior*, 26
Parliament: Exclusion Crisis, 222, 231, 235; Fortescue as member, 48; High Court of, 112, 128, 129, 203; House of Lords, 170; legislative authority of King and, 148–49; licensing of printing, 182, 187; role in mixed monarchy, 94, 217–18; of 1628, 129, 171, 172, 173–74; sovereignty, 29, 132; speeches of James I, 4–5, 85–91, 92; Tudor monarchs and, 26. *See also* Long Parliament
Parmenter, Thomas, 137
Peacham, Edmund, 125–26
Perjury, 160, 202

Perkins, John, 107
Perpetuities, 117–18
Petition of Right (1628), 24, 28, 129, 132, 174
Pevsner, Sir Nikolaus, 136
Phelips, Sir Robert, 172
Pigott, Sir Christopher, 88
Pius V, Pope, 62, 244n6
Plato, *Republic*, 190
Plucknett, Theodore, 12, 37, 39
The Political Works of James I, *see* James I of England and VI of Scotland, *The Political Works of James I*
Poor Laws, 143, 145
Popham, John, 108, 140–41
The Poulterers' Case, 162
Presbyterians, 95, 180, 230
Printing industry, 33; cultural impact, 185–86; law books, 33; licensing, 182–85, 187; political pamphlets, 185–87
Privy Council: activities at local level, 143; assizes and, 145; Coke as member, 127, 162; oversight of justices of the peace, 144; in Star Chamber, 6, 153; use of torture, 155
Property law: perpetuities, 117–18; students, 33, 34. *See also* Littleton, Sir Thomas, *Tenures*
Protectorate, 29, 149, 196, 207, 210, 227–28, 229
Protestants: *adiaphora* (things indifferent), 63, 77, 180; Calvinism, 62, 63, 71–72, 76; city-states, 189; disputes among, 69–72, 76, 85; Reformed, 66, 186. *See also* Church of England; Puritanism; Reformation
Proverbs, 104
Prynne, William: as Keeper of Tower Records, 183, 254n12; libel trials, 183–84, 185, 193; Milton and, 193–94; papers searched, 8, 193–94; political pamphlets, 183, 184, 186, 187
Pulton, Ferdinando, 146, 147, 159
Puritanism: calls for further reform, 76, 80, 186; controversies with other Protestants, 63, 69, 77; covenant theology, 72; English Revolution and, 77; Laud's opposition to, 77, 145–46. *See also* Civil War, English
Pym, John, 59
Pynchon, William, 151
Pynson, Richard, 141; *Magna Charta cum aliis Antiquis Statutis*, 27
Raleigh, Sir Walter, 47, 81–82, 120, 131
Ray, John, 223
Reformation, 58, 62–63; *adiaphora* (things indifferent), 61–62; effects on law, 65; legislation, 73; new landowners, 72. *See also* Church of England; Protestants
Reformed Protestantism, 66, 186
Renaissance, twelfth century, 19–20
Republicanism: in England, 28–29, 186–87, 196, 254n17; European, 196–97, 207; Magna Carta and, 28–29; in Massachusetts Bay Colony, 204
Reynolds, John, 81
Riccio, David, 79, 87
Richard fitz Neal, 21
Richard I, King of England, 13
Richard III, King of England, 206
Richardson, Sir Thomas, 146
Rolle, Henry, *Abridgement*, 222, 258n3
Roman Catholic Church: canon law, 19, 64–65; English Catholics, 86–87, 119; papacy, 94–95, 189; response to Reformation, 62, 244n6
Roman law, 17, 19, 104, 109, 148, 156
Roosevelt, Theodore, 14
Rousseau, Jean-Jacques, 94
Royal Society, 10, 223–24
Rudyard, Sir Benjamin, 219
Rule of law, 29, 150, 204
Rules: Bacon on, 107, 109; Coke on, 113; common law, 6; relationship to laws, 107
Ryman v. Bickley, 162

St. Germain, Christopher, *Dialogue between a Doctor and Student*, 39, 57
Salisbury, Earl of, 210–11
Science, *see* Natural philosophy
Scotland: invasion of England, 185, 214–15, 216; lairds, 94; Parliament, 94, 96; politics, 95; Presbyterians, 95, 180; Reformed Protestantism, 66; union with England, 88–89
Sedition, 161
Selden, John: character, 167; Fortescue and, 59; *History of Tithes*, 169; James I and, 169; legal practice, 175, 253n8; legal writings, 168–69; life, 170–75; *Mare Clausum*, 169–70; as member of Parliament, 172, 173–74; Milton and, 189; political involvement, 170–74; *Privilege of the Baronage of England*, 170; publication of Fortescue,

47; scholarly works, 167–70, 175; *Table Talk*, 8–9, 167, 175–76
Settled Land Act of 1882, 118
Sèze, Raymond-Romain de, 209
Shakespeare, William: *Henry IV Part 2*, 205–6; *Henry VI Part 3*, 46; history plays, 26–27, 205; *King John*, 26–27; *Merry Wives of Windsor*, 152; *Richard III*, 206; sonnets, 72, 205
Shapiro, Barbara, 224–25, 232
Shelley's Case, 117
Sheriffs, handbooks for, 139
Short Parliament, 174, 185
Sidney, Algernon, 206
Simpson, A. W. B., 2–3, 6–7
Slander, 161
Smith, Adam, 131
Smith, Sir Thomas, *De Republica Anglorum*, 58
Social contract theory, 59–60, 75
Soviet Union, 207–8
Sparks (binder-bookseller), 183, 184
Spencer, Thomas, 137
Spenser, Edmund, *The Faerie Queene*, 189
Star Chamber: abolition, 152, 162, 163, 165–66; activism, 160; barristers, 138, 157, 253n8; cases, 127, 165–66; contribution to common law, 158–64, 166; examinations of witnesses, 154; judges, 153, 159, 162–63, 165; jurisdiction, 122, 157, 159; origins, 156; procedures, 153–54, 156–57; punishments, 155, 184; regulation of printing, 182, 184–85; reputation, 152–56, 164; sophisticated crimes prosecuted, 5, 146, 158–62; *A Treatise of the Court of Star Chamber* (Hudson), 5, 6, 157–58, 164, 166; trials, 153
"The Star Chamber" (film), 153
Statute of Uses, 34, 42, 43, 44, 100, 117, 118
Staunford, William, 107
Stenton, Doris May, 25
Stephen, Sir James Fitzjames, 36, 147
Stephen, King, 13–14, 16, 19
Stephen, Sir Leslie, 188
Strafford, Thomas Wentworth, Earl of, 149, 172, 174, 216

Table Talk of John Selden, 8–9, 167, 175–76
Taltarum's Case, 40–41
Taylor, Roderick, 153
Thomas Aquinas, *De Regimine Principum*, 53
Thorne, Samuel E., 105, 133
Tillieres, Comte de, 81, 85, 87, 92
Tillotson, John, 224
Torture, 155
Tottell, Richard, 33
Tractatus de Legibus et Consuetudinibus Regni Anglie qui Glanvilla Vocatur, *see* Glanvill, *Tractatus de Legibus et Consuetudinibus Regni Anglie qui Glanvilla Vocatur*
Travers, Walter, 68–69, 245n10
Treason, 125, 146, 155, 161, 202–3, 217–18
A Treatise of the Court of Star Chamber (Hudson), 5, 6, 157–58, 164, 166
Tribonian, 109
Tudor monarchs: Parliament and, 26; prominence of law, 72–73; strength, 114
Two Treatises on Civil Government (Locke), 28, 59–60, 75, 177, 235
Tyrannicide, 96, 97

Unbarrable entails, 40–41
United States Constitution: Bill of Rights, 31; Fifth Amendment, 27; First Amendment, 161; foundations, 30; judicial review, 163; Magna Carta's influence, 30–31; Milton's influence, 177, 181
United States Supreme Court, 163
Uses: contingent remainders, 41–42, 117–18; Littleton on, 42–44; Statute of Uses, 34, 42, 43, 44, 100, 117, 118

Van Caenegem, Raoul C., 12, 16
Van Dyck, Anthony, 213
Venice, 196
Virtuosi, 223–24
Vivès, Ludovico, 66

Walter, Hubert, 13
Warburton, Peter, 141
Ward, Nathaniel, "Body of Liberties," 30
Warren, W. L., 15
Wars of the Roses, 26, 32, 46–47, 50, 55–56, 206
Wentworth, Sir Thomas, *see* Strafford, Thomas Wentworth, Earl of
Westminster Palace, Camera Stellata, 153. *See also* Star Chamber
Whig historians, 111, 130–31
White collar crimes, 146, 158–62
Whitelock, Bulstrode, 219, 257n25
Whitgift, John, 68
Wilkins, John, 224

William I, King of England, 16, 18, 19, 232, 233
William II, King of England, 18
William III, King of England, 10, 24, 235–36
Wilson, Arthur, 82
Winfield, Percy, 37
Wingate, Edward, *Maximes of Reason*, 111
Winthrop, John, Sr., 30, 199, 200, 201, 255–56n3
Writs: of assistance, 135; Glanvill on, 2, 17–18, 22, 156; institution of system, 155–56; of prohibition, 90, 123, 124
Wyclif, John, 189
Wyndham, Sir Thomas, 219
Wythe, George, 135

Yale, D. E. C., 232
Year Books, 35, 39, 40, 47–48, 105, 112–13, 133. *See also* Rolle, Henry, *Abridgement*
Yelverton, Henry, 172
York, house of, *see* Wars of the Roses

Jurists: Profiles in Legal Theory

GENERAL EDITOR

William Twining

William E. Conklin, *Hegel's Laws: The Legitimacy of a Modern Legal Order*

Neil MacCormick, *H. L. A. Hart*, Second Edition

Wouter de Been, *Legal Realism Regained: Saving Realism from Critical Acclaim*

Allen D. Boyer, *Sir Edward Coke and the Elizabethan Age*

John Dinwiddy, edited by William Twining, *Jeremy Bentham*

Roger Cotterrell, *Emile Durkheim: Law in a Moral Domain*

Colin Imber, *Ebu's-su'ud and the Islamic Legal Tradition*

Edited by Robert W. Gordon, *The Legacy of Oliver Wendell Holmes, Jr.*

Robert S. Summers, *Lon L. Fuller*

The authorized representative in the EU for product safety and compliance is:
Mare Nostrum Group
B.V Doelen 72
4831 GR Breda
The Netherlands

www.ingramcontent.com/pod-product-compliance
Lightning Source LLC
LaVergne TN
LVHW091515200926
848483LV00005B/425/J
* 9 7 8 0 8 0 4 7 5 7 1 4 0 *